George Herbert and the Mystery of the Word

Gary Kuchar

George Herbert and the Mystery of the Word

Poetry and Scripture in Seventeenth-Century England

Gary Kuchar
University of Victoria
Victoria, British Columbia, Canada

ISBN 978-3-319-44044-6   ISBN 978-3-319-44045-3   (eBook)
DOI 10.1007/978-3-319-44045-3

Library of Congress Control Number: 2016962102

Cover image © Peter Horree / Alamy Stock Photo
Cover design by Fatima Jamadar

Printed on acid-free paper

This Palgrave Macmillan imprint is published by Springer Nature
The registered company is Springer International Publishing AG
The registered company address is: Gewerbestrasse 11, 6330 Cham, Switzerland

For Troy and in memory of my father Joseph Kuchar

A NOTE ON REFERENCES

- References to George Herbert's English poetry are given in text by line number and are from *The English Poems of George Herbert* ed. Helen Wilcox (Cambridge: Cambridge UP, 2007).
- References to George Herbert's prose are given in text by page number and are from *The Works of George Herbert* ed. F.E. Hutcheson (Oxford: Clarendon Press, 1959).
- References to George Herbert's Latin poetry are given in text by page number and are from *The Latin Poetry of George Herbert: A Bilingual Edition*. trans. Mark McCloskey and Paul R. Murphy (Athens: Ohio UP, 1965).
- Unless noted otherwise, references to the sermons of Lancelot Andrewes are given in text by volume and page number and are from *Lancelot Andrewes: Ninety-Six Sermons 5 Volumes* (Oxford: John Henry Parker, 1841–1843).
- Unless noted otherwise, references to the work of Richard Sibbes are given in text by volume and page number and are from *The Complete Works of Richard Sibbes 7 Volumes* ed. Alexander Grosart (Edinburgh: James Nichol, 1863).
- References to Edward Herbert's *De Veritate* are given in text by page number and are from Edward Herbert, *De Veritate* trans. Meyrick H. Carré (London: Routledge, 1937).
- References to Edward Herbert's *A Dialogue Between a Tutor and His Pupil* are given in text by page number are from the 1678 London edition printed by W. Bathoe.

- References to Edward Herbert's *De Religione Laici* are given in text by page number and are from *De Religione Laici* ed. Harold R. Hutcheson (New Haven: Yale University Press, 1944).
- References to John Donne's Sermons are given in text by volume and page number and are from *The Sermons of John Donne* 10 vols. ed. George R. Potter and Evelyn M. Simpson (Berkeley: University of California Press, 1953–1962).
- Except when otherwise noted, references to St. Augustine are given in text by volume and page number and are from *The Works of St. Augustine* (2nd Release) ed. John E. Rotelle (Charlottesville: Intelex Corp., 2001).
- References to Henry Vaughan's poetry are given in text by line numbers and are from *The Works of Henry Vaughan* ed. L.C. Martin 2nd edition (Clarendon: Oxford UP, 1957).
- Unless noted otherwise, references to Martin Luther are given in text by volume and page number and are from *Luther's Works 55 Volumes*. ed. Jaroslav Pelikan and Helmut T. Lehmann (Fortress Press: Philadelphia, 1955–1986).
- Unless noted otherwise, all references to the bible are given in text by chapter and verse and are from *The Holy Bible: King James Version a Reprint of the edition of 1611* (Peabody, MA: Hendrickson, 2005).

You see, the Word stands apart as at once the foundation for all things to stand on, and the ceiling for them to stand under ... all things are in it.[1]

—St. Augustine

A problem is something which I meet, which I find complete before me, but which I can therefore lay siege to and reduce. But a mystery is something in which I myself am involved, and it can therefore only be thought of as a 'sphere where the distinction between what is in me and what is before me loses its meaning and its initial validity.' A genuine problem is subject to an appropriate technique by the exercise of which it is defined; whereas a mystery, by definition, transcends every conceivable technique. It is, no doubt, always possible (logically and psychologically) to degrade a mystery so as to turn it into a problem. But this is a fundamentally vicious proceeding, whose springs might perhaps be discovered in a kind of corruption of the intelligence.

—Gabriel Marcel[2]

We say amiss,
This or that is:
Thy word is all, if we could spell.

—George Herbert, "The Flower."

---

[1] 13.210.

[2] Gabriel Marcel, *Being and Having* trans. K. Farrer (New York: Harper and Row, 1965), 101.

ACKNOWELDGMENTS

I am very grateful to have the opportunity to thank the friends, colleagues, and institutions that helped make this book possible. This project began with a generous invitation from Hannibal Hamlin to write on poetry and prayer. During that time, I enjoyed the support of the Social Sciences and Humanities Research Council of Canada. Paul Dyck commented on an early draft of the whole manuscript while Sara Beam, Matthew Koch, John Money, Ed Pechter, Terry Sherwood, Judith Weil, and Chauncey Wood provided advice on individual sections. I am also very grateful to my anonymous readers who offered crucial advice and to Phillip Getz and Alexis Nelson for their editorial support. My biggest intellectual debt is to Paul Cefalu for commenting on multiple drafts and for allowing me to draw on his magisterial book project in manuscript form, *The Johannine Renaissance in Early Modern English Religion and Literature* (Oxford University Press: Forthcoming). I am also grateful to all those who generously provided me with a venue to test out my ideas at various stages in the project, including Margaret Cameron, Paul Dyck, Kenneth Graham, Ryan Mcdermott, Heather Easterling Ritchie, Paul Stevens, Linda Tredennick, Alden Turner, and Jennifer Waldron. I also benefitted from conversations with Christopher Douglas, Erin Kelly, Jim Knapp, Allan Mitchell, Linda Morra, and many others. Thanks also go to my many RAs over the last decade, especially Rose Morris who helped me through the book's final stages. A Faculty Fellowship in 2016–2017 from the Faculty of Humanities at the University of Victoria allowed me to complete this project. Finally, I am grateful to the editors of the following publications for kindly allowing me to reprint some of the material from the following publications: "Sounding The Temple: George Herbert and the Mystery of Hearkening" *Figures of the Sacred in English Poetry.* eds. Jennifer Kilgore-Caradec, Ineke Bockting, and Cathy Parc (New York: Peter Lang, 2013); "Prayer Terminable and Interminable: George Herbert and the Art of Estrangement" *Religion and Literature.* 42.3 (2010), 132–143; and "Exegesis and Experience in Herbert and Calvin: A Review Essay of Daniel Doerksen's *Picturing Religious Experience: George Herbert, Calvin, and the Scriptures*" in *George Herbert Journal* 34. 1–2 (2010–2011), 119–136. It goes without saying that errors are mine alone.

CONTENTS

CHAPTER 1

Herbert's Neatness

> Welcome sweet and sacred cheer,
> Welcome deare;
> With me, in me, live and dwell:
> For thy neatnesse passeth sight,
> Thy delight
> Passeth tongue to taste or tell.
>
> "The Banquet." (1–6)

In a celebrated essay on transformations in English protestant culture across the sixteenth and seventeenth centuries, Patrick Collinson identifies three historically discrete ways in which reformers answered George Herbert's question: "Is there in truth no beauty?"[1] At first, Collinson explains, Tudor protestants drew on existing cultural media as they taught people the new faith while exposing the corruptions of the old one. In this early stage of reformation, religious drama and other forms of art were widely deployed in proselytizing and polemical efforts. By around 1580, however, during the puritan ascendancy in Elizabethan England, protestant publicists began rejecting forms of cultural representation associated with England's Catholic past. In this second phase of cultural change, protestants began seeing older forms of art and media as an active threat to

---

[1] Patrick Collinson, *The Birthpangs of Protestant England: Religious and Cultural Change in the Sixteenth and Seventeenth Centuries* (Basingstoke: Macmillan, 1988), 98.

© The Author(s) 2017   1
G. Kuchar, *George Herbert and the Mystery of the Word,*
DOI 10.1007/978-3-319-44045-3_1

the new faith, as a corrupting expression of anti-Christ.[2] But things started to change again a couple of decades later when "protestant Biblicism delivered its positive answer in ever fuller measure to Herbert's question, heard most clearly in some of the greatest of the English poets. And it was at this point that an authentically protestant literary culture emerged."[3] Although these three broad phases describe some of the general transformations English protestant culture underwent after the Reformation, they do not explain how or why a fully mature biblical literature emerged in early Stuart England. To be sure, such questions demand many answers from a host of different perspectives. Taking George Herbert as its focus, this book offers one.

In my estimation, Herbert's biblical poetics was born out of a religious culture which was rediscovering the virtues of uncertainty, the value of doubt, and the force of mystery, all things lyric poetry does well. While these values were by no means unprecedented and while they had never truly disappeared, a number of influential writers in early Stuart England, working from different doctrinal standpoints and varying styles of piety, nevertheless found it necessary to reemphasize these features of Christian faith in the hopes of giving them new life. Revealingly, such emphases were often articulated as embattled achievements. Those who emphasized the importance of wise ignorance generally did so as a response to religious overconfidence and the despair that it sometimes inadvertently engendered. In particular, such writers expressed wariness about conceiving of the bible as a book of binding rules that could be cataloged or interpretively controlled for the sake of spiritual security and exegetical certainty. Responding to such perceived dogmatism, a number of early Stuart writers began emphasizing scripture's estranging qualities without losing sight of its comforting promises or ethical strictures.

Other forces were thought to be behind the eclipse of mystery that some saw taking place in England as well. Throughout the course of the European Reformation, protestant leaders worried about the rise of impious forms of rationalism. In England, this fear was stoked by Edward Herbert's

---

[2] For a fuller discussion of this second phase, see Collinson's "From iconoclasm to iconophobia: the cultural impact of the Second English Reformation" in *The Impact of The English Reformation 1500–1640* ed. Peter Marshall (London: Arnold, 1997), 278–307. For an assessment of some of the qualifications of Collinson's account of second-phase English reformation culture, see Peter Marshall, "(Re)defining the English Reformation" *Journal of British Studies* 48.3 (2009), 564–586, 576–7.

[3] Collinson, *Birthpangs*, 98.

De Veritate (1624) only to be more fully realized later in works such as John Toland's aptly named *Christianity not Mysterious* (1696). It was within this set of pressures, most of which were internal to Protestantism itself, that George Herbert forged his spiritual and poetic vision.

To explain Herbert's poetic and spiritual vision, I take a two-pronged approach in this book: one broadly philosophical and one more locally historical. First, I suggest that Herbert participated in a transhistorical exegetical tradition running from the Christian bible through Augustine up to present-day theological hermeneutics in which scriptural revelation is thought to consist of a mode of revelation-in-concealment and concealment-in-revelation. According to this tradition, spiritual reading is participatory in the sense that the reader remains fully immanent within the horizon of divine revelation. The underlying principle here is captured in the patristic figure of the bible as a mirror which Augustine explains in his commentary on Psalm 103. According to Augustine, in scriptures God

> has provided … a mirror for you, and there you are told, *Blessed are the pure of heart, for they shall see God* (Mt 5:8). In that text a mirror is held out to you. See whether you are one of the pure-hearted it mentions, and grieve if you are not yet like that; grieve in order to become so. (19.110)

Construed as what Herbert calls "the thankfull glasse, / That mends the lookers eyes," the significance of scripture evolves in its ongoing disclosure across time, space, and persons ("The H. Scriptures (I)," 8–9). From this perspective, the ethical assimilation of scriptural revelation to oneself is not one mode of reading among others; instead, it is a constitutive part of the interpretive process as such. As Herbert writes early in "The Church-porch": "Beware of lust: … / It blots thy lesson written in thy soul; / The holy lines cannot be understood. / How dare those eyes upon a Bible look, / Much lesse towards God, whose lust is all their book?" (7, 9–12).

Second, in stressing the mysterious and evolving nature of biblical revelation, Herbert participated in a broader cultural project of resisting more dogmatic approaches to religious life in seventeenth-century England. As I have begun to suggest, Herbert shared the concern of others in his generation that the drive for certainty within post-reformation Christianity results in a reductive form of faith, one that obscures wonder and awe in favor of stability and security. Viewed this way, Herbert's project as a writer appears as a sustained attempt to negotiate two competing impulses within post-reformation thought, two contrary aspects of reformation spirituality as he inherited it: the impulse to certainty, assurance, and security and the impulse to mystery, wonder, and nescience. As part of this project, Herbert participated in the ongoing dialogue about the role of the church as an interpretive community. Importantly, this dialogue was partly structured by the way that shifting theological concepts of mystery helped engender competing claims about the relative authority of scripture and church.[4] Consequently, Herbert's approach to questions of religious authority partly turn on his view of what it means to identify the church as the *corpus mysticum*. Along with others in the period, particularly Hooker and Andrewes, Herbert conceived of the church as a mystery more in the sense of a sacramental community unfolding in time than as a statically conceived body rooted in an apostolic ideal. To this extent, concepts of mystery not only inform Herbert's biblical poetics but also his broader ecclesiastical and sacramental vision. Perhaps most significantly, he showed that poetry could convey the experience of reading scripture in different situations in more flexible ways than other mediums generally can. In doing so, his lyrics emphasize the social and spiritual advantages of maintaining a slightly more open-ended role for the church as an interpretive and sacramental community than was the case in the more polarized decades of the early European Reformations.

One benefit of this two-pronged approach is that it gives us a fuller understanding of why religious poetry flowers in the age of Herbert and Donne rather than in the age of Wyatt and Surrey. As Helen Gardner once observed, sixteenth-century England

> is an almost completely blank period for the lover of religious verse, in spite of the overwhelming concern with religion and the fervour of religious feeling that sent Protestants to the stake and Catholics to Tyburn ... Perhaps the Ages of Faith were unpropitious for the writing of religious poetry in being too propitious.[5]

---

[4] Along with Chap. 2 see Henri de Lubac, *Corpus Mysticum: The Eucharist and the Church in the Middle Ages* trans. Gemma Simmonds (Notre Dame: University of Notre Dame Press, 2006); Michel de Certeau, *The Mystic Fable: The Sixteenth and Seventeenth Centuries* trans., Michael B. Smith (Chicago: University of Chicago Press, 1992); and Jennifer R. Rust, *The Body In Mystery: The Political Theology of the* Corpus Mysticum *in the Literature of Reformation England* (Evanston, Illinois: Northwestern University Press, 2014).

[5] Helen Gardner, *Religion and Literature* (Oxford: Oxford UP, 1971), 138.

The qualifying addendum here seems particularly apt. The relative lack of religious verse in sixteenth-century England was likely because of rather than despite the intensely polemical nature of the period's faith. If this is correct, then the full consequences of Gardner's basic insight have yet to be sufficiently integrated into literary histories of the seventeenth century. This book is an attempt to flesh out the implications of her claim that diachronic differences between sixteenth- and seventeenth-century Protestantisms are often more significant than the ostensibly synchronic differences (between say Anglican and Puritan, or even Catholic and Protestant) witnessed in the period, especially as far as literary history is concerned.

HERBERT AND THE MYSTERY OF PLAINNESS

Given Herbert's enormous influence on English Christianity in following generations, his spiritual poetics offers a privileged view of how and why a mature protestant biblical literature emerged when it did in reformation England. One major reason for his influence lies in the way he often expresses pious awe with beguiling understatement, as in the opening lines of "The Banquet" cited above. Beneath the restrained formalities and ostensible simplicity of "The Banquet" pulses a profound sense of mystery, one that motivates every corrective turn, every push and pull, the lyric takes. On the one hand, the poem opens by praising God's "neatness" as manifested in the decorous elegance of the eucharist, its "fine aspect in fit array" as he says elsewhere of the English liturgy, echoing St. Paul's command that all things be "done decently and in order" (OED, 2; "The British Church" 7; 1 Cor. 14:40). This celebration of God's well-ordered rite conforms to the opening sestet's unassumingly ornate structure, with its crisp trochees and triplets processing through two linked tercets in which a second couplet is tightly couched in an envelope of rhyme (*aabccb*). On the other hand, however, the speaker's buttoned-up formality does not repress what is quietly evoked in the Pauline phrases "passeth sight … Passeth tongue to taste or tell," which slow the sestet to an end and a hush (Cor. 2:9; Phil. 4:7). By this point in the stanza, a widened perspective opens as God's neatness now entails not only "fineness" but also "cleverness of expression in language or speech; pithiness; brevity" (OED, 1). The implication here is that the eucharist gives plain expression to an inexhaustible mystery, hence the claim that communion "Fills my soul, / Such as is, and makes divine!" (8–9).

Balancing stately refinement with the familiarity of the local pub, "The Banquet" presents the Lord's Supper as an everyday miracle in which all the promises and teachings embodied in the person of Christ become accessible. As the speaker says in the penultimate stanza, in the act of communion "I wipe mine eyes, and see / What I seek, for what I sue; / Him I view, / Who hath done so much for me" (45–48). This account of the eucharist as holding all scriptural truth *in potentia* revealingly parallels Lancelot Andrewes' treatment of the passion in a 1605 Good Friday sermon before the king at Greenwich. According to Andrewes, St. Luke captures the whole of Christ's story "in plain and express terms [when] he calleth the Passion θεωριαν 'a theory or sight'" (2.158). So richly condensed is the passion, Andrewes declares, that "were all philosophy lost, the theory of it might be found there [in the passion] ... All virtues are there visible, all, if time would serve" (2.179). Implicit in these accounts of the eucharist and the passion is the Pauline idea that the "mystery of Christ" (Eph. 3:4; Coloss. 4:3) unifies or gathers together "all things ... which are in heaven and which are in earth" (Eph. 1:10). For Andrewes and Herbert, the Word's capacity to express this recapitulation (*anakephalaiosis*) of all things in the person of Christ is the ultimate expression of its neatness.

Having caught a glimpse of Christ's gathering together of all things in the eucharist, the speaker of "The Banquet" concludes by praying to become part of the "mystery of Christ" in both flesh and word, both "lines and life":

> Let the wonder of this pitie
> > Be my dittie,
> And take up my lines and life:
> Hearken under pain of death,
> > Hands and breath;
> Strive in this, and love the strife. (49–54)

One of the culminating moments in *The Temple*, this desire to unite with Christ in "Hands and breath" shows Herbert's speaker revealing signs of deification (*theosis*), the idea captured in the patristic adage, "God has become man, that man might become God" which is evoked in stanza two's claim that the eucharist "makes divine!" (9).[6] In the context of "The

---

[6] For a discussion of this concept with reference to Andrewes, see Nicholas Lossky, *Lancelot Andrewes, The Preacher* (1555–1626): *The Origins of the Mystical Theology of the Church of England* trans. Andrew Louth (Oxford: Clarendon Press, 1991), 32–33. For an account of the puritan interest in this idea, see Theodore Dwight Bozeman, *The Precisianist Strain:*

Church" as a whole, this process of sanctification has special authority. The speaker of "The Banquet" is one of the most spiritually mature in the sequence not least because of the way he deftly balances simplicity and richness, confidence and wonder. Formally mirroring the divine neatness that it celebrates, "The Banquet" exemplifies the hard to describe but enduringly appealing way in which *The Temple* is simultaneously lucid and challenging at once. To read this poem is to experience the combination of clarity and bewilderment that coreligionists like Andrewes sought to cultivate in fellow Christians. From Herbert's perspective, there is no contradiction between rhetorical economy and spiritual inexhaustibleness. Where the Lord dwells, he teaches, "all is neat" ("The Familie," 8).

As "The Banquet" intimates, Herbert's pursuit of poetic neatness is part of a broader desire to participate in the "mystery of Christ" as expounded in Ephesians. The basic idea here is that Christ embodies all virtues and unifies all differences within himself in a way that is plainly revealed and yet not fully comprehensible. To this extent, one of the key biblical concepts animating Herbert's conception of poetic neatness is the Greek term *mysterion*, a hotly contested notion that, among other things, conveys the idea that God's revelation remains incompletely understood despite its having been fully and clearly revealed. Partly based on the book of Daniel, the biblical notion of mystery occurs throughout the New Testament, especially the Pauline corpus and to a lesser extent the gospels and book of Revelation.[7] Though fiercely debated, the New Testament's concept of the Word has long been recognized as presupposing a dimension of mystery in the restricted sense that its meaning, manner, and timing are unpredictable and rarely without an element of irony or unexpectedness.[8] As Herbert declares in "The Temper," with a series of metrical stresses expressive of both surprise and wonder, the Word "suddenly dost raise and race, / And ev'ry day a new Creatour art" (7–8). By reversing expectations and deploying paradox, scripture was thought from at least Augustine forward, but especially among protestants, to sustain plainness and mystery simultaneously. From this standpoint, Herbert's culturally influential concept of neatness implies not simply plainness but more precisely and paradoxically mystery-in-plainness and plainness-in-mystery.

Disciplinary Religion & Antinomian Backlash in Puritanism to 1638 (Chapel Hill: University of North Carolina Press, 2004), 31, 109.

[7] G.K. Beale and Benjamin L. Gladd, *Hidden But Now Revealed: A Biblical Theology of Mystery* (Downers Grove: IVP Academic, 2014).

[8] Ibid.

As in many other matters pertaining to the bible, Herbert's understanding of scriptural neatness shows the influence of his Westminster
schoolmaster Lancelot Andrewes.[9] In a 1607 Nativity Sermon on 1
Timothy 3:16, "And without controversy great is the mystery of godliness," Andrewes explores the dynamics of scriptural mystery at some
length. Intriguingly, this sermon does not make the standard patristic
point repeated throughout the Reformation that the difficult parts of
scripture are clarified by the plain ones. Instead, Andrewes argues that
even the most fully evident, plainly expressed, parts of scripture possess
a bewildering richness of meaning. In making this distinction, Andrewes
criticizes those who misconstrue the gospel's ostensible simplicity. A "false
conceit," he warns,

> is crept into the minds of men, to think the points of religion that be mani-
> fest to be certain petty points, scarce worth the hearing. Those—yea those
> be great, and none but those, that have great disputes about them. It is
> not so ... Those are necessary He hath made plain; those that [are] not
> plain not necessary. What better proof than this here? This here a mystery, a
> great one—religion hath no greater—yet manifest, and *in confesso*, with all
> Christians. (1.35)

Rather than identifying mystery with abstruse passages, Andrewes locates it
in the act of applying to scripture to oneself. Deeply invested in the problem of participatory reading, he begins the sermon by drawing a distinction
between the evangelists' description of the incarnation as an historical event
and Paul's discovery in it of a personally significant, inexhaustibly profound,
narrative. The very fact that Andrewes feels the need to make, let alone
stress, such a distinction is telling. According to Andrewes,

[9] In *A Priest to the Temple*, Herbert advises country parsons to avoid the kind of text crum-
bling deployed in sermons before learned audiences in the period (235). This is context-
specific advice about how preachers should speak before rural audiences and should not be
construed as revealing any sort of general partisan or stylistic difference from Andrewes. On
this point, see Peter McCullough ed., *Lancelot Andrewes: Selected Sermons and Lectures*
(Oxford: Oxford UP, 2005), xlii. For an important dismantling of the anachronistic distinc-
tion between plain and metaphysical preaching often imposed on Herbert's *A Priest to the
Temple*, see Mary Morrissey, "Scripture, Style and Persuasion in Seventeenth-Century
English Theories of Preaching" *The Journal of Ecclesiastical History* 53. 4 (2002), 686–706.
For a discussion of puritan uses of similar rhetorical strategies as Andrewes, see Janice Knight,
Orthodoxies in Massachusetts: Rereading American Puritanism (Cambridge, Mass.: Harvard
UP, 1994), 130–163. Whatever their differences, both Herbert and Andrewes shared a com-
mitment to neatness and mystery in the senses described here.

The manifestation of God in the flesh the Evangelists set down by way of an history; the Apostle goeth farther, and findeth a deep mystery in it, and for a mystery commends it unto us. Now there is difference between these two, many—this for one; that a man may hear a story, and never wash his hands, but a mystery requireth both the hands and heart to be clean that shall deal with it. (1.32)[10]

Without a sense of scripture as a living mystery, Andrewes worries, participatory reading becomes impoverished, if not impossible, hence his emphasis on reading with "hands and heart," just as Herbert later stressed participating in the sacraments with "Hands and breath." Seeking to revitalize the tradition of spiritual reading for those living in the Jacobean church, Andrewes stresses the compatibility of plainness and richness. In doing so, he advocates the sort of neatness that Herbert identifies in the English word *son*, its capacity to bear a host of "fresh and new" spiritual meanings in a beguilingly economical way. Herbert writes:

> How neatly doe we give one onely name
> To parents issue and the sunnes bright starre!
> A sonne is light and fruit; a fruitfull flame
> Chasing the fathers dimnesse, carri'd farre
> From the first man in th' East, to fresh and new
> Western discov'ries of posteritie. ("The Sonne," 1–6)

Here, the revealing power of the Logos is seen to be tersely conveyed in a single word, the contemplation of which reduces the obscurity of God's hiddenness by discovering the paradoxical tension between humility and glory that is embodied in Christ, hence the sonnet's pithy conclusion: "For what Christ once in humblenesse began, / We him in glorie call, *The Sonne of Man*" (13–14). Herbert's meditation on the word *son* further recalls Andrewes' treatment of the phrase "By his Son" in his Nativity Sermon on Hebrews 1:1–3. According to Andrewes, the scripture writers devised strategies to ensure that such phrases would be patiently and slowly read rather than quickly consumed. In his account of Hebrews, the writer feared that "we would not weigh these words 'by His Son' as were meet but hear them slightly and pass them lightly over" (1.107). As a result, "the rest of the text he spends in making a commentary of this word Son; that we may consider how great this Party is" (1.107).

---

[10] For a closely related sermon, see Andrewes, 2.383–403.

Just as Andrewes encourages his auditors to hear enormous richness and depth hidden within the ostensible simplicity of the phrase "by His Son" (*in Filio*), so Herbert asks us to do the same with the phrase "The Son of Man," especially as it resonates in English. The aim in both cases is to estrange common scriptural idioms so as to encourage a mode of biblical reading that results in interpretive wonder and spiritual participation more than exegetical control or purely objective meaning.

Viewed in these contexts, Herbert's career as a poet-priest begins to appear as an ongoing pursuit of spiritual and aesthetic neatness. Crucially, though, this effort was not simply a conventional expression of Christian plainness. On the contrary, it was a response to the eclipse of mystery being broadly diagnosed in Jacobean England. This is why it is now important to qualify the strong stress placed on the more assured side of Herbert's poetics in recent criticism. To date much critical emphasis has been placed on how Herbert's "ceaseless drive towards 'simplicity'"[11] arises from sixteenth-century protestant attitudes toward scripture. Christopher Hodgkins summarizes this side of the poet's thought when he suggests that for Herbert "the Bible is assumed clearly to answer all questions of faith and provide explicit general rules that govern in obscurer matters of external practice ... Like Cranmer, he believes that he and others can arrive at a clear knowledge of the Bible's message."[12] Yet, Herbert's scripturalism not only informs his pursuit of simplicity and plainness; it also animates his abiding sensitivity to the mystery of the biblical Word, to its spiritual unpredictability and relative open-endedness. For Herbert, no less than for Augustine, or even Milton in a different register, biblical truth

[11] John Drury, *Music at Midnight: The Life and Poetry of George Herbert* (London: Allen Lane, 2013), 134–5.

[12] Christopher Hodgkins, *Authority, Church, and Society in George Herbert: Return to the Middle Way* (Columbia: University of Missouri Press, 1993), 53. Hodgkins sees Herbert as longing for the solidity of the Elizabethan settlement, particularly its more Calvinist elements. For a reading of Herbert in relation to a similar view of the Jacobean consensus, see Daniel W. Doerksen, *Conforming to the Word: Herbert, Donne, and the English Church before Laud* (Lewisburg: Bucknell UP, 1997) and his *Picturing Religious Experience: George Herbert, Calvin, and the Scriptures* (Newark: University of Delaware Press, 2011). For a study of Herbert in relation to basic reformed ideas of grace and redemption, see Richard Strier, *Love Known: Theology and Experience in George Herbert's Poetry* (Chicago: University of Chicago Press, 1983). This body of scholarship has undermined any attempt to read Herbert as a Laudian poet. The challenge now is to reassess Herbert in light of post-revisionist historiography, especially its reconfiguring of what used to be called the Calvinist consensus.

is a streaming fountain that cannot be held or possessed in the same way in all times, places, and persons. But to appreciate this other side of Herbert's biblical imagination, we need to push our contextual frame both backward and forward from the sixteenth-century contexts most often adduced by recent critics. This means looking back to Augustine and the hermeneutic traditions he inspired and then forward again to the seventeenth-century protestants who had become wary of the exaggerated certainties that had developed within Protestantism over the previous century.

By turning to the tensions within Herbert's immediate contexts, we will better appreciate how he articulates an experience of faith in which the event of "fresh and new discov'ries" deepens rather than dispels the experience of mystery. For Herbert, poetry provides access to modes of discovery which enhance our sensitivity to the limits of human knowledge while at the same time furthering rather than frustrating our desire for further discovery. In this way, he construes good devotional poetry as akin to Augustinian prayer: it provides intelligibility within mystery, religious meaning without excessive, schismatically generating certitude, hence its spiritual and social as well as aesthetic value. Ultimately for Herbert, poetry is a species of prayer in which one continually rediscovers the mysteries of faith as situated within the unbounded context of the divine Word, the "mystery of Christ" as expounded in the Pauline-Augustinian tradition of scripture as mirror.[13]

The crux here, however, is that *poetry, prayer, mystery,* and *discovery* were all hotly contested terms in post-reformation Europe. Taken together, these contestations formed, as it were, the furnace in which Herbert's neatness was forged. Accordingly, to understand his poetics is to understand how he responded to the way that changing interpretations of these four key terms altered the framework in which hermeneutic and spiritual activity took place in reformation England. While we know the bible was central to Herbert's poetics, it remains to be seen how his approach to scripture constitutes a response to increasing tensions within seventeenth-century protestant hermeneutics and the forms of piety at stake in them.[14]

[13] My approach to Herbert and Augustinian prayer aims to expand, update, and in some instances modify, Elizabeth Clarke, *Theory and Theology in George Herbert's Poetry: 'Divinitie, and Poesie, Met'* (Oxford: Oxford UP, 1997).

[14] For a sustained study of Herbert and the bible, see Chana Bloch, *Spelling the Word: George Herbert and the Bible* (Berkeley: University of California Press, 1985).

STYLES OF PIETY AND THE EARLY STUART CHURCH

Herbert was by no means alone in seeking to negotiate the competing impulses of wonder and certainty in seventeenth-century England. Such tensions permeate post-reformation culture as a whole, often shaping the works of individual writers who helped define the fluctuating parameters of orthodoxy in Elizabethan, Jacobean, and Caroline polities. Consequently, such tensions cannot be mapped onto one ecclesiastical party over and against another within the Stuart Church. If puritans sometimes claimed exaggerated assurance about salvation and the visible church, then Laudians often displayed disastrous administrative arrogance in their pursuit of ecclesiastical uniformity. As for those between these extremes, conformists sometimes used the language of moderation as a means of social control that presupposed modes of certainty no less rigid than that of their opponents.[15] Even the rhetoric of mystery was routinely deployed by state authorities as a weapon of suppression and control, especially under Archbishop Laud and after the Restoration. The thesis of this book is not that Herbert perfectly balanced tensions between mystery and certainty because he adhered to a narrowly partisan version of the *via media*. My thesis is that Herbert's admirable but imperfect effort to balance these tensions helps account for some of the most compelling features of his work, and that in making this effort he participated in developing a relatively nondogmatic style of piety that emerged in early Stuart England. Better understood as a work in diachronic progress than as a synchronically identifiable or unified group, this strain of English piety sought to avoid exaggerated claims to religious security along with the ecclesiastical exclusivism coincident with them.

Part of what made Herbert's style of piety possible was timing. He came to maturity at a moment when some members of the Jacobean church were softening the doctrinal and pastoral rigidities of certain parts of the Elizabethan clergy. One impetus for these changes came from parishioners who reacted against the more divisively dogmatic elements of

---

[15] For this phenomenon, see Ethan H. Shagan, *The Rule of Moderation: Violence, Religion, and the Politics of Restraint in Early Modern England* (Cambridge: Cambridge UP, 2011) and Peter Lake, "The moderate and irenic case for religious war: Joseph Hall's Via *Media* in context" in *Political culture and cultural politics in early modern England* eds. Susan D. Amussen and Mark A. Kishlansky (Manchester: Manchester UP, 1995), 55–83.

godly religion.[16] Emphasizing accommodation over confrontation, some ministers in Herbert's generation developed a more generously comprehensive pastoral style. In this strain of piety, a strong emphasis was also placed on the socially unifying power of liturgy.[17] Herbert's *A Priest to the Temple* has been shown to exemplify this new kind of sociable pastorate, one in which the minister seeks to integrate himself into the community so as to more effectively carry out a wider range of duties than was often the case in Elizabethan England, hence Herbert's concern with "The Parson in Contempt" and his general insistence that an effective priest "is a Lover of old Customes" (268–269, 283).[18] The extent to which *The Temple* also participates in this cultural shift, however, still remains to be explained.

The softening of reformed piety in early Jacobean England also took place in the rarified world of theological discourse far beyond the immediate practicalities of pastoral life. This period saw the rise of a brand of moderate puritan piety that was attentive to anti-puritan critique and the dangers of polarized debate that was often heard in the 1580s and 1590s. As Jonathan D. Moore observes, in the late Elizabethan period

> it was fashionable to draw up very clear battle lines. Either Christ came to save the elect only or he did not; either God desires to save all or he does not ... A reconciliatory *via media* seems to have been as unnecessary as undesirable; no appeasing grey areas; no paradoxical mysteries.[19]

---

[16] Christopher Haigh, "The Taming of Reformation: Preachers, Pastors, and Parishioners in Elizabethan and Early Stuart England" *History* 85.280 (October 2000), 572–588, 584; *The Plain Man's Pathways to Heaven: Kinds of Christianity in Post-Reformation England, 1570–1640* (Oxford: Oxford UP, 2007), 1–78 and "Anticlericalism and the English Reformation" in *The English Reformation Revised* ed. Christopher Haigh (Cambridge: Cambridge UP, 1987), 56–74. See also Judith Maltby, *Prayer Book And People In Elizabethan And Early Stuart England* (Cambridge: Cambridge UP, 1998). For a critical response to early formulations of this school of thought, see Patrick Collinson, *From Cranmer to Sancroft* (London: Hambledon Continuum, 2006), 55–74. For a detailed and definitive response, see Haigh, *The Plain Man's Pathways*.

[17] Haigh, "Taming of the Reformation," 584.

[18] Ibid., 576–7. For a study of Herbert's pastoral art see Greg Miller, *George Herbert's 'Holy Patterns': Reforming Individuals in Community* (New York: Continuum, 2007).

[19] Jonathan D. Moore, *English Hypothetical Universalism: John Preston and the Softening of Reformed Theology* (Grand Rapids: Eerdmans, 2007), 68. On the softening of reformed piety in early Stuart England, see also Anthony Milton, *Catholic and Reformed: The Roman and Protestant Churches in English Protestant Thought* 1600–1640 (Cambridge: Cambridge UP, 1995), 413–417 and Arnold Hunt, *The Art of Hearing: English Preachers and Their Audiences, 1590–1640* (Cambridge: Cambridge UP, 2010), 369. For discussions of assurance

Driven by religious and social insecurity, Elizabethan puritans made assurance of salvation the center of devotional life. In the process, they developed highly systematized theories of conversion that explained in minute detail how the Holy Spirit works on the soul.[20] Instead of emphasizing the inevitability of doubt or the value of mystery, as later puritans such as Richard Sibbes would, Elizabethan writers such as William Perkins taught that "God commands us ... not to doubt."[21] In Perkins, the process of conversion was so elaborately delineated that even if Christians did not know when their own conversion occurred, they could nevertheless be reasonably certain of its underlying structure, thereby gaining mastery over its meaning and direction.[22] If the pietist "campaign against doubt" ultimately proved counterproductive in some respects, its primary aim was nevertheless to provide soteriological and exegetical certainty.[23] The result was a spiritual ethos characterized by the pursuit of *affiance* or the confidence of one's salvation as based on the solidity of a Word that means the same thing in all times, places, and persons.[24] Though very much in the Augustinian tradition, such an approach nevertheless differs from Augustine's later work, so crucial to Herbert, in which the bishop of Hippo strenuously avoided trespassing on God's inscrutability.[25]

The relative dominance of this Elizabethan style of pietism, however, was not to last. In place of the "stark simplicity" of Elizabethan formulations on key theological issues arose a more flexible, less dogmatic style of

among Elizabethan Puritans, see Joel R. Beeke, *Assurance of Faith: Calvin, English Puritanism, and the Dutch Second Reformation* (New York: Peter Lang, 1991) and Norman Pettit, *The Heart Prepared: Grace and Conversion in Puritan Spiritual Life* (New Haven: Yale UP, 1966), 1–21, 48–85.

[20] For an overview of the social dimensions of the puritan drive for control and assurance and a discussion of the wide body of scholarship on the issue, see Bozeman, *The Precisianist Strain*, 40–62.

[21] Cited in Charles Lloyd Cohen, *God's Caress: The Psychology of Puritan Religious Experience* (Oxford: Oxford UP, 1986), 100.

[22] Pettit, *The Heart Prepared*, 6; Cohen, *God's Caress*, 75, 79; Bozeman, *Precisianist Strain*, 192; Knight, *Orthodoxies*, 4, 53, 87, 174.

[23] Bozeman, *Precisianist Strain*, 147.

[24] For a discussion of affiance as a key puritan term, see Stephen Foster, *The Long Argument: English Puritanism and the Shaping of New England Culture, 1570–1700* (Chapel Hill: University of North Carolina Press, 1991), 70. For puritan approaches to scripture, see Bozeman, *Precisianist Strain*, 30; John S. Coolidge, *The Pauline Renaissance in England: Puritanism and the Bible* (Oxford: Oxford UP, 1970); and Knight, *Orthodoxies*, 130–163.

[25] Paul van Geest, *The Incomprehensibility of God: Augustine as a Negative Theologian* (Peeters: Paris, 2011), 214.

reformed piety.[26] Often focusing more on mystagogy than theology, this new religious style developed rhetorical and pastoral strategies designed to lead believers into the mystery of God's love rather than focusing on what could be communicated as information. In doing so, puritan writers began demonstrating greater sensitivity to the way that more rigid forms of protestant piety could undermine the pursuit of holy living within a broad-based national fellowship. In this respect, some aspects of the anti-puritan critiques launched by Hooker, Andrewes, and others began to register in the divinity of moderate puritans who came to maturity in Jacobean England such as John Preston and Richard Sibbes. Despite many differences, all of these writers placed increased emphasis on biblical conceptions of mystery as they qualified the pursuit of assurance and the simplicity of scripture more characteristic of earlier phases of reformation piety. In the process, rhetorically flexible and interpretively generous genres such as the devotional lyric found a more amenable social environment than had existed in previous decades. In the wake of the softening of reformed piety, religious poetry provided further avenues of expression for those who were wary of dogmatism and ecclesiastical exclusivism but were nevertheless deeply committed to spiritual transformation, Christian fellowship, and the beauty of holiness. It was within this context that Herbert structured *The Temple* around St. Paul's long-contested concept of *mysterion*, making it a central feature of how readers experience his particular form of poetic and spiritual neatness.

It is important to note here that in their pursuit of religious and social security, leading puritans like Perkins did not sunder faith from assurance in any strict doctrinal sense.[27] As far as fundamental doctrines about sin and salvation go, there is little meaningful difference between Calvin and mainstream English puritans. Pietists such as Sibbes agreed with Calvin

---

[26] Moore, *English Hypothetical Universalism*, 139; Knight, *Orthodoxies*.

[27] Richard A. Muller, *The Unaccommodated Calvin: Studies in the Foundation of a Theological Tradition* (Oxford: Oxford UP, 2000), Ch. 9 and *After Calvin: Studies in the Development of a Theological Tradition* (Oxford: Oxford UP, 2003); Joel R. Beeke, *Assurance of Faith*; Mark E. Dever, *Richard Sibbes: Puritanism and Calvinism in Late Elizabethan and Early Stuart England* (Macon: Mercer UP, 2000); and Moore, *English Hypothetical Universalism*. Although this body of scholarship is widely recognized as having superseded R.T. Kendall's, *Calvin and English Calvinism to 1649* (Oxford: Oxford UP, 1979), it has thus far had little effect on Herbert studies. One rarely cited exception is Lisa M. Gordis, "The Experience of Covenant Theology in George Herbert's 'The Temple'." *The Journal of Religion* 76.3 (July 1996), 383–401.

that works righteousness amounted to Catholic heresy and that one must ultimately ground assurance in Christ not through personal signs of justifying sanctification. There are, however, significant differences of emphasis and style within the puritan tradition, especially between Elizabethan pietists and a number of those writing in the following generation when puritanism was at its least militant (1603–1633). This generational difference helps explain why Herbert's work shows much greater affinity with Sibbes than with Perkins or even, for that matter, with Calvin. Sibbes and Herbert both belonged to a generation of churchmen who reemphasized the virtue of wonder, the centrality of the incarnation, the importance of divine and human love (especially as expressed in the Johannine corpus), and a more open-ended approach to scripture.

To be sure, though, these emphases often transcend parties and factions. If critiques of dogmatic certainties are audible in "avant-garde" churchmen such as Andrewes and Hooker and if they register in moderate puritans such as Sibbes and Preston, then they are also characteristic of dissenters such as Richard Baxter and Francis Rous. Despite many important differences, all of these writers recognized the spiritual and social dangers of religious polarity and exaggerated certitude. As a result, they all display a lyrical openness to mystery and a general wariness about dogmatism that is more characteristic of Collinson's third than second phase of the English Reformation. In their own context, however, these writers do not form a coherent group with an identifiable name.[28] Often differing about the role of the church as an interpretive community and on the nature of the two remaining sacraments, as well as other issues, men as different as Andrewes and Sibbes nevertheless responded to the internal pressures that had built up within protestant culture over the last century in similar, if not always identical, ways.[29]

[28] In fact, Andrewes conspired against Preston perhaps even aiming to expel him from Cambridge. See Moore, *English Hypothetical Universalism*, 15 and Irvonwy Morgan, *Prince Charles's Puritan Chaplain* (London: George Allen & Unwin Ltd., 1957), 46–50.

[29] As far as the conformist strain of this tradition goes, the term *Anglican* inevitably comes to mind as the best of a series of inadequate terms. As even Patrick Collinson admits, the term *Anglican*, which is anachronistic for the seventeenth century, is "perhaps justified if we are speaking of Lancelot Andrewes or John Donne or even of George Herbert, with his unusual devotion to the particular, maternal genius of the 'British Church'." *The Puritan Character: Polemics and Polarities in Early Seventeenth-Century English Culture* (UCLA: William Andrews Clark Memorial Library, 1989), 16. Collinson makes a similar point when he situates Herbert's *A Priest to the Temple* in relation to Hooker's *Laws of Ecclesiastical Polity* in *From Cranmer to Sancroft*, 55–56. See also Diarmaid MacCulloch's wry description of

Among the most important of these shared responses was the developing recognition that religious identities were often a matter of style and temperament as well as dogma. By the early Jacobean period, it was becoming increasingly clear that one's spiritual and expressive orientation could be as consequential as the substance of one's theology; or more precisely, that one's theology could only be construed through its rhetorical mediations and practical applications. In the case of the puritan movement, for example, much more was at stake than a doctrinal consensus. At issue was the manner in which key doctrines were communicated through practical divinity, how they were applied in pastoral and polemical contexts.[30] While this generally meant that puritans held basic protestant beliefs more rigorously than others, it also resulted in a wide variation of religious styles within puritanism itself. This variation was so pronounced that puritanism ultimately had "no stable ideological valence"; it could be "moderate, hierarchical, repressive and orthodox, but it could also be divisive, extreme, and heterodox. Which aspect of this complex … ideological mixture predominated … depended on a whole series of social … and intellectual forces."[31]

Like Herbert, puritans seeking to avoid social divisiveness often drew on the nondogmatic strains of St. Augustine as a way of tempering the more polemical features of godly piety. As William Haller observes in his foundational study of puritanism, preachers such as Sibbes may have been Calvinist to varying degrees but the "French reformer's positive, clear, dogmatic intelligence" did not, on the whole, provide "a model of discourse which they chose to imitate when they mounted the pulpit."[32]

Richard Baxter, a dissenter, as the "first of the Anglicans" in "The Latitude of the Church of England" in *Religious Politics in Post-Reformation England: Essays in Honour of Nicholas Tyacke* eds. Fincham and Lake (Woodbridge: Boydell Press, 2006), 41–59, 58–59.

[30] Peter Lake, *Moderate puritans and the Elizabethan church* (Cambridge: Cambridge UP, 1982) 7; Patrick Collinson, "The Jacobean Religious Settlement: The Hampton Court Conference" in *Before the English Civil War: Essays on Early Stuart Politics and Government* ed. Howard Tomlinson (London: Macmillan, 1983), 27–52, 29–30; J. Sears McGee, *The Godly Man in Stuart England: Anglicans, Puritans, and the Two Tables, 1620–1670* (New Haven: Yale UP, 1976), 7–11.

[31] Peter Lake, "'A charitable Christian hatred': the godly and their enemies in the 1630's" in C. Durston and J. Eales eds. *The Culture of English Puritanism 1560–1700* (Basingstoke: Macmillan, 1996), 145–83, 182–3.

[32] William Haller, *The Rise of Puritanism* (New York: Columbia UP, 1938; rpt. Harper and Row, 1957), 85. Haller's basic view is given fuller elaboration in Knight's, *Orthodoxies in Massachusetts*.

Actually, Haller continues, some puritan preachers "referred as often to
St. Augustine as to the author of the *Institutes*."[33] Mark E. Dever's recent
study of Sibbes confirms Haller's basic view in somewhat more nuanced
terms. According to Dever, Sibbes was a conforming puritan with an irenic, nondogmatic Augustinian sensibility. Celebrated for his ability to convert dissenters to the English church, Sibbes emphasized the cognitive
and illuminative dimensions of conversion to the point that he has been
misread as denying the gratuitous nature of grace. For Sibbes, as Dever
explains, "The [Holy] Spirit did not simply persuade; rather He enlightened the elect by opening the eyes of the soul to God because 'A carnal
eye will never see spiritual things.'" Sibbes thus "presented conversion as a
more Augustinian notion—the Spirit's action in enlightenment is a transforming event in the soul."[34] These kinds of emphases suggest some of the
ways Sibbes modified aspects of the puritan tradition that often worried
its conformist critics, particularly Elizabethan puritanism's somewhat programmatic emphasis on assurance and security.

Yet, what most concerned Sibbes was not the overconfidence of fellow puritans but "the atheism of these times," the way in which so many
"stand in awe of nothing" (7.302). Throughout his sermons, Sibbes can
be heard lamenting that "coldness and deadness is a spiritual disease in
these days" (6.41). For "we live," as he says elsewhere, "in a soiling age ...
[and] an infected air" (7.309). More than just a pastoral convention or
ministerial reflex, these claims constitute a sustained cultural diagnosis,
one that significantly differs from the sense of optimism that John Jewel
expressed at the beginning of Elizabeth's reign when he declared, "The
sun is risen; the day is open ... The night is past."[35] No longer in the dawn
of reformation glory, Sibbes saw Christendom as undergoing an eclipse of
mystery, the result of which was violence, idolatry, and spiritual deadness.
Through this cultural diagnosis, Sibbes cultivated a religious and expressive sensibility illuminatingly similar to Herbert's.

[33] Ibid. Owen C. Watkins makes the same point with reference to Richard Norwood's
spiritual autobiography in *The Puritan Experience* (London: Routledge and Kegan, 1972),
61, 80.
[34] Mark E. Dever, *Richard Sibbes*, 122. Seeing Sibbes' thought in the context of the softening of reformed theology helps explain a feature of his thought that Pettit observed but
didn't account for, namely Sibbes' practice of writing with "a minimum of concern for the
rigors of dogma." See *The Heart Prepared*, 67.
[35] Cited in Christopher Haigh, "Success and Failure in the English Reformation" *Past and
Present* 11.173 (2001), 28–49, 28.

Viewed in these contexts, it becomes evident that Herbert's emphasis on mystery emerged out of a broadly reformed and relatively ill-defined mixture of varying positions rather than anything that can be accurately summarized as Calvinist or even, strictly speaking, consensual. Even revisionist historians like Collinson note that the "label 'Calvinist' ... by no means accurately describes the doctrine of grace taught in the Thirty-nine Articles, or even its treatment in Archbishop Whitgift's Lambeth Articles of 1595."[36] But now that ecclesiastical historiography has moved into a so-called post-revisionist phase, increasing stress has been placed on the extent to which Elizabethan and Jacobean polities were "knitted together in a manner whose complexity is not adequately captured by the notion of a Calvinist consensus."[37] As a result, there is an increasing awareness that many Jacobean churchmen cannot be meaningfully understood as Calvinist or anti-Calvinist.[38]

One influential example of this cultivated ambiguity is John Overall (1559–1619), bishop of Coventry and Lichfield and later Norwich. Highly revered in the 1620s by churchmen of differing styles of piety, Overall argued that the English church maintained a theory of saving grace that stood midway between Calvinist predestinarianism and Arminian freewill views.[39] By no means alone in his theology, Overall adopted a religious style that has been attributed to Hooker and which has been shown to have influenced other church leaders.[40] If this kind of synthesis is even

[36] Patrick Collinson, *The Elizabethan Puritan Movement* (Oxford: Clarendon Press, 1967; rpt. 2004), 37.

[37] Charles W.A. Prior, *Defining the Jacobean Church: The Politics of Religious Controversy, 1603–1625* (Cambridge: Cambridge UP, 2005), 10.

[38] See Peter White, *Predestination and Polemic: Conflict and Consensus in the English Church from the Reformation to the Civil War* (Cambridge: Cambridge UP, 2002), 140; and Julian Davies, *The Caroline Captivity of the Church: Charles I and the Remoulding of Anglicanism 1625–1641* (Oxford: Clarendon Press, 1992), 93. Even those who sharply disagree with White's critique of revisionary accounts of the Jacobean and Caroline churches agree that Stuart religious culture is better defined as a complex spectrum riven with tensions than a set of fixed binaries structuring a static consensus. See, for instance, Peter Lake, "Predestinarian Propositions" *Journal of Ecclesiastical History* 46.1 (1995), 110–123.

[39] Anthony Milton, "'Anglicanism' by Stealth: The Career and Influence of John Overall" in *Religious Politics in Post-Reformation England: Essays in Honour of Nicholas Tyacke* eds. Kenneth Fincham and Peter Lake (Woodbridge: Boydell Press, 2006), 159–176, 175, 173. See also Lake, "The moderate and irenic case for religious war," 75–6.

[40] See Moore, *English Hypothetical Universalism*, 203. For Hooker, see Nigel Voak, *Richard Hooker and Reformed Theology: A Study of Reason, Will, and Grace* (Oxford: Oxford UP, 2003).

roughly true of some in the Stuart clergy, then it is doubly so of a poetic work as deeply sensitive to the varying, even competing, spiritual dispositions available in seventeenth-century England as Herbert's *The Temple*. Ultimately, such syncretism helps explain why categories like Calvinist and Arminian do not serve as sufficient context for *The Temple*. In Herbert's tradition, what is sometimes more decisive than explicitly stated dogma is a general wariness about exaggerated claims to religious certitude, be it obnoxious assertions of personal assurance or overly refined statements of transparently clear dogma.[41]

This anti-dogmatic wariness reflects a nuanced understanding of the complexities of religious doctrine as a cultural phenomenon. Many in the period recognized that doctrine consists of much more than propositional statements synchronically enshrined in articles of faith. It emerges over time out of generically and rhetorically discrete speech acts evolving through both written and oral discourse.[42] Viewed this way, Herbert's religious culture appears to be defined by differences in style and disposition as well as by generalized forms of doctrinal consensus. This is one of the reasons we will never be able to determine the religious contexts informing Herbert's *The Temple* according to a specific, preexisting theological framework. It is too thoughtful, dynamic, and open-ended a response to an ecclesiastical synthesis shot through with competing impulses, one that remained irreducible to predicate statements about belief and worship or binaries such as Calvinist and Arminian. When taken as a whole, revisionist and post-revisionist ecclesiastical historiography reads like an explanation of the "generous ambiguity" for which Herbert is sometimes celebrated.[43]

---

[41] Hence the calculated ambiguity of Herbert's "The Water-course," a poem that says nothing to which Augustine, Aquinas, Luther, Calvin, Perkins, or Andrewes could object on strict theological grounds. For the relevant issue of God's judgment pertaining to the poem, see Richard A. Muller, "The Myth of 'Decretal Theology'" *Calvin Theological Journal* 30.1 (1995), 159–67, 163. I discuss the poem in Chap. 5. Here it is also helpful to recall that the rise of a Calvinist orthodoxy in protestant Europe was partly the result of the Frenchman's capacity for highly precise definitions, a virtue that churchmen of Herbert's generation often avoided. For this feature of Calvin's thought, see Muller, *The Unaccommodated Calvin*, 184.

[42] Brian Cummings, *The Literary Culture of the Reformation: Grammar and Grace* (Oxford: Oxford UP, 2002), 285. See also P.G. Lake, "Calvinism and the English Church 1570–1635" *Past & Present* 114.1 (1987), 32–76, 49–50; Prior, *Defining the Jacobean Church*, 6; and McGee, *Godly Man*, 7–11.

[43] For the most nuanced statement along these lines, see Cummings, *The Literary Culture*, 281–327. Although Cummings observes that the Calvinist/anti-Calvinist binary often breaks down in the period, I see this as more self-consciously typical, more purposefully

Needless to say, this does not mean that doctrine is irrelevant for understanding Herbert's poetry. On the contrary, it means that we must attend
to the formal mediations of theology in his lyrics. Rather than being a
statement of faith, a Herbert poem is a complex aesthetic process consisting of an implied backstory, a beginning, a middle, and an end, all of
which are mediated by voice, form, figure, and allusion. And although the
application of doctrine to life is often a crucial feature of Herbert's spiritual aesthetic, it constitutes part of the poetic experience rather than being
its ultimate, synchronically translatable result. On the one hand, then,
Herbert's generous ambiguity is a function of his attention to poetic form
and the experience that particular lyric forms represent and generate. As a
first-rate critical theorist, Herbert recognized that a lyric poem is an event
in the participating consciousness of the reader as well as a representation
of an unfolding experience on the part of the speaker. On the other hand,
however, Herbert's generous ambiguity is also as an expression of a spiritual ethos taking shape within Herbert's own lifetime. While this ethos
possesses deep continuity with earlier phases of the Reformation, it also
shows important differences of style and emphasis as Herbert responded
to the period's shifting contexts and changing exigencies alongside men as
different as Andrewes and Sibbes.

THE KING JAMES BIBLE AND THE ECLIPSE OF MYSTERY

The productive ambiguity characteristic of some Jacobean religious thought
is consistent with and perhaps in some sense a product of the Authorized
Version of the bible (1611), which Overall had a hand in translating as
a member of Lancelot Andrewes's First Westminster Company.[44] As is
often noted, the Authorized Version is remarkable for its self-conscious
openness to variable meanings, especially on matters of doctrine and discipline. The translators consciously embraced formulations susceptible to
different, even competing interpretations, always aware, it would seem, of

characteristic, of early Stuart divinity than he does. See also Louis Martz, "The Generous
Ambiguity of Herbert's *The Temple*," in ed. Mary A. Maleski. *A Fine Tuning: Studies of the
Religious Poetry of Herbert and Milton* (Binghamton NY: MRTS, 1989), 31–56 and Bruce
A. Johnson, "Theological Inconsistency and Its Uses in George Herbert's Poetry" *George
Herbert Journal* 15.2 (Spring: 1992), 2–18.

[44] See Adam Nicolson, *God's Secretaries: The Making of the King James Bible* (New York:
Perennial, 2004), 251 and Benson Bobrick, *Wide as the Waters: The Story of the English Bible
And The Revolution It Inspired* (New York: Penguin, 2002), 313.

partisan criticism and an unnecessary narrowing of exegetical possibility.[45] Where Tyndale and the Genevan translators sought clarity and straightforwardness, the King James translators chose phrases for their suggestive resonances. The result was an accessible text that nevertheless sustained some of the alien and thus potentially estranging features of the Hebrew and Greek originals.[46] Moreover, where the Geneva bible controlled interpretation through doctrinally charged marginal notes, the Jacobean translators were instructed by Archbishop Bancroft to avoid all such glossing. They were even told to eschew explaining Greek and Hebrew terms in marginal notes if their meanings could be conveyed via *circumlocutions* within the text, a term that means both explain and conceal.[47] A self-consciously nondogmatic distillation of previous translations, the King James Bible is Jacobean England's most influential expression of neatness in Herbert's sense of the term.[48]

Indeed, Herbert's *The Temple* is an exquisite expression of the same flexibility that gave rise to the Authorized Version and the climate of synthesis and compromise in which its translators worked. Like the Authorized Version, *The Temple* was written out of an intellectually vigorous belief in the virtues of wise ignorance and the complex simplicity that follows from it. Perhaps this was because Herbert was unusually well positioned to internalize the styles of piety and expression enshrined in the AV. When he was a student at Westminster (1604–1608), the school's dean, Lancelot Andrewes, was heading the committee responsible for translating Genesis through 2 Kings of which Overall was a member. And by the time Herbert was elected scholar of Trinity College, Cambridge, in 1609, critiques of religious certainty had been resonating in Oxbridge and London for over a generation. While this conversation came to something of a climax at the Hampton Court Conference in 1604, questions about religious certainty preoccupied and, in many senses, came to define English protestant culture over the course of the coming century. Herbert very much came of

[45] Gerald Hammond, "English Translations of the Bible" in *The Literary Guide to the Bible* eds. Robert Alter and Frank Kermode (Cambridge, Massachusetts: Harvard UP, 1987), 647–667, 661.

[46] Nicolson, *God's Secretaries*, 77–78; David Norton, *A History of the English Bible As Literature* (Cambridge: Cambridge UP, 2000), 62–3.

[47] See Nicolson, *God's Secretaries*, 77, 145 and appendices 3, 4, and 5 of Bobrick, *Wide as the Waters*, 301–317.

[48] This nondogmatic attitude is articulated in the prefatory letter "Translators to the Reader," which I discuss in Chap. 3.

age in a world in which many of the things that mattered most in English Protestantism hinged on differences over questions of security and clarity. And few, if anyone, in Jacobean England had more scholarly authority on such issues than Lancelot Andrewes whom Herbert praised in the dedicatory address to *Musae Responsoriae* as a "watchman of heaven, / Whose learning none on earth can equal, / Whose matchless holiness the stars are witness to" (*quo sanctius astra vident*) (4–5).

Beginning around 1592, Andrewes began publicly criticizing the spiritual overconfidence of "a great many [who] think that presumption in being secure of their salvation is good divinity" (5.531).[49] He was particularly concerned with protestants who were reducing faith to a systematic exercise graspable through reason. He thus mocked those who had "God's secret decrees ... at their fingers' ends ... the number and order of them just with 1, 2, 3, 4, 5" (3.32). Behind such efforts, Andrewes spied an unrealistic expectation of total assurance of salvation through faith alone, one that had negative spiritual and social consequences. Fearing that God's mystery was being eclipsed in the period, Andrewes complained how "even some that are far enough from Rome ... think they perceive all God's secret decrees, the number and order of them clearly; and are indeed too bold and too busy with them" (3.328). As loaded terms like *bold* and *busy* indicate, Andrewes' intended target at such moments were puritans, particularly those who behaved as though the "word of God had come ... to them only, and none besides" (2.408).

However broadly Andrewes intended such anti-puritan remarks, his critique applies much more to the programmatic style of divinity associated with the "Intellectual Fathers" William Perkins and William Ames than it does to the lyrical and affective piety of the "Cambridge Brethren" led by Sibbes and Preston.[50] After all, what ultimately worried Andrewes

[49] Although I modify emphases and make some additions, the following account of Andrewes derives largely from Peter Lake, "Lancelot Andrewes, John Buckeridge, and avant-garde conformity at the court of James I" in *The Mental World of the Jacobean Court* ed. Linda Levy Peck (Cambridge: Cambridge UP, 1991), 113–133. Many of my quotes are used to similar effect in his article. See also Nicholas Tyacke, "Lancelot Andrewes and the Myth of Anglicanism" in *Conformity and Orthodoxy in the English Church*, c. 1560–1660 eds. Peter Lake and Michael Questier (Woodbridge: Boydell, 2000), 5–33 and Lori Ann Ferrell, *Government By Polemic: James I, The King's Preachers, and the Rhetorics of Conformity* 1603–1625 (Stanford: Stanford UP, 1998). For strong evidence that Andrewe's "radical reassessment of the English Reformation" extended "well back into the 1580's," see McCullough, *Lancelot Andrewes*, xiii, xvi.

[50] For the use of these categories, see Knight, *Orthodoxies in Massachusetts*.

was the over-rationalization of the *ordo salutis*, the process of conversion through which one can know that one is of the elect and the reductive biblicism that undergirded it, both of which also concerned Sibbes and Preston though in different ways and to different degrees. In a subtle but sustained effort to combat puritan intellectualism, Andrewes cultivated a lively sense of spiritual reading and a deeply affective mode of piety that often bears important similarities with Sibbes.

Perhaps even more than the Cambridge Brethren, however, Andrewes often stressed the estranging paradoxes of scripture while exploring its linguistically alien idioms. But like them, he stressed the importance of applying scripture to one's own spiritual condition. In doing so, he emphasized Augustine's view that exegesis and application are inextricably bound up with one another rather than being separate interpretive processes. The overall result is a style of piety centered on wonder over the incarnation and a deep sense of awe over scriptural richness, especially as embodied in the liturgy; hence his teaching that Christians should find ways to participate in the unfolding mystery rather than seek mental control of God's attributes as when he warns: "We hear those [speculative] points too often, and love them too well: points of practice are less pleasing, but more profitable for us; namely how we may get into the partnership of this mystery" (1.41). For Andrewes, it was crucial that members of the church understand that divinity is a field of knowledge which simply does not permit the kind of certainty one enjoys with sciences such as mathematics. In theology, he insists, one arrives at truth through deduction, sometimes working from the "twentieth hand" (5.527). And, even then, "There is a part of divinity that dazzles; if we look too long on it, we may well lose our sight" (1.228).

As Peter Lake notes, Andrewes was fundamentally concerned with how too many churchmen had "reduced religion to the transfer and assimilation of information,"[51] hence Andrewes's complaint about men who behave "as though Christian religion ... had but certain *theses* to be held, dogmatical points, matters of opinion" (1.288). He says something similar elsewhere when he observes that too many fellow protestants misconstrue religion as a simple matter of knowledge rather than a bewildering affair of the heart: "Such is the imagination in our days of carnal Gospellers; that, so he forget not his creed, he cannot miscarry. These be the Gnostics of our age" (5.58). In making such claims, Andrewes maintained a degree of vagueness about whom he was attacking exactly. One of his aims in doing

---

[51] Lake, "Andrewes ... and avant-garde conformity," 115.

so may have been to bring a critique of reductive conceptions of edification typical of anti-puritan leaders such as Archbishop Whitgift under the umbrella of exaggerated claims to assurance characteristic of some puritan divines. By means of this strategy, Andrewes was able to disguise a partial critique of conformist piety under the appearance of a strictly anti-puritan one.[52] Here it is helpful to recall that in his response to the puritan charge that the rites of the English church were unedifying, Whitgift lowered the threshold of what counts as edifying by saying that some things in the church "pertain to instruction and some to order and comeliness."[53] In doing so, Whitgift equated edification with the teaching of basic doctrine through preaching while associating ceremonies with the maintenance of decency and order. Wary of such a reductive view of conformist piety, Andrewes appears to have buried an implicit critique of Whitgift's view of edification and ceremony within his broader critique of puritan presumption. The result is a style of piety that differs in some respects from both puritans and conformists in the period; hence Lake's use of the term *avant-garde* to describe it.

However unusual Andrewes' style of piety may have been in early Jacobean England, his critique of puritanism was echoed throughout the seventeenth century, caricature and all, by anti-puritan writers such as Anthony Farindon, Ralph Cudworth, Humphrey Sydenham, Archbishop Laud and others.[54] In many respects, this critique of puritanism marks a return to early reformation emphases on the mysteriousness of God's ways, especially the Luthero-Calvinist insistence on God's inscrutability. At the same time, however, Andrewes stressed the estranging, polyphonic richness of scripture and the high mystery of sacraments in ways that often went beyond what early reformers were willing to say on such topics.[55]

Yet the issue here is perhaps less a matter of theological substance than broadly shifting exigencies. After all, Luther and Calvin faced very different pastoral challenges than Andrewes and Herbert. For early reformers, the key challenge was to overcome the spiritual anxiety generated by the Roman Catholic church's privileging of works righteousness and

---

[52] For Whitgift's arguably reductive view of edification, see Coolidge, *Pauline Renaissance* 23–54 and Lake, *Anglicans and Puritans: Presbyterianism and English Conformist Thought from Whitgift to Hooker* (London: Unwin Hyman, 1988), 19, 39, 65.

[53] Cited and explained in Lake, *Anglicans and Puritans*, 39.

[54] See McGee, *Godly Man*, 105–7 and Morgan, *Prince Charles's Puritan Chaplain*, 39–40.

[55] For Andrewes' figuring of biblical polyphony as song, see his 1619 Nativity Sermon (1.215–232).

the interpretive confusion engendered by its allegorical traditions, hence the early reformation emphasis on scripture's monological clarity and the Pauline idea that assurance comes by faith alone. Andrewes, however, faced something like the opposite threat. He found it necessary to critique overly systematic approaches to assurance and an exegetical style motivated by a desire for interpretive control for the sake of spiritual security. The result is a different set of emphases than we find in earlier stages of the Reformation coupled with a distinct exegetical and spiritual style. Crucially, many of these emphases were shared by men who did not wholly embrace Andrewes' anti-Calvinism, including James I and Herbert as well as, to some extent, the Cambridge Brethren centered around Sibbes. If churchmen as different as Sibbes and Andrewes shared some emphases vis-à-vis scriptural mystery, it is partly because seventeenth-century exigencies differ from those of the previous century. To read Herbert historically, we need to draw distinctions of time and style as well as distinctions of bare, synchronically conceived doctrine. Doing so will help us better understand how the works of Henry Vaughan, Thomas Traherne, and Richard Baxter were made possible by the generation to which Herbert belonged.

It is also important to remember that Andrewes' concern with religious and interpretive overconfidence animates the formal structure of his sermons as well as their thematic content. Through a range of formal strategies, he incorporates listeners into his text, sometimes by concluding with an invitation to participate in the eucharist and sometimes by promising listeners future participation in the banquet of the kingdom.[56] For Andrewes, scripture is not simply a text to be interpreted but also a song to be sung, a chorus to be joined.[57] In this respect, his sermons teach listeners how to experience scripture as a living mystery, a dynamic text which cannot be possessed in the same way in all contexts. And however avant-garde such an approach may have been, Andrewes remained one of the most powerful men in the Jacobean church, exercising influence not only through court sermons but also through church appointments, biblical translation, and shrewd political calculations. His influence, especially on Herbert, should not be underestimated, particularly when it comes to biblical hermeneutics and the edifying power of liturgy.[58]

---

[56] For a discussion of some of these strategies, see Lossky, *Lancelot Andrewes*, 32–100.

[57] See, for example, 1.215–232.

[58] For important correctives to the view that Hooker and Andrewes constituted an avant-garde style of piety, see Ferrell, *Government By Polemic*; Prior, *Defining the Jacobean Church*; and White, *Predestination and Polemic*.

HERBERT AND THE ECLIPSE OF MYSTERY

If Herbert came to agree with those who were concerned about a post-Elizabethan eclipsing of mystery, it was perhaps because he was unusually well positioned to see two of the diametrically opposed ways in which it manifested in the period. As a young man at Cambridge, a member of parliament for the borough of Montgomery, and priest in the English church, Herbert had occasion to confront dogmatic claims to certainty grounded in crude forms of scriptural interpretation and the forms of spiritual inspiration that often and irritatingly accompanied them. Such experience may help explain why Herbert suggests in *The Country Parson* that the minister's greatest threat is "Spirituall pride" and "selfe-conceite" (238). But as the younger brother of Lord Cherbury, whose 1624 treatise *De Veritate* was probably the most influential work of rational theology in seventeenth-century England, Herbert was also close to the dreaded threat of "deism" which Pierre Viret and Robert Burton both warned of prior to Cherbury's bombshell.[59] Despite their enormous differences from one another, these two tendencies share something essential in Herbert's view: they both foreclose the place of mystery in religious life in favor of certainty and confidence. But where dogmatists do this on the basis of scriptural authority and personal experience of the Holy Spirit, rationalists do it on the basis of universal reason and the forms of natural religion to which it gives rise.

Herbert understood these dynamics rather well. Wary of both dogmatism and rationalism, Herbert perspicuously recognized how the spiritual and hermeneutic sustenance provided by the experience of mystery was coming under pressure from two very different flanks. In response, he exploited the resources of the religious lyric to revitalize long-standing but newly threatened Christian investments in the idea of revelation as a *mysterion*. Many of the key formal features of Herbert's verse, including its patterning of correction and revision, work to estrange common scriptural idioms, thereby generating wonder about its neatness. Ultimately, Herbert's conception of poetry as a particular kind of spiritual practice is concomitant with, and perhaps even to some extent an outgrowth of, his view of scripture as a living mystery. In poetry, that is to say, Herbert saw much more than a medium for personal expression or noncontroversial pastoral care; in it, he saw a privileged way of sustaining the vitality of mystery at an historical moment when it no longer went without saying.

---

[59] See Chap. 6 for references.

Situated as he was, Herbert shared some of his contemporaries' concerns with the way that dogmatism and rationalism could serve as defensive postures against authentic spiritual experience. Throughout his poetry, Herbert explores what, exactly, happens when a human being understands something in a way that does much more than add to a previous storehouse of information for the sake of intellectual mastery. His poetry routinely explores the differences between understanding as a form of personal edification versus knowledge as a correspondence between mind and world via information-transfer. These issues preoccupied Herbert because he shared the concern that his culture was losing the capacity to articulate the full force of this distinction due to extreme forms of fideism and rationalism. Crucially for him, these two interrelated dispositions disguised a psychological defense against spiritual mortification, the experience of "dying" that has been astutely described as "the deepest poetic rhythm of *The Temple*."[60] In Herbert's view, genuine spiritual experience involves the breaking down of one's defenses, one's prior assumptions, and thus one's habitual way of being as a self-centered isolated being. By providing the certainty and stability that Milton's Satan calls a "fixed mind," dogmatism and rationalism prevent this kind of transformative experience from taking place. Understood as attitudinal dispositions as well as intellectual stances, dogmatism and rationalism constitute, for Herbert, two different ways in which pride expresses itself. As the earthy wisdom of Sibbes would have it, "A proud nature arms itself with defences, as a hedgehog winds himself round and defends himself by his pricks" (7.358).

In Herbert's tradition, one of the key roles of the Holy Spirit is to overcome such hedgehog-like defenses. Despite his post-Restoration reputation as the "sweet singer of Bemerton," Herbert generally assumes that there is something stupefying about God's presence in the world. As the speaker of "Justice" complains, first in thumping tetrameter and then in an exasperated, metrically stressed opposition between God's creative and destructive action in the soul:

> I cannot skill of these thy wayes.
> *Lord, thou didst make me, yet thou woundest me;*
> *Lord, thou dost wound me, yet thou dost relieve me;*
> *Lord, thou relievest, yet I die by thee.* (1–4)

---

[60] Esther Gilman Richey, "The Property of God: Luther, Calvin, and Herbert's Sacrifice Sequence" *ELH* 78.2 (2011), 287–314, 302.

With typical Herbertian irony, the answer to this confusion brings with it yet another level of bewilderment. In the following stanza, the speaker reflects upon himself only to conclude, with the emphasis on the penultimate syllable: "I cannot skill of these my wayes" (12). Like Christianity's greatest critic of rationalism Søren Kierkegaard, Herbert assumes that experiences worthy of the name edifying are, more often than not, dismaying, for such experiences estrange and surprise even as they may ultimately enrich, expand, and console. As Kierkegaard writes:

> Where there is nothing at all dismaying and no dismay, there is nothing at all edifying and no edification ... One should not be terrified by the dismay, as though it might stand in the way of edification, nor keep it timorously at a distance, in the hope of making the edification acceptable; for with the fear of dismay the edification vanishes. But on the other hand it is precisely in dismay that edification lies.[61]

Herbert's critique of uncritical dogmatism on the one hand, and unfettered rationalism on the other, is a critique of those practices which preclude the shocking dimensions of edification, the building up of the "new man" by first the tearing down of the old: "*Lord, thou dost kill me, yet thou dost reprieve me*" ("Justice," 5). These are precisely the experiences that Andrewes and Sibbes both worried were declining in English Protestantism.

For Herbert, the dismaying experience of edification is interpretive or hermeneutic as well as spiritual or psychological. In his view, the process of regeneration is fundamentally biblical in nature; it happens, as we have seen, through an encounter with a Word that "suddenly dost raise and race, / And e'ry day a new Creatour art" ("The Temper (II)," 7–8). Deeply sensitive to the idea that the divine Word is a double-edged sword that both destroys and renews (Heb. 4:12), Herbert came to see dogmatism and rationalism as strategies for keeping the dismayingly creative force of the Word at a distance. For him, these dispositions are ways of timorously defending against the unpredictability of the divine Word. After all, they both falsely presuppose that one knows what "fresh and new discov'ries" the Word will reveal in advance of its actually doing so. In short, Herbert diagnosed dogmatism and rationalism as both powerful, if pathetic, means of not having to endure spiritual change. This is why

---

[61] Søren Kierkegaard, *Christian Discourses* trans. Walter Lowrie (New York: Oxford UP, 1961), 102.

one of the most powerful challenges Herbert's speakers confront in *The Temple* is the temptation to imagine oneself "past changing," to misconstrue peace as emotional, psychological, or worse yet, professional, stability ("The Flower," 22). As the speaker of "Dotage" writes, such is the "folly of distracted men" seeking after "False glozing pleasures, casks of happinesse … / Shadows well mounted, dreams in a career" (13, 1, 3). Herbert's primary theme is religious understanding as a species of ongoing and often excruciating spiritual transformation, the sort of transformation one might sooner resist than endure. But what makes these dispositions truly dangerous in Herbert's view is that all Christians have something of the dogmatist and rationalist lurking in them potentially preventing them from becoming a "stormie working soul" who "Dare[s] to be true" ("The Church-porch," 76–77).

Given Herbert's spiritual orientation, it is easy to see why he routinely qualifies claims about scripture's simplicity, often emphasizing that "Bibles laid open," offer "millions of surprises" ("Sinne (I)," 8). Correlatively, his spiritual vision also helps explain why so many of his poems enact processes of discovery. Unlike medieval religious lyrics which tend to be organized paratactically, such that one could reorganize the sequence of stanzas without significantly altering the poem's meaning or effect, Herbert's speakers often develop in the course of a lyric through careful stanzaic arrangements, complex shifts in tone, and subtle patterns of correction and revision.[62] While these processes are inherently formal in nature and must thus be understood in poetic terms, they are nevertheless mediated by a host of historical pressures and investments, almost all of which come back to questions of biblical exegesis.

In Chap. 2, I outline these pressures and investments by explaining the hermeneutic notions of mystery and revelation animating *The Temple*. Then in Chap. 3, I explain the intellectual and cultural pressures being brought to bear upon Augustinian concepts of biblical mystery by tracing the rise and fall of exegetical optimism in reformation thought. Chapter 4 then considers how these pressures constitute the spiritual exigency behind Herbert's depiction of spiritual adoption in his verse, especially in his celebrated lyric "Perseverance" and the doctrinally significant "Assurance." Developing this analysis, Chaps. 5, 6, and 7 examine Herbert's response to

---

[62] For a discussion of the paratactic structure of medieval religious lyrics, see Patrick S. Diehl, *The Medieval European Religious Lyric: An Ars Poetica* (Berkeley: University of California Press, 1985), 15.

dogmatism and rationalism, first with reference to *Briefe Notes on Valdesso*, then in relation to Herbert's reaction to his elder brother Edward, and lastly with reference to the productive role that error plays in Herbert's anti-methodological hermeneutics. Taken together, these six chapters show how many of Herbert's poetic strategies constitute formal, literary responses to the eclipse of mystery diagnosed in the period, many of which have important social and ecclesiastical as well as aesthetic and spiritual consequences.

While the next six chapters focus on Herbert's depiction of the bible as a text to be read, the final chapter examines how Herbert assumed that scripture was a book to be heard. In doing so, I explain how early modern ideas about sound and hearkening inform Herbert's practice of mystagogy, the way he leads readers into the mysteries of faith. Developing a line of inquiry initiated in Chap. 7, the final chapter considers how it was likely through his reading of Bacon that Herbert came to recognize the spiritual and aesthetic dangers of reducing mysteries into problems which brings me to one of the major aims of this book.[63]

Throughout this study, I try to demonstrate how Herbert routinely explores what happens when inexhaustible conditions of human existence devolve into riddles that one might solve once and for all, like so many Gordian knots. The great temptation with which Herbert is often concerned in his poetry is the temptation to fully comprehend the Christian narrative by implicitly exempting oneself from it, thereby *slipping the collar* as Andrewes says in a sermon that may have given Herbert an idea for a poem (3.98). Indeed, when Andrewes worries about an eclipse of mystery within English Protestantism, it is precisely this tendency to assume an objective rather than participatory stance with respect to scripture that he is addressing. For him, a hermeneutically robust notion of mystery is the *sine qua non* of Christian faith. Without it, as Sir Thomas Browne later confirmed, a scripturally centered religion is simply not sustainable. If scripture is not a living narrative in which one spiritually moves, then it has devolved into a dead letter, either because it has become mere history or because it is only legible as a set of rules for ethical behavior or the promise of individual salvation. Once such hermeneutic degradation sets in, the idea of Christianity as a fellowship of the mystery becomes meaningless and with it the very idea of faith itself.

---

[63] For an explanation of the distinction between mysteries and problems, see the quote from Gabriel Marcel in my epigraph to this book.

While these dangers were known to early reformers like Luther and Calvin, they greatly increased in the following century. Writing in the wake of such pressures, Herbert also came to see that a hermeneutically robust notion of mystery is the *sine qua non* of any Christian poetry worthy of the name. And out of this awareness came not only a little volume of poetry printed in duodecimo format called *The Temple* but also a set of formally mediated spiritual and exegetical insights that would play a decisive role in nourishing subsequent biblical literature in England and beyond.

CHAPTER 2

Mystery in *The Temple*

The Temple's investment in biblical notions of mystery is evident from the very outset of "The Church," first appearing in "Superliminare" (meaning lintel above the door):

> Avoid profanenesse; come not here:
> Nothing but holy, pure, and cleare,
> Or that which groneth to be so,
> May at his perill further go. (5–8)

Reminiscent of the prohibitive tone in the prayer book's prefaces and rubrics, this warning functions like the hortatory signs placed outside of pagan temples which reveal that even the heathens, as Richard Sibbes explains, "Carry themselves reverently in their mysteries; *Procul este profane*, Away, begone all profane" (5.465). This declaration thus claims for poems what *The Country Parson* maintains for sermons, that they "are dangerous things ... none goes out of Church as he came in, but either better, or worse" (233). More precisely, "Superliminare" suggests that to faithfully cross the "The Church's" threshold means confirming one's participation in a community that is grounded on an identification with the death and resurrection of Jesus, a living temple of "one body in Christ" (Rom. 12:5). Based on St. Paul's parallels between Christian revelation and Hellenistic mystery cults, "Superliminare" summons readers to "approach, and taste / The churches mysticall repast" (3–4) but at their own risk.

© The Author(s) 2017
G. Kuchar, *George Herbert and the Mystery of the Word*,
DOI 10.1007/978-3-319-44045-3_2

In doing so, it signals Herbert's role as *mystagogue* or the poet-priest who leads initiates through the mysteries as a means of sanctification.

By establishing Herbert's role as mystagogue, "Superliminare" structures *The Temple* around the New Testament notion of *mysterion*. A central but highly contested biblical concept, the term *mysterion* appears in the New Testament 27 or 28 times.[1] In its pre-Christian usage, *mysterion* unites a variety of meanings, including "the sacred, arcane or hidden, and initiation (*sacra, arcanum, initia*)."[2] Partly due to this range of meanings, biblical uses of *mysterion* raise difficult exegetical questions. Most significantly for medieval and reformation interpreters, Paul's use of the term was thought to imply a play of similarity and difference between Christian fellowship and the Eleusinian mysteries, the exact nature of which continues to exercise scholars.[3] Like later Christian exegetes, the early fathers were anxious to differentiate pagan mystery rites from Ephesians' "fellowship of the mystery" (3:9). Tertullian did this by sharply distinguishing between *sacramenta*, which had no associations with Greek religion, and *mysteria*, which did.[4] Ambrose took an even more precise approach to the issue. In his writings, *sacramentum* generally refers to the sensibly experienced aspect of Christian worship while *mysterium* denotes the invisible reality at work in it.[5]

---

[1] Raymond E. Brown, S.S. *The Semitic Background of the Term 'Mystery' in the New Testament* (Philadelphia: Fortress Press, 1968), 3.

[2] Daniel G. Van Slyke, "The Changing Meanings of *Sacramentum*: Historical Sketches" *Antiphon* 11.3. (2007), 245–279. The following discussion leans heavily on Slyke's article along with the scholarship noted in footnote 3.

[3] See G. Bornkamm, "Mysterion" in *Theological Dictionary of the New Testament* Vol. 4. ed. Gerhard Kittel trans. and ed. Geoffrey W. Bromiley (Grand Rapids: Eerdmans 1967), 802–828; Hugo Rahner, *Greek Myths and Christian Mystery* (New York: Biblo and Tannen, 1971); Chrys C. Caragounis, *The Ephesian Mysterion: Meaning and Content* (Lund: CWK Gleerup, 1971); Louis Bouyer, *The Christian Mystery: From Pagan Myth to Christian Mysticism* trans. Illtyd Trethowan (Edinburgh: T&T Clark, 1990). Beale and Gladd, *Hidden But Now Revealed*, 305–319. For a discussion of these issues in the context of political theology see Giorgio Agamben, *Opus Dei: An Archaeology of Duty* trans. Adam Kotsko (Stanford: Stanford UP, 2013), esp. Chap. 2.

[4] Slyke, "Changing Meaning," 250–251. For a fuller treatment of Tertullian's use of *sacramentum* see J. De Ghellinck, *Pour l'histoire du mot* sacramentum, vol. 1, *Les Pères Anténicéens* (Louvain: Spicilegium Sacrum Lovaniense, 1924), 59–152.

[5] Ibid., 264. Lubac makes the same point with reference to Algerius of Liège in *Corpus Mysticum*, 49.

Other writers, however, including Ambrose's younger contemporary Augustine, obscured the difference between these two terms.[6] In Augustine, *sacramentum* became largely indistinguishable from *mysterium* with both terms identifying one's participation with Christ's saving presence as manifested within the church.[7] Augustine's usage proved highly influential as many subsequent Latin commentators elided the difference between *sacramentum* and *mysterium* for both theological and linguistic reasons.[8] Linguistically, the practice of eliding these terms is partly a function of the Latin penchant for doublets, the use of two or more words for the same concept.[9] But in this instance, as Henri de Lubac explains, the Latin penchant for doublets did theological work. Conflating *sacramentum* and *mysterium* helped convey the paradox that biblical mysteries remain obscure or hidden even in the very process of being revealed.[10] On the basis of these idioms, the Vulgate translates *mysterion* as *sacramentum*, giving it the sense of a sign that is both hidden and disclosed.[11] Developing this perspective through a specific set of Latinate idioms, Augustine articulated a view in which revelation is a mystery in at least two main senses. First, it is a mystery because God conceals his will in the very act of disclosing it (*mysterium*). But second, it is a mystery because those who have faith are immanent within the act of disclosure, experiencing it as participants rather than just exegetes (*sacramentum*). Importantly, both definitions are broadly consistent with the use of *mysterion* in Ephesians in which the Greek term refers not only to Christ's cosmic gathering of all things into himself, nor simply to God's plan of salvation, but also to the unpredictable manner of their divine disclosure.[12] After Augustine, *sacramentum* and *mysterium* began working together to convey this dialectical

[6] Emmanuel J. Cutrone "Sacraments" in *Augustine through the Ages: An Encyclopedia* eds. Allan D. Fitzgerald et al. (Grand Rapids: Eerdmans, 1999), 742.

[7] Ibid.

[8] Slyke, "Changing Meaning," 267. For Augustine's view of this term see C. Couturier "'Sacramentum Et Mysterium' Dans L'Oeuvre de Saint Augustine," *Études Augustiennes* (Paris: Aubier, 1953), 161–332.

[9] Henri de Lubac, *Medieval Exegesis: The Four Senses of Scripture* trans. E. M. Macierowski (Edinburgh: Eerdmans, 1998), 2.20. For an explanation of some of the shortcomings in Lubac's overall study of exegesis, see Ryan Mcdermott "Henri De Lubac's Genealogy of Modern Exegesis and Nicholas of Lyra's Literal Sense of Scripture" *Modern Theology* 29.1 (2013), 124–156.

[10] See, for example, Lubac, *Medieval Exegesis*, 2.83–98.

[11] Slyke, "Changing Meaning," 259; Lubac, *Corpus Mysticum*, 41–54.

[12] Caragounis, *The Ephesian Mystery*, 139–140, 143, 145.

and immanentist view of revelation. The general result was a vision of Christianity as "nothing but a continued mystery, a continuation of mysteries, a chaining together of mystery upon mystery" (Sibbes 5.462).

THE POETRY OF REVELATION: UNGRATEFULNESSE

One of the poems in which Herbert explicitly addresses this mode of revelation-in-concealment and concealment-in-revelation is "Ungratefulnesse." A poem of both praise and definition, "Ungratefulnesse" hinges on an opposition between the plain visibility of the incarnation which "allure[s] us with delights" and the "sparkling light" of the Trinity which "accesse denies" (22, 14, 16). But rather than being a commonsense distinction between showing and hiding, the distinction is really between two forms of generosity: one that is reassuringly familiar in its modesty and one that is frighteningly alien in its excessiveness. So, while the "sweets" and "mercies" of the incarnation delight by offering a "box we know," (i.e., an embodied God), the "rare cabinet" of the Trinity "affrights" us with its blinding light (7, 19, 20, 23, 14).

In praising these two pillars of Christian revelation, "Ungratefulnesse" goes out of its way to define them not as intellectually dazzling riddles but as something else entirely. Instead of figuring these mysteries as intellectual problems that might be circumscribed, "Ungratefulnesse" presents them as constituting the context in which believers live and move, the environment, as it were, in which God simultaneously gives and withholds himself. Over the course of the poem, Herbert explores how various biblical idioms express the ways in which God accommodates himself to human understanding. In doing so, the poem enacts scripture-like processes of revelation as initially puzzling images and idioms become clearer retrospectively. The final result is a poem that asks if human beings have the courage to brave the estranging lines of communion between God and humanity. At work in the poem, then, is a sensitive understanding that, "Mystery arises at that point where different kinds of beings are in communication. In mystery there must be strangeness; but the estranged must also be thought as in some way capable of communion."[13]

Our first description of Christianity's mysteries comes in stanza two when the speaker calls them "rare cabinets full of treasure" (7). Contrasting the false "casks of happinesse" in "Dotage" (1), each of these two cabi-

---

[13] Kenneth Burke, *A Rhetoric of Motives* (Berkeley: University of California Press, 1969), 115.

nets is a "secret receptacle, treasure-chamber, store-house; *arcanum*" (OED, 6). While there may be a suggestion here that each cabinet is a *Kunstkammer* or chamber of exotic wonders, it is more likely that Herbert is referring to the kind of antechamber that a 1598 visitor of Hampton Court Palace described when he notes that there was a "cabinet called Paradise (*Paradisus appellatur*), where besides that everything glitters so with silver, gold, and jewels, as to dazzle one's eyes."[14] Yet, neither of these definitions accounts for the puzzling use of the verb "made" that follows:

> Thou hast but two rare cabinets full of treasure,
> The *Trinitie*, and *Incarnation:*
> Thou hast unlockt them both,
> And made them jewels to betroth
> The work of thy creation
> Unto thy self in the everlasting pleasure. (7–12)

Instead of showing or revealing their treasure, these two cabinets are suddenly "made" jewels by which God plights his truth to humankind ("betroth," OED, 1). While this combined image may appear straightforward at first, it nevertheless amounts to a mixed metaphor in which God's being, having, and doing are conflated in ways that belie logical categories and normal syntactical expectations. Even more, this odd catachresis is further estranged through the speaker's somewhat altered reference to the marriage of Christ and the church in Ephesians 5:32, which St. Paul calls a "great mystery" (*to musterion touto mega estin*). Rather than just marrying the church, God is now said to generously embrace all of creation. Yet if these images and allusions resist easy analysis, their very opacity is revealing. They intimate that the mysteries being praised are not objects, like just so much bijoux, nor even persons in any normal sense of the term, but something altogether different, something more like the basis of a relationship. But this remains to be seen.

A somewhat clearer view of Christianity's twin mysteries emerges in the following stanza when the term *cabinet* comes to denote a secret council, hence the claim that the Trinity denies full access to its inner recesses (15). At this point, Herbert's speaker alludes to the kind of royal council that

[14] *A Journey into England by Paul Hentzner in the Year MDXCVIII*, ed. Horace Walpole (Strawberry Hill: 1757), 82.

the Old Testament associates with God's secret judgments through the Hebrew term *sod* which is a rough equivalent of the Greek *mysterion*.[15] This is the Hebraic idiom that Lancelot Andrewes presupposes when he complains of "Men that sure must have been in God's cabinet," having, as they do, "God's secret decrees ... at their fingers' ends" (3.32). In a logic-defying way, Herbert's "rare cabinets" morph from being objects containing treasure into inaccessibly divine persons passing judgments and withholding secrets. Only retrospectively, then, can we connect the verb "made" with the image of the cabinet. Viewed from this widened perspective, the "rare cabinets" turn out to have been councils with the power to make things happen by fiat. Our earlier confusion is now partly clarified as the poem's idioms accumulate in meaning over time in the process of exploring the significance of Colossians' depiction of "the mysteries of God, and of the Father, and of Christ, In whom are hid all the treasures of wisedome, and knowledge" (Col. 2:2–3).

Herbert's unexpected use of the verb "made" in stanza two further recalls the biblical idiom that is often deployed in the New Testament to figure God's incarnation, such as Galatians 4:4–5 which Andrewes systematically estranges in his 1609 Christmas Day sermon. In this sermon, Andrewes declares: "When the fullness of time was come, God sent His Son, *made* of a woman, *made* under the Law" (my emphasis).[16] Andrewes' dialectical approach to these idioms parallels the movement of mystery and clarity unfolding in Herbert's lyric. On one hand, Andrewes turns these phrases over and over so as to accumulate a host of meanings and associations. On the other, however, he repeats Paul's idioms with such frequency that the verb "made" becomes unmoored from its referent, like a precocious child playing word games. One result of this latter movement is to genuinely estrange whatever it is Paul may be saying about the incarnation exactly; or as Andrewes puts it with self-conscious confusion: "To make Him any thing is to mar Him, be it what it will be" (1.52). Taken as a whole, Andrewes' multilingual dialectic of meaning and mystery engenders a renewed sense of how Paul's idioms disclose the extraordinary generosity of the incarnation. Praising and estranging God's kenotic self-emptying in the act of incarnation (Phil. 2:5–8), Andrewes teaches that

---

[15] See Brown, *Semitic Background*.

[16] Andrewes pursues a similar strategy in his 1611 Christmas Day sermon before the king at Whitehall. See 1.90–91.

whatsoever else He had been 'made', it would have done us no good. In this then was 'the fulness' of His love, as before of His Father's—that He would be made, and was made, not what was fittest for Him, but what was best for us; not what was most for His glory, but what was most for our benefit and behoof. (1.53)

The strangeness of the verb "made" and the semantic instability of the word "cabinet" are only two ways in which "Ungratefulnesse" imitates scriptural processes of unfolding revelation in similarly estranging ways as Andrewes.

Another important formal device Herbert deploys in the poem involves stanza structure. Each of the first four sestets moves outward toward openness and generosity, then inward toward the intimate or unknown or both, and then outward again. This breath-like movement is partly expressed through shifting meters as Herbert's sestet holds four short lines between two longer pentameter ones, all in a poem that is exactly 30 lines long. Appropriately enough, he uses this movement in stanza 3, beginning at line 13, to both disclose and conceal the trinitarian mystery:

> The statelier cabinet is the *Trinitie*,
>   Whose sparkling light access denies:
>   Therefore thou dost not show
>   This fully to us, till death blow
>   The dust into our eyes:
> For by that powder thou wilt make us see. (13–18)

While eternal life and the inner reaches of the Trinity remain tucked away in the middle of the stanza, like jewels in a rare cabinet, the promise of fuller revelation returns in the distending assonance of the closing line. Happening within each stanza as well as across the poem as a whole, the lyric's movement of disclosure and concealment is rhythmic and palpable, as well as semantic and numerological. Each stanza is thus figured as though it were itself a little cabinet revealing and withholding treasure.

The penultimate stanza further clarifies the kind of divine generosity being praised in "Ungratefulnesse." Only now the language is more homely as the incarnation is figured as God's attempt to alleviate the anxiety caused by his enormous gap in station with his bride(s)-to-be. Like an unconflicted Mr. Darcy, God generously stoops beneath his status in order to offer humanity a "box we know" in the person of Christ (23).

Obviously referring to the human body, this image allows us to breathe a sigh of interpretive relief as the poem has finally given us a "cabinet" that is easy to grasp. Yet, the assurances and accommodations of familiarity have their limits, as the poem's conclusion unexpectedly shows.

Up until the final stanza, everything but the poem's title has led us to believe that we are headed toward a celebration of the mystical marriage of Christ and the soul. After all, this is a poem in praise of how God's "bountie and rare clemencie" have "redeem'd us from the grave" thereby making us "gods" (1, 2, 6). But instead of deification, what we witness in the last stanza is man's cowardly rejection of Christ's proposal as the bride unexpectedly leaves the groom at the altar:

> But man is close, reserv'd, and dark to thee:
> When thou demandest but a heart,
>   He cavils instantly.
> In his poore cabinet of bone
>   Sinnes have their box apart,
> Defrauding thee, who gavest two for one. (25–30)

As a result of this churlish refusal of Christ's advances, the mystery of the Godhead is now replaced by the mystery of sin. Revealingly, Andrewes also thinks the *mysterium iniquitatis* is characterized by self-protective secrecy and shame, as when he preaches: "O it is naturally given us to hide our abasing what we can. Our misery must be kept in a mystery, and that mystery not manifested in any wise" (1.34).[17] As the meaning of Herbert's title finally becomes clear, the poem raises the possibility that sin is fundamentally a failure of nerve, a function of "a deficient will" arising from the mutually reinforcing dynamics of pride and shame.[18] With the sadness and frustration of a wedding that does not go off, Herbert's generic Christian chooses the familiar box he knows, the privative "box apart," rather than entering into the positive estrangements of God's "rare cabinets," the Lord's "tabernacle" (OED, 1b). And why? Because he cannot admit that divine communion begins with a bare but humbling admission of gratitude, the simple realization that the jewels on offer are gifts only in the sense that life itself is a gift. In this instance, sin is to sleep as gratitude is to waking. And out of a fearful lack of trust driven by a deep-rooted

---

[17] See Sibbes 1:73 for a discussion of how sinners "churlishly refuse" Christ's mercy.

[18] John Preston, *Irresstiblenesse of Converting Grace, 15*, cited in Moore, *English Hypothetical Universalism*, 74, 81.

sense of shame coupled with not a little hint of pride, Herbert's bride-to-be chooses slumber.[19]

The rejection of divine intimacy bemoaned in "Ungratefulness" is also of concern in *The Country Parson*, especially "The Parson's Dexterity in Applying Remedies." Teaching ministers how to comfort those who despair of God's mercy, Herbert somewhat equivocally asserts that Christians have the "pledges of Gods Love" in two ways:

> the one in his being, the other in his sinfull being: and this as the more faulty in him, so the more glorious in God. And all may certainly conclude, that God loves them, till either they despise that Love, or despaire of his Mercy: not any sin else, but is within his Love; but the despising of Love must needs be without it. The thrusting away of his arme makes us onely not embraced. (283)

On the one hand, the passage seems to imply that although the human will cannot reject God's love entirely, it can nevertheless refuse his embrace thereby obscuring the signs of God's love. On the other hand, however, there is a lurking sense here that despising God's love in the final instance amounts to something like the unforgivable sin against the holy ghost of Mark 3:28–30. If the latter reading has any legitimacy, it is because Herbert stresses the idea that God's embrace of sinners is his greatest act of charity (*agape*). While God is said to love his creation in the way an artist loves his work, he ultimately loves sinners in the way that a loving parent loves his children (283). To reject such love, Herbert implies, is to reject God's fullest act of self-revelation.

REVELATION AND INTIMACY IN THE SEARCH AND LOVE (III)

However we parse this sequence from *The Country Parson*, the failure of spiritual union lamented in "Ungratefulnesse" is answered later in *The Temple* in poems that further portray God's revelation-in-concealment

---

[19] Frances Cruikshank overlooks the revelatory nature of Herbert's poetics in her otherwise valuable *Verse and Poetics in George Herbert and John Donne* (Farnham: Ashgate, 2010) when she asserts: "The metaphors by which God communicates His nature and His activities are not mysterious but efficacious. They are not given as a code to be deciphered, but as instructions to be followed, a 'bidding' to be heeded" (46).

and concealment-in-revelation. In "The Search," for example, the question of God's love is again a matter of learning how to cope with the paradoxes of divine communication and the modes of intimacy engendered by it. After failing to locate God in the earth, sky, and stars, the speaker reaches a point of exasperation, crying out: "Where is my God? what hid den place / Conceals thee still?" (29–30). This crisis returns the speaker to the insight that God is the non-circumscribable environment in which he lives and moves rather than an object in space and time. This insight is intimated in the double meaning of "intrenching" and the surprised discovery that God transcends all modes of linguistic difference that is attendant upon it: "Thy will such an intrenching is, / As passeth thought: / To it all strength, all subtilties, / Are things of nought" (37–40).[20] On one hand, "to entrench" means to "surround," "safeguard," "fortify" with trenches (OED, 1, 2). The implication here is that God is the mystery sustaining all life. After all, "Preservation is," as Herbert says elsewhere, "a Creation, and a creation every moment" (*Country Parson*, 281). On the other hand, however, to entrench means "To make (a wound) by cutting" (OED, 3). The implication here is that God reveals himself to those who are wounded, indeed to those he wounds, hence the speaker's subsequent realization that "my grief must be as large, / As is thy space" (45–46). Intimating a deeper understanding of the dialectics of regeneration as a movement between a God of power and a God of love, the speaker also realizes that God transcends all forms of perceptual and conceptual difference, including the difference between immanence and transcendence. Thus, rather than being a practiced instance of negative theology, in which one systematically approaches God by means of verbal negations, this stanza shows the speaker suddenly discovering the underlying exigency for such forms of prayer: that God is a mystery, not a problem.[21]

Having further clarified the significance of God's transcendence, the speaker of "The Search" arrives at a renewed sense of his "nearness" thereby regaining the capacity for intimacy that is absent in "Ungratefulnesse":

---

[20] For a similar reading of "The Search" but in the context of early modern discourses of godly sorrow, see my *The Poetry of Religious Sorrow in Early Modern England* (Cambridge: Cambridge UP, 2008), 18–24.

[21] *Pace* Hillary Kelleher, "'Light thy Darknes is': George Herbert and Negative Theology" *George Herbert Journal* 28.1–2 (2004–2005) pp. 47–64, I see no evidence that Herbert deploys distinctly Pseudo-Dionysian strategies or imagery in his verse. While negative theology is certainly important to Herbert, as Kelleher persuasively shows, its forms are generally more Augustinian than Dionysian in idiom and structure.

When thou dost turn, and wilt be neare;
    What edge so keen,
What point so piercing can appeare
    To come between? (53–56)

The weight of the enjambment in this stanza's penultimate line is difficult to overstate. When we hover on the word *appeare*, the imagery of wounding reaches a point as sharp as a spear that pierces Christ or a sin that pricks the conscience. Yet, the following line denies any such cut, as God's nearness is now said to overcome all divisions.

Although the penultimate stanza of "The Search" constitutes a perfectly satisfying conclusion, Herbert nevertheless pushes the level of intimacy with God even further. In doing so, "The Search" both echoes and answers the ending of "Ungratefulnesse":

For as thy absence doth excell
    All distance known:
So doth thy nearnesse bear the bell,
    Making two one. (57–60)

Teasing us out of thought, these lines further collapse the distinction between immanence and transcendence, manifestation and concealment toward which the conclusion has been working. The result is a poetic depiction of the kind of intimacy Augustine envisions when he describes God as "more inward to me than my most inward part."[22] In this way, "The Search" conveys Augustine's notion that the more intimate one becomes with God, the less one understands him.[23] At the same time, the final phrase amounts to an etymological translation of the verb "reconcile" (*re-conciliare*), or to be brought back together, thus evoking its theological sense of being brought back into peaceful unity with God. Importantly, then, "The Search" concludes by rewriting the final lines of "Ungratefulnesse" where we learned that "Sinnes have their box apart, / Defrauding thee, who gavest two for one" (29–30). Only now the strange unity of God's being, doing, and having inspires a mysterious intimacy

---

[22] For this and other Augustinian contexts in "The Search," see my *The Poetry of Religious Sorrow*, 18–24.

[23] See sermon 117 in *The Works of St. Augustine* (2nd Release), 13.209–223 and Paul van Geest, *The Incomprehensibility of God*, 18, 138.

rather than fearful ingratitude as the phrase "two for one" is replaced with God's miraculous "Making two one."

If "The Search" explores God's apparent absence, then the final poem in "The Church," "Love (III)," depicts the effects of his overpresent generosity. In this respect, Herbert's poem dilates on the communion rite in *The Book of Common Prayer*, particularly its claim that "Ye know howe grevous and unkynde a thing it is, when a manne hath prepared a riche feaste: decked his table with al kynde of provisyon, so that there lacketh nothinge but the gestes to site downe: and yet they whych be called wythout anye cause, mooste unthankfully refuse to come."[24] In responding to this passage, "Love (III)" further develops the dynamics of revelation and divine generosity at issue in "Ungratefulnesse" and "The Search." The difference in "Love (III)" is that God's presence manifests in the single form of incarnate Love rather than the dual form of immanent and transcendent deities of the earlier poems. Revealingly, the exigency for and the idioms of "The Church's" concluding poem further parallel the concerns expressed in "The Parsons Dexterity in applying of Remedies." It is almost as though this highly enigmatic lyric stages the "unanswerable argument" that Herbert encourages country parsons to use on those who despair of God's love. According to Herbert, if the country parson sees Christians

> neerer desperation, then Atheisme; not so much doubting a God, as that he is theirs; then he dives unto the boundlesse Ocean of Gods Love, and the unspeakable riches of his loving kindesse. He hath one argument unanswerable. If God hate them, either he doth it as they are Creatures, dust and ashes; or as they are sinfull. As Creatures, he must needs love them; for no perfect Artist ever yet hated his owne worke. As sinfull, he must much more love them; because notwithstanding his infinite hate of sinne, his Love overcame that hate; and with an exceeding great victory, which in the Creation needed not, gave them love for love, even the son of his love out of his bosome of love. (283)

Like the despairing Christians portrayed here, Herbert's speaker in "Love (III)" is welcomed into God's presence, but he nevertheless draws back, first out of "dust and sinne" and then out of unkindness, ingratitude, and shame (9, 13). In this way, Herbert dramatizes the fear that God's overpresence inspires in scriptural passages such as Job 13:21 "Withdrawe thine hand far from me; and let not thy dread make mee afraid" and Canticles 6:5 "Turne away thine eyes from me, / for they have overcome me." Only now the scene is more quietly domestic than sublime, its ostensible familiarity both revealing and concealing the drama's life-defining profoundness:

> Love bade me welcome: yet my soul drew back,
> Guiltie of dust and sinne.
> But quick-ey'd Love, observing me grow slack
> From my first entrance in,
> Drew nearer to me, sweetly questioning,
> If I lack'd anything. (1–6)

Fleshing out what remains relatively implicit in the final stanza of "Ungratefulnesse," this opening scenario exposes the human tendency to avoid love and recognition simultaneously, to "cavil instantly" in the face of God's love. To this extent, "Love (III)" addresses the *mysterium iniquitatis* that Stanley Cavell diagnoses when he remarks that there "are no lengths to which we may not go in order to avoid being revealed, even to those we love and are loved by. Or rather, especially to those we love and are loved by."[25] In further dramatizing the dynamics of shame, "Love (III)" develops one of the most disquieting impulses expressed in *The Temple*, namely the desire to "reuenge me on [God's] love" first introduced in "The Thanksgiving" (17). In naming such a desire, Herbert recognizes, with Cavell, that "For some spirits, to be loved knowing you cannot return that love is the most radical of psychic tortures," hence the insight that "Christ was killed by us, because his news was unendurable."[26] If "Love (III)" succeeds poetically, it is because it offers an eloquently persuasive picture of a person finally breaking out of this psychic torture while being freed from the "box apart" that is shame and sin. If not killed with kindness, the speaker of "Love (III)" is nevertheless shamed to exhaustion by it.

Facing straight into the unendurable heart of God's overpresence, the speaker of "Love (III)" recoils out of fear of being recognized and loved simultaneously, crying out: "Ah my deare, / I cannot look on thee" (9–10). In doing so, however, he further betrays a desire to see face to

---

[25] Stanley Cavell, *Disowning Knowledge In Seven Plays of Shakespeare* (Cambridge: Cambridge UP, 2003), 56.
[26] Ibid., 61, 68. I discuss this feature of "The Thanksgiving" in Chap. 8.

face in love, hence the term of endearment he uses in the very gesture of withdrawing from God: "Ah my deare." Being pulled in two directions at once, the speaker cannot bear God's generosity even as he wishes to accept it. The dynamic here is similar to the one Bernard of Clairvaux identifies in his commentary on the Song of Songs when he observes how "The spirit is filled with dread even while it is stirred."[27] Instead of meeting God's gaze, the speaker only perceives his own shame reflected back to him and thus he recoils back into his "box apart." Realizing that the speaker is still clinging to the privacy and isolation of "Sinnes Round," Love immediately responds to his misprision, taking his hand and asking: "Who made the eyes but I"? In this tender gesture, Love echoes "The Country Parson's" advice that pastors should counsel those in despair by insisting that God loves all that he has made (283). Insufficient as a strategy, however, Love then adopts a more frank tone, asking: "know you not ... who bore the blame" for your sin (15)? Here again, Love continues with the advice given in "The Country Parson" now echoing Herbert's advice to counsel those anxious of salvation by insisting that in taking sin upon himself "Love overcame that hate [of transgression]" (283). Finally succeeding, this second approach implies the Pauline idea that when the time of judgment comes, Christ will cover his sins, thereby making unmediated intimacy possible: "For now we see in a mirror dimly; but then face to face: now I know in part; but then shall I know even as also I am known" (1 Cor. 13:12). Accepting the extraordinary conditions of Love's invitation and the promise of fullness that it entails, the speaker, no longer shrinking and hiding, is now finally able to "sit and eat" (18).

The ending of "Love (III)" is graceful in its simplicity. Its sweetly comic final line calls to an end all the struggling and recoiling that goes on in the lyric, as though to say, with almost Jane Austen like irony: What took you so long? Was it really so hard? Delicate and subtle, the sense of release achieved in the final line is nevertheless exquisitely, even unspeakably, liberating. It suggests that for Herbert faith amounts to the intellectually simple but spiritually excruciating commitment that God recognizes, loves, and accepts sinners simultaneously and that the name for this transcendently inhuman generosity is grace.

The carefully qualified confidence achieved at the end of the poem is signaled in the speaker's chosen physical posture at *The Temple's* final

---

[27] Bernard of Clairvaux, *On the Song of Songs IV* trans. Irene Edmonds (Kalamazoo: Cistercian Publications, 1980), 4.

feast: "I did sit and eat." In "The Parson in Sacraments," Herbert interprets sitting at the eucharist as a sign of spiritual preparedness. Recalling King James I's view that physical posture during communion is a matter indifferent,[28] Herbert teaches that

> the Feast indeed requires sitting, because it is a Feast; but man's unpreparednesse asks kneeling. Hee that comes to the to the Sacrament, hath the confidence of a Guest, and hee that kneels, confesseth himself an unworthy one, and therefore differs from other Feasters: but hee that sits, or lies, puts up to an Apostle: Contentiousnesse in a feast of Charity is more scandall then any posture. (259)

The crisply frank line "I did sit and eat" resolves the drama played out in "Ungratefulnesse" as the speaker now enjoys the confidence requisite to divine intimacy, at least for the moment. Less an ending than an initiation, the final stanza of "Love (III)" complements the turn to last things at the end of "The Church." After all, it suggests that the speaker is readying himself for the arrival of the son of Man in the rather beguiling sense demanded by the Gospel of Luke: "Be yee therefore ready also: for the sonne of man commeth" at an unexpected hour, "an houre when yee thinke not" (Luke 12:40). In its broader context, then, "Love (III)" presents us with a feast that is both present and eschatological, enigmatic and homely, at once. In this respect, it conveys the *already-and-not-yet* nature of God's kingdom, a spiritual process that is present and happening but not yet complete. As such, "Love (III)" ends "The Church" much as the final stanza of "The Banquet" completes its celebration of the eucharist: as an invitation to the banquet of the kingdom that is now, forever, and yet to come.

Despite the highly elevated scenario that it depicts, "Love (III)" focuses attention on its neat coincidence of mystery and plainness. This deftly handled balancing of familiarity with strangeness partly rests on the depiction of divinity in the poem. On one hand, the divine majesty that engendered alienation in poems such as "Ungratefulnesse" is now more modestly concealed. As a result, "Love (III)" creates better conditions for a fuller reception of God's overwhelming mercy than most earlier poems. On the other hand, however, Love is now literally present, speaking directly to

---

[28] Roland G. Usher, *Reconstruction of the English Church* (New York: Appleton and Company, 1910), 2:354

the speaker without the mediations of prayer. Stilling the dialectics of revelation and concealment, this balance of tensions dissolves the distances between human and divine more fully than perhaps any other poem in "The Church." Most importantly, the plain language used for the poem's elevated scenario has the paradoxical effect of engendering wonder and estrangement while nevertheless conveying a sense of spiritual comfort and religious readiness. Maintaining such tension is a delicate task. Even more, it is a pressing cultural exigency for Herbert, hence the placing of "Love (III)" at the climax of "The Church."

What is achieved over the course of these three interrelated poems, and thus *The Temple* as a whole, is a carefully calibrated and hard-won spiritual confidence, a delicate sense of holiness. If "Love (III)" expresses and instills a sense of assurance, it is one that is nevertheless strikingly modified by awe over the simplicities and terrors of God's communicating will, and its patterning of revelation-in-concealment and concealment-in-revelation.

MYSTERY IN TRANSLATION: ST. AUGUSTINE

This brings us back to St. Augustine. If Augustine promiscuously conflated the terms *mysterium* and *sacramentum*, it is because he needed a set of idioms that would adequately capture in prosaic form the dynamics of revelation and concealment that Herbert explores poetically in *The Temple*. After all, Augustine inherited a theological tradition in which not only the divine plan of redemption but the very process of revelation was a mystery. As Henri de Lubac has shown, Latin translations of *mysterion* and the theological idioms that grew up around it helped convey the sense that readers are immanent within the mystery whether they are reading scripture or participating in the sacraments. For Augustine, he explains, the "Bible is essentially the 'writing of the mysteries' and its books are the 'books of the divine sacraments.' The two words are often simply synonyms."[29] So, when Augustine describes the bible as a "firmament" that encompasses the world like a translucent skin, he conveys a view of scripture as the spiritual environment in which one lives, moves, and breathes.[30]

One of Augustine's most explicit articulations of this view of the divine Word occurs in Sermon 117 "On the Words of the Gospel of John 1:1–3:

---

[29] Lubac, *Medieval Exegesis*, 2.20.

[30] For a discussion of this usage, see Peter M. Candler Jr., *Theology, Rhetoric, Manuduction or Reading Scripture Together on the Path to God* (Grand Rapids: Eerdmans, 2006), 3.

In The Beginning Was the Word." This sermon provides a striking gloss on Herbert's general exegetical sensibility, especially as encapsulated in the epiphany "We say amiss, / This or that is: / Thy word is all, if we could spell" ("The Flower," 19–21). According to Augustine, the opening chapter of the Gospel of John

> can only be understood in ways beyond words; human words cannot suffice for understanding the Word of God. What we are discussing and stating is why it is not understood. I am not speaking in order that it may be understood, but telling you what prevents it being understood (*Non nunc dicimus ut intelligatur, sed dicimus quid impediat ne intelligatur*). You see, it is a kind of form, a form that has not been formed, but is the form of all things that have been formed; an unchangeable form, that has neither fault nor failing, beyond time, beyond space, standing apart as at once the foundation for all things to stand on, and the ceiling for them to stand under … all things are in it (*omnia in illo sunt*). And yet because it is God, all things are under it. What I am saying is how incomprehensible is the passage that was read to us. But in any case, it wasn't read in order to be understood, but in order to make us mere human beings grieve because we don't understand it, and make us try to discover what prevents our understanding, and so move it out of the way, and hunger to grasp the unchangeable Word, ourselves thereby being changed from worse to better. The Word, after all, does not make progress, or grow, when someone who knows it comes along. But it is whole and entire if you abide in it, whole and entire if you fall away from it; whole and entire when you return to it; abiding in itself and making all things new. (13.210–11)[31]

While acknowledging the wholeness of the Word, this sermon simultaneously demonstrates a deep sensitivity to the principle of perspectival awareness. For example, Augustine insists that "whatever you look at, you are not looking at the whole of it. When you see someone's face, you don't see their back while you see their face; and when you see their back, you don't at that moment see their face" (13.211). Because human beings stand within the compass of the divine Word, Augustine teaches, they cannot grasp the whole of it at any one moment. This principle helps explain the ending of "Ungratefulnesse," for what makes the lyric poignant is our frustrating sense that Herbert's generic Christian refuses to open his eyes in order to acknowledge the spiritual environment supporting and

---

[31] References to the Latin text are from *Sancti Augustini Opera Omnia* ed. D.A.B. Caillau (Parisiis: Paul Mellier, 1842), 19.16.

encompassing him, namely the abiding presence of God's love that brings the bewildered, even slightly frustrated speaker of "Mattens" into speech: "I cannot ope mine eyes, / But thou art ready there" (1–2).

Sermon 117 also illuminates the rather qualified forms of negative theology animating "The Search." By the end of this poem, the speaker realizes that one should not teach Christians *how to* understand God so much as how *not to* understand him. Much more invested in mystagogy than theology, "The Search" leads readers into a relationship with God by showing his speaker discovering the value of the negative way, especially in the clear yet elusive ending in which the promise of unity is expressed in a manner that not only sustains but deepens the divine mystery. "The Search's" discovery of the negative way both contrasts and complements "Love (III)," which shows a speaker how to approach God through divine love (*via amoris*). While "The Search" begins with negation and non-understanding only to end by expressing the *via amoris*, "Love (III)" unfolds the *via amoris* throughout, thereby bringing it to fulfillment within the context of *The Temple*. In doing so, it suggests that the experience of divine love begins with an avowal of non-understanding. Such interweaving of the negative way and the way of love is very much in keeping with St. Augustine's approach to mystagogy, especially as conveyed in Sermon 117.[32]

Even more importantly, Herbert's celebration of God's mystery in *The Temple* is animated by Augustine's idea of the bible as mysteriorum scriptura, divinorum sacramentorum libri.[33] From this perspective, scripture is the living Word of God into which one continually re-enters, as though into an ever-renewing tabernacle or marriage. On this account, the Christian reader of scripture is more like a character in an unfolding story than a subscriber to a constitutional charter or philosophical system. In Augustine's view, the mysteries of scripture constitute a dynamic spiritual context more than a static set of messages; they are a sacrament of God experienced in the first person rather than a set of divine statements that can be abstracted into a third-person standpoint or possessed once-and-for-all in the form of a message or statement. And because readers stand within scripture's evolving compass, they cannot, in principle, comprehend the whole of it. This is why Andrew of St. Victor can say that divine

---

[32] See Geest, *Incomprehensibility of God*, Chap. 5.

[33] For a reference to this Augustinian usage, see Couturier, "Sacramentum Et Mysterium," 190–1.

mysteries are "discovered in such a way that there always remains something to discover" and Saint Gregory can claim that scripture "advances
with those who read it."[34] This is likely also why when discussing the
Christian's arduous pursuit of wisdom, Augustine uses the terms *circuitus*
and *ambulatio* to suggest a parallel with Hellenistic mystery rites.[35] These
hermeneutic and sapiential principles inform the dialectical structure of
poems such as "Ungratefulnesse" as biblical idioms are simultaneously
clarified and estranged. In the case of "Ungratefulnesse," this process leads
to an open-ended conclusion in which readers are implicitly challenged
to differentiate themselves from the generic Christian with whom they
must also inevitably identify. By correcting the generic Christian's rejection of God at the end of "Ungratefulnesse," readers reopen the "mystical
repast" that is suddenly foreclosed at the poem's end. Through this process, readers find themselves reinitiated in the *mysterion* as the primordial
drama of "Superliminare" replays itself anew.

When Herbert presents the act of entering *The Temple* in the Pauline
context of pagan mystery rites in "Superliminare," he intimates the connection between initiation and mystery that is concomitant with an Augustinian
view of scripture. According to such a view, the moment of religious understanding is, by definition, an experience of (re)initiation, a waking up to
a relationship that situates or grounds one's overall perspective and being.
The idea that spiritual understanding constitutes a point of reentry into the
corpus mysticum helps explain Herbert's tendency to treat initiation as a kind
of master trope, especially with respect to the way he concludes poems. Like
Andrewes' sermons, Herbert's poems often end by reopening the scriptural
or sacramental mystery rather than by concluding in a fully close-ended way.
"Superliminare" and "Love (III)," which begin and end "The Church,"
exemplify the invitational nature of Herbert's endings, just as "The Banquet"
does. Implicit in this literary strategy is the idea that an event of spiritual
understanding involves becoming part of the light by which one perceives.
At bottom, *mysterion* is a hermeneutic concept identifying the interpenetration of reader and text, of interpreter and Word, in exactly this way.

This structure of participatory understanding is opposed to the more
objective knowledge that Herbert's friend Francis Bacon championed
in the realm of natural philosophy. For Bacon, the interpenetration of

[34] Cited in Henri de Lubac, *The Splendour of the Church* trans. Michael Mason (London:
Sheed and Ward, 1956), 11 and Lubac, *Medieval Exegesis*, 2.205.
[35] Eugene TeSelle, *Augustine The Theologian* (London: Burns and Oates, 1970), 76.

interpreter and interpreted is precisely the hermeneutical problem to be overcome. Yet, Augustinian understanding also differs from the kind of comprehension that is assumed by those who reduce "religion to the transfer and assimilation of information."[36] Aware of poetry's capacity to keep these different modes of understanding distinct from one another, Herbert adopts a set of formal strategies that emphasize that Christian life takes place within the compass of a divine Word whose excessive light both illuminates and blinds precisely because its glow, as the speaker of "Divinitie" says, surpasses "in brightnesse any flame" (16). If "Superliminare" warns of the costs of stepping into the blinding light of the Word, and if "Ungratefulnesse" laments what is lost in not doing so, then "Love (III)" celebrates the soul's entry into the light of mystery.

THE HERMENEUTICS OF FAITH

To put this another way, the Augustinian view of scripture animating Herbert's poetry presupposes that faith is a hermeneutic principle as well as an expression of belief. Rather than simply denoting a Christian's avowal of particular creeds, faith, for Herbert, identifies a specifically participatory way of experiencing scripture. Given the centrality of this exegetical principle to Herbert's bible-centered spirituality, it is perhaps no surprise that he outlines it in his poem "Faith." Here again, the plainness of his imagery in this poem matches the shocking modesty of Christ's incarnate presence, in this case his nativity. Describing sanctifying grace as a podiatric medicine before going on to stress the "lowness" of Christ's "common manger," or what Andrewes often calls his "cratch," Herbert again achieves a form of plainness that is little short of bizarre (the allusion to the serpent's wounding of Adam's heel in Genesis 3:14–15 notwithstanding):

> There is a rare outlandish root,
> Which when I could not get, I thought it here:
> That apprehension cur'd so well my foot,
> That I can walk to heav'n well neare ...
>
> Faith makes me any thing, or all
> That I beleeve is in the sacred storie:
> And where sinne placeth me in Adams fall,
> Faith sets me higher in his glorie.

[36] Lake, "Lancelot Andrewes ... and avant-garde conformity," 115.

If I go lower in the book,
What can be lower then the common manger?
Faith puts me there with him, who sweetly took
Our flesh and frailtie, death and danger. (9–12, 17–24)

This account of faith recalls Richard Sibbes' claim that "faith knoweth no distance of place, as well as no distance of time … to the eye of faith all … things are present" (7.118) and so it "is a great art in faith to apprehend Christ suitable to our present condition" (7.214). But what is crucial is the way Herbert translates this view of faith into a specifically hermeneutic context. In doing so, he implies that believers can no more be done with the gospel than they can be done with the environment in which they live, a point he intimates in "Christmas" when he declares to God that "The pasture is thy word: the streams, thy grace" (19). In this view of things, scripture is more a context than a set of messages; it cannot be fully reduced to a set of problems that can be answered or promises that can be possessed. Instead, scripture is a relationship or environment into which one is continually reinitiated. In other words, rather than a set of propositions faith primarily consists of a widening of perception as the opening of "Faith" suggests: "Lord, how couldst thou so much appease / Thy wrath for sinne, as when mans sight was dimme, / And could see little, to regard his ease, / And bring by Faith all things to him?" (1–4). This is the hermeneutic attitude presupposed by Herbert's description of scripture as a "book of stars."

MYSTERION REFORMED: MARTIN LUTHER

As "Faith" indicates, the Augustinian view of scripture as the living word of God (*viva vox Dei*) was crucial to protestant reading practices in post-reformation Europe. Despite the decline of the fourfold allegorical method of interpretation, which was central to medieval traditions of *lectio divina*, spiritual reading remained a vital part of protestant culture. From the very beginning of the Reformation, laymen were widely taught to read scripture as a story that fully discloses its meaning only when read with the belief that is about the personal experience of individual Christians. Rooted in the distinction between letter and spirit, this reformation hermeneutic emphasizes the extent to which the bible is something that cannot simply be preserved and passed on in the form of a collectively received tradition; instead, it must be continuously read from a first-person point of view, a process that can never be fully completed once and for all.[37] In intellectual circles, however, the renewed importance of this practice was complicated by the fact that protestants were coming to terms with the increasing gap between a biblical text now studied in Hebrew and Greek and an outdated theological system rooted in church Latin.[38]

As modern biblical scholarship developed over the course of the seventeenth century, the idea that scripture is the living Word of God came under increasing pressure. While some historians blame this process on the supposed scholasticism of seventeenth-century protestant orthodoxy, Richard A. Muller sees it as an inevitable casualty of the changing hermeneutical landscape of early modern Europe.[39] In his view

> the farther the hermeneutics moved away from the *quadriga* (or fourfold allegorical method) toward a strict literal, grammatical, linguistic, and contextual analysis of the text itself, the less tenable did the interpretive concept of *viva vox Dei*—and related concepts, like the christological *scopus scripturae*—become. And it was the age of orthodoxy in the seventeenth century that saw the further flowering of textual criticism and of the study of the cognate languages of the Bible. If existential language of the *viva vox Dei* became more difficult to maintain hermeneutically in the seventeenth century, it would become impossible in the eighteenth and nineteenth. Critique of the Protestant orthodox for the (partial!) loss of this dimension of the Reformation view of Scripture amounts to little more than an unrequited and unrequitable theological nostalgia.[40]

Whatever combination of forces led to the partial loss of a spiritually vital conception of scripture as the living Word of God the process was overdetermined, the result of several intersecting pressures that built up in the course of more than a century. From legalistic reading practices to

[37] See Gerhard Ebeling, *Luther: An Introduction to his Thought* trans. R.A. Wilson (London: St James's Place, 1970), 98–99.

[38] Richard A. Muller, *Post-Reformation Dogmatics Volume 2. Holy Scripture: The Cognitive Foundation of Theology* (Grand Rapids: Baker Books, 1993), 488.

[39] For the idea that protestant orthodoxy betrayed the gains of the early Reformation, see, for example, Gerhard Ebeling, *Word and Faith* trans. James W. Leitch (Philadelphia: Fortress Press, 1960), 305–332. For the view that Luther had an inadvertent hand in this process, see Paul Althaus, *The Theology of Martin Luther* trans. Robert Schultz (Philadelphia: Fortress Press, 1966), 52.

[40] Muller, *Post-Reformation Dogmatics*, 93–4. See also 321 and de Certeau, *Mystic Fable*, 12–13.

exaggerated claims to assurance, to excessive forms of rationalism and the pursuit of intellectual methods for arriving at objective truth, especially in the realm of biblical scholarship, the defense of religious mystery was a war fought on multiple fronts.

One of the early events in this post-reformation history was Martin Luther's translation of the term *mysterion* in *The Babylonian Captivity* (1520). Writing in the wake of Erasmus' 1516 Greek New Testament, Luther critiqued Catholic ecclesiology by way of the Vulgate's rendering of the Greek word *mysterion*, especially the church's claim that marriage is a sacrament. Deeply sensitive to the principle that scripture is the living Word of God, Luther stressed the idea that the divine Word is not just God's message but is, in a very real sense, Christ himself. In his view, the real presence of God is to be found as much in the words of scripture as in the sacrament, in spiritual reading as in sacramental eating. For Luther, God's Word is the text of scripture itself, the very words on the page rather than just Christ alone as in protestant neoorthodoxy.[41] Readers remain alert to this dimension of scripture as the living presence of God when they feel themselves assimilated to the saving presence of the Word; but when this confidence subsides and one does not read with Spirit, then one only encounters the text as a dead letter.[42] Luther gives a striking articulation of this view of scripture in his 1520 treatise *The Babylonian Captivity*, where he explains why *mysterion* should not be translated as *sacramentum*. Developing the sacramental and ecclesiological implications of Erasmus' rejection of the Vulgate's translation of *mysterion*, Luther declares:

> Nowhere in Holy Scripture does the noun, 'sacrament', bear the meaning which is customary in the church, but rather the opposite. In every instance, it means, not a 'sign of something sacred', but the sacred, secret, and recondite thing itself.[43]

In Luther's view, the translation of *mysterion* as *sacramentum* turns a signified into a signifier, thereby watering down its power and presence. As a result, the Vulgate translation obscures the meaning and accessibility of mystery, centering it within the ecclesiastical domain rather than the scriptural firmament. Luther was thus showing readers that they were closer to

---

[41] Ibid., 2.55.

[42] See, for example, the three prefaces to his first lecture on the Psalms LW: 10.3–10.

[43] Martin Luther, "The Pagan Servitude of the Church" in *Martin Luther: Selections from His Writings* ed. John Dillenberger (New York: Anchor Books, 1958), 327.

God than they realized. In his view, "The words of Christ are sacraments by which he works our salvation" because "The Gospel words and stories are a kind of sacrament, that is, *a sacred sign, by which God effects what they signify* in those who believe."[44] Remediating medieval sacramental theology in the context of biblical exegesis, Luther believed that Christians could approach the deity through the words of scripture in a manner once reserved for the altar.

Luther's redefinition of *mysterion* is a striking example of the ecclesiastical and spiritual consequences arising from changes in definitions of mystery outlined in Michel de Certeau's *The Mystic Fable*.[45] As de Certeau explains, over the course of the twelfth through the seventeenth centuries, the term *mystic* and its various correlates ceased to mediate the threefold body of Christ (historical, sacramental, and scriptural). The result was a fundamental change in the meaning of *corpus mysticum* along with a general breakdown of the mutually supportive relations among scripture, church, and sacrament. Prior to the twelfth century, the term *corpus mysticum* subtly distinguished the eucharist from the physico-historical body of Christ. Functioning liturgically and sacramentally, it expressed an interactive, mutually dependent relation between the eucharist and the production of the church as a living body growing in time. In the centuries following, however, the *corpus mysticum* degenerated into a more static sociological term for the ecclesial body alone. Through this process, a dynamic sense of the eucharist's interaction with the church as a developing body of lay and clerical participants gave way to a more bifurcated and institutionally rigid sense of the church as a hierarchical instantiation of divine authority.

In other words, in its pre-twelfth-century form the term *mystery* was "more an action than a thing."[46] And as an action, it denoted a dynamic interplay among Christ's historical, scriptural, and ecclesial manifestations. But from the twelfth-century onward, the three parts of Christ's body became more rigidly distinguished as patristic mystery idioms failed to mediate among the different dimensions of Christ's threefold body. Consequently, a more rationalized and politicized conception of the church arose along with a more narrowly construed view of the eucharist

---

[44] Christmas Sermon (1519) as cited in Phillip Cary, *Outward Signs: The Powerlessness of External Things in Augustine's Thought* (Oxford: Oxford UP, 2008), viii.

[45] de Certeau, *The Mystic Fable*, 82–85. As de Certeau explicitly indicates, his argument constitutes a kind of sequel to Lubac's *Corpus Mysticum*. See also Rust, *The Body in Mystery*, 8–9.

[46] Lubac, *Corpus Mysticum*, 49; cited in Rust, *Body in Mystery*, 7.

in terms of real presence. Ultimately, this splitting apart of the threefold body set the stage for a post-reformation contest over the relative authority of scriptural and ecclesiastical corpuses.

It was only in the wake of such a contest over the meaning of Christ's various bodies that Luther could displace *mystery* from Christ's ecclesial body to his scriptural body in the highly consequential manner that he did. However philologically accurate he may have been in attacking the Vulgate's translation of *mysterion* as *sacramentum*, his interpretation took place within a broader theological context in which the shifting meanings of *mystery* were in play in ecclesiastically decisive ways. Hence, his conclusion "that Christ and the church are a 'mystery', or something at once hidden and of great importance, a thing which can, and should be spoken of metaphorically, and of which matrimony is a sort of material allegory."[47] In redefining *mysterion* this way, Luther recognized that he was also necessarily redefining the church as a *corpus mysticum* and thus the very idea of Christian fellowship as such. After all, by rejecting *sacramentum* as a translation of *mysterion* he transferred some of the authority previously granted to the mass as an arm of ecclesial power to the living presence of Christ in the bible. What is thus at issue in *The Babylonian Captivity* is not just the number of sacraments but the very nature of the Christian community as a *corpus mysticum*. Properly understood, Luther's interpretation of *mysterion* was part of a broader reconfiguration of the relations among God's manifestations in history, scripture, and the church taking place across several centuries.

Of particular significance for Herbert is the way Luther's view of mystery informs his biblical hermeneutics. For Luther, mystery lies less in scripture's allegorical obscurity than in what is plainly shown forth. So, although Luther rejects the imposition of allegory onto scripture when it is not warranted and although he lambasts Erasmus' skepticism about the possibility of theological certainty, he nevertheless stresses the paradox of mystery in simplicity as Herbert and Andrewes later would. Even in polemical situations such as *The Bondage of the Will*, where he is led to strongly emphasize scripture's clarity, Luther nevertheless manages to sustain a sense of scripture's mystery. In this decisive work, he teaches that with the bible

Matters of the highest majesty and the profoundest mysteries are no longer hidden away, but have been brought out and are openly displayed before the

[47] Luther, "Pagan Servitude," 328.

very doors. For Christ has opened our minds so that we may understand the Scriptures ... See, then, whether you and all the Sophists can produce any single mystery that is still abstruse in the Scriptures.[48]

The paradox guiding Luther's defense is the one Donne expresses in Satire 3 when he says that scriptural "mysteries / Are like the sun, dazzling, yet plain to all eyes" (87–88).[49]

While Luther stressed the paradox of mystery-in-plainness, he also recognized that such a view was not without spiritual and hermeneutic dangers, especially in the wake of humanist scholarship. When overemphasized, scripture's monological clarity can lead to legalistic dogmatism or, even worse, historicism. The potential for a reductive biblicism is always present in a theology which stresses a literal-grammatical approach at the expense of spiritual reading, especially when it serves to bolster the need for a mode of assurance that is greater than the conjectural certainty offered by the medieval church (a point to which I shall return). In order to be assured of one's salvation with the confidence that early reformers desired, one must be certain of what scripture says on the matter. Cognizant of the reductive potential within the co-related principles of faith alone and scripture alone, Luther developed a number of strategies to ward off threats posed by historicism, legalism, and radical spiritualism. One of the most potent of these was his particular interpretation of the dialectic between law and gospel.

For Luther, the dialectic of law and gospel served to combat the foreshortening of the bible that he saw in the historicism of late medieval writers such as Nicholas of Lyra as well as in the radical spiritualism of Anabaptists.[50] In Luther's view, Lyra stressed scripture's historical dimensions at the expense of its saving and promissory aspects thereby weakening the bible's vitality. In a different way, he saw Anabaptists privilege the

---

[48] Luther, *Bondage of the Will,* 111.

[49] *John Donne: The Major Works* ed. John Carey (Oxford: Oxford UP, 2008), 29–31.

[50] The following discussion of Luther's dialectic of law and gospel is informed by Gerhard Ebeling, *Luther: An Introduction to His Thought,* 110–140; *Word and Faith* (Philadelphia: Fortress Press, 1963), 305–332; Gerhard O. Forde "Law and Gospel in Luther's Hermeneutic" *Interpretation* (37.3: 1983), 240–252; and Gerald Bruns, *Hermeneutics: Ancient and Modern* (New Haven: Yale UP, 1992), 139–158. For Luther's response to Anabaptism see Luther, *Preface to Romans, LW*: 35: 368; *LW,* 40:83; *Karlstadt's Battle with Luther: Documents in a Liberal-Radical Debate* ed. Ronald J. Sider (Philadelphia: Fortress Press, 1978); and Louise Schreiner, *Are You Alone Wise: The Search for Certainty in the Early Modern Era* (Oxford: Oxford UP, 2011), 88–93.

motions of the Spirit over scriptural revelation, thereby dislocating God from his Word. Seeking to avoid the spiritual costs of historicism and radical spiritualism, Luther developed a particular understanding of the dialectic between law and gospel. In his view, law and gospel do not refer to two parts of scripture's content as a sacred history so much as two different ways of experiencing the Word as an ongoing story. Where law commands and instructs, gospel gives and comforts. His formula for this is that, "The promises of God give what the commandments of God require," a formulation that slightly tweaks Augustine's prayer in *The Confessions*: "Give what you command, and command what you will."[51] Operating dialectically in the reader's own life and soul, Luther's law/gospel distinction prevents scripture from devolving into abstraction or legalism insofar as they both presuppose a fully first-person response. In short, Luther's key hermeneutic distinction was partly motivated by the need to sustain a first-person mode of spiritual reading absent of the resources that the fourfold allegorical method had provided.

Luther sustained a profound sense of mystery within Christian thought in other ways as well. Perhaps most important here is the stress he put on God's terrifying inscrutability, something Calvin would develop for similar ends. Throughout his work, Luther insists that God "has not bound himself by his word, but has kept himself free over all things" thus remaining infinitely inscrutable.[52] This inscrutability becomes the site of awesome sublimity in Luther's thought, a *mysterium tremendum* so great that he warns: "May you as you are yourself never be confronted by the unclothed God" (12:312).[53] If Luther's belief in predestination and his emphasis on scriptural clarity diminish the place of mystery in Christian faith by limiting the dialectic of revelation and concealment at the level of the scriptural sign, his theology of the hidden God nevertheless goes a long way in sustaining a sense of the Christian *mysterion*.[54] We have already heard echoes of this view of God in Herbert's suggestion

[51] Luther, *The Freedom of a Christian*, LW 31:349 and Augustine, *Confessions*, 10:40, 10:45, 10:60 as cited in Phillip Cary, *Inner Grace: Augustine in the Traditions of Plato and Paul* (Oxford: Oxford UP, 2008), 84.

[52] Luther, *Bondage of the Will*, 201.

[53] For this and other key passages on the *deus absconditus* in Luther see Althaus, *Theology of Martin Luther*, 20–21.

[54] For the idea that Luther's emphasis on the hidden God played a kind of prophylactic function in his thought, protecting the sphere of mystery from other aspects of his theology, see John Dillenberger, *God Hidden and Revealed: The Interpretation of Luther's Deus*

that the divine will "such an intrenching is, / As passeth thought" ("The Search" 37–38) and in his description of the Trinity which "access denies" and "affrights" ("Ungratfulnesse" 14, 21). At such moments, Herbert stresses the Luthero-Calvinist belief that in communicating his presence God simultaneously conceals his essence so as not to overwhelm humans with his power.[55]

Judging by Lancelot Andrewes' sermons, however, Luther's emphasis on the hidden God and his dialectic of law and gospel did not go far enough in sustaining a sense of Christian mystery, at least not as it was needed within the context of early Stuart England. At various points in his sermons, Andrewes expresses a degree of impatience with the drive for certainty and clarity that is necessarily bound up with sixteenth-century translations of *mysterion*. In his 1607 Christmas Day sermon on 1 Timothy 3:16, for example, Andrewes insists that the mystery of godliness "or exercise of godliness—call it whether ye will … we call the Sacrament; the Greek hath no other word for it but *Μυνστεριον*, whereby the Church offereth to initiate us into the fellowship of this day's mystery" (1.43). This relatively generous translation of *mysterion* rebuts Calvin's rigorous disambiguation of the Vulgate's translation of godliness as a *sacramentum* in his biblical commentary on 1 Timothy 3. Rebuking papist ecclesiology much as Luther did, Calvin rails against the Vulgate's promiscuous use of the term *sacramentum* and the uncertainty that it generates. For Calvin, "It is a shocking blasphemy to say, that the word of God is uncertain, till it obtain from men what may be called a borrowed certainty."[56] In this instance, the exegetical differences between Calvin and Andrewes are partly a matter of context. Preaching for a king with ecumenical aspirations, Andrewes was less motivated by anti-Catholic polemic than Calvin was. As a result, he was able to adopt a more liberal attitude toward translation, one that not only sustained but even reveled in ambiguity and mystery. Thus, rather than disambiguating the Vulgate text, Andrewes unfolds the meaning of godliness from multiple points of view so as to initiate

Absconditus and its Significance for Religious Thought (Philadelphia: Muhlenberg Press, 1953), 16 and Althaus, *Theology of Martin Luther*, 285.

[55] For discussions of Calvin's development of the *deus absconditus* see Edward A. Dowey, JR. *The Knowledge of God in Calvin's Theology* (Grand Rapids: Eerdmans, 1994), esp., 12 and Susan E. Schreiner, *Where Shall Wisdom Be Found?: Calvin's Exegesis of Job from Medieval and Modern Perspectives* (Chicago: University of Chicago Press, 1994), 91–155.

[56] Calvin, *Calvin's Commentaries* 23 *Volumes* trans. William Pringle (Grand Rapids: Baker Books, n.d.), 21.90–91.

readers into a "*gravida mysteriis*, 'one mystery … [that] hath many mysteries with it'" (1.34). His aim in doing so is not to provide exegetical certainty but to recreate the experience of discovering scripture as though for the first time. To do this, Andrewes openly draws on a Latin translation of *mysterion* that earlier reformers had rejected on philological grounds.

COLOSS. 3.3 OUR LIFE IS HID WITH CHRIST IN GOD

It was out of this same emergent need to sustain a deepened sense of scriptural mystery that Herbert gave expression to the dynamics of revelation-in-concealment and concealment-in-revelation in *The Temple*. Consequently, the exigency behind many of Herbert's key poetic strategies only becomes fully intelligible when seen in context of an emerging eclipse of mystery. Responding to the threats of dogmatism and exaggerated certainty that had built up over the course of the Reformation, Andrewes and Herbert developed a range of formal strategies for conveying mystery within simplicity, including those Herbert deploys in "Coloss. 3.3 *Our Life is hid with Christ in God.*" If "Ungratefulnesse" depicts revelation-in-concealment through stanza structure and if "The Search" does it with imagery, then "Coloss. 3:3" does so visually.

Read on Easter Day in *The Book of Common Prayer*, "Coloss. 3:3" stresses the constitutively hidden dimensions of Christian revelation: "yee are dead, and your life is hid with Christ in God." This passage was evidently dear to Herbert, who, according to John Aubrey, had it painted "at his Wive's Seate" in Bemerton church.[57] Stressing the interpenetration of reader and text, the poem's formal structure visualizes the reader's immanence within the scriptural mystery alongside Christ's immanence within the soul. In doing so, it offers a textual-visual depiction of scripture as a living *mysterion*.

Like Andrewes, Herbert takes liberties in "Coloss. 3.3" with the biblical text that he is poeticizing. First, he introduces a grammatical incongruity into the text by altering "your" to "our." Second, he conflates an earlier passage in Colossians with 3.3, the passage in which Paul praises the "mystery of God, and of the Father, and of Christ, In whom are hid all the treasures of wisdom, and knowledge" (Col. 2:2–3).[58]

---

[57] Cited in Wilcox, 303.
[58] Chauncey Wood makes this observation in "A Reading of Herbert's 'Coloss. 3.3,'" *George Herbert Journal*, 2.2 (1979), 15–24, 22.

Stitching these scripture passages together, Herbert conveys in striking visual form the Pauline notion of mystery as that infinite treasure which is hidden in the very act of being revealed:

> *My* words & thoughts do both expresse this notion,
> That *Life* hath with the sun a double motion.
> The first *Is* straight, and our diurnall friend,
> The other *Hid*, and doth obliquely bend.
> One life is wrapt *In* flesh, and tends to earth:
> The other winds towards *Him*, whose happie birth
> Taught me to live here so, *That* still one eye
> Should aim and shoot at that which *Is* on high:
> Quitting with   daily   labour   all   *My*   pleasure,
> To   gain   at   harvest   an   eternall   *Treasure.*

In the Bodlean manuscript, the acrostic dimensions of the lyric are even more obscure as the diagonally set words are not consistently expressed typographically. In both texts, though, the poem captures the paradoxes inherent in St. Paul's concept of *mysterion* as a mode of divine manifestation that remains partly out of sight despite its being fully disclosed. In this way, Herbert's poem articulates something like Sibbes' claim in "The Hidden Life" that "A Christian is a strange person. He is both dead and alive … The life of a Christian is a secret life. It is a peculiar life … It is secret because it is hid … God's children are secret ones. They are not known to the world, nor to themselves oftimes" (5.206–7).

Taking the form of a confession, "Coloss. 3.3" presupposes a rich back-story. Rather than presenting one of the many "spiritual Conflicts that have past betwixt [himself] and God," the poem presents the results of an encounter with God. More a fully realized epiphany than an unfolding meditation, the poem functions as a spiritual portrait, an image of the Christian as simultaneously sinner and saved, dead and alive. Despite its analogies with portraiture, however, this ten-line poem is not static. As its organizing metaphors of celestial orbiting imply, the lyric expresses a view of spiritual life as a life of motion and movement, an eternal journey as it were.

Ernest Gilman and Eric B. Song have independently demonstrated that the spiritual motion expressed in the poem involves allusions to anamorphic perspectives.[59] A kind of pictorial conceit, an anamorphic image

---

[59] Ernest B. Gilman, *The Curious Perspective: Literary and Pictorial Wit in the Seventeenth Century* (New Haven: Yale UP, 1978), 190–191 and Eric B. Song, "Anamorphosis and the

presents two discrete images that are both visible within one visual plane, thereby creating a sense of movement and dynamism. This is the kind of visual image that Herbert alludes to when he says that devils are but sins in "perspective" ("Sinne (II)," 10). According to Song, Herbert's poem exploits the anamorphic image's uncanny capacity to make viewers feel as though they are inside rather than outside the visual frame. He begins by noting that the grammatical incongruities of "*Our life* is hid with Christ" are doubled by the coexistence of two incongruous images, one corresponding to the life of the flesh and one to the life of Christ. What is crucial, however, is that both of these images define us as Christian readers, visually externalizing and thereby mirroring our condition of being. Through these anamorphic doublings, Song explains, "'Coloss 3.3.' not only arrests our gaze as readers/viewers ('as subjects, we are literally called into the picture, and represented here as caught') but also mirrors or enacts our condition as divided subjects."[60] To fully understand the visual dynamics of this poem, however, and to better appreciate it as an example of Herbert's revelatory poetics, we need to take its exegetical contexts into closer account.

To start with, Herbert's use of anamorphic figures in "Coloss. 3.3" likely arises from his reading of Luther's commentaries on the New Testament. As Eugene Cunnar observes in his interpretation of Herbert's "The Windows," "Luther consistently equates Paul's words with painting … particularly anamorphic vision."[61] Evidently fascinated by the recent development of anamorphic perspective, Luther draws on perspectival metaphors in order to express the interpretive process of spiritual reading. As Cunnar indicates, this is especially evident in Luther's explanation of John's discussion of typology. According to Luther, the Gospel of John explains the sense in which Christ is the *skopos* or ultimate goal of scripture. In the Gospel, the Lord

> shows us the proper method of interpreting Moses and all the prophets. He teaches us that Moses points and refers to Christ in all his stories and illustrations. His purpose is to show that Christ is the point at the center of a

Religious Subject of George Herbert's 'Coloss. 3.3" *SEL 1500–1900* 47.1 (2007), 107–121. Song does not cite Gilman.

[60] Song, "Anamorphosis and the Religious Subject," 116.

[61] Eugene R. Cunnar, "Herbert and the Visual Arts: *Ut Pictura Poesis:* An Opening in 'The Windows' in eds. Edmund Miller and Robert DiYanni. *Like Season'd Timber: New Essays on George Herbert* (New York: Peter Lang, 1987), 101–138, 108.

circle, with all eyes inside the circle focused on Him. Whoever turns his eyes on Him finds his proper place in the circle of which Christ is the center. All the stories of Holy writ, if viewed aright, point to Christ.[62]

Luther's account of Christ as both origin and ultimate horizon of all scriptural meaning turns on a striking modification of Nicolas of Cusa's influential thesis about the nature of God's gaze. In *De Visione Dei*, Cusa explains God's gaze by figuring it as analogous to the seemingly omnivoyant gaze of a painted face which is positioned at the center of a room, thereby creating the effect it "seems to behold everything around it."[63] Giving a characteristically modern twist to his fellow German's late-medieval thinking, Luther deepens the decentered position of the viewing subject that Cusa presumes. For Luther, the experience of reading scripture aright is like viewing an anamorphic image which, fully seen, reveals the perspectival omnivoyance and scriptural omnipresence of Christ as God. And in the act of feeling our decentered selves beheld by an absolutely centered deity, we recognize our proper place has been prepared for us and we can then settle into it as right-reading, right-seeing Christians. Indeed, we recognize that *we are*, in effect, the place that God has determined for us within the compass of his grace. The visual dimensions of "Coloss. 3.3" constitute a formal means of conveying this exegetical principle, this idea that the Christian reader is within rather than without the scriptural frame.

Luther's and Herbert's uses of anamorphic tropes to describe the experience of finding oneself in scripture reveal at least two things. First, they suggest that both writers use such figures as a way of communicating a particular version of the *de te fabula* principle, the idea that the text's meaning is only revealed once we realize that we are in the story itself. And second, they suggest that in becoming a Christian subject one is thrown out one out of oneself as worldly being in order to discover oneself by means of a return journey made through and by Christ. In other words, it is not human desire but God's desire in Christians that makes them sons of God. As Richard Sibbes says: "Let us labour to be righteous men, labour to be in Christ, to have the righteousness of Christ to be ours, to be out of ourselves in Christ" (7.7). Herbert's "Coloss. 3.3" not only conveys the

[62] Cited in Cunnar, "Herbert and Visual Arts," 108. Cunnar cites this passage as LW, 21.337. It is actually 22.339.
[63] Jasper Hopkins, *Nicholas of Cusa's Dialectical Mysticism: Text, Translation, and Interpretive Study of De Visione Dei* (Minneapolis: Arthur J. Banning Press, 1985), 113.

dialectic of sin and sanctity inherent to Pauline soteriology, but it also conveys the exegetical sense of scriptural immanence underwriting it.

Closer to home, Herbert may have known that Lancelot Andrewes developed Luther's anamorphic figures in his 1605 Good Friday sermon before the king at Greenwich. Carefully analyzing the way that Greek prepositions express modes of spiritual perception in the gospels, Andrewes encourages Christians to perceive Christ as a living mystery as well as a dying man. Here again, the distinction between history and story is crucial to Andrewes's investment in participatory reading:

> ...the Passion is a piece of perspective, and ... we must set ourselves to see it if we will see it well, and not look superficially on it; not on the outside alone, but ... 'pierce into it', and enter even into the inward workmanship of it, even of His internal Cross which He suffered, and of His entire affection wherewith He suffered it. (2.178)

The mode of perception that Andrewes outlines here helps explain what Herbert's poem demands of its readers. Herbert's reader must not see the outside alone but must "pierce into" the text so as to participate in the dialectic of revelation and concealment orienting the poem which figures the spiritual presence of Christ within the viewer's soul. In this way, Herbert's lyric visually enacts how the Christian subject comes to know himself as divided between flesh and spirit. In turn, it enacts how Christians recognize themselves as Christians by experiencing themselves being seen by Christ. Luther conveys this decisive phenomenon with reference to Nicholas of Cusa's image of a divine gaze peering out at us from the center of a circle. Herbert conveys the same basic point by placing "*In Him*" at the geometrical center of the poem, thereby granting it semantic priority.[64] In both instances, anamorphic figures remind us that we are not just beholding the divine image/Word from the outside, but rather we are participants within it and are thus shaped by it. In this way, we are not just looking at the poem, but the poem is looking back at us. Here again, the spiritual process of understanding consists of initiation, the double movement of assimilating and being assimilated by the Word.

---

[64] For this point see Robert McMahon, "Herbert's 'Coloss. 3.3' as Microcosm" in *George Herbert Journal* 15.2 (Spring 1992), 55–69, 61.

The visual dynamics at work in "Coloss. 3.3" suggests some of the ways in which participatory exegesis engenders two dialectically opposed responses. From the perspective of the flesh, the Christian's encounter with the Word is self-alienating and unsettling in the way expressed in the final stanza of "Ungratefulnesse." But from the perspective of the Spirit, it is recuperative and thus enchanting as realized in the conclusion to "Love (III)." Through this latter movement, "Coloss. 3:3" invites a process of initiation, an entry into the mystery. Robert McMahon provides a rich sense of what the reader of "Coloss 3:3" is being initiated into when he observes that the poem enacts the process of recapitulation already noted with reference to "The Banquet" (*anakephalaiosis*). This is the idea that the beginning of all things is integrated into their end and that the process of integration unfolds in a movement that is at once teleological and circular, much like the movement of *The Temple* as a whole that is described at the end of "Paradise": "such beginnings touch their END" (15). By tracing these processes, "Coloss. 3.3" "mimes the movement of salvation history: Christ is the center ('*Him*' l. 6) and end ('*Treasure*,' l. 10) sustaining the whole, redeeming the fragmentations and divisions of life wrought by the Fall (ll. 3–5)."[65] In Ephesians 1:9–10, this process of recapitulation is defined as "the mystery of [God's] will," "the dispensation of the fullness of times." To enter into this dispensation is to undergo an experience of being thrown ahead of oneself into a Christological future. Gregory of Nyssa calls this kind of throwness *epektasis*, the tension of striving after God in the wake of the incarnation but before the final coming.[66] This is the eschatological experience that Herbert summarizes when he says Christians should have one eye "aim and shoot at that which *Is* on high" (8). The Easter context within which Herbert's readers would have received this poem accentuate this *already-and-not-yet* dimension of eschatological hope. In celebrating the life hidden in him, Herbert anticipates the future promise of that which "*Is* on high" as well as that which is yet to come.

Herbert's later seventeenth-century imitator Nathaniel Wanley also perceived an eschatological dimension at work in Herbert's "Coloss. 3.3." Reworking Herbert's visual trope in a poem titled "The Divorce," Wanley places even greater emphasis on God's providential action. He does this through a call and response pattern in which the diagonal acrostic is presented as God's answer to the main poem's petition:

[65] Ibid., 64.
[66] See Bouyer, *The Christian Mystery*, 176.

All wheels Lord in my soule are out of order
On **things** forbid I dote and still the border
Thou says **shall** be the bound to keepe mee in
My mind doth **worke** to passe ; my soule & sin
Long since were joind **together** ; wth remorse
I therefore sue to thee **for** a divorce
Let but one line be written wth **thy** blood
And then I shall be sure it will hold **good**.[67]

Playing on Herbert's poetics of spiritual motion and prayerful dialo-gism, this poem involves two basic movements. First, there is the divorc-ing of the soul from God through sin; and second, there is the uniting of the soul with Christ through grace. This unification happens in the word *good*, which semantically combines the two axes upon which the poem is built, bringing human and divine voices together in one unified intention. The use of the word *good* functions here much as the word *rhyme* does in the final line of Herbert's "Deniall" where it is the only instance in which a stanza's final word rhymes with any of the previous lines. The suggestion being that God has finally provided the order and harmony whose absence set the poem into motion in the first place. Such word magic is typically Herbertian.

Herbert's and Wanley's poems are both eschatological in a very spe-cific sense. They are concerned with *epektasis* as a dialectical experience of uncertainty in hope and anxiety in promise. Of all the visual modes available to Herbert, none convey the sense of uncertainty inherent in this experience more viscerally than anamorphosis. Indeed, this visual mode perfectly expresses Augustine's perspectival awareness vis-á-vis scripture. Accordingly, the poem ends by defining the tension between certainty and uncertainty inherent in the experience of *epektasis*. It does this by concluding with a mixed metaphor derived from the gospels as the speaker hopes "To gain at harvest an eternall Treasure" (10). The catachresis that ends the poem derives from John 4:35, which Thomas Wilson's *Rules for the understanding and practice of holy scrip-tures* identifies as an example of how the bible often puts "one word twise in one sentence, with a different signification."[68] The verse in John reads: "Say not ye, There are yet foure moneths, and then com-

---

[67] *The Poems of Nathaniel Wanley* ed. L.C. Martin (Oxford: Clarendon Press, 1928), 19.
[68] Thomas Wilson, *Theological Rules ... serving to guide us in the understanding and prac-ticse of holy Scripture* (1615), 21.

meth harvest? Behold, I say unto you, Lift up your eyes, and looke on the fields : for they are white already to harvest." In the first instance, the reference is to a temporal harvest but in the second it refers to the harvest of eternity through grace, a harvest that is both now and ever. Herbert expresses the gap between these two meanings through the anamorphic play of reference, emphasizing the leap of faith one must take in order to perceive the eternal within and through the temporal. Revealingly, this is precisely what the speaker of "Home" remains unable to do. Adopting a strong *contemptus mundi* attitude that is out of keeping with the Advent season occasioning the poem, the speaker of "Home" complains that although "We talk of harvests; there are no such things, / But when we leave our corn and hay" (55–56), further recalling the ironic complaint in "The Collar": "Have I no harvest but a thorn" (7). Impatient with Christ's absence, the speaker of "Home" dislocates the paradox of eternity within time that the Gospel of John introduces. This refusal to take the leap of faith that accounts for the impatience of "Home's" refrain: "O show thy self to me, / Or take me up to thee!" Unlike the speaker of "Coloss. 3.3.," the speaker of "Home" seeks after absolute certainty in the here and now. As a result, he is unable to avow Sibbes' insight that "there are two contrary principles always in a believer," doubt and faith, assurance and mystery (5.476). Without an awareness of this duality, the Christian seeks a premature way out of this "weary world" rather than being able to "love the strife" ("Home," 37, "The Banquet," 54).

Failing to sustain John's paradox that Christ makes an eternal harvest present even in the dark of winter, the speaker of "Home" not only succumbs to a disenchanted view of the natural world but also to a deadening view of scripture. Ultimately, the final corrective turn belongs to the reader as we must decide if the final stanza's break in rhyme marks the arrival of Christ or not. Herbert does not decide for us:

> Come dearest Lord, passe not this holy season,
>   My flesh and bones and joynts do pray:
> And ev'n my verse, when by the ryme and reason
>   The word is, *Stay*, sayes ever, *Come*.
>   O show thy self to me,
>   Or take me up to thee! (73–78)

CONCLUSION: THE ECLIPSE OF BIBLICAL NARRATIVE

As we have begun to see, Herbert modeled his volume of verse on a conception of scripture as a living mystery. One enters *The Temple* as one enters the bible: in the hopes of experiencing sanctifying transformation through the vivifying limits of an inexhaustibly rich Word. Yet Herbert developed his poetics within the shifting contexts of seventeenth-century protestant orthodoxy, the period in which conceptions of scripture as a book of mystery began to decline in intellectual circles (ca. 1565–1640). By the late seventeenth century, this pressure culminated in what Hans Frei has described as the eclipse of the biblical narrative, the disappearance not of the biblical story but of the hermeneutical assumption that the reader is immanent, as it were, within the scriptural frame.[69]

Those who resisted the eclipse of mystery in England during the period of protestant orthodoxy found themselves in a world where some believers were becoming newly cognizant of the virtues of nescience while others avidly pursued certainty and where all had to find some kind of balance between shifting extremes. If early Stuart England witnessed the rise of a fully mature biblical literature, it is partly because the historical tide was beginning to move against the spiritual and hermeneutic conditions requisite to such writing. As is often the case in literary history, traditions come into full maturity at the very moment when their underlying conditions of possibility begin to pass. As pressure mounted on the idea that scripture is the living Word of God, there emerged an exquisitely self-conscious sense of what it takes for faithful Christians to live a life guided by the experience of spiritual reading. It was within this set of intellectual and spiritual pressures that Herbert developed a range of formal strategies to convey the idea that scripture is the living Word of God. In doing so, he participated in the seventeenth-century critique of religious certitude and spiritual overconfidence to which we now turn.

---

[69] Hans W. Frei, *The Eclipse of Biblical Narrative: A Study in Eighteenth and Nineteenth Century Hermeneutics* (New Haven: Yale UP, 1974). Gerard Reedy, S.J. briefly mentions the passing of participatory exegesis among late seventeenth-century Anglican preachers in *Robert South* (1634–1716): *An Introduction to His Life and Sermons* (Cambridge: Cambridge UP, 1992), 74.

CHAPTER 3

The Critique of Certitude in Seventeenth-Century England

With the rise of modern biblical scholarship and the success of the protestant Reformation, seventeenth-century England witnessed a decline in exegetical optimism, the fading of conviction in scripture's simplicity.[1] If interpretive confidence had been a virtue when reformers were fighting a rearguard action in the early Reformation, it became a potential liability once protestants found themselves in positions of ecclesial and political authority. What is worse, it became increasingly difficult to sustain such a view of scripture in light of ongoing philological and theological debate. So, while Luther faced a polemical situation that led him to stress scripture's perspicuity, John Hales found it necessary to warn his 1617 Oxford audience that there is more obscurity in scripture than "in any writing that I know secular or divine."[2]

In making such a case, Hales was stating in strong terms what the translators of the AV had publically acknowledged half a decade earlier. In his prefatory letter "The Translators to the Reader," Miles Smith declared that as far as difficult passages are concerned "fearfulnesse would

---

[1] For the use of the phrase "exegetical optimism" to describe post-reformation exegetical developments, see Susan E. Schreiner, "'The Spiritual Man Judges All Things': Calvin and Exegetical Debate about Certainty in the Reformation" in *Biblical Interpretation in the Era of the Reformation* eds. Richard A. Muller and John L. Thompson (Grand Rapids: Eerdmans, 1996), 189–215, 197 and David C. Steinmetz, *Luther in Context* (Bloomington: Indiana UP, 1986), 96.

[2] John Hales, *Sermon ... Concerning The Abuses ... of holy scripture* (Oxford: 1617), 36–37.

© The Author(s) 2017
G. Kuchar, *George Herbert and the Mystery of the Word*,
DOI 10.1007/978-3-319-44045-3_3

better beseeme us then confidence, and if we will resolve, to resolve upon
modestie with *S. Augustine* ... it is better to make doubt of those things
which are secret, then to strive about those things that are uncertaine"
(n.p.). This is a different set of emphases than the ones we find in the
Edwardian and Elizabethan homilies on the reading of scripture.[3] Where
earlier protestant authorities stressed the plainness of scripture, even to
the point of addressing it as a scandal for learned readers, the King James
translators found it important not to "conclude or dogmatize upon this
or that peremptorily" because "to determine of such things as the Spirit
of God hath left ... questionable, can be no lesse then presumption"
(n.p.). The exegetical surety that had once been a central protestant
virtue was now being greatly qualified in light of both philological
advances and changing ecclesiastical and national circumstances. It was
out of these contexts that Herbert developed the spiritual ethos encapsulated in "The Flower's": "We say amiss, / This or that is: / Thy word is
all, if we could spell."

BIBLICAL COMPLEXITY: ANDREWES, LUTHER, CALVIN

Even before the Authorized Version appeared, some of its leading translators were already placing a firmer emphasis on scripture's ambiguity
than previous generations of protestants had done. In a sermon on the
controversial epistle of James preached before the king at Greenwich in
1607, Andrewes adopts the Vulgate's outdated mystery idioms in order to
emphasize the importance of works. Taking Gregory and Augustine as his
models, Andrewes depicts religious acts as analogous to the miracle of real
presence, thereby demonstrating a remarkably open-ended, if not doctrinally innocent, approach to bible translation and commentary. Deploying
the same strategy of correction and revision characteristic of Herbert's
verse, Andrewes preaches:

> To be a doer of the word is, as St. Gregory saith well, *convertere scripturas
> in operas*, to change the word which is audible into a work which is visible,
> the word which is transient into a work which is permanent.
>   Or rather not to change it, but, as St. Augustine saith, *accedat ad verbum*,
> unto the word that we hear let there be joined the element of the work,

---

[3] See Thomas Cranmer, *Certayne sermons, or homelies* (*N.P.* 1547), B2v-B3r and *The seconde tome of homelyes* (London: 1563) Fol. 159v-160, 169.

that is, some real elemental deed; *et sic fit magnum sacramentum pietatis*, and so shall you have 'the great mystery' or sacrament of 'godliness'. For indeed godliness is as a sacrament … if it be not a sacrament it is not true godliness. (5.195)

By adopting *sacramentum* for *mysterion*, Andrewes further rejects the overscrupulosity of those interpreters who, as the prefatory letter says, tie themselves "to an uniformitie of phrasing, or to an identitie of words" (n.p). Rather than restricting meaning for the sake of precision and purity, Andrewes chooses idioms that open the text up to creative glossing, thereby making the text more conducive to the first-hand assimilation.

To be sure, though, Andrewes' approach to scripture and translation does not mark any kind of radical break from mainstream Protestantism. It goes without saying that his exegetical style owes much to the Reformation, especially Luther. After all, Andrewes' wariness about religious certitude has its roots in Luther's debates with Karlstadt and Müntzer. After his encounter with the radicals, Luther became increasingly sensitive to the politically subversive and hermeneutically reductive potential within Anabaptism. As a result, he carefully privileged the Word over the Spirit in the restricted sense that all spiritual motions confirm rather than supplement what is written in scripture. By the early 1520s, he insisted that "the Holy Spirit is not given except in, with, and by faith in Jesus Christ … through God's Word" (35:368), hence his sardonic accusation that Anabaptist "fanatics" who make supra-scriptural claims on the basis of spiritual motions have swallowed "the Holy Spirit feathers and all" (40:83). As we have seen, when coupled with his approach to the dialectic of law and gospel, Luther's conception of the Word closely guarded against the interrelated dangers of radical spiritualism, dogmatic codification, and historicism. The result was a formidable sense of scripture as the living voice of God, one that Andrewes and Herbert both sought to deepen in light of the increasing pressures being brought to bear upon it.

At the same time, however, Luther, like other early reformers, was motivated by a desire for soteriological and exegetical certainty. One of the main exigencies of the Reformation was to provide Christians with a greater sense of assurance about religious truth than the conjectural certainty proffered by late-medieval religion.[4] For Luther and Calvin, true

---

[4] See Susan Schriener *Are You Alone Wise?* and "The Spiritual Man Judges All Things"; Richard H. Popkin *The History of Skepticism From Savonarola to Bayle* revised and expanded

faith offers the fully persuasive certainty of first-hand experience of God's redemptive action grounded in the plainness of the Word as verified by the motions of the Spirit.[5] On this account, faith and assurance are inextricably related because salvation comes through faith alone. As Luther warns in *The Pagan Servitude of the Church*, only

> ungodly men ... declare that no man can be certain of the forgiveness of his sins ... For faith is the work, not of man, but of God alone, as Paul teaches. God does the other works through us and by us; in the case of faith, He works in us and without our co-operation.[6]

On the basis of these assumptions, Luther skewered Erasmus' skeptical approach to theological matters, confidently declaring that "The Holy Spirit is no Skeptic, and it is not doubts or mere opinions that he has written on our hearts, but assertions more sure and certain than life itself and all experience."[7] While Luther and Calvin carefully guarded against antinomian extremes and while they acknowledged the reality of doubt and sin, their Pauline-centered theologies were strongly grounded in the need for personal assurance of salvation and the exegetical clarity requisite to it. As a result, the drive to certainty lay at the very center of their overall spiritual and biblical vision.

Nowhere is this impulse more evident than in Luther's practice of distinguishing between the righteous and the wicked in terms of certainty. As he writes in his exposition of Psalm 37:

edition (Oxford: Oxford UP, 2003); Barbara Pitkin, *What Pure Eyes Could See: Calvin's Doctrine of Faith in Its Exegetical Context* (Oxford: Oxford UP, 1999); J.P. Callahan, "'Claritas Scripturae': The Role of Perspicuity in Protestant Hermeneutics" *Journal of the Evangelical Theological Society*. 39.3 (1996), 353–372; Joel R. Beeke, *Assurance of Faith*; Edward A. Dowey, Jr., *The Knowledge of God*; and T.H. L Parker, *Calvin's Doctrine of the Knowledge of God* (Edinburgh: Oliver and Boyd, 1969). I draw heavily on Schreiner in the following sequence.

[5] On this point, see Pitkin, *What Pure Eyes*, 36. For a discussion of medieval concepts of faith as a voluntary certainty (*voluntaria certitudo*), see G.R. Evans, *Getting it Wrong: The Medieval Epistemology of Error* (Leiden: Brill, 1998), 166–176.

[6] Luther, *Pagan Servitude*, 296.

[7] Luther, *Bondage of the Will*, in *Luther and Erasmus: Free Will and Salvation* eds. E. Gordon Rupp and Philip S. Watson (Philadelphia: Westminster Press, 1969), 109. See Popkin, *History of Skepticism*, 9–10.

the steps of the righteous do not slip but go straight ahead, safe and sure, in good conscience, because he is certain of his cause … But the wicked always fall and slide around, and their step is uncertain. (14:224)

By extension, he uses the same kind of distinction to distinguish true from false belief. We true believers, Luther writes, "are able to declare and judge with certainty, on the basis of the Word, about the will of God toward us" but "the papists and the fanatic spirits are unable to judge with certainty about anything."[8] More than simply a motivating desire, certainty became a criterion of theological truth in the sixteenth century. In many instances, being right meant being assuredly confident. At such moments, the redeemed mind was, by definition, a certain mind.[9]

This strain within reformation orthodoxy self-consciously differed from medieval conceptions of belief. Immediately prior to the Reformation, true belief consisted first and foremost of adherence to dogmas guaranteed by the councils and traditions of the church. In the case of such "historical faith," true belief is a matter of correspondence between what one professes and what the church declares, the result of which is a less personally assured form of certainty. For medieval Christians, certainty was "*ecclesiastical* (rather than Christological) and *sacramental* (rather than pneumatological)" or Spirit-based.[10] Luther's concept of belief operates differently and as a result so too does his stronger version of personal certainty. In his view, true belief involves the first-hand experience of the Spirit confirming the truth of the Word in one's heart, hence his rejection of Erasmian skepticism on the grounds that there is nothing "more miserable than uncertainty."[11] By redefining right belief in the light of the dialectic of Word and Spirit, Luther claimed to have freed Christendom from the bonds of doubt and uncertainty. On the basis of such claims, he was able to declare: "Thank God … that we have been delivered from this [Roman] monster of uncertainty and that now we can believe with certainty that the Holy Spirit is crying and issuing that sigh too deep for words in our hearts."[12]

Despite his many critiques of reason, Luther's redefinition of faith results in a form of certitude that is very different than the one encapsulated in

---

[8] Cited in Schreiner, *Are You Alone*, 97.
[9] See Ibid., 37–130.
[10] Beeke, *Assurance of Faith*, 13.
[11] Luther, *Bondage of the Will*, 108. See Schreiner, "The Spiritual Man Judges," 189.
[12] As cited in Schreiner, *Are You Alone Wise*, 60.

Tertullian's phrase: "It is certain because it is impossible." Rather than aligning certainty with a leap of faith based on the authority of God as collectively and institutionally received, Luther experiences certainty because he has been fully persuaded by the Word as confirmed by the motions of the Spirit. In making such claims, Luther participated in a broader sixteenth-century reformation discourse in which the Spirit served as an agent of certainty. As such, the Spirit was thought to ground exegetical claims to the objectivity of scriptural authority as well as personal, subjective, claims to assurance.[13] Paul Althaus is thus right to suggest that, for Luther, "the certainty that God's word is true is … something completely different from any axiomatic or a priori certainty. The self-certainty of reason, the evidential character of rational truths, is far removed from the 'testimony of the Holy Spirit'."[14]

None of this is to deny Luther's sensitivity to experiences of doubt or near despair. Luther knew better than most how terrifying it can be to work out one's salvation in fear and trembling. The concept of *Anfechtung* or tempting-trial is crucial to his overall spiritual vision. This side of Luther's work becomes particularly evident in the pastoral context of private correspondence. For instance, in a 1545 letter to a woman anxious about her election, Luther teaches that seeking out certainty of predestination absent of reference to Christ is a sin and so "we should think of [Christ] daily and follow him. In him, we shall find our election to be sure and pleasant."[15] Nor do I wish to deny Luther's awareness of scriptural complexity, something that he acknowledged in some circumstances. What I am suggesting, however, is that the polemical situations in which Luther wrote led him to emphasize spiritual confidence in matters of grace and clarity in matters of interpretation, the first resting on the second. By the time we reach seventeenth-century England, the polemical need for these emphases had largely subsided as a new set of spiritual exigencies arose in their place. If Luther sought to provide comfort for those overcome by the anxieties of late-medieval religion, then Andrewes and Herbert faced very different, even in some sense opposing, challenges. In their new context, Luther's capacity for doubt, along with his striking penchant for paradox, became far more valuable than his strong capacity for certainty.

---

[13] Schreiner, "The Spiritual Man," 190 and *Are You Alone*, 84–129, esp., 103.

[14] Althaus, *Theology of Martin Luther*, 50.

[15] Martin Luther, *Letters of Spiritual Counsel* trans. and ed. Theodore G. Tappert, (Vancouver: Regent College Publishing, 2003), 137–138.

Rather than emphasizing purity of doctrine and rather than encouraging a rigorously Pauline ethos grounded in an uncompromising confidence through faith alone, Herbert participated in a religious culture characterized by a greater degree of theological syncretism and a renewed emphasis on the mystery of scripture than was the case in previous decades. The result was a religious culture unusually well suited to the production of aesthetically and spiritually engaging devotional poetry.

CALVIN'S CERTAINTY

By the time Calvin wrote, some of the dangers involved in making certitude a criterion of biblical truth had already become increasingly visible. As Susan Schreiner explains, in Calvin we can discern "a kind of reserve that seems to reflect the awareness of past difficulties posed by claiming the Spirit as the source of certainty." Unlike earlier reformers, "Calvin was much more reticent to cite the familiar passages from Romans, Galatians, and the Gospel of John in order to validate his interpretations" with reference to the Spirit.[16] And like Luther, Calvin rejected any attempt to ground one's assurance in speculation about predestination separate from faith in Christ. "They are madmen," Calvin taught, "who seek their own salvation or that of others in the whirlpool of predestination, not keeping the way of salvation which is exhibited to them." For Calvin, this way of salvation lies in faith through an effectual calling: "To every man, therefore, his faith is a sufficient attestation of the eternal predestination of God." Holding to the view that "the testimony of the Holy Spirit is nothing else than the sealing of our adoption" (Rom. viii.15), Calvin maintained that the experience of calling via sanctification can strengthen faith and hence assurance but it cannot ground them.[17]

But if Calvin qualified the assurance one can derive from the Spirit, he nevertheless augmented the security made available through faith. In the course of revising *The Institutes*, Calvin evolved a definition of faith that went from primarily meaning "trust" to eventually meaning "certain knowledge."[18] While early editions of *The Institutes* tended to define faith

---

[16] Schreiner, *Are You Alone Wise*, 103.
[17] Calvin, *Commentary on the Gospel According to John* trans., William Pringle (Grand Rapids: Baker Books), 17:254.
[18] See Pitkin, *What Pure Eyes*, 40; T.H.L Parker, *Calvin's Doctrine of the Knowledge of God*, 5; and Schreiner, *Are You Alone Wise*, 66.

as *fiducia*, later editions evolved a definition of faith as a *firmam certamque cognitionem* or firm and certain knowledge. By the time Calvin completed the definitive 1559 edition of *The Institutes*, he had carefully distilled his definition of *fides* as a form of understanding that is irreducible to strictly natural modes of knowing. Making faith formally equivalent to supernatural, spiritually regenerated knowledge, Calvin now attributed to it a newly solid form of certainty, one that was irreducible to natural or noninspired modes of knowing. For the mature Calvin of the 1559 edition of *The Institutes*,

> we shall possess a right definition of faith if we call it a firm and certain knowledge [*firmam certamque cognitionem*] of God's benevolence toward us, founded on the truth of the freely given promise in Christ, both revealed to our minds and sealed [*obsignatur*] upon our hearts by the Holy Spirit.
> We add the words 'certain' and 'firm' in order to express a more solid constancy of persuasion. For, as faith is not content with a doubtful and changeable opinion, so it is not content with an obscure and confused conception; but requires full and fixed certainty such as men are wont to have from things experienced and proved.[19]

On this account, believers can be certain of their salvation precisely insofar as they have an exact conception of their faith. Spiritual confidence is concomitant with theological clarity and interpretive assuredness.

On the basis of these interrelated principles, Calvin made the practice of becoming assured of one's own salvation the center of his spiritual vision. As Schreiner explains, "Calvin told his congregation that when we 'cry' through the Spirit, we do so 'with full certainty that we know and acknowledge that we are members of [God's] Son and by means of Christ we are accepted by God into his celestial kingdom'."[20] Even when preaching on a biblical text that stresses the importance of mystery such as 1 Timothy 3:16, Calvin focuses on how to "be certeine of his [Christ's] truth to obteine salvation."[21] Such an approach is consistent with Calvin's general emphasis on scripture's objective meaning, its *genuinus sensus, germanus sensus, simplex sensus,* and *litteralis sensus,* all of which imply the constant, unchanging, and intended meaning of the text.[22]

---

[19] Calvin, *Institutes*, 3.2.15 as cited in Schreiner, *Are You Alone Wise*, 66.

[20] Schreiner, *Are You Alone Wise*, 67.

[21] *Sermons of M. John Calvin on the Epistles of St. Paul to Timothy and Titus* (London: 1579), 321. Subsequent references are given in text.

[22] T.H.L Parker, *Calvin's New Testament Commentaries* 2nd edition (Edinburgh: T&T Clark, 1993), 102. See also Muller, *After Calvin*, 164–165, and Schreiner, *Where Shall*

As his sermon on the mystery of godliness suggests, Calvin's general exegetical focus is on recovering authorial intention in order to provide all believers with assurance of salvation. Published in English in 1579, Calvin's sermon on 1 Timothy 3:16 approaches the incarnation by admitting how difficult the idea is for the human mind to grasp, remarking that hearing of it is like listening to a "strange language" (324). Moreover, he describes the incarnation as a miracle that even the "Angells could never have thought upon," thus cross-referencing his primary text with 1 Peter 1:12 as is commonly done. Yet this estranging of the idea of incarnation soon gives way to something very different. The crescendo of Calvin's oration comes when he remarks that if God can create man with a visible body and an invisible soul, then "why should we think it strange in Jesus Christ that God used a far greater miracle in him" (330). Rather than dwelling on the incarnation as an occasion for wonder, Calvin approaches it as an obstacle to knowing that one is saved, what he elsewhere calls the gospel's primary "intrinsic stumbling-block" or "scandal."[23] He concludes the sermon with an attempt to mitigate the intellectual difficulties posed by the incarnation. He does this by stressing the believer's full assurance of redemption through Christ which he accomplishes by cross-referencing 1 Colossians 2:2–3 with Ephesians 3:18–19. Except where Paul emphasizes the experience of Christ's love as the root of fellowship in both passages, Calvin concludes by emphasizing the believer's confident assurance in Christ's saving power. So, while Paul's focus is both social and soteriological, Calvin telescopes the passage in order to focus on personal assurance alone. And while Paul balances understanding with mystery, Calvin stresses the idea that the elect fully grasp the mystery of salvation. According to Calvin,

---

Wisdom Be Found?, 91. This attitude is perhaps even more true of William Tyndale for whom the Word, as John Bossy notes, was "addressed to no one and everyone, like the Ten Commandments which were to replace statues and images behind the altars of English churches." John Bossy, *Christianity in the West 1400–1700* (Oxford: Oxford UP, 1987), 99. For a strongly stated view of the interpretively reductive and socially divisive aspects of this kind of early reformation hermeneutics, see James Simpson, *Burning to Read: English Fundamentalism and its Reformation Opponents* (Cambridge: The Belnkap Press of Harvard UP, 2007). For a related set of conclusions arrived at from an entirely different methodological standpoint, see Haigh, *The Plain Man's Pathways to Heaven*

[23] John Calvin, *Concerning Scandals* trans. John W. Fraser (William B. Eerdmans Grand Rapids Michigan 1978), 7–22.

Jesus Christ did not only appeare man, but shewed in deed that he was God almightie … If we once know this, wee may well perceive that it is not without cause, that Saint Paule sayeth, that all the treasures of wisdome are hidden in our Lorde Jesus Christ. So then, we shall knowe the height and depth, the length and largenesse, yea, whatsoever is necessarie for our salvation. (333)

Streamlining his biblical sources toward the question of personal assurance, Calvin depicts faith as overcoming mystery rather than serving as a way into it.

Taken as a whole, Calvin's treatment of his biblical sources in this sermon on 1 Timothy confirms the thesis that for him justifying faith inheres in a sense of trust grounded in certainty more than on an experience of God's love as expressed within the *communitas* of the church.[24] Viewed in a wider perspective, it also exemplifies the claim that more puritan forms of post-reformation Christianity tend to stress sins against God and the need for personal assurance much more than sins against neighbors and the need for social reconciliation.[25] As John Bossy concludes, post-reformation Christianity "was less well adapted to inspiring a sense of the Church as a *communitas*, a feeling for sacraments as social institutions, or simply the love of one's neighbor" as pre-reformation Christianity was. One of the rationales Bossy gives for this claim amounts to a virtual paraphrase of what we have already seen from Andrewes, namely that post-reformation Christendom tended to reduce Christianity "to whatever could be taught and learnt."[26] Sensitive to these increasingly visible shortcomings within post-reformation spirituality Andrewes approaches Paul's text in his 1607 sermon on 1 Timothy 3:16 very differently than Calvin.

Lancelot Andrewes and the Mystery of Godliness

Andrewes counters Calvin's approach to 1 Timothy 3:16 in several ways. First, he modifies Calvin's highly focused emphasis on Paul's assurance through faith with the Johannine emphasis on assurance through love. He does this by focusing particular attention on a series of widely debated

---

[24] Schreiner, "Spiritual Man Judges," 193.

[25] Bossy, *Christianity in the West* and McGee, *The Godly Man in Stuart England*. For a strongly worded but by no means devastating revisionist critique of McGee, see Nicholas Tyacke's review of *The Godly Man* in *The Journal of Ecclesiastical History* 20.1 (January 1978), 123–124.

[26] Bossy, *Christianity in the West*, 120.

passages, including John 13:34–45 and 1 John 3:18–20, the latter of which reads: "My little children, let us not love in word, neither in tongue, but indeede and in trueth. And hereby we know that wee are of the trueth, and shall assure our hearts before him."[27] But perhaps the most significant passage for understanding Andrewes' view of assurance is 1 John 4:16–21:

> God is love, and hee that dwelleth in love, dwelleth in God, and God in him. Herein is our love made perfect, that wee may have boldnesse in the day of Judgment, because as hee is, so are we in this world. There is no feare in love, but perfect love casteth out feare.

The Johannine claim that assurance of salvation comes through love was widely debated in the Reformation, sometimes resulting in significant tensions within individual writers, most notably Luther. Over the course of his career, Luther struggled to reconcile Johannine notions of assurance through brotherly love with his dominantly Pauline view of assurance via faith alone.[28] This led subsequent reformers like Calvin to simplify and streamline Johannine texts along Pauline lines. As Barbara Pitkin observes, the Gospel of John "threatens Calvin's view that there is really only one kind of faith and that this faith is certain."[29] As she goes on to show, Calvin protected Pauline notions of faith from Johannine complications in two ways.[30] First, he imposed a distinction between John's "doctrine" of faith and his "exhortation" to love. Second, he reinterpreted John's notion of faith and his discourse of seeing as knowledge. Both strategies allowed Calvin to sustain his view that faith is equivalent to subjective certainty of justification. Privileging Paul over John this way, Calvin warded off Johannine threats to the idea of faith as certain knowledge of salvation. Long before Pitkin, Andrewes had already recognized that Calvin's pursuit of certainty led him to simplify the rather beguiling set of relations among New Testament notions of faith, love, and godliness.

---

[27] My discussion of Herbert's and Andrewes' use of Johannine concepts of assurance is informed by Paul Cefalu's magisterial study *The Johannine Renaissance in Early Modern English Religion and Literature* (Oxford UP: Forthcoming) and from personal conversation with him.

[28] Althaus, *Theology of Martin Luther*, Appendix Two, 446–459 and Cefalu, *Johannine Renaissance*, Chap. 4.

[29] Pitkin, *What Pure Eyes Could See*, 91.

[30] Ibid., 83–97.

Rather than imposing Pauline notions of assurance onto John, Andrewes' sermon on 1 Timothy 3:16 moves in the opposite direction. Glossing Paul via John, Andrews adopts a more both/and logic than Calvin. In so doing, his 1607 oration gives much greater scope to the idea of assurance through neighborly love than one often finds in early reformation thought. Glossing Paul's letter to Timothy via 1 John 4, Andrewes not only unequivocally extends the promise of salvation to all men, much as Herbert does at the end of "The Invitation," but he also stresses the assurances Christians can derive from charity. The exigency for this emphasis comes from "the complaint, that in our godliness, nowadays, we go very mystically to work indeed; we keep it under a veil, and nothing manifest, but *opera carnis*" (1.42). In other words, Andrewes insists that Christians not keep faith "all within; for we deal not with a mystery alone, but with a manifestation too" (1.42). Insisting on the dialectical nature of *mysterion* as revelation-in-concealment and concealment-in-revelation, Andrewes counters the tendency to obscure outward works in favor of inward faith. In making this critique, he further reemphasizes the social dimensions that Calvin obscured. For Andrewes, godliness

> is not only faith, which referreth to the mystery as we have it directly at the ninth verse, the 'mystery of faith;' but it is love too, which referreth to the manifestation. For in *hoc cognoscimus*, saith St. John, 'by this we know, ourselves;' and, in *hoc cognoscent omnes*, saith Christ, 'by this shall all men know' that we are His. (1.42)

Following both John and Paul, Andrewes suggests that it is through the manifestation of love in the context of Christian fellowship that believers derive a sense of assurance and an understanding of godliness. Moreover, rather than downplaying wonder and mystery at the dynamics of faith and love, Andrewes stresses them. The result is a text that counters the underlying assumptions that sometimes made Calvinist preaching "divisive in its psychological and social consequences" and thus potentially "limited in its intellectual and spiritual appeal."[31] Viewed in his wider European and historical contexts, Andrewes ultimately appears like of one of Bossy's "nervous conservatives" diagnosing the fissiparous forces unleashed by

---

[31] Patrick Collinson, *The Religion of Protestants: The Church in English Society* 1559–1625 (Oxford: Clarendon Press, 1982), 108.

the prioritization of "the perspicuous word over the mysteriously integrative rite, of faith over charity."[32]

From the strict *sola fides* standpoint of early reformed thought, what Andrewes offers is not really true assurance at all because it relies too heavily on visible human actions in the world. Nevertheless, this more Johannine orientation animates Jacobean religious culture in ways that often run much deeper than overt theological statement and which oftentimes transcend parties and factions.[33] After all, the exigency for Andrewes' sermon extends back to the theological culture of Elizabethan Cambridge with its relatively narrow focus on personal assurance, its somewhat dogmatic striving for security, and its overall systematizing methods. Here again, the influence of Calvin is important. Although Luther generally avoided conflating certainty with security, Calvin used the terms interchangeably.[34] Calvin's view of security is especially significant when we bear in mind that his soteriology was systematically elaborated by Cambridge theologians such as William Whitaker, who, as H.C. Porter notes, regarded "his aim as Regius Professor to teach *de certitudine et securitate salutis*: and he, with the other Calvinist heads ... could emphasize the 'spiritual security' of the Christian."[35] In the process, Elizabethan Calvinism accentuated some of the underlying differences between Augustine and Calvin on questions of grace and perseverance. For Augustine, Christians do not enjoy assurance of faith (*securus*) in Calvin's very strong sense, though they do live in the hope that they shall persevere to the end.[36] In subtle but crucial respects, Herbert's spiritual and poetic sensibility emerged from a broadly felt need to engender an alternative style of reformed piety than the one found in Elizabethan Calvinism, one more attentive to the both/and logic that Andrewes deployed when confronting the tensions between Pauline and Johannine traditions.

---

[32] Bossy, *Christianity in the West*, 140.
[33] For a fuller elaboration of this thesis, see Cefalu's *The Johannine Renaissance* (Forthcoming). For a broadly related approach to Herbert, see Terry Sherwood, *Herbert's Prayerful Art* (Toronto: University of Toronto Press, 1989).
[34] Beeke, *Assurance of Faith*, 24; H.C. Porter, *Reformation and Reaction in Tudor Cambridge* (Cambridge: Cambridge UP, 1958), 319.
[35] Ibid.
[36] See Cary, *Inner Grace*, 119.

Richard Hooker and the Critique of Certainty

Another important harbinger of this alternative style of Augustinianism was Richard Hooker. In his sermons on Habakkuk delivered in the Temple Church, London, between 1585 and 1586, Hooker offers a stark, if subtly expressed, alternative to Whitaker's "spiritual security." Of particular significance here is Hooker's first extant sermon, printed posthumously in 1612: "A Learned and Comfortable Sermon on The Certainty and Perpetuity of Faith In The Elect." Somewhat deceptive in title, Hooker's sermon qualifies the kind confidence many protestants should expect of themselves. One major aim in doing so is to console those worried about their unbelief. In his view, anyone sincerely anxious about their lack of faith stands within the light of grace even if they do not realize it. Hooker thus implies that the truly reprobate would presumably not worry over their salvation to any great extent. At the same time, however, Hooker warns against the dangers of presumption. He takes this dialectical perspective in order to show how spiritual desperation is often the result of a misguided expectation of spiritual security. In making this case, he strongly qualifies the idea of faith as firm and secure knowledge. The result is a sermon that offers spiritual advice to those in despair which is as pastorally insightful as it is politically calibrated.

Hooker begins his sermon by lowering his auditors' expectations about what kind of faith they can expect of themselves through a distinction between "certainty of evidence" and "certainty of adherence." In the case of many natural phenomena, Hooker explains, we enjoy "certainty of evidence" such as the knowledge that "a part of any thing is less than the whole."[37] In matters of faith, however, we only enjoy "certainty of Adherence" or the confidence that is felt when the heart cleaves to the things in which it believes. On the basis of this distinction, Hooker concludes "that we have less certainty of evidence concerning things believed [through faith], than [we do] concerning [things] sensible or naturally perceived" (470–471). Hooker further warns against presumption by challenging preachers who take Abraham as a model of perfect faith on the grounds that "He did not doubt" (472). He answers such exegetes by remarking that while it is true that Abraham did not doubt from infidelity, he nevertheless doubted from infirmity (472). Following on this distinction, he explains how it is sometimes better for a soul to be humbled

---

[37] *The Works of Mr. Richard Hooker Volume 3* 3rd edition ed. John Keeble (Oxford: Oxford UP, 1845), 470. Subsequent references to this sermon are given in text by page number.

by desolation than "exalted above measure" (474). So, rather than focusing on doubt as an obstacle to be overcome, Hooker stresses its spiritually positive functions.

Hooker then turns to address those who fall into despair as a result of an unrealistic expectation of assurance. In a sequence that is as pastorally moving as it is politically calculated, Hooker explains that in really severe cases of religious despair clerics cannot offer solace by explaining the "privy operations" of the Spirit in our heart as can be done in more common cases. Instead, ministers comforting those in true despair must

> favour them a little in their weakness; let that be granted which they do imagine; be it that they are faithless and without belief. But are they not grieved for their unbelief? They are. Do they not wish it might, and also strive that it may, be otherwise? We know they do. Whence cometh this, but from a secret love and liking which they have of those things that are believed? No man can love things which in his own opinion are not. (475)

The exigency behind this remarkable sequence derives from the kinds of pastoral and theological problems posed by self-proclaimed reprobates such as Francis Spiera whose story first appeared in England around 1550 only to recur in popularity, especially among puritans, in the 1580s and 1590s.[38] So well known was the Spiera case that Hooker could take it for granted that his audience would recognize it as a major subtext of this particular sequence.[39]

After renouncing a number of his protestant beliefs before the Inquisition, Spiera suffered terrible pangs of conscience and died apparently convinced of his own damnation. In the process, he became the most well-known figure of the Italian Reformation and the subject of intense scrutiny across Europe for over a century.[40] From the time of his self-accusations, theologians debated whether there was ever any hope

---

[38] See Michael MacDonald, "The Fearefull Estate of Francis Spira: Narrative, Identity, and Emotion in Early Modern England" *Journal of British Studies* 31.1 (Jan. 1992), 32–61, 38. The following discussion of Spiera leans heavily on Macdonald's article.

[39] For the ubiquity of the Spiera case in Tudor England, see Erin E. Kelly, "Conflict of Conscience and Sixteenth-Century Drama" *ELR* 44.3 (2014), 388–419, 391–392.

[40] For Spiera's Italian reception, see M.A. Overall, "The Exploitation of Francisco Spiera" *The Sixteenth Century Journal* 26.3 (1995), 619–637.

for an apostate as spiritually desperate as him. One major voice in this conversation was John Calvin. Unhappy with the ambiguity of Italian interpretations of Spiera, Calvin wrote a response to the affair which was included in some of the early English editions of Spiera's life.[41] In it, he concludes that the Italian's fate exhibits "how earnest vengeance [God] will take upon those that scorne his majestie."[42] While this certainty about someone else's reprobation is out of keeping with Calvin's general views on grace, it is nevertheless consistent with his attitude toward false belief, which he wrote about extensively.[43] Recalling his third sermon on Deuteronomy 13, Calvin thought that Spiera was a clear object lesson in the dangers of conforming to a false church for the sake of personal expediency (Nicodemism). In his view, the moral of Spiera's story was evident: protestants who outwardly conform to the Catholic faith were subject to the despair of the nonelect. On the basis of this reading, many dissenting puritans took Spiera's horrifying end as a warning against outward conformity to an imperfectly reformed church. Others were less confident and more compassionate.

In his sixth sermon on the Lord's Prayer (1552), Hugh Latimer commented on the Spiera case by suggesting that even those who sin against the Holy Ghost can "Ask remission of sin in the name of Christ."[44] While Latimer does not outright contradict Calvin's conclusion that Spiera was damned, he softens the Frenchman's moral by suggesting that there is always hope even for the worst of sinners. Revealingly, Hooker went much further than Latimer in departing from Calvin. Rather than claiming that those in despair can still seek grace, Hooker emphasizes the extent to which they show signs of already possessing it.

Of course it didn't hurt that Hooker's offer of consolation to puritans suffering from despair just happened to undermine a major rationale for dissent. In the 1580s, when Hooker was preaching at The Temple, threats to the individual soul were often inextricable from

[41] Ibid., 631.

[42] Matthew Gribaldi, *A Notable and Marveilous Epistle* (London, n.d.), Aiii; cited in MacDonald, 46.

[43] See Wulfert De Greef, *The Writings of John Calvin: An Introductory Guide* trans. Lyle D. Bierma (Westminster: John Knox Press, 2006), 118–126.

[44] Hugh Latimer, *The Works of Hugh Latimer Volume 1* ed. George E. Corrie (Cambridge: Cambridge UP, 1844), 425.

threats to a properly reformed church, especially where the Nicodemite specter of Spiera was concerned.[45] Hooker's first extant sermon thus needs to be seen in its broader ecclesiastical contexts, namely the effort to establish a state church in which papists and the hotter sort of protestants could all find a place. Viewed this way, it becomes apparent that Hooker's sermon implicitly counters anti-Nicodemist readings of despairing souls. Accordingly, Hooker's empathic account of puritan despair in "The Certainty of Faith" confirms the view that *The Laws of Ecclesiastical Polity* is grounded on a number of keen psychological insights into puritan piety.[46] Crucially, Hooker recognized that the threat of despair was not the opposite of spiritual security but its necessary correlate, its flip side as it were, hence the "turbulence of spirit" he saw as characteristic of puritans. On the basis of this insight into Calvinist psychology, Hooker concluded that puritans overconflated the pursuit of assurance with the externals of worship due to an unrealistic expectation of spiritual security, one that too easily led to either presumption or despair, or mutually reinforcing oscillations between the two.

Hooker's diagnosis of puritan despair has important consequences for his overall approach to puritan piety. Instead of being heretics who dishonored God, Hooker thought that puritans were simply mistaken about the dynamics of faith. Out of their drive for security they developed an overly literal reading of scripture in which the bible was made to bear more prescriptive weight than the Holy Spirit intended. In the process, they inadvertently developed a potentially harmful spiritual psychology. Armed with this diagnosis, Hooker concluded that problems of conscience would have to be resolved through mutual understanding and dialogue rather than by raw power or vitriolic polemic. After all, the problem as he saw it was as much psychological as theological.

---

[45] See Overall, "The Exploitation of Francisco Spiera," 634.
[46] See W. Speed Hill's, "The Evolution of Hooker's *Laws of Ecclesiastical Polity*" in *Studies in Richard Hooker: Essays Preliminary To an Edition of His Works* ed. W. Speed Hill (Cleveland: Case Western Reserve, 1972), 117–158. The following two paragraphs reiterate and try to build on Hill's reading of Hooker.

THE BARRETT CONTROVERSY AND THE HAMPTON
COURT CONFERENCE

If controversies over religious security remain beneath the surface of Hooker's sermons on Habakkuk, then they erupted in the wake of William Barrett's sermon to clergy in St. Mary's Church on 29 April 1595.[47] It was in the wake of such controversies that churchmen of Herbert's and Sibbes' generation developed their spiritual and expressive styles.

A chaplain of Gonville and Caius College, Barrett appears to have taken direct aim in his infamous sermon at what he understood to be Calvinist notions of perseverance and assurance. In doing so, he sought to undermine some of the basic reformation ideas about justification as he thought they were currently being interpreted. Judging by extant summaries of the sermon, Barrett explicitly suggested, "No *Man can entertain such an Assurance*, &c. *as that he ought to be secure of his Salvation*" (*ut de salute sua debeat esse securus*).[48] Adopting what must have been an unusually confrontational style, he attacked some of the ways Calvinism arguably turned spiritual confidence into naked presumption. A flurry of controversy ensued and Barrett was soon censored and forced to recant by the heads of Cambridge University.

One of the most significant results of the university's disciplining of Barrett was the production of the Lambeth articles, a series of nine statements on the dynamics of predestination which register a period of controversy more than they enshrine a univocal statement of faith.[49] Of particular importance to the articles is the question of whether the elect necessarily persevere in justifying grace throughout the whole of their lives. The Calvinist party hoped to end debates about spiritual security by having the articles adopted as an official declaration of church dogma. When Elizabeth rejected this request, it became increasingly evident that

---

[47] For a summary of the Barrett controversy along with his retraction of the nonexistent sermon for which he was censored, see John Strype, *The Life and Acts of the Most Reverend Father in God, John Whitgift* (London: 1718), 4.443–459.

[48] Lancelot Andrewes, "A Review of the Censure passed upon Dr. Barrett's Opinion concerning Certainty of Salvation" in J. Ellis, *Defence of the Thirty Nine Articles* (London: 1700), 121. For the original, see Andrewes, "Censura D. Barreti De Certitudine Salutis" in *A Pattern of Catechistical Doctrine* (Oxford: John Henry Parker, 1846), 301.

[49] Cummings, *Literary Culture*, 288. For an account of how the articles came into being, see Peter Lake, *Moderate Puritans in Elizabethan Church*, 201–242. For competing views see Peter White, *Predestination, policy, and polemic*, 101–109 and H.C. Porter, *Reformation and Reaction*, 344–390.

the major tensions within the church were going to remain unresolved. Peter Lake puts the point sharply when he asserts that the Barrett episode marks the moment when "the foundations of high Elizabethan protestantism started to crumble ... With the collapse of the Lambeth Articles, the Calvinist claim to represent the sole fount of orthodoxy in the Church of England was definitively discredited."[50] In short, the Barrett affair helped give rise to the more eclectic and ultimately less stable synthesis of beliefs and practices characteristic of writers in Herbert's and Sibbes' generation.

Much more was at stake in the Barrett controversy than the personal question of election. At issue was the broader question of certainty itself. Given that certainty often functioned as a criterion of biblical truth, rather than just a by-product of right belief, the spiritual and theological stakes were very high. Since the issue of certainty had become methodological as well as soteriological, the act of questioning assurance of salvation was equivalent to deflating religious confidence as such.[51] Little surprise, then, that these controversies did not go away for long.

Debates over spiritual security remerged at the beginning of James' reign during the Hampton Court Conference in January of 1604. The conference witnessed a number of leading bishops square off against influential moderate puritans, including John Reynolds, president of Corpus Christi, Oxford, and future translator of the King James Bible. On the second day of the conference, Reynolds tried to persuade King James to adopt the Lambeth Articles in order to clarify the church's stance on questions of grace, especially the matter of perseverance.[52] According to William Barlow's official narration of events, the bishop of London and future Archbishop, Richard Bancroft warned against Reynolds's proposal. As Barlow tells it, Bancroft "took occasion to signifie to his majesty, how very many in these daies, neglecting holiness in life, presumed too much of persisting of grace, laying all their religion upon predestination."[53] James is then said to have concurred, remarking that

---

[50] Lake, *Moderate Puritans*, 239.

[51] Schreiner, *Are You Alone Wise*, 37–130. For a related account of the Barrett affair, see Cummings, *Literary Culture*, 290.

[52] William Barlow, *The Summe and Substance of the Conference ... at Hampton Court* (1605), printed in E. Cardwell ed. *A History of Conferences and Other Proceedings connected with the Revision of the Book of Common Prayer*, 1558–1690 3rd edition (Oxford, 1849), 178.

[53] Ibid., 180.

the doctrine of predestination might be very tenderly handled, and with great discretion, lest on the one side, God's omnipotency might be called in question, by impeaching the doctrine of his eternal predestination, or on the other, a desperate presumption might be arreared, by inferring the necessary certainty of standing and persisting in grace.[54]

No anti-Calvinist on such matters at this point in his kingship, James I nevertheless warned against spiritual security in a way that shows real understanding of why, during the Hampton Court Conference, John Overall requested that the 39 Articles include the Augustinian idea that "the Elect might often fall from grace and faith."[55] At the very least, James' statement would have done nothing to dissuade the Venetian ambassador from his opinion, reached by April of 1603, that "His Majesty's religion is not, as was said, Calvinist, but Protestant" and that he thought the "Puritans a very plague."[56] By cultivating a degree of ambiguity on key issues, the king helped engender an ecclesiastical climate in which churchmen could adopt positions that often remained irreducible to the conventional categories of Calvinist and Arminian. In the wake of the Hampton Court Conference, the theological waters of the English church became increasingly muddied. The cultural conditions were now set for theologically syncretistic visions that are more characteristic of the period and its religious poetry than is often thought.

PAX ECCLESIA: RICHARD HOOKER AND ROBERT SANDERSON

The defeat of the puritan party at Hampton Court resulted in a diminished association between certainty and truth than had been the case in earlier stages of the English and European Reformation. With more than 80 years of hindsight, the dangers of doctrinal purity had become increasingly clear to many English churchmen. One important example is Robert Sanderson, royal chaplain to Charles I and later Bishop of Lincoln (1660).

---

[54] Ibid., 181.

[55] Usher, *Reconstruction of English Church*, 336. For an important account of James' shifting views of Calvinism and puritanism and for his probable strategy at the Hampton Court Conference, see Kenneth Fincham and Peter Lake, "The Ecclesiastical Policy of King James I," *Journal of British Studies* 24.2 (April 1985), 169–207.

[56] 'Venice: April 1603', in *Calendar of State Papers ... Venice*, Volume 10, 1603–1607, ed. Horatio F Brown (London, 1900), 2–16.

In a 1625 sermon before parliament called *Pax Ecclesia*, Sanderson suggests that overstated claims to certainty are spiritually naive and socially
divisive. Written in the wake of the Arminian controversies stirred up by
Richard Montague's *A New Gag for an Old Goose* (1624), *Pax Ecclesia*
applies some of the insights of Richard Hooker's *Laws* to the context of
the early Caroline church. Like Hooker, Sanderson stresses the value of
adopting "tender" or generously ambiguous definitions of key doctrines
and certain practices. While such claims to moderation could serve as a
polemical means of silencing opposition, Sanderson's 1625 work adopts
a brand of reformed thinking that was generously ambiguous enough to
have broader appeal than Montague's bombshell which had nevertheless
earned the support of an increasingly anti-puritan King James.[57]

According to *Pax Ecclesia*, churches need to give a degree of latitude
on some doctrinal and liturgical matters; otherwise, they run the risk
of generating needless schism. And the way to do this is to socratically
acknowledge

> that they who have the greatest serenity of natural understanding, and the
> largest measure of Divine Revelation withal, must yet confess the unfath-
> omed depth of the judgments and ways of God, which are *abyssus multa*,
> rather to be admired than searched into.[58]

The implication is that those who are most spiritually mature are those
most sensitive to what they do not know.

Peter Lake's suggestion that Sanderson's investment in mystery was a
rhetorical ploy designed to ingratiate himself with the Laudian establishment may not do the man full justice.[59] After all, Sanderson's investment
in mystery is fully in evidence in the anti-Arminianism of *Pax Ecclesiae* in
1625. More importantly, this kind of emphasis on mystery is one of the
ways Jacobean religious culture avoided dogmatic extremes and the conflict it engenders. To be sure, though, Sanderson's 1625 sermon does not

---

[57] For a subtle account of why the king came to endorse Montague's works, see Fincham
and Lake, "The Ecclesiastical Policy of James I," 202–207.

[58] Robert Sanderson, "Pax Ecclesiae" in *The Works of Robert Sanderson: Six Volumes*
(Oxford: 1854), 5.256. The work was first printed in Izaak Walton's 1678 *Life of Sanderson*.

[59] Peter Lake, "Serving God and the Times: The Calvinist Conformity of Robert
Sanderson" *Journal of British Studies*, 27.2 (April, 1988), 81–116, 104.

show the strain of polarization that his later, Laudian, work does.[60] The difference is so pronounced that after the Restoration he evidently sought to suppress *Pax Ecclesiae* for fear that it was too tolerant of moderate division.[61] This is probably because by the time of the Restoration the rhetoric of mystery had become more of an authoritarian reflex for suppressing dissent than an irenic avowal of human and institutional limitations. In any case, behind *Pax Ecclesia* lay many of the lessons that Richard Hooker had taught, especially those pertaining to the issue of certainty and theological disagreement.

Indeed, the shift from Elizabethan rigidities to Jacobean anti-dogmatism that so informs Herbert's poetic and spiritual style is partly animated by Hooker's views on scripture and tradition. While Calvin tended to see conflicts over scripture in somewhat absolutist terms, viewing them as a symptom of sinfulness that should ultimately be overcome, Hooker tended to see them as normative and unavoidable.[62] As a result, Hooker presupposes that all scriptural interpretation, at least at some level, is partial and vulnerable to error. While Calvin acknowledged the inevitability of disagreement over scripture among people of true faith, he did not integrate this principle into his understanding of the biblical tradition in as broad a way as Hooker did.[63] Writing in more viciously polemical contexts, Calvin found it necessary to view disagreement as an unavoidable consequence of human sinfulness and the limitations of human reason, especially as it was further corrupted by the perversions of nonbiblical traditions. For Hooker, on the other hand, disagreement over scripture is an inherent feature of the dynamic unfolding of faith and reason in action over time in the form of tradition. Unlike his puritan opponents, Hooker believed that Christian tradition constitutes an ongoing, socially and historically mediated conversation about the nature of faith and revelation. What it

---

[60] Compare, for example, Sanderson's 1625 *Pax Ecclesia* with his more partisan 1639 court sermon on 1 Timothy 3.16 delivered at Berwick, July 16 collected in *XXXVI Sermons* (London: 1689 8th edn.), 479–491.

[61] David Novarr, *The Making of Walton's Lives* (Ithaca: Cornell, 1958), Chap. 11, especially 412–430.

[62] John K Stafford, "Scripture and the Generous Hermeneutic of Richard Hooker" *Anglican Theological Review* 84.4 (2002) 915–928 and Prior, *Defining the Jacobean Church*, 260.

[63] In the preface to his commentary on Romans, Calvin echoes Augustine's claim that some disagreement over scripture among the truly faithful is to be expected (*Commentaries*, 19. xxvii).

does not consist of is a set of fixed beliefs and practices derived from an unmediated encounter with scripture. To this extent, Hooker accentuates a muted strain within Augustine's thought. In his letter *To Simplicanus*, Augustine hints at the historical contingency of dogmatic formulae, the idea that words about God are never immutably true and thus subject to change and correction.[64] Developing Augustine's capacity for a "pluralism of interpretations as of formulations,"[65] Hooker sought to define the acceptable parameters within which members of the Church of England could peacefully disagree with one another about what it means to be a member of the true church. Possessing a different view of tradition than Calvin, Hooker assumed that being a member of a living church necessarily meant participating in a debate about what it means to be a member of such a church. The problem involved limiting the debate in such a way as to preclude unnecessary dissent and division.[66]

In cultivating this kind of attitude, Hooker was not defending a preexisting Elizabethan orthodoxy so much as he was trying to frame the debate going forward.[67] Rather than simply firming up the state church as he found it, Hooker was arguing that the Christian tradition necessarily consists of self-consciously imperfect acts of interpretation unfolding within the social context of an inevitably flawed church. His general aim was to loosen the necessary connections among protestant claims to scriptural simplicity, authority, and assurance. In doing so, Hooker articulated the degree of uncertainty inherent in religious tradition as a socially existing reality in ways that were conducive to a nondogmatic poetics such as Herbert's. Indeed, Hooker's irenicism and nonpolemical rhetorical style are part and parcel with his assumption that disagreement is a basic condition of ecclesiastical and national life. In adopting such an attitude, Hooker developed

---

[64] Van Geest, *Incomprehensibility of God*, 75.

[65] Chretién, *Under the Gaze of the Bible* trans. John Marson Dunaway (New York: Fordham, 2015), 53.

[66] My formulations here are inspired by Alasdair MacIntyre, *After Virtue: A Study in Moral Theory* 2nd Edition (Notre Dame: University of Notre Dame Press, 1984), 222. What Hooker may not have fully appreciated was the paradoxes involved trying to control the framework of religious tradition while writing from within it. It would require a Shakespeare to see that problem. See Alasdair MacIntyre, "Epistemological Crises, Dramatic Narrative, and the Philosophy of Science," *Monist* 60.4 (October 1977), 453–472.

[67] See Lake, *Anglicans and Puritans?*, 145–252 and "The Anglican Moment? Richard Hooker and the Ideological Watershed of the 1590's" in *Anglicanism and the Western Catholic Tradition* (Norwich: Canterbury Press, 2003), 90–121. See also, Nigel Voak, *Richard Hooker and Reformed Theology*.

a relatively empathic rather than vitriolic approach to those with whom he disagrees. And he was not alone in doing so. While the real force of his influence was to come after the Restoration, his anti-dogmatism was part of a broader movement afoot within the early Stuart church.

Richard Sibbes and the Mystery of Godliness

To be sure, this ecclesiastical development included a number of conforming puritans who contributed in important ways to the general softening of English protestant piety in Jacobean England. Even William Perkins came to recognize the pastoral and political dangers of Calvin's uncompassionate response to Francis Spiera. In his 1600 edition of *A Golden Chaine*, Perkins rebukes Calvin's certainty about the whole affair, asserting that "they which will avouch *Spira* to be a reprobate, must ... prooue ... that he despaired both *wholly* and *finally:* which if they cannot proove, wee for our parts must suspende our iudgements."[68] If Perkins did not go as far as Latimer in suggesting that all can be saved by calling upon Christ, he nevertheless rediscovered the virtue of Latimer's uncertainty.

By the late 1620s, English puritans had found a subtle critic of spiritual security and a stark defender of religious mystery in Richard Sibbes. Master of Katherine Hall, Cambridge, and a preacher at Gray's Inn, Sibbes was educated at St. John's College, Cambridge, which he entered in the fateful year of 1595. As a leading puritan in the early Caroline church, Sibbes had to walk a fine line between resisting the Laudian establishment while simultaneously defending the Church of England from the dangers of radical dissent. This awkward position helps explain his insistence in *The Bruised Reed* that "in a contentious age, it is a witty thing to be a Christian" (1.54). One of the things that most characterizes Sibbes' extensive body of writing is its sustained investment in the importance of mystery. Aware that Laudians had made mystery central to their sacramentally centered form of piety, often with authoritarian results, Sibbes countered with a puritan mystery-theology of his own. One major example of his practice of mystagogy occurs in his 1635 treatise on 1 Timothy 3:16 *The Fountain Opened or The Mystery of Godliness Revealed.*

As a preacher at Gray's Inn where Francis Bacon had quarters, Sibbes addressed a church populated not only by lawyers but also by nobility,

<hr>

[68] William Perkins, *A Golden Chain* (Cambridge: 1600), 478.

gentry, and the citizenry. Unlike Herbert's Bemerton flock, this was a highly educated, powerful, and probably somewhat puritan group. The potential for separatist dissent within such a group may help explain his qualified defense of the ministry in *The Fountain Opened*. In defending the ministry's pastoral role, Sibbes aims to establish the grounds for a firm, broad, and peaceful fellowship, one consisting of spiritually revitalized believers who accepted the authority of the state church even as he critiqued some aspects of it. In making his case Sibbes has several audiences in mind, the two most obvious of which are dissenting puritans and Laudian authorities. On the one hand, Sibbes stresses the importance of the ministry as a sacramental stewardship in order to mitigate puritan skepticism about the priesthood. But on the other hand, he makes sure not to carry more water for the Laudian establishment than he must. The result is a treatise that focuses on the inevitability of doubt and ignorance in the pursuit of holiness with very little concern for spiritual security or scriptural simplicity. Moreover, he stresses the importance of love as a ground for Christian fellowship. Taken together, these emphases show Sibbes discovering the most lyrical, social, and nondogmatic aspects of reformed piety.

Unsurprisingly, Sibbes always treads carefully when criticizing fellow puritans. At one point, for example, he softens his defense of the ministry by grounding it on an oblique but unmistakable anti-Catholic premise:

> Divine truths are mysteries; therefore they may not be published to people. Nay, divine truths are mysteries; therefore they must be unfolded. Hence comes the necessity of the ministry; for if the gospel be a mystery, that is, a hidden kind of knowledge, then there must be some to reveal it. (5.469)

Typical of Sibbes, he here uses anti-Catholic polemic to minimize differences within his English protestant audience. After all, the implied association between pagan mystery rites which demand great secrecy and the Catholic resistance to publishing scripture in the vernacular cushions the relatively strong emphasis on the role of the ministry in this sermon. He does the reverse moments later when he uses anti-Catholic polemic to veil a swipe at Archbishop Laud's privileging of sacraments over sermons. According to Sibbes, "The papists … make the sacrifice of the Mass a means to apply Christ, and other courses; but the ministerial means to apply to Christ is the preaching of the gospel" (5.515). As is often the case with conforming puritans in the period, anti-Catholic polemic serves to unify disparate constituencies within the Church of England.

Rather intriguingly, *The Fountain Opened* takes 1 Timothy 3 as the occasion for explicitly addressing a minister's need to be cagey when dealing with matters of controversy. Sibbes broaches this topic at the outset of the treatise by explaining that Paul's style of speech is designed to teach Timothy the proper way of conversing in the church. Self-reflexively embodying Paul's rhetoric of mystery, Sibbes explains that Paul "makes way to raise up the spirit of Timothy, and in him us, unto a reverent and holy attending to the blessed mysteries that follow" (5.460). Here the difference from Calvin's sermon on 1 Timothy is palpable. Where Calvin strives toward certainty of salvation through faith, Sibbes stresses the importance of sustaining a sense of wise ignorance before the gospel, insisting that "We must be content 'to become fools', that we may be wise" (1 Cor. 5:10). And where Calvin disambiguates the text so as to focus almost entirely on the Christological basis of salvation, Sibbes approaches it from multiple angles holding various perspectives in view simultaneously. Most significantly, *The Fountain Opened* suggests that the mystery truly worthy of wonder is not justification per se but the impulse to holiness, the very way in which grace "stir[s] us up to godliness" (5.527). In Sibbes' treatise, the central question is not, *how are we saved?* Instead, it is, *why do human beings want to be holy in the first place?* For him, the proper disposition toward this "mystery of godliness" is not to strive after certainty but to seek to become part of Christ's fellowship by being answerable to the call to sanctity, hence the strong, if carefully calibrated, emphasis on works and holiness in his exposition on mystery.

Central to Sibbes' inquiry is an unusually sustained interrogation of the question: "What is a mystery"? According to Sibbes, Paul presents mystery as referring to something that is "*a secret*, not only for the present" but which "was a secret, though it be now revealed; for the gospel is now discovered. It is called a Mystery, not so much that it is secret, but that it was so, before it was revealed" (5.462). Sibbes also stresses that the gospel "is a mystery, in regard of what we do not know, *but shall hereafter know*" (5.463). More strikingly, though, Sibbes further claims that one is in the midst of a divine mystery "When there is any great reason, that we cannot search into the depth of the thing, though the thing it self be discovered" (5.462). From this Augustinian view of *mysterion*, Christian mystery is not so much an instance of the purloined letter paradox as it is the spiritual context of life itself. By definition, Christians live, move, and find their being within a divine Word that both orients and awes, hence Sibbes' emphasis on the complexities of scriptural interpretation rather than its clarity. For Sibbes, the gospel "is a mystery in regard of the things themselves, and in regard of us" (5.467). At such moments, he stresses the Pauline idea that the revealed mystery remains hidden to those who do not see with the Spirit (1 Cor 2:14; 2 Cor. 3). Pushing this point a little further than Paul does, Sibbes translates a standard set of sixteenth-century idioms into a new ecclesiastical and interpretive context, one where the demands of fellowship and spiritual seeking require different emphases than those Calvin gives in his responses to 1 Timothy 3:16. Without denying the objective authority or partial clarity of scripture, Sibbes nevertheless warns that excessive passions distort our perception of the gospel by turning it into our own sinful image. "Take heed," he declares, "*of passion and prejudice*, of carnal affections that stir up passion, for they will make the soul that it cannot see mysteries that are plain in themselves" (5.470–1). On this account of mystery, holiness and moderation are hermeneutic necessities even as they are signs of grace. The implication here is that the overconfidence animating both puritan dissent and Laudian extremism can be mitigated by acknowledging that scripture is a book of mysteries subject to misinterpretation and misuse.

It is within this set of distinctly seventeenth-century pressures that Sibbes takes the mystery of godliness as the occasion to rediscover nescience and awe rather than to assert full assurance of salvation via faith alone. At one particularly crucial moment, he declares that when Paul

> entered into a depth that he could not fathom, doth he cavil at it? No. 'Oh the depth! Oh the depth!' So in all the truths of God, when we cannot comprehend them, let us with silence reverence them, and say with him, 'Oh the depth! Divine things are mysteries, the sacraments are mysteries. Let us carry ourselves towards them with reverence. (5.465)

Due perhaps to their shared context and likeminded commitment to religious latitude, if not their differing politics and theologies, Sibbes sounds more like Browne than Calvin here. As Browne famously declared:

> I love to lose my selfe in a mystery to pursue my reason to an *oh altitudo* … I can answer all the objections of Satan, and my rebellious reason, with that odde resolution I learned of *Tertullian Certum est quia impossibile est.*[69]

[69] Sir Thomas Browne, *The Major Works* ed. C.A. Patrides (London: Penguin, 1977), 69–70.

Despite their significant differences, Sibbes and Browne both clearly believed that a peaceful Christian fellowship must be grounded in a hermeneutically and spiritually robust concept of mystery. To this extent, J.K. Jordan was right to identify both men as forerunners of latitudinarian developments later in the century.[70] But rather than emphasizing the role of reason in religious life as later Anglicans would, they both express a strong Augustinian commitment to mystery as a central feature of Christian faith. In this respect, they are both much closer to Andrewes and Herbert than to Stillingfleet and Tillotson.

In fact, Sibbes explicitly addresses the dangers of rationalism that would later ground Anglican latitudinarianism as it sought to cope with the deist threat. At a key moment in the treatise, Sibbes does double-duty by warning that, "If we set upon this mystery only with wits and parts of our own, then what our wits cannot pierce into, we will judge it not to be true, as if our wits were the measure of divine truth" (5.467). On the one hand, this critique echoes the growing concern with trying to understand God's ways via human reason registered in Andrewes' sermons. From this perspective, the critique seems aimed at the more rationalist features of systematic theology. On the other hand, however, this sequence also applies to more unfettered forms of rationalism. From this angle, Sibbes reminds us that rationalism in the first half of the seventeenth century was more culturally significant than is often presupposed. Viewed in its full context, Sibbes' treatise participates in a tradition of anti-rationalist critique that reaches back at least to 1563 when Pierre Viret warned of the danger posed by deists as well as to Calvin's polemics against Sebastian Castellio and other liberal Christians. Crucially though, such anxieties increased in the 1620s and 1630s, which are thought to have constituted a distinct stage in the prehistory of deism, especially in France.[71] Perhaps this is why Archbishop Laud expressed concern about the rise of rationalism in his debate with Fisher.[72] And perhaps it also helps explain how an early seventeenth-century Buckinghamshire gentleman like Sir William Drake could die a deist.[73]

[70] W.K. Jordan, *The Development of Religious Toleration in England* (1603–1640) (Gloucester, Mass.: Peter Smith, 1965), 358–361, 446–453.

[71] C.J. Betts, *Early Deism in France: From the so-called 'déistes' of Lyon* (1564) *to Voltaire's 'Lettres philosophique'* (1734) (Boston: Martinus Nijhoff, 1984), 31.

[72] See Kevin Sharpe, *The Personal Rule of Charles I* (New Haven: Yale UP, 1996), 385.

[73] See Kevin Sharpe, *Reading Revolutions: The Politics of Reading in Early Modern England* (New Haven: Yale UP, 2000), 139.

Despite the absence of any publically professed deists in early Stuart England, there almost certainly was an intellectual milieu conducive to such ideas in the period.[74] The clandestine existence of such a milieu helps explain the exigency of Sibbes' treatise as well as Herbert's *The Temple*. Wary of rationalism, Sibbes approaches scriptural mystery idioms in a way that is not altogether different than Thomas Smith's anti-deist *A Sermon of the Credibility of the Mysteries of the Christian Religion, Preached before a Learned Audience* (1675). If dogmatism and authoritarianism were the primary threats to mystery in Sibbes' treatise, the looming specter of rationalism remains not far off in the distance.

CONCLUSION: TRADITION AND DEBATE

Although concerns with the eclipse of mystery had real doctrinal inflections in early Stuart England, they ultimately transcended partisan differences. A broad range of protestants can be found trying to cultivate a religious culture that was wary of making methodological links between truth and certainty and which recognized the limitations of a piety narrowly focused on personal salvation. In many respects, the agenda here was set by King James I. For instance, in his 1619 meditation on the Lord's Prayer James complained of how "our *Puritans* may be justly called *Chymicall* doctors in Divinity, with their Quintessence of refined and pure doctrine."[75] This is the same ethos James is said to have adopted at the Hampton Court Conference when he is recorded as saying that a theology "of the necessary certainty of standing and persisting in grace' entails 'a desperate presumption'." Coming close to repeating William Barrett's critique of Calvinist perseverance without explicitly doing so, James warned against presuming that believers will sustain a sense of certainty about being in state of justifying grace throughout the course of their lives. To ask if Calvin would agree with the substance of this sentiment or not amounts to anachronism. Early reformation ideas were now being articulated and applied within a significantly new ecclesiastical and cultural context, one in which people were rediscovering much more than the virtues of Erasmian vagueness; they were coming to feel that disagreement is an inherent part of any living tradition, especially one rooted in the idea of the bible as the

---

[74] Harold R. Hutcheson, *Lord Herbert of Cherbury's De Religione Laici* (New Haven: Yale UP, 1944), 59.
[75] King James I, *Meditation Upon the Lord's Prayer* (1619), 10.

living voice of God. From this standpoint, the uncertainties within tradition could give rise to further discovery which would in turn reinvigorate the experience of divine mystery. Such a view allows for the idea that revelation is a mystery in the sense that it is as an ongoing action developing "fresh and new discov'ries" rather than an impenetrable assertion. Instead of being a fixed set of propositions to which one must declare undying allegiance, tradition was now increasingly being conceived as the context in which personal and collective spiritual discovery could happen in the course of time.

Needless to say, this view of tradition gave plenty of room for political maneuver. James' strategy at the Hampton Conference involved some sleight of hand as he pitted moderate puritans against more extreme precisians, making relatively empty promises about further reform and dialogue.[76] To this extent, the fragile peace of his church may have come to rest more on the illusion of accommodation than its reality.[77] But even that was quite an accomplishment, bettering most of the likely alternatives, the worst of which would be realized under his son Charles I. Faced with this situation, Herbert had to avoid a number of pitfalls, including spiritual blandness, mind-numbing fideism, radical doubt, or outright ecclesiastical cynicism. Doing so would require a supple exegetical ethos and a deft capacity for balancing spiritual and theological tensions, including the tensions between assurance and doubt to which we now turn.

---

[76] Fincham and Lake, "The Ecclesiastical Policy of King James I."
[77] Ibid.

CHAPTER 4

Adoption, Doubt, and Presumption: From *Perseverance* to *Assurance*

Two important poems in which Herbert deftly balances the desire for spiritual confidence with the realities of doubt are "Perseverance" and "Assurance." In both lyrics, Herbert registers Andrewes' concerns that some early modern English Christians were grounding their sense of assurance on bare repetitions of Pauline texts in which the Holy Spirit is said to operate as an agent of certitude for those who are truly sons of God. Worried about the dangers of presumption arising from a narrowed reading of the Pauline epistles in which gospel wholly obscures law, Andrewes preaches:

> Gospel it how we will, if the Gospel hath not the *legalia* of it acknowledged, allowed, and preserved to it; if once it lose the force and vigour of a law, it is a sign it declines, it grows weak and unprofitable, and that is a sign it will not long last. We must go look our salvation by some other way than by *Filius Meus Tu*, if *Filius Meus Tu* (I say not be preached, but) be not so preached, as Christ preached it; and Christ preached it as a law. And so much for *legem*. (1.289)

Andrewes here rails against those who reduce the experience of saving grace to a formula, to the idea that one can simply cry out to God on the model of Romans 8:15–16 in order to know that one is saved: "whereby we cry, Abba, father. The spirit it selfe beareth witness with our spirit,

© The Author(s) 2017
G. Kuchar, *George Herbert and the Mystery of the Word*,
DOI 10.1007/978-3-319-44045-3_4

that we are the children of God."[1] For Andrewes, too many protestants in England confused spiritual adoption with presumption. In his view, the result was a spiritually and exegetically reductive conception of faith in which gospel was emphasized to the apparent exclusion of law, the inadvertent result of which is a vicious return of the law upon the conscience. Showing even greater pastoral sensitivity, Hooker, as we have seen, thought that too many protestants suffered despair due to an unrealistically high expectation of joyful assurance. From this perspective, an unchecked drive to certainty of salvation through faith alone inadvertently generated spiritual despair and ecclesiastical conflict.

Herbert addresses these issues in his emotionally devastating lyric "Perseverance," which appears in the Williams Manuscript but not in the final version of *The Temple*. Because "Perseverance" is almost universally celebrated for its affective power, it is not immediately clear why Herbert removed it from his final sequence. The most widely held explanation is that the lyric expresses an unusually naked fear of reprobation, a fear articulated most directly in stanza three when, as Louis Martz notes, the speaker worries "that his own sins may yet forbid the banns that might announce his welcome to the marriage-supper of the Lamb."[2] As Joseph Summers concludes, the lyric most likely left out of the final version "because Herbert did not believe that it would 'turn to the advantage of any dejected poor soul'."[3] Elizabeth Clarke confirms this view when she describes the poem as "unremittingly pessimistic." In her reading, "Perseverance" dramatizes the unintended implications of Calvinist assurance by showing the speaker in "a desperate act of will, represented [in the final stanza] as of someone clinging to the edge of a precipice by his fingertips."[4] In Clarke's account, the poem remains wholly ambiguous on the question of perseverance, leaving us dangerously unsure of whether the speaker is elect or not.

While I agree that "Perseverance" was excised for pastoral reasons having to do partly with despair, I do not think it is unremittingly pessimistic. Properly understood, the poem depicts a speaker who shows distinct signs

[1] See also Andrewes, 5.337. For one example of this type of reduction, see John Forbes, *How a Christian man may discerne the testimonie of Gods spirit* (Middleburgh: 1616), 60–64.
[2] Joseph H. Summers, *George Herbert: His Religion and Art* (London: Chatto and Windus, 1954), 62; Louis L. Martz, "Generous Ambiguity" in *A Fine Tuning* ed. Maleski, 37.
[3] Summers, *George Herbert*, 62.
[4] Clarke, *Theory and Theology*, 7, 280.

of being in the throes of spiritual adoption, which is a definitive event in the order of salvation. This is why it appears in the Williams sequence as the 71st of 76 poems, a choice Herbert would almost certainly not have made had he intended it to be an unresolved expression of potential reprobation. Viewed this way, it becomes clear that the true pastoral challenge Herbert took up in "Perseverance" was to express the experience of adoption in a way that avoids the exaggerated certainties that often accompanied accounts of election in sermons and treatises in the period. In other words, "Perseverance" was written with the awareness that despair and security are often two sides of the same coin. Avoiding one necessarily involves avoiding the other. Thus, to say that Herbert rejected the poem on the grounds that it is too despairing is not incorrect so much as incomplete.

By situating "Perseverance" within the broader context of Herbert's depictions of spiritual adoption throughout *The Temple*, we gain a fuller view of how he carefully balances the need for assurance with the reality of doubt. Of particular importance here is how Herbert approaches the scriptural texts that reformers most often turned to when defining the event of spiritual adoption within the broader process of conversion and regeneration. As is so often the case with Herbert, his formal and scriptural mediations of key doctrines are more revealing than attempts to nail down the doctrines themselves according to one specific framework or category of belief. Ultimately, though, Herbert was unhappy enough with his negotiations of hope and despair in "Perseverance" to leave it out of the final version of *The Temple*. In its place, we find "Assurance" which is absent from the Williams Manuscript and which was thus presumably composed later. On the one hand, "Assurance" concludes with greater explicit optimism than "Perseverance." On the other, however, it does not make as decisive a claim for personal adoption as the older lyric implicitly does. Less flamboyantly dramatic and more doctrinally wary than "Perseverance," "Assurance" is subtly syncretic, especially with respect to its handling of some key differences within the Pauline and Johannine traditions that we saw Andrewes negotiate in the previous chapter. As these lyrics suggest, how Herbert formally negotiates spiritual and doctrinal pressures ultimately proves more revealing than trying to isolate one single theological context for individual poems.

PERSEVERANCE AND THE MOTIONS OF PRAYER

The theological issues at stake in "Perseverance" are encoded in the poem's less-than-transparent title. On the one hand, Herbert's title might imply the technically vague idea expressed in the New Testament that those who endure in faith until the end shall be saved (Mat. 10:22, Mark 13:13, and Heb. 3:14). On the other hand, however, Herbert may be evoking Augustine's view that if one enjoys perseverance, it is because God wills it to be so, but if one falters, it is one's own fault. Alternatively, it may allude to Calvin's stricter version of the perseverance of the saints in which saving grace, once given, cannot be lost, a subtle but distinct variation of which was enshrined in the Lambeth Articles of 1595. Part of the difficulty that the poem presents lies in the way these varying notions of perseverance combine in the lyric without any one obviously dominating.[5] Such ambiguity may partly reflect the fact that perseverance was an unusually hot topic in Stuart England. If it was central to the William Barrett crisis and the Hampton Court Conference in 1604, then it became an even more dangerous issue after the 1622 Directions to Preachers forbade ministers below the rank of bishop or dean to preach about election and reprobation.[6] Like "Assurance," the theological vision expressed in "Perseverance" remains syncretistic and is ultimately subordinated to spiritual and aesthetic concerns. Its purpose is not to teach one stable doctrine so much as to convey the felt-experience of a believer struggling to persevere in faith at the darkest of hours.

Complicating matters further is the fact that the question of perseverance is inextricable from the experience of spiritual motions. Throughout protestant theology, perseverance in grace is thought to occur through the motions of the Holy Spirit, especially as expressed in Pauline texts such as Galatians 4:6: "because yee are sonnes, God hath sent foorth the spirit of his Sonne into your hearts, crying Abba, Father." On the basis of such passages, Luther and subsequent reformers identified the Holy Spirit as an agent of certitude guaranteeing one's election. As Richard Strier notes in his reading of "Assurance," Luther believed that it was only "the ungodly"

---

[5] Such theological open-endedness is not altogether surprising when we bear in mind that Arthur Lake, a bishop who had acted as a consultant to the British delegation at the Synod of Dort, was quite willing to leave the question of final perseverance unresolved. See Arnold Hunt, *The Art of Hearing*, 382. Clearly, such open-endedness reflects cultural as well as literary exigencies.

[6] For a discussion of the Barrett controversy and subsequent events, see Chap. 3.

who "declare that no man can be certain of the forgiveness of his sins."[7] If Christians had faith in Christ and could call upon God with the confidence that a child calls upon a loving parent, then they could be assured of justification through the ongoing presence of the Spirit.[8] The opening stanza of "Perseverance" assumes these associations when the speaker corrects his mistaken belief that he is responsible for his prayer rather than the Spirit:

> My God, ye poore expressions of my Love
> W^{ch} warme these lines, & serve them up to thee
> Are so, as for the present, I did move
>   Or rather as thou movedst me. (1–4)

On the one hand, these lines are a humbling expression of the view that the merit of prayer is not antecedent to grace. In making this point, however, the speaker somewhat awkwardly places responsibility for his lack of inspiration at the feet of the Holy Spirit much as Herbert does in stanza two of "The Church-lock and key": "I do lay the want of my desire, / Not on my sinnes, or coldnesse, but thy will" (7–8). Stanza one thus raises the question of where the Spirit's motions end and the human will begins or as Andrewes asks in his sermon on Romans 8:26: "When the Apostle saith, 'The Spirit maketh intercession for us' ... What groanings are these? are they thine or mine?" (5.339). In this respect, the opening stanza establishes the poem's broader concern with the widely assumed connection between spiritual motions and the perseverance of those adopted into Christ.

By admitting that his prayer may be motivated by God rather than himself, the speaker of "Perseverance" evokes St. Paul's claim that the soul does not always know what is really happening at the moment of prayer. According to Paul, the conscious intention of the mind is not necessarily coincident with the intention of prayer itself because "the Spirit ... maketh intercession for us with groanings which cannot be uttered. And he that searcheth the hearts knoweth what is the minde of the Spirit, because he maketh intercession for the saints, according to the will of God" (Rom. 8:26–27).[9] What is crucial at the moment of prayer is not

---

[7] Luther, *Babylonian Captivity*, cited in Strier, *Love Known*, 307.

[8] For a fuller discussion of this aspect of reformation thought, see Chap. 3 and Louise Schreiner, *Are You Alone Wise?*, 57–58.

[9] For Clarke's groundbreaking discussion of this passage in relation to Herbert, see *Theory and Theology*, 165.

that the soul understand everything which is happening in her and cer‐
tainly not that her own words transparently express a holy intent. What
is important is that the will of God be realized through the motions of
the supplicant's heart, a process that, as Thomas Goodwin explains in
his 1643 treatise, *The Returne of Prayers*, may be partly unconscious.
Following Augustine, Goodwin explains how prayer is often initiated "by
a gracious pre‐instinct, though unbeknown to them [who pray]."[10] John
Donne makes a related point in a sermon on Romans 13:7 when he para‐
phrases St. Bernard's assertion that "God heares the very first motions
of a mans heart, which, that man, till he proceed to a farther consider‐
ation, doth not heare, not feele, not deprehend in himself" (4.310). As
Goodwin and Donne indicate, prayer often begins and ultimately unfolds
not in words but in heartfelt movements. Moreover, prayer's mysteri‐
ous origins sometimes lie in "pre‐instincts" that can be more remote to
will and understanding than what Augustine calls the "abyss of human
conscience."[11] It is only later, upon meditative reflection, or at a subse‐
quent, unforeseen moment within the prayer itself that the supplicant
may come to understand what was revealed by the divine will during the
act of prayer. From this perspective, prayer is more a mode of discov‐
ery than a form of expression, "a plummet sounding heav'n and earth"
("Prayer (I), 4").

In explaining the importance of listening for God's answer to one's
petitions, Thomas Goodwin teaches his auditors to

> observe if in the end God doth not answer thee still according to the *ground*
> of thy prayer: that is, see if that holy end, intention, and affection, which
> thou hadst in prayer, be not in the end fully satisfied, though not in the
> thing thou didst desire: for God answers, *Secundum cardinem*, according to
> the hinge which the prayer turnes upon.[12]

Following Goodwin's cardiological pun, God answers prayer by opening
the heart that is the hinge upon which prayer turns. According to this the‐
ory, prayer is an opening to a wider perspective of understanding—one that
retrospectively reveals the real meaning of what one originally intended
without fully knowing it. If prayer doesn't fundamentally change one's

[10] Goodwin, *The Returne of Prayers* (London: 1643), "Epistle Dedicatory," *3v.
[11] St. Augustine, *Confessions*. Loeb Classical Library. With an English translation by William Watts (Cambridge: Harvard UP, 1961), 74.
[12] Goodwin, *Returne of Prayers*, 69.

intention, in the sense of totally redefining it, it nonetheless reveals hidden or unanticipated aspects of the "ground" underneath one's intention at the moment of praying itself, and this might feel like much the same thing. That God listens to a prayer "according to the hinge which the prayer turnes upon" means that God responds from a vantage point that includes things one doesn't comprehend at the moment of a petition or confession. This is as much as to say that one really doesn't know what one means when one prays, even and especially if the Holy Spirit moves in the heart during prayer without the supplicant knowing it. Prayer, in order to be prayer, must remain open to the possibility that what one truly prayed for comes back from the future in the form of God's response to his own intention. Prayer might thus be said to be "Gods breath in man returning to his birth" ("Prayer (I)," 2).[13]

Goodwin's account of prayer assumes two crucial features of Augustine's view on the topic. As Rebecca Weaver explains, Augustine thought that the prayerful act of putting one's spiritual desires into words "serves to clarify for oneself the actual content of the desires." And that "this imposition of form through words necessarily modifies the desires themselves."[14] In other words, prayer teaches one what one truly desires even if that desire remains unconscious, thereby modifying or even replacing any wrongly oriented desire. Taken as a whole, "Perseverance" couples this Pauline-Augustinian conception of prayer with closely associated ideas about spiritual adoption.

To be precise, the Pauline conception of prayer as a dialogue with the Spirit orients the basic movement of "Perseverance" from the explicit doubt of the opening stanzas to the hope and qualified assurance of its conclusion. The final stanza of "Perseverance" is extraordinary for the way it dramatically avoids any kind of formulaic depiction of adoption. It does this by juxtaposing two conventional but nevertheless incongruous images of God: Christ as the rock upon which one stands and God as the parent to whom one clings. Agonizing over the state of his soul, the poet concludes with the startling expostulation:

> Onely my soule hangs on thy promisses
> W[th] face and hands clinging unto thy brest,
> Clinging and crying, crying without cease,
>   Thou art my rock, thou art my rest. (13–16)

---

[13] For a related discussion of prayer and spiritual motions in Herbert's poetry, see Clarke, *Theory and Theology*.

[14] Rebecca Weaver, "Prayer," *Augustine through the Ages*, 672.

In this extraordinary ending, Herbert avoids any risk of presumption by conflating the starkly opposing spiritual states of certainty and uncertainty that Ezekiel Culverwell distinguishes in his popular 1623 work, *Treatise of Faith*. According to Culverwell, "When there is resting … on God's word after temptation, there is true faith; but where there is nothing but hanging in suspense, and uncertainty, that is wavering."[15] At first blush, Culverwell's distinction between resting and hanging makes it look like Herbert's poem is designed to be purposefully ambiguous as the speaker is doing both at the same time. Undeniably, the poem opens up the Augustinian possibility that "he who falls, falls through his own will, but he who stands, stands through the will of God" (Voluntate autem sua cadit qui cadit, et voluntate Dei stat qui stat), a formulation that Calvin tweaked when he made the stronger claim that "Man slips according to God's decree; but he slips because of his vice."[16] This is perhaps why Sidney Gottlieb argues that the "psalmic phrases that are the substance of his cries—'thou art my rock, thou art my rest—perhaps look forward to but do not bring him any relief within the borders of this poem."[17] Yet, in context the poet's cry is an exemplary, if highly anguished, instance of the Pauline experience of adoption that St. Augustine explains in his treatise *On The Gift of Perseverance*. According to Augustine,

> since *we do not know what we should pray for as we ought, but the Spirit himself*, says the Apostle, *pleads for us with unutterable groanings* … What does this mean: *the Spirit himself pleads*, unless 'to make one plead' … For it is He of Whom the Apostle speaks in another passage: *God has sent the Spirit of his Son into our hearts, crying 'Abba, Father.'* And what does this word *crying* mean except 'making one cry,' through the use of that figure of speech by which we call a day a happy one which makes us happy? And this he makes plain in another place: *Now you have not received a spirit of bondage so as to be again in fear, but you have received a spirit of adoption as sons, by virtue of which we cry, 'Abba! Father!'* In that passage, he said *crying*, but in this one, *by virtue of which we cry*, explaining clearly how he meant *crying*, that is, as

[15] Ezekiel Culverwell, *A Treatise of Faith*. Seventh Edition. (London: 1633), 50–51.

[16] Augustine, *De Dono Perseverantiae* trans. Sister Mary Alphonsine Lesousky (Washington D.C.: Catholic University of America, 1956), 128–129; Calvin *Institutes* 3.80 cited in George Tavard, *Holy Writ or Holy Church : The Crisis of the Protestant Reformation* (New York: Harper, 1959), 105.

[17] Sidney Gottlieb, "The Two Endings of George Herbert's 'The Church'" in *A Fine Tuning*, 57–76, 64.

I have already explained, 'making one cry.' Thus we understand that this is also a gift of God, that we cry to God with a sincere and spiritual heart.[18]

The spiritual core of Herbert's "Perseverance" lies in Augustine's Pauline theory that one is adopted into Christ through the motions of the Spirit as conveyed in the act of crying (inwardly or outwardly). After all, it is precisely this process that is requisite to, and thus a sign of, the gift of perseverance. Read in this context, Herbert's lyric implies that just as the poem ultimately originates not with his own will but with a divine motion, so too his capacity to cry originates not with himself but with the cry of the Spirit in him. The spiritual weeping that ends the lyric thus makes the poem's opening complaint about the lack of motions rather ironic as the Spirit moves the speaker in unexpected ways. Rather than being a rhetorical tactic, the cry shows the speaker displaying the gift of *parrehesia*, the capacity enjoyed by the adopted soul to boldly cry out to God as a child cries out to a benevolent parent. But fearing to overstate the case for adoption, Herbert tones down the confidence often associated with *parrehesia* in protestant culture. Going for a soft touch, Herbert marks the Spirit's presence in the poem's conclusion by smoothing out of verb tenses as the manic oscillations between past and present tenses initiated in stanza one now cease as the speaker remains thoroughly in the present. The suggestion here is that a spiritual change has occurred even if it has not yet taken full root in the speaker's soul. Whatever comfort the poet may consciously gain by the end of the poem, he does not display assurance in the sense of *securitas*.

GOD AS PARENT; GOD AS ROCK

If "Perseverance" leaves some readers with a nagging sense that its spiritual drama remains dangerously open-ended, it is partly because even by its conclusion the emphasis is almost entirely on the speaker's act of will, his clinging to Christ the rock. Importantly, though, such imagery recalls the practice among protestant preachers of describing the soul's relation to Christ as parallel to a child that is being held in his mother's arms. Richard Sibbes explains the power of the human will in spiritual matters with exactly this image:

---

[18] Augustine, *De Dono Perseverantiae*, 209.

> We are comprehended of [Christ], as the child is of the nurse or of the mother. The child holds the nurse, and the nurse the child. The child is more safe from falling by the nurse and the mother's holding of it, than by its holding of them. Those that are at years must clasp and grasp about Christ, but Christ holds and comprehends them; much more doth God comprehend those that are children, that are not to comprehend him. (7.486–7)

If Herbert's poem exaggerates the possibility of falling from persevering grace that is evoked by such imagery, it is because he wanted to avoid the overconfident depictions of adoption which, according to Hooker, are the route to real despair. He did this by making the speaker's experience of adoption implicit in the poem.

Because the event of adoption remains unconscious in "Perseverance," Herbert's speaker sounds no more confident than the voice at the end of "Gratefulnesse." In this lyric from *The Temple*, the speaker artfully plays the role of precocious child tugging, as it were, on the sleeve of a benevolent parent:

> Thou hast giv'n so much to me,
> Give one thing more, a gratefull heart.
> See how thy beggar works on thee
>   By art. (1–4)

The cleverly sly tone of this childlike speaker becomes exquisitely wise by the poem's end:

> Wherefore I crie, and crie againe;
> And in no quiet canst thou be,
> Till a thankfull heart obtain
>   Of thee
>
> Not thankfull, when it pleaseth me;
> As if thy blessings had spare dayes:
> But such a heart, whose pulse may be
>   Thy praise. (25–32)

Sibbes provides another helpful gloss to Herbert when he writes:

> a Christian soul that hath union with Christ, that hath a being and station in him, *may know it*. There are always some pulses from this heart. As we know there is some life by the beating of the pulses, so Christ's dwelling in the heart is known by these pulses. (5. 211)

In both "Perserverance" and "Gratefulnesse," the speaker desires Christ's presence without confidently possessing it, a desire that may nevertheless suggest, without necessarily confirming, such presence in the first place. By implying a fundamental change that has not yet taken full root, "Perseverance" concludes in a very similar way as "Longing," which begins:

> With sick and famisht eyes,
> With doubling knees and weary bones,
>   To thee my cries,
>   To thee my grones,
> To thee my sighs, my tears ascend:
>   No end? (1–6)

This excruciating cry of interminable prayer might seem to be just as unanswered as the implied petition orienting "Perseverance" may appear to be, as it concludes:

> My love, my sweetnesse, heare!
> By these thy feet, at which my heart
>   Lies all the yeare,
>   Pluck out thy dart,
> And heal my troubled breast which cries,
>   Which dyes. (79–84)

But as Helen Wilcox notes, "Several critics have observed that the first line of next poem, *The Bag,* 'reveals that grace has intervened at last—his petition has been answered'" (512). The same dynamic occurs with respect to "Perseverance," which is followed in the Williams manuscript by the ironically titled "Death." This confidence is evident in "Death" right at the outset and is then developed throughout the poem as a whole: "Death, thou wast once an uncouth hideous thing ... / But since our Saviours death did put some bloud / Into thy face; / Thou art grown fair and full of grace" (1, 13–16).[19] The moderately confident assurance expressed in "Death" is latent in "Perseverance," indicating the motions of the Spirit in ways unbeknownst to the speaker. While Herbert does not literally have the speaker of "Perseverance" cry out "Abba! Father!" he does what amounts to the same

[19] *The Williams Manuscript of George Herbert's Poems: A Facsimile Reproduction With An Introduction Amy M. Charles* (Delmar NY: Scholars Facsimiles and Reprints, 1977), 76.

thing; he has him cry out unceasingly as a child to God in the expectation that he will respond as a loving parent.

That this expectation of saving grace is not misplaced is implied in the way the final stanza of "Perseverance" presents a kind of rebus, a visual puzzle disclosing a verbal sign. As we have seen, the central image of the concluding stanza involves an image of a child clinging to a parent who is figured as a rock: "my soule hangs on thy promisses" (13). On the face of it, the word *hangs* is hardly the likeliest verb here, certainly not as likely as "to cleave" or "to cling."[20] For one thing, it connotes capital punishment. But when read in the context of spiritual adoption, however, the word's negative connotations are negated by a biblical idiom in which trusting God is figured as hanging upon him. Two central passages on assurance in Isaiah are crucial here, the first being 32:17: "And the worke of righteousness shall be peace, and the effect of righteousness, quietness and assurance for ever" (Isa. 32:17) and the second 30:15: "In quietness and confidence shall be your strength." In Hebrew, the word for "quietness" (*Shâqat*) "signifies to hang upon something, and accordingly the meaning is 'trust'."[21] In biblical Hebrew, then, to trust God is to hang upon him. The implication of Herbert's idiom is that the act of hanging upon God is coincident with the experience of adoption and the assurance it engenders both of which are the work of the Spirit.

But there is even more going on in the final stanza's carefully chosen idioms. The most common metaphor reformers use to describe the process of spiritual adoption is the Pauline figure of being engrafted into Christ as in Donne's declaration that "the spirit of adoption hath ingraffed us" into God's covenant (5.102). When Herbert's speaker says he "hangs" upon God's promises, he testifies to his having been engrafted into Christ through the actions of grace. Just as God motioned him to pray and to cry, so too does he support the very action of "hanging." Not only is God with him now, the conclusion implies, God has been with him from the start, indeed from before the start. So, while the poem's two final images of God are in literal tension with one another, betraying the speaker's lack of conscious assurance, their biblical idioms nevertheless suggest the unconscious or "pre-instinctual" workings of the Spirit. The poem's ending implies that an experientially registered assurance may yet arrive but it has not yet

[20] *Institutes* 3.2.31.497.
[21] W.E. Vine, *Vine's Expository Dictionary of Old and New Testament Words* (Nashville: Thomas Nelson, 1997), 21–22.

come. Seen this way, the poem endorses a carefully modified form of protestant perseverance, one that is modest, agonized, and implicit. In short,
this is perseverance without anything remotely resembling presumption.

HERBERT'S "FOULING-PEECE"

Herbert's tempering of the kind of assurance associated with adoption
in "Perseverance" is further evinced in stanzas two and three. To start
with, these stanzas come very close to mooting the spiritual motions intimated at the outset. In the second stanza, the speaker makes the mistake
of assuming full responsibility for the origins and significance of both his
prayer and his poems, asking what shall issue from "*my* words" (5, my
emphasis). His anxiety continues to register through shifting verb tenses
which are now exacerbated by an awkward repetition of conjunctions:

> But what shall issue, whither these my words
> Shal help another, but my iudgment bee;
> As a burst fouling-peece doth save ye birds
> But kill the man, is seald wth thee. (5–8)

The anxiety that the speaker registers in his repetition of "but" three
times in four lines involves the distinction between a general rather than
a special witness of the Spirit, the idea that although the speaker believes
Christ saves he remains unconvinced of his own justification. John Forbes
explains this distinction in his 1616 treatise on *How a Christian man
may discerne the testimonie of Gods spirit* with reference to a preacher in
Herbert's position, noting that such a man "may bee a Preacher, and be
witnes of all the promises of God in Christ to others, & yet have no parte
in them him selfe."[22] The danger of remaining in the state of general witnessing is that it is "no warrant of adoption."[23] Read from Forbes' standpoint, "Perseverance" asks whether the speaker moves from a general to a
special witnessing of the Spirit, from an objective belief in Christ's saving
power to a subjective persuasion that he enjoys the fruits of such power.

The speaker's disturbing awareness that his own words may have unintended effects is also expressed in stanza two through one of Herbert's
most violent images. The speaker's poem prayers are compared to a mis-

---

[22] Forbes, *How a Christian May Discerne*, 17.
[23] Ibid.

firing gun that blows up in the shooter's face, saving others but killing oneself. The force of the aptly named "fouling-peece" rests, in part, on an association going back to the patristic period of ejaculatory prayers with "darts."[24] The suggestion here is that the poet is not even confident enough to assume that his verse qualifies as what Donne describes in a 1620 sermon as "weak prayers":

> The words of man, in the mouth of a faithfull man ... are a Canon against God himselfe, and batter down all his severe and heavy purposes for Judgements. Yet, this comes not, God knows, out of the weight or force of our words, but out of the easinesse of God. God puts himselfe in the way of a shot, he meets a weak prayer, and is graciously pleased to be wounded by that: God sets up a light, that we direct the shot upon him, he enlightens us with a knowledge, how, and when, and what to pray for; yea, God charges, and discharges the Canon himself upon himselfe. (3:152)

Where Donne situates God, Herbert's poet situates himself. Where Donne sees God as both the inspirer and the receiver of prayer, Herbert's speaker remains unsure about both the true authorship and the real significance of his prayers. Assuming that the substance of his prayer remains *his* rather than God's, the poet inevitably worries that his prayers are self-destructive rather than "an Engine against the almighty" ("Prayer (I)," 5). Ultimately, "Perseverance" resolves these tensions by intimating several ways in which the Spirit speaks through a poet who is in the throes of adoption.

ADOPTION IN *THE TEMPLE*

As I noted, Herbert placed "Perseverance" near the end of the sequence because adoption occurs late in the order of salvation. Had he put it earlier, he would only have increased the danger of presumption he sought to avoid in writing a lyric about the experience of adoption.[25] While Herbert probably removed "Perseverance" from the final version of *The Temple*

---

[24] For a discussion of this aspect of the word, see Clarke, "George Herbert's House of Pleasure? Ejaculations, Sacred and Profane," *George Herbert Journal,* 19.1–2 (1996), 55–71.

[25] As William Perkins explains, adoption is co-extensive with justification and thus occurs late in the experience of sanctification. See *The Golden Chain or the Description of Theology* (London: 1591), Q2v.

for pastoral reasons, the issues at stake in the poem cannot be reduced to despair alone. If the only thing preventing "Perseverance's" inclusion in the final version of *The Temple* were its despairing elements, Herbert could simply have changed its title. Had he called the poem "Adoption" or "The Holy Spirit" or "Romans 8:15," he would have clearly pointed to the salvific event depicted in the final stanza. But had he done so, he would have made the poem an obnoxiously direct declaration of election.

Deeply sensitive to the Johannine principle that the Spirit blows where it lists, Herbert took up the challenge of composing a poem about adoption without making it an expression of security. In doing so, he avoided the risks that William Perkins ran into when the Cambridge theologian offered a formula for election wherein "The judgment and discerning of a man's own predestination is to be performed by means of these [eight] rules which follow."[26] In composing "Perseverance," Herbert not only worried about the pastoral problems posed by self-proclaimed reprobates such as Francis Spiera but he also worried about overconfident reactions to him such as those of Calvin and Matthew Gribalde.[27] This is why the same reticence about exaggerated certainty animating "Perseverance" is audible in other poems that evoke the experience of adoption.

In Herbert's most famous depiction of spiritual adoption "The Collar," the speaker hesitatingly concludes: "Me thoughts I heard one calling, *Childe* / And I reply'd, *My Lord*" (35–36). The speaker's response here is an act of faith based on the hope that it is God speaking and that he is being addressed with the spiritually consequential term *child*. The uncertainty of this ending is even more pronounced than Augustine's confusion in Book 8 of *The Confessions* when he says that the voice which called out "tolle lege," leading him to fully convert, sounded as if ("quasi") it were that of a boy or a girl but ultimately he could not be sure. Uncertain of the source and context of the phrase, Augustine nevertheless takes a leap of faith and interprets the voice calling "take up and read" as a divine injunction beckoning him to read holy scripture with renewed vigor. And yet, the uncertainty and surprise of "The Collar's" ending appears remarkably assured when compared with the bewildered and defensive speaker of "Dialogue." In this poem, the tortured speaker rejects being called "Child" by Christ due to the excruciating burden that the atonement places on him. He thus responds to Christ's explanation "*I did freely part*

---

[26] Ibid., A4r.
[27] For a discussion of the Spiera case, see Chap. 3.

/ *With my glorie and desert,* / *Left all joyes to feel all smart*—" by abruptly ending the conversation: "Ah! no more: thou break'st my heart" (29–32). Similarly, in "Holy Baptism (II)," the speaker wants to see himself as a child in the eyes of God but it remains wholly petitionary: "O let me still / Write thee great God, and me a childe: / Let me be soft and supple to thy will" (6–8). In each of these poems, the experience of adoption is attended by uncertainty, interpretive error, and the underlying but unarticulated promise "blessed are the poor in spirit." By also stressing these features in "Perseverance," Herbert sought to avoid the mutually implicating dangers of presumption and despair, though he appears, in the end, to have felt himself to have failed. To be sure, this lyric exemplifies the extent to which theological substance in post-reformation England is inextricably related to rhetorical and communicative style. While "Perseverance" is not properly legible without reference to Augustinian notions of prayer and adoption, what the poem finally gives us is an irreducibly personal expression of a single man, at a particular moment in time, taking Richard Sibbes' advice to "Hold God fast in the dark night, although we see nothing … Cast anchor in him" (3.150).

Assurance

It may not be entirely true to say that "Perseverance" is the only poem Herbert wrote in which the threat of reprobation is seriously entertained. For it is precisely this "spitefull bitter thought" that brings the speaker of "Assurance" into speech, giving the lyric its underlying, if slightly muted, spiritual exigency. In this respect, the question the poem raises is how the speaker manages to overcome the anxiety that is too terrible to speak its name. According to Richard Strier, "Assurance" shows Herbert gaining a sense of spiritual confidence through a rejection of covenant theology. Instead of seeking *affiance* by examining himself for signs of grace, the speaker, Strier argues, turns entirely to God through faith.[28] There is good reason for seeing the poem as a reaction against some of the more systematized approaches to conversion and sanctification evident in covenant theology. After all, the speaker's "spitefull bitter thought" was triggered by the kind of "gnostic" desire that Andrewes mocks when he criticizes "this licentious touching, nay tossing [God's] decrees of late; this sounding the depth of His judgments with our line and lead, too much

[28] Strier, *Love Known*, 108–113.

presumed upon by some in these days of ours" (3.32). The point is made in line five of stanza one of "Assurance":

> O spitefull bitter thought!
> Bitterly spitefull thought! Couldst thou invent
> So high a torture? Is such poison bought?
> Doubtlesse, but in the way of punishment,
>   When wit contrives to meet with thee,
>   No such rank poyson can there be. (1–6)

In other words, the speaker's fear that his "league" with God was "broke, or neare it" arose because he tried to gain a sense of assurance by understanding God's ways through his own "wit" (11, 5). The implication here is that Herbert also sees some kinds of terrifying doubt as an inadvertent consequence of the desire to gain total assurance by reducing God's ways to a rationally conceivable plan. As with Hooker, despair is diagnosed here as the flip side of presumption rather than its genuine opposite. In this sense, Strier is entirely right to see "Assurance" as a reaction against the way that some puritans trespassed on the mystery of God's ways. Nevertheless, he overstates the point when he says that the poem wholly rejects the covenant idea.

Rather than rejecting covenant ideas, Herbert's "Assurance" presents a speaker coming to a proper notion of them. More precisely, the speaker arrives at a view of the covenant that is broadly similar to Richard Sibbes' theory, especially the distinction between conditional and absolute promises that he stresses in his commentary on 2 Corinthians. Some promises, Sibbes writes,

> (2.) be *conditional* in the manner of propounding, but yet absolute in the real performance of them. As, for example, the promises of grace and glory to God's children. The promise of forgiveness of sins,—God will forgive their sins if they believe, if they repent. They are propounded conditionally, but in the performance they are absolute, because God performs the covenant himself; he performs our part and his own too. (3.394)

Viewed in this context, there is no contradiction between Sibbes' brand of covenant theology and the resolution of "Assurance." On the contrary, Herbert deploys covenant idioms in very similar ways as Sibbes, especially in the poem's ante-penultimate stanza:

> But thou art my desert:
> And in this league, which now my foes invade,
> Thou art not onely to perform thy part,
> But also mine; as when the league was made
>   Thou didst at once thy self indite,
>   And hold my hand, while I did write. (25–30)

The idea that the covenant promise is conditional in its "manner of propounding" but absolute in its performance delimits and defines human will without altogether annulling it, hence the highly qualified joint action of this stanza's final line. At a strictly theological level, then, there is no real contradiction between the covenant idioms of "Assurance" and the deficiency of the human will lamented in "Ungratefulnesse."[29] Similarly, what we see in "Assurance" is a less histrionic balancing of grace and human will than the one expressed in the final stanza of "Perseverance." This is partly because "Assurance" leans more cautiously on God's role in the process but without, at the same time, wholly effacing human action and will.

Concomitantly, there is no suggestion in "Assurance" that faith cannot be strengthened through the experience of sanctification, something both Calvin and the poem's final stanza permits, though in slightly different ways.[30] What is emphasized in the poem is not the question of resting in God rather than relying on one's own personal sanctification; instead, its exigency arises from the dangerously intimate relation between despair and the forms of assurance that are dependent on man's "wit" which Andrewes often attacks. This emphasis is affirmed in the poem's final stanza:

>   Now foolish thought go on,
> Spin out thy thread, and make thereof a coat
> To hide thy shame: for thou hast cast a bone
> Which bounds on thee, and will not down thy throat:

---

[29] For a discussion of "Ungratefulnesse," see Chap. 2.

[30] See Calvin, *Institutes* 3.14 *sections* 18–20, pp. 785–86 particularly as cited and discussed in Steven Ozment, *The Age of Reform 1250–1550: An Intellectual and religious History of Late Medieval and Reformation Europe* (New Haven: Yale UP, 1980), 378. See also Calvin's commentary on 1 John 3:14 *Commentaries on the Epistle of Paul the Apostle to The Hebrews* trans. John Owen (Grand Rapids: Baker Books, n.d.), 217–218, especially as discussed in Pitkin, *What Pure Eyes Could See*, 88. As we saw in the last chapter, Herbert, like Calvin, takes it for granted that the "pledges of Gods Love" are visible to Christians. See *The Country Parson*, 283.

> What for it self love once began,
> Now love and truth will end in man. (37–42)

The proverbial bone imagery of the final stanza returns us to the ante-cedent scenario alluded to in stanza one: the systematization of God's ways through human wit for the sake of total assurance rebounds back in the form of despair and doubt. In this sense, the speaker's shame lies in his having trespassed on a divine mystery that God's love nevertheless overcomes. Instead of resting on his own efforts of wit and unsanctified will, he turns to 1 John 13–17 and the assurance of God's love promised there.[31] Like Andrewes, Herbert roots the experience of assurance not just in Pauline concepts of faith alone but also in the Johannine idea that divine love manifests in the human soul through fellowship and spiritual intercourse with God, hence the affirmation of a qualified form of reciprocity between man and God in the final two lines: "What for it self love once began, / Now love and truth will end in man" (37–42). This Johannine emphasis on the reciprocal dynamics of love between the soul and God modifies the strong Pauline emphasis on faith alone in the poem's penultimate stanza. Here again, Sibbes offers a helpful parallel:

> Can a man know God's love in Christ incarnate, and Christ's suffering for us, and his sitting at the right hand of God for us, the infinite love of God in Christ, and not be carried in affection back to God again, in love and joy and true affiance, and whatsoever makes up the respect of godliness? It cannot be. (5.461)

This is precisely the kind of reciprocity envisioned in the final lines of "Assurance" as God's love returns to God through man, much as his breath does in "Prayer." Rather than voiding human responsibility altogether, the poem's final lines reassert it in light of God's loving, covenantal, promises as remanifested "in man." In this way, the final lines make man the medium or agent of God's loving work that Andrewes sees as grounding both assurance and fellowship. The result is a lyrical synthesis of covenantal and Johannine ideas that transcends, if it does not

---

[31] For a related reading of "Assurance" to which I am very much indebted, see Cefalu, *The Johnnanine Renaissance*, Chap. 4.

outright offend, categories such as Calvinist and Arminian. Ultimately, "Assurance" exemplifies how Herbert responded in his poetry to the post-Elizabethan eclipse of mystery as it manifested around questions of assurance and certainty. So, while it may be less spiritually tortured than "Perseverance" and while it may not emphasize the Augustinian idea that one can fall from grace, it nevertheless deftly balances the virtue of assurance with the vice of presumption. Preferring scriptural mystery to biblical formulae, Herbert resists dogmatism while nonetheless avowing the value of *parrehesia*, the confidence required to "Hold God fast in the dark night, although we see nothing" (Sibbes, 3.150).

CONCLUSION: COVENANT THEOLOGY

In this chapter, I have sought to modify a major narrative in Herbert studies. It is still often maintained by Herbert scholars that seventeenth-century protestant orthodoxy, especially as manifested in covenant theology, marks a substantial break from the early Reformation and that in rejecting this break Herbert was returning protestant spirituality to a more original, more pure, form.[32] There are at least two problems with this contextualization of *The Temple*. The first is that as far as reformed theology goes it overstates differences of style with differences of substance. As Richard Muller and others have shown, the idea that covenant theologians fundamentally betrayed the early Reformation constitutes a form of "theological nostalgia" more than a convincing historical thesis.[33] Second, it obscures differences of approach between the systematic theology of Elizabethan-reformed theologians and the more lyrical approaches of conforming puritans of Herbert's generation such as Sibbes and Preston. In doing so, it makes it appear that Herbert is best contextualized with reference to early reformers such as Luther and Calvin. Yet, this interpretive frame obscures crucial features of Herbert's own immediate religious and literary culture. As I have suggested, Herbert participated in the softening of reformed theology witnessed during his generation, a softening that was broadly responsive to the emphasis on mystery characteristic of churchmen such as Andrewes, Hooker, and Sanderson and which was highly conducive to the development of religious poetry as an important cultural and spiritual

[32] See footnote 12 of the Introduction for references.
[33] See footnote 27 of the Introduction for references.

practice. In this respect, Herbert is better understood in relation to some key contemporaries than he is with reference to sixteenth-century reformers. One major reason for this is that he shared the view that a spiritually destructive eclipse of mystery was taking place in seventeenth-century England, especially with respect to scriptural hermeneutics to which we now turn.

CHAPTER 5

Herbert, Scripture, and Fellowship

In this and the following chapter, I explain how Herbert's investment in mystery finds expression in his critical reaction to two very different theological visions. First, I examine Herbert's response to the trivializing hermeneutics that he combats in *Briefe Notes on Valdesso's Considerations* (1638). Then in the following chapter, I consider his reaction to the rational theology evinced by his elder brother Edward's philosophy, particularly as expressed in *De Veritate* (1624). Despite their enormous differences from one other, the evangelical Valdés and the rationalist Cherbury share something essential in Herbert's view. They both diminish the space within which a scripturally centered mystery flourishes, thereby threatening the bonds of biblical fellowship. Herbert responded to the kinds of pressures exemplified by Valdés and Cherbury by stressing that the mystery of the Word constitutes the ground out of which the fellowship of the mystery grows. In Herbert's spiritual aesthetic, there is an intimate connection between learned ignorance and fellowship, the experience of cultivated nescience and the life of common prayer.[1]

[1] For important discussions of the more positive side to Herbert's reading of Valdés, see Clarke, *Theory and Theology*, 179–223, and Ilona Bell, "Herbert's Valdésian Vision," *ELR* 17 (1987), 303–328.

© The Author(s) 2017
G. Kuchar, *George Herbert and the Mystery of the Word*,
DOI 10.1007/978-3-319-44045-3_5

BRIEFE NOTES ON VALDESSO

Herbert's *Briefe Notes on Valdesso* was first published in 1638 as part of Nicholas Ferrar's English translation of Valdés' sixteenth-century theological treatise, *The Hundred and Ten Considerations* (1550). To Ferrar and Herbert, Valdés was a noble-born Spanish statesman whose status as a Roman Catholic did not prevent French and Italian protestants from embracing his works of experimental and practical divinity. Valdés was particularly celebrated by protestants for his Pauline-centered views on justification and mortification.[2] Within Italian Catholic circles, he was known for heading an evangelical reform group or *spirituali* center which included a number of influential members including Peter Martyr Vermigli.[3] After his death in 1540, Valdés' work was further championed by Cardinal Reginald Pole who was probably more responsible than Valdés himself for the spread of Valdesian heresy within reformed Catholic circles.[4] In twentieth-century scholarship, Valdés has been described as one of the most authentic religious geniuses of sixteenth-century Europe, a thinker whose ideas emerged from a fertile blend of Lutheranism, Erasmianism, and distinctly Spanish forms of spiritual radicalism.[5]

Valdés was trained in the evangelical-Franciscan ethos of the University of Alcalá under the directorship of Cardinal D. Fra. Franciso Ximénez de Cisnernos, one-time confessor of Queen Isabel, Archbishop of Toledo, Supreme Inquisitor, and twice regent of the kingdom.[6] Strongly committed to reforming the church, Cisneros encouraged translation of devotional material into the vernacular while strongly supporting rigorous biblical scholarship. Through his efforts to train future leaders in the newest advances in biblical study, the university eventually produced the enormously influential *Biblia Poliglota Complutense*, a six-volume multilingual edition of the bible which includes the first printed version of the

[2] See "The Publisher to the Reader" in *The Hundred and Ten Considerations of Signior John Valdèsso* (Oxford: 1638; rpt. John Lane: New York, n.d.), xxiii–iv.
[3] Daniel A. Crews, *Twilight of the Renaissance: The Life of Juan de Valdés* (Toronto: University of Toronto Press, 2008), 5, 106.
[4] Ibid., 154. See also Massimo Firpo, *Juan de Valdés and the Italian Reformation* trans. Richard Bates (Farnham: Ashgate, 2014), 123–176.
[5] See J.N. Bakhuizen van den Brink, *Juan de Valdés: réformateur en Espagne et en Italie 1529–1541* (Genève: Librairie Droz, 1969), 95 and Firpo, *Juan de Valdés*, 1–40.
[6] José C. Nieto, *Juan de Valdés And the Origins of the Spanish and Italian Reformation* (Genève: Libraire Droz 11 Rue Massot 1970), 51–54 and Firpo, *Juan de Valdés*, 6. The following paragraph derives mostly from Nieto.

Greek New Testament. It was within this scholarly context that Valdés developed an exegetical style that has been celebrated for its objectivity and modernity. In his exegetical work, Valdés applied recent developments in scholarship "to penetrate into the meaning of the biblical text and bring out the results in a brief, sober, and objective manner."[7] His concern was with the objective meaning of scripture independent of his own subjectivity, hence his refusal to sacrifice the grammatical meaning of the text in favor of pious mystical allegory.[8] This exegetical approach arose from Valdés' assumption that the bible is not a verbally inspired or divinely dictated book "but an expression of the right concepts about God, by men who had been moved by the Spirit."[9] Working from these assumptions, he concluded that scripture "is not always the word of God 'for me'."[10] Instead, it is a work that provides information on questions of ethics that is true in the same way in all times, places, and persons.

Valdés combined this scholarly approach to scripture with a very strong sense of the Holy Spirit's role in the individual Christian's life. Scholars have traced this spiritualist aspect of his piety to the so-called *Alumbrados* movement of early sixteenth-century Spain.[11] A Spanish word meaning "Enlightened ones," the term *Alumbrados* denotes a complex spiritual phenomenon which stressed the importance of personal experience through the motions of the Holy Spirit oftentimes at the expense of ecclesiastical authority, scripture, and tradition. In 1559, the Dominican theologian Melchor Cano identified the unorthodox dimensions of this movement when he observed that unlike Lutherans who "deduced the certainty of grace from faith, they deduced it from a feeling of experiencing the faith and the love of God, which they deluded themselves to be feeling."[12] Combined with a rather modest view of scripture's inspiration, this aspect of Valdés' spirituality worried not only the Spanish Inquisition but also the leaders of the Genevan Reformation. In a letter dated 2 September 1566, the ministers of Geneva, led by Theodore Beza, criticized a pastor of the French Church at Emden for publishing a Flemish translation of Valdés' *Considerations*. According to the letter, Valdés' work swarms "with many

[7] Nieto, *Juan de Valdés*, 195.
[8] Ibid.
[9] Ibid., 253.
[10] Ibid., 254.
[11] See Nieto, *Juan de Valdés* 56–60 and Firpo, *Juan de Valdés*, 5–16.
[12] Explained and cited in Firpo, *Juan de Valdés*, 16.

errors and even blasphemies against God's sacred word."[13] The ministers' general concern was not that Valdés was too Roman Catholic, but that his evident privileging of spiritual motions over scripture looked suspiciously Anabaptist.

Although Beza published a more positive assessment of Valdés in his 1580 work *Icones*, celebrating him and Vermigli for their reforming work in Naples, concern about the more radical dimensions of the Spaniard's thought lingered into the seventeenth century.[14] In his 1648 anti-sectarian work *A Survey of the Spirituall Antichrist*, Samuel Rutherford warns that Valdés provides the "grounds and poysonable principles of *Familisme, Antinomianisme, Enthusiasme*, for he rejecteth the Scriptures, [and] magnifieth Inspirations."[15] Responding to the positive reception of Valdés among civil war sectarians, Rutherford restates Herbert's basic criticisms of *Considerations* in more sharply polemical language. In particular, Rutherford shares Herbert's concern with Valdés' reducing of scripture to just so much information and the antinomian spiritualism attendant upon it. For Herbert, however, dogmatism and rationalism are not only dangerous because they take the form of social movements threatening Christians from the outside. More subtly, they are dangerous because they embody spiritual and interpretive postures that protect oneself from mortifying affliction, the spiritual suffering attendant upon sanctifying change. Ultimately, Herbert did not see the threat posed by Valdés as isolated to the antinomian or Anabaptist fringe. More significantly, he saw it as an inherent tendency arising from within the modern scriptural tradition, hence the sharpness of his critique.

Herbert's concerns with Valdés are initially broached in the prefatory letter to Ferrar. While congratulating Ferrar on his translation of a valuable treatise, Herbert nevertheless indicates that "there are some things which I like not in him" (304). Once having voiced such concern, he notes that the treatise is nevertheless worth publishing for "three eminent things observable therein" (304). First, the treatise is of historical interest as a proto-protestant work written in the midst of popery (304). Second, Valdés gives "great honour and reverence" to Christ, an observation that rightly notes the Christocentric nature of Valdés' anthropology. Third, Herbert admires Valdés' "pious rules" for the "ordering our life" (304–5).

---

[13] The letter is given as Appendix IV in van den Brink, *Juan de Valdé*s, 112–13.
[14] See Nieto, 15 and Massimo, 197–208.
[15] Rutherford, *A Survey of the Spirituall Antichrist* (London: 1648), 164.

Ultimately though, Herbert is forced to admit that he finds the treatise's treatment of biblical exegesis "unsufferable" (318).

Herbert's major critique of *Considerations* centers on his belief that Valdés severs God's word from God himself. Rather than identifying scripture as the bearer of the living Word, Valdés reduces scripture to a set of catechistical-style messages. Herbert thus complains:

> These words about the H. Scripture suite with what he writes elsewhere, especially Consid. 32. But I like none of it, for it slights Scripture too much: holy Scriptures have not only an Elementary use, but a use of perfection, and are able to make the man of God perfect, 2 *Tim. 3.* (306)

For Herbert, the pursuit of holiness happens in and through scripture as the context of spiritual life. This is what he means when he insists:

> All the Saints of God may be said in some sence to have put confidence in Scripture, but not as a naked Word severed from God, but as the Word of God: And in so doing they doe not sever their trust from God. But by trusting in the word of God they trust in God. (306–7)

The basic problem Herbert diagnoses is that Valdés nullifies the Word's power to generate ongoing significance in the life of the individual believer. Valdés kills off the Spirit's inspiration of the living Word by wrongly presupposing that the bible's horizon of expectation can be reached and even surpassed. This is why Herbert later claims that the gospel is "ever outrunning the Teacher" (310), ever surpassing both priest and layman alike. In emphasizing this dimension of scripture, Herbert echoes Saint Gregory's assertion that the Word "advances with those who read it" thereby sustaining the *pro nobis* principle so central to orthodox reformation hermeneutics.[16]

At stake in Herbert's critique of Valdés is nothing less than the ontology of scripture. In it he asks if the bible is a story that circumscribes one within its ever-receding frame, making the Christian believer more like a character in an evolving story than a subscriber to a philosophy or constitutional charter. In other words, does the bible continue to function as a book of mysteries? Or is it better understood as a book of promises that one can take possession of once and for all? Is it essentially dynamic,

---

[16] Cited in Lubac, *Medieval Exegesis*, 2.205.

ongoing, and richly complex, thereby involving a strong sense of uncertainty and open-endedness? Or is it static, propositional, and straightforwardly simple, thereby involving real certainty? How Herbert answers these questions is as crucial to his poetics as it is to the social and ecclesiastical vision that his poetry serves.

From a hermeneutical standpoint, the differences between Herbert and Valdés are fundamental. Where Herbert insists that the significance of scripture is constantly beyond our full grasp, Valdés assumes that the message of scripture can be attained once and for all. Valdés thus perceives the gospel as only so much information, something one can absorb and possess, like an image or the alphabet. Recognizing the spiritual implications of this eclipse of biblical narrative, Herbert expresses dismay:

> I much mislike the Comparison of Images, and H. Scripture, as if they were both but Alphabets and after a time to be left. The H. Scriptures (as I wrote before) have not only an Elementary use, but a use of perfection, neither can they ever be exhausted, (as Pictures may be by a plenarie circumspection) but still even to the most learned and perfect in them, there is somewhat to be learned more. (309)

According to Herbert, Valdés does not allow for the idea that biblical revelation speaks to individual believers over the course of their lives in varying contexts. He thus worries aloud that without a view of scripture as a story in which one is a character moving toward but never fully reaching "perfection," Christianity leaves room for nothing but "catechizing and ... Enthusiasmes" (310). In other words, if the Word can be learned as though it were no different than an alphabet, then all that is left for Christianity, Herbert worries, are propositional statements of the sort one finds in catechisms or, worse yet, the nonsensical delusions of fanatical "visionaries" moved by the "Spirit." For Herbert, Valdés exemplifies some of the most reductive aspects of post-reformation scriptural hermeneutics.

Reacting to Valdés' "abuse ... of Holy Scriptures" (309), Herbert makes an important distinction between two major features of biblical revelation, its doctrines and its promises. In the scriptures, Herbert explains, are " *[Doctrines, these ever teach more and more.* [And] *[Promises, these ever comfort more and more. Rom. 15.4"* (310). Crucially, for Herbert, these two dimensions of scripture do not have equal standing. As he explains, the "use of the Doctrinall part, is more, in regard it presents us not with the same thing only when it is read as the promises doe, but enlightens us with new Considerations the more we read it" (310). This distinction implies Herbert's awareness that the Latinate sense of *doctrina* captures some of what Augustine thought Paul's sense of *mystery* entails. Rather than denoting a statement or philosophy, doctrine signifies teaching, lesson, or even more broadly culture or tradition, as in Augustine's *De Doctrina Christiana*.

Herbert's twofold distinction of scripture's contents collapses the four-fold definition offered in *The Country Parson* when he argues that scripture contains "Precepts for life, Doctrines for knowledge, Examples for illustration, and Promises for Comfort" (228). In *Valdesso's Considerations*, the first three are folded into the doctrinal dimension. Notably, though, this dimension involves not just the "plain and evident declaration" of the biblical text that Herbert's country parson should explicate for his largely uneducated audience; it now also consists of "observations drawn out of whole text," its potential consequences for different readers in different situations. In this respect, the concept of doctrine in *Valdesso's Consideration* denotes the sort of teaching that one never finishes with, a Christian *paideia* involving ongoing edification rather than the sort of training involved in a catechism which can be done with at a certain point.

In stressing the point that scripture involves more than bare messages or information, Herbert pursues an exegetical vision similar to the one Jeremy Taylor advocates in his 1647 work *The Liberty of Prophesying*. Explaining the multiform nature of scriptural revelation, Taylor argues that the bible's richness constitutes the very condition for charity and fellowship. While acknowledging that basic creeds are expressed clearly in scripture, Taylor also admits that

> there are innumerable places, containing in them great mysteries, but yet either so inwrapped with a cloud, or so darkened with umbrages or heightened with expressions ... that God may seem to have left them as trials of our industry, and arguments of our imperfections, and incentives to the longings after heaven.[17]

Writing in the wake of the civil war, Taylor sees the complexity and mystery of scripture as providing the "occasions and opportunities of our mutual charity and toleration to each other and humility in ourselves, rather than the repositories of faith, and furniture of creeds, and articles

---

[17] Jeremy Taylor, *The Whole Works in Ten Volumes* (London: Longman, 1862), 5.410.

of belief."[18] Deepening elements in Hooker's thought, Taylor argues that what should bind the community together is not only a commitment to a set of fixed creeds or doctrinal propositions but a shared pursuit of the truth carried out in open-ended honesty regarding the reality of human limitations. There is a striking emphasis here on the way wonder and the ongoing pursuit of truth ground Christian fellowship. For Taylor, the proper interpretive disposition is one that admits its own provisionality. This is why he argues that misinterpreting scripture is perfectly excusable, so long as it is committed "by a mind prepared to consent in that truth which God intended," a mind, that is, that can admit its mistakes.[19]

Like Herbert, Taylor assumes that reading scripture is concomitant with misreading it. After all, Taylor admits, scripture has "very many senses" and there are many different "designs of expounding" it.[20] What is more, there are no infallible rules of interpretation, no sure method for guaranteeing the validity of one's exegesis. As Taylor observes, even the literal or grammatical meaning can cause no end of problems,

> for there is in very many scriptures a double sense, a literal and a spiritual … and both these senses are subdivided. For the literal sense is either natural or figurative: and the spiritual is sometimes allegorical, sometimes anagogical; nay, sometimes there are divers literal sense in the same sentence.[21]

What is even worse for those eager to fix the divine Word into one meaning is the realization that there is no infallible rule for determining whether a passage is literal or figurative in the first place.[22]

Perhaps most disconcerting for those in search of certainty is the spiritual disposition required for proper exegesis. Following the same Augustinian tradition that Sibbes extends, Taylor assumes that there is no ultimate distinction between the subjective state of readers and the significance they derive from scripture. The two are intimately co-related precisely insofar as "there are some *secreta theologiae*, which are only to be understood by persons very holy and spiritual."[23] Given this interpenetration of reader and

---

[18] Ibid.

[19] Ibid., 411. For the limits of Taylor's irenicism vis-à-vis the state of emergency, see Novarr, *Making of Walton's Lives*, 372.

[20] Ibid., 414.

[21] Ibid., 414.

[22] Ibid., 416–417.

[23] Ibid., 419.

Word, no one can be infallibly certain of his own interpretation of scripture. As a result, error is an inevitable, even sometimes productive, dimension of spiritual reading. Taylor thus concludes that there is "a very great necessity in allowing a liberty in prophesying, without prescribing authoritatively to other men's consciences, and becoming lords and masters of their faith."[24]

Despite some obvious differences, much of what Taylor says in *The Liberty of Prophesying* closely squares with Herbert's *Briefe Notes* and *The Temple*. Ultimately, what Herbert saw in Valdés was a tendency to reduce scripture to an inventory of messages, a reduction that he saw as equivalent to the kiss of spiritual death. Once scripture is perceived primarily in terms of message and promise rather than teaching and mystery, one can take hold of it as though it had the status of an account book rather than experiencing it as a living context in which one moves. Herbert's critique of Valdés thus lies in the way he sees him as privileging scripture's objective or promissory dimensions over its mysteriously edifying and thus necessarily personal aspects.

Like Taylor, Herbert believed that exaggerated claims to certainty were falsely reassuring, providing believers with a delusional sense of being in possession of simple, propositional truth. By emphasizing doctrine over promise, and by defining *doctrina* as an evolving spiritual context rather than a collection of propositional statements, Herbert sought to curtail reductive approaches to scripture. This critique of certainty is clearest in Herbert's commentary on Valdés' 63rd Consideration. According to Herbert,

> The Authour doth still discover too slight a regard of the Scripture, as if it were but childrens meat, whereas there is not onely milk there, *but strong meat also. Heb. 5. 14. Things hard to bee understood. 2 Pet. 3.1.6. Things needing great Consideration. Mat. 24. 15.* (317)

Importantly, Herbert's emphasis on the complexity of scripture here goes further than the Elizabethan Homilies. While the Homilies admit "that many things in the Scripture be spoken in obscure mysteries," they qualify the point by insisting that "there is no thing spoken under darke mysteries in one place, but the selfe same thing in other places, is spoken more familiarly and plainly, to the capacity both of learned and unlearned."[25] This is a standard view easily found in a huge range of medieval and reformed thinkers. But like Andrewes' sermon on 1 Timothy 3:16, it is not the point

---

[24] Ibid., 421.
[25] *Certain sermons or homilies* (London: 1551), B2v.

that Herbert stresses. Avoiding the standard claim about biblical simplicity, Herbert quotes scripture in order to make the point that the bible possesses *"Things hard to bee understood"* and *"Things needing great Consideration."* As Herbert implies, the word *consideration* deployed here and in Valdés' title is a relatively technical term referring to a process of combined meditation and prayer.[26] The implication of Herbert's critique is that scripture is the site of ongoing, prayerful, meditation rather than information-transfer. More than simply read, the scriptural text must be lived in order to be understood.

What emerges from Herbert's response to Valdés is a palpable concern that a particular mode of reading scripture was at risk of being overshadowed in seventeenth-century Europe. According this vision, the bible confers meaning upon believers in a way that is difficult to control or know in advance precisely insofar as the story of revelation includes readers within its unfolding narrative structure.

THE H. SCRIPTURES (I) AND (II)

At the center of Herbert's *Briefe Notes* is a distinction between the bible's message-centered and mystery-bearing features, its promises and its doctrines. In *The Temple,* this basic distinction forms the main thread connecting "The H. Scriptures (I)" and "The H. Scriptures (II)." In these two poems, Herbert gives us his most explicit description of the bible as a beloved with whom the loving reader forms a relationship. The result is nothing less than a new kind of sonnet, one that instead of addressing a human beloved praises scripture as "quick and powerful," living and active (Heb. 4:12). Taken together, these two poems trace an increasingly mature view of scripture, one that moves from the relative stability and certainty of promise to the wonder of *sacra doctrina.*

In both sonnets, the bible is addressed as a living presence orienting the life of the believer. But in the first of the two lyrics, scripture is praised for offering consolation as though it were like an account book in which one could calculate God's promises, as some seventeenth-century autobiographers sought to do.[27] Yet the poem goes even further, expressing what a 1992 study of Christian Prayer describes in a different context

[26] For a discussion of Valdés' use of this term, see Nieto, 188.
[27] See Watkins, *The Puritan Experience,* 21.

as the fundamentalist tendency to view scripture "as if it were a medicine chest: full of disparate remedies but each useful for a specific malady."[28] James Boyd White notices this too, remarking that Herbert "imagines Scripture as a kind of snake-oil that will cure all 'grief', all 'pain'."[29] Such a limited view emerges from the speaker's description of the bible through images of ambassadorial messages, ledgers (account books), handsells (or initial installments of payment), and medicinal drugs, all of which figure the bible as a book of promises:

> Oh Book! infinite sweetness! let my heart
>   Suck ev'ry letter, and a hony gain,
>   Precious for any grief in any part;
> To cleare the breast, to mollifie all pain.
>
> 5   Thou art all health, health thriving, till it make
>   A full eternitie: thou art a masse
>   Of strange delights, where we may wish & take.
> Ladies, look here; this is the thankfull glass,
>
> 10 That mends the lookers eyes: this is the well
>   That washes what it shows. Who can indeare
>   Thy praise too much? thou art heav'ns Lidger here,
> Working against the states of death and hell.
>
>   Thou art joyes handsell: heav'n lies flat in thee,
> 14 Subject to ev'ry mounters bended knee.

The opening stanza recalls Herbert's description of scripture in *The Country Parson* as "the storehouse and magazine of life and comfort … There he sucks, and lives" (228). But rather than being a literal restatement of prose ideas into poetry, "The H. Scriptures (I)" shows a speaker developing toward a fuller understanding of scripture; hence the speaker's naïve desire to "suck ev'ry letter" as though he could eventually be done with scripture the way one finishes with a meal. This is precisely the kind of reductive biblicism that the preface to the King James Bible rejects when

---

[28] Lawrence S. Cunningham, *Catholic Prayer* (New York: Crossroad, 1992), 81.
[29] James Boyd White, '*This Book of Starres*': *Learning to Read George Herbert* (Ann Arbor: University of Michigan Press, 1995), 164.

Miles Smith warns that scripture "is not a pot of Manna, or a cruse of oil, which were for memory only, or for a meal's meat or two, but as it were a shower of heavenly bread sufficient for a whole host, be it never so great" (n.p.). The speaker's limitations are further conveyed by his huckster-like cry of a barker or street vendor: "Ladies, look here; this is the thankfull glasse" (8).[30] The tone here sharply contrasts Augustine's more austere depiction of scripture as "a mirror [that] is held out to you. See whether you are one of the pure-hearted it mentions, and grieve if you are not yet like that; grieve in order to become so. The mirror will reflect your face to you" (19.110).[31] So, while it is probably too much to say that the praise Herbert's speaker "utters is distorted and mistaken from the beginning,"[32] his focus remains largely on "the letter" and thus the promissory dimension of scripture. This association of the bible's promise with its letter prevents Herbert's speaker from falling prey to an overly deadening view of scripture, something he further avoids by asserting that scripture cannot be praised "too much" as though its "strange delights" were incalculable.

The description of scripture changes significantly in sonnet two. Now images of payment and ambassadorial message-bearing evolve into images of light and illumination. Rather than describing scripture as though it were a medicine that one could take once and be done with, "The H. Scriptures (II)" describes it as a light that continually shows the way. Yet, the limited understanding of scripture as a book of promises still lingers in the first stanza of sonnet two as the speaker hopes to grasp how all of scripture's parts unite into one totalizing whole. This is the basic, Valdésian error that the poem will eventually correct:

> Oh that I knew how all thy lights combine,
>   And the configurations of their glorie!
>   Seeing not onely how each verse doth shine,
> But all the constellations of the storie. (1–4)

The speaker begins by making the standard assumption that a reading of the bible is complete when the individual parts of the work are recon-

---

[30] The term *huckster* is John Drury's, *Music at Midnight*, 9; the terms *barker* and *street-vendor* are White's, *This Book of Starres*, 164.

[31] This and other patristic articulations of the idea of scripture as mirror are discussed in Chretién, *Under the Gaze of the Bible*, 6–22.

[32] White, *This Book of Starres*, 164.

ciled with the whole. This view, however, obscures the extent to which the bible discloses the living Word of God as its ethical and spiritual teachings are overshadowed by its soteriological promises. The turn toward this insight occurs when the speaker reorients his perspective in order to accommodate the view that scripture is a *sacramentum* in which one participates even before it is a promise that one receives. In other words, the speaker begins to appreciate the extent to which the Logos has an ontological as well as an historical dimension; it is a Being in which one moves as well as an event to which one must respond.[33] Without such a dynamic view of scripture, reading can devolve into a legalistic, closed-ended activity in which meaning becomes a predictable matter of obtaining information rather than a surprising process of discovering oneself anew.

This widening of perspective occurs in the third quatrain of "The H. Scriptures (II)" with the introduction of the term *secrets*, a close synonym of Paul's *mysteria*:

> Such are thy secrets, which my life makes good,
>   And comments on thee: for in ev'ry thing
>   Thy words do finde me out, & parallels bring,
> And in another make me understood. (9–12)

This sequence outlines a reading process in which the text confers meaning on the reader even as the reader interprets the text. Crucially, this exegesis happens through first-hand apprehension rather than abstract intellectual comprehension. It is through "life" that he discovers and rediscovers the significance of the holy text, a process that presupposes the hermeneutical openness of scripture, its capacious ability to incorporate individual experience within an open-ended pattern that adapts to him as he readapts to it. Bearing this in mind, the text's "secrets" refer not only to specific meanings within scripture but to the inexhaustible process of discovery that happens in and through it. This is why Herbert follows Augustine in insisting that the bible not only possess mysteries but is, itself, a mystery. Such is the Herberterian view that Henry Vaughan explores in "The Agreement" when he addresses the bible as "The mount, whose white ascendents may / Be in conjunction with true light! (15–16)."

---

[33] For a brief explanation of the distinction between the Word as Being and the Word as Deed, see Jaroslav Pelikan, *Luther's Works*, 56:54.

Vaughan's astrological figure suggests that the bible's meaning is like "the point of the ecliptic, or degree of the Zodiac, which at any moment ... is just rising about the eastern horizon."[34] The implication here is that Christians are immanent participants within the scriptural narrative not transcendent observers of it.

Behind Herbert's and Vaughan's astronomical figures lies the theological tradition of describing scripture's *skopos*, its "goal," "aim," "target," "design," or "method" with the navigational sighting of a star for the sake of orientation. As Margaret O'Rourke Boyle explains, the term *skopos* acquired this particular theological valence in Erasmus, especially his *Enchirdion*. For the Catholic reformer, "the true astrotheologian does not gawk at pagan deities frozen into constellations like Cynosura [Ursa Minor]. He fixes on Christ alone" because Christ is the fixed-sign or *praefixum signum* that orients the spiritual life.[35] Intriguingly, Herbert and Vaughan avoid this association of scriptural *skopos* with a "fixed sign" (76–77). Once it becomes clear that scripture confers ongoing and dynamic meaning, the analogy between the bible and constellations at the beginning of "The H. Scriptures (II)" diminishes in significance. Acknowledging the limitations of his astronomical analogy, the speaker of "The H. Scriptures (II)" arrives at a view of the bible as a medium in which one moves as well a series of unfolding messages to which one should be responsive. He realizes that "Starres are poore books, & oftentimes do misse: / This book of starres lights to eternall blisse" (11–12). The implication here is that scripture is not only a guide but also a path, not only, or even primarily, a specific set of directions or regulations but more crucially a spiritual orientation or relatively open-ended way. Herbert thus drops the idea that the bible's *skopos* can be compared with astronomical forms of sighting precisely because they imply a somewhat fixed or predictable mode of reading. If the bible lets in "future times," as Herbert says in "The bunch of grapes," it does so in a way that is unpredictably dynamic ("bunch of grapes," 13) from the standpoint of the first-person reader. Herbert makes much the same point in "The Temper" when he describes the Holy Spirit as a power who "suddenly dost raise and race / And ev'ry day a new Creatour art" ("The Temper (II)," 7–8). As these lines imply, the

---

[34] OED Cited in Martz, *George Herbert and Henry Vaughan* (Oxford: Oxford UP, 1986), 534.

[35] Marjorie O'Rourke Boyle, *Erasmus on Language and Method in Theology* (Toronto: University of Toronto Press, 1977), 81.

Spirit not only destroys and makes new on a quotidian basis, but it also runs ahead, blazing "fresh and new discov'ries," hence the repeated rediscovery in *The Temple* that the speaker is behind, before, and within the Word. For example, when he regretfully says in "The Reprisall" "though I die for thee, I am behind" (3), he stumbles on an insight that is repeatedly rediscovered throughout the whole of *The Temple*. The movement between the two "H. Scriptures" poems encapsulates this sequence-long process of assimilating and being assimilated by the Word.

The Bunch of Grapes

The spiritual and exegetical movement that takes place between "The H. Scriptures (I) and (II)" in *The Temple* also occurs within single poems, most notably perhaps "The bunch of grapes." This lyric exemplifies Herbert's sense that reading scripture is concomitant with misreading it. The common, even perhaps inevitable, mistake that the speaker makes involves the legalistic error of assuming that one can freeze God's Word in place, as though its medium were stone rather than voice, visual image rather than living Spirit. This mistaken desire for interpretive control gives "The bunch of grapes" its spiritual and exegetical exigency. The poem stages a crisis of reading in which the desire for spiritual fixity gives rise to a reductive understanding of scripture as a closed-ended text in which everything is predictably laid out beforehand. In this way, the poem depicts how scripture's saving and sanctifying power can devolve into an abstract and deadening letter when Christians expect to possess gospel without law and joy without affliction. For Herbert, as we have seen, the life of grace lies in fully embracing strife rather than hoping that one might be exempted from suffering.

The spiritual and interpretive crises played out in "The bunch of grapes" are evinced earlier in *The Temple* when the speaker of "The Temper" asks:

> ...how should my rymes
> Gladly engrave thy love in steel,
> If what my soul doth feel sometimes,
> My soul might ever feel! (1–4)

While the sentiment here is admirable, the idioms are askew. The desire to *engrave* God is potentially idolatrous, a point that is further conveyed when the word *engrave* is echoed in the speaker's feeling that though the world is too small for God it remains "A grave too big for me" (12). The same mistake is repeated in the following poem of the same title when the speaker asks God to "fix [his] chair of grace" so that he might be reduced to human control and domination (2, 9). This immature tendency to equate divine love with emotional stasis recurs throughout *The Temple*, giving rise to poems such as "The Glimpse" which begins: "Wither away delight? / Thou cam'st but now; wilt thou so soon depart, / And give me up to night?" (1–3). In each of these poems, the desire for stasis intimates a defensive posture against the mortifying force of the Word as law.

In these moments of psycho-spiritual defense, Herbert diagnoses the tendency among Christians to enjoy the grace of gospel without the justice of law that Lancelot Andrewes and Richard Sibbes both warn against. In a 1623 Nativity Sermon at Whitehall, Andrewes, as we have already seen, critiques those who downplay the importance of law so as to accentuate the experience of assurance under grace, declaring:

> We had well hoped, Christ would have preached no law, all Gospel He. That He would have preached down the old Law, but not have preached up any new. We see it otherwise. A law He hath to preach, and preach it He will … If we love not to hear of a law, we must go to some other Church; for in Christ's Church there a law is preached. (1.287)

The problem with expecting joy without affliction, Andrewes continues, is that it does not have the desired spiritual effect. In fact, it makes matters worse as locking up joy inadvertently results in a forceful return of the law that can cause a severe spiritual crisis. As Andrewes warns:

> Gospel it how we will, if the Gospel hath not the *legalia* of it acknowledged, allowed, and preserved to it; if once it lose the force and vigour of a law, it is a sign it declines, it grows weak and unprofitable, and that is a sign it will not long last. We must go look our salvation by some other way than by *Filius Meus Tu*, if *Filius Meus Tu* (I say not be preached, but) be not so preached, as Christ preached it; and Christ preached it as a law. And so much for *legem*. (1.289)

In other words, the desire for the gospel without the law is an inadvertent form of legalism; it reduces the dynamic interplay of Word and Spirit that is of the very essence of scripture as a living presence, thereby making

God's actions predictable and comprehensible. In this respect, exaggerated expectations of assurance come at a high spiritual and interpretive cost because it deludes Christians into thinking that they are in control of God's Word. Ultimately, the more one tries to repress law, the more it returns in the form of an inadvertent legalism. Herbert's "The bunch of grapes" begins at the very moment when the force of law suddenly returns from being repressed, thereby shocking his speaker into speech. Rather than recording a displacement of the law, "The bunch of grapes" shows a speaker learning the hard way that the law is "our Schoolmaster *to bring us* unto Christ, that we might be justified by faith" (Gal. 3:24). In this poem, then, the implied backstory returns us to the pattern explored in "Affliction, (1)": "My dayes were straw'd with flow'rs and happinesse; / There was no moneth but May. / But with my yeares sorrow did twist and grow, / And made a partie unawares for wo" (21–24). Only now the issue is more explicitly exegetical as the speaker over-identifies with the experience of Jewish exile at the brook of Eshcol when the Jewish elders cut down a large cluster of grapes to prove the bounty of the giant-inhabited Canaan to the other Hebrews (Num. 13:23–24).

Richard Sibbes addresses these same themes regarding law and gospel in his 1630 treatise *The Bruised Reed*. Fascinatingly though, he adopts a very different perspective than the anti-puritan one detectable in Andrewes' sermon. According to Sibbes,

There is a dangerous slighting of the work of humiliation, some alleging this for a pretence for their overly dealing with their own hearts, that Christ will not break the bruised reed; but such must know that every sudden terror and short grief is not that which makes us bruised reeds … but a working our hearts to such a grief as will make sin more odious unto us than punishment. (1.47)

Here the critique is leveled at those who are not rigorous enough in their self-analysis, letting themselves off the hook too easily. So, rather than identifying exessive optimism with "carnal Gospellers" (5.58) as Andrewes does, Sibbes identifies it with those who are spiritually lazy. Always careful to avoid polemic with fellow protestants, Sibbes balances his implied critique of nonpuritan conformists by admitting: "It is dangerous, I confess, in some cases with some spirits, to press too much and too long this bruising, because they may die under the wound and burden before they be raised up again" (1.47). For Sibbes, "Where most holiness is, there is most moderation" (1.57). His ultimate concern in *The Bruised Reed*, however, is with the overemphasis on saving grace which is "the cause oft of relapses and apostasies, because men never smarted for sin at the first; they were not long enough under the lash of the law" (1.44). In his view, "Weakness with watchfulness will stand out, when strength with too much confidence faileth" (1.86).

Like the misguided efforts to render God's revelation statically unchanging that Andrewes warns against, the speaker of "The bunch of grapes" confesses to having tried to "lock up" Joy. Having not spent enough time "under the lash of the law," the speaker now finds himself undergoing the kind of relapse that Sibbes diagnoses in *The Bruised Reed*. Herbert's speaker begins:

> Joy, I did lock thee up: but some bad man
> > Hath let thee out again:
> And now, me thinks I am where I began
> > Sev'n yeares ago: one vogue and vein,
> > One aire of thoughts usurps my brain.
> I did toward Canaan draw; but now I am
> Brought back to the Red sea, the sea of shame. (1–7)

The spiritual crisis motivating this poem is initiated by the speaker's desire to possess a mind unchanged by place or time. Unfortunately, this expectation overlooks the inherently multifaceted or "crazy" dimension of the human personality ("The Windows," 2). For Herbert, the human soul is more a "medley" of voices than an individuated unity ("Mans medley"). Absent of real self-knowledge, the speaker finds himself shocked by the "bad man" whom he does not see coming, namely a different aspect of himself. Even worse, his spiritual disposition prior to the poem denies the extent to which "Mans joy and pleasure / Rather hereafter, then in present, is" ("Mans medley," 5–6), a realization that many of Herbert's speakers struggle with.

In stanza two of "The bunch of grapes," the speaker projects this desire for stasis onto the signifying force of the Word. In doing so, he gains a perspective from which the Word appears to mean the same thing for all Christians everywhere at all times. This allows him to recover a sense of control, the loss of which brought him into speech in the first place. Unexpectedly, though, the Word now begins to feel like a noose tightening around him:

> For as the Jews of old by Gods command
> Travell'd, and saw no town:
> So now each Christian hath his journeys spann'd:
> Their storie pennes and sets us down. (8–11)

What is important here is not only what he says, but the position of presumed transcendence from which he thinks he says it. Rather than being fully immanent within the scriptural narrative (on the journey that it outlines), the speaker presumes that he is temporally behind the Word while nevertheless remaining exegetically ahead of it. The illusion here lies in his assumption that he can fully comprehend his spiritual state from a third-person point of view, a position that ultimately nullifies the conditions of hope and faith, thereby giving rise to either presumption or despair. By adopting this attitude, the speaker makes the same type of mistake disclosed in the final lines of "Miserie," where an ostensibly objective account of man's miseries turns out, rather shockingly, to be a first-person narrative: "Now he is / ... A sick toss'd vessel, dashing on each thing; / Nay, his own shelf: / My God, I mean my self" (73, 77–78). And yet, despite his interpretive presupposition of transcendence, the speaker of "The bunch of grapes" nevertheless complains that he is penned in and by the Word, claustrophobically impaled by it to use a startling image from "The Church-porch" (21). The expectation of constant joy has engendered an interpretive attitude in which the divine Word is fixed in place resulting in a sense of alienation from God. In a terrible reversal of expectation, the speaker achieves the stasis he desired but in the opposite way he had hoped.

The crisis explored in "The bunch of grapes" arises from the speaker's wrongheaded expectation to be in a constant state of emotionally legible assurance by enjoying the fruits of gospel without the thorns of law. In this respect, the poem dramatizes the dangers of adopting an overly objective view of scripture in the spiritually opposite way that "Self-condemnation" does. If "The bunch of grapes" exposes how unrealistic expectations of constant joy can give rise to spiritual deadness, then the speaker of "Self-condemnation" warns against spiritual pride and self-conceit. In both cases, however, readers are warned against assuming that they know what significance scripture may hold out for them. As the speaker of "Self-condemnation" warns

> Thou who condemnest Jewish hate,
> For choosing Barabbas a murderer

> Before the Lord of glorie;
> Look back upon thine own estate,
> Call home thine eye (that busie wanderer)
> That choice may be thy storie. (1–6)

In these two poems, Herbert connects spiritual overconfidence with interpretive overconfidence, both of which result in a dangerously reductive version of Christianity. The parallels here with Valdés are striking. Recall, for example, how Herbert criticizes Valdés for articulating the doctrine of reprobation or God's hardening of the heart in dangerously blunt ways, cautiously remarking: "This doctrine, however true in substance, yet needeth discreet, and wary explaining" (314). Conversely, Herbert warns against the antinomian potential within Valdés' thought by reasserting the distinction between divine and civil law, observing that a war may be legally just on both sides as it indeed was for both Canaanites and Israelites (316). What clearly worries Herbert about Valdés is the overconfidence subtending his overall spiritual disposition, an overconfidence that expresses itself exegetically, soteriologically, and politically through its theologically naïve assumption of pure objectivity. These same interconnections between spiritual and interpretive dispositions animate the crisis unfolding in "The bunch of grapes" as unrealistic expectations of joy drive the speaker to an interpretively reductive and spiritually deadening objectivism.

In his effort to sustain an unrealistic sense of constant assurance, the speaker in "The bunch of grapes" is driven to a spiritually deadening interpretation of Christian life as circumscribed by the narrative of Jewish exile. In the speaker's mind, there is no difference between Jewish history and Christian narrative in the sense that both are complete; their significance is predictable and unchanging. With law having supplanted gospel and letter having absorbed spirit, the history of Jewish exile looks identical to the story of Christian life. Emptied of all mystery, the bible can now be read the same way in all times and places and by all people; or as the speaker would have it: "So now each Christian hath his journeys spann'd: / Their storie pennes and sets us down" (10–11). This reified typological connection between Jewish history and Christian story is a spiritually dangerous example of what Luther means by law as an exegetical attitude rather than a specific narrative content. For Luther, as we have seen, law and gospel are two different ways of talking about and experiencing God's revelation. Where law speaks primarily in the imperative mood, placing demands upon readers, gospel speaks in the declarative mood, proclaiming and giving what the law demands. According to Luther, "The law *commands that we should have love and that we should have Jesus Christ,* but the gospel *offers and presents* both to us."[36] In this respect, gospel is the dimension of scripture that prevents a living story from becoming a deadening history. Rather than being a thematic description of the bible's content, the law/gospel distinction is Luther's answer to the threat of historicism that he saw in exegetes such as Nicholas of Lyra. Taking the form of a dialectic, the movement between law and gospel sustains the possibility of living a scripturally oriented life in which the bible is both history and story, both commanding law and saving spirit. By reducing the Christian journey to the history of Jewish exile, Herbert's speaker occludes the saving dimension of the biblical narrative, turning a living story into something past and complete. For Luther, this is what scripture looks like when viewed from the pseudo-objective perspective of history and law rather than the first-person point of view of mystery and Spirit. And as Herbert and Andrewes both warn, it is how scripture comes to look when one expects to live in a permanent state of spiritual confidence.

Understood hermeneutically, the truth of gospel in Luther's sense of the term does not denote the objective correspondence between interpretation and text. Instead, it signals the individual believer's unfolding relationship to Christ. Consequently, the goal of interpretation is personal assimilation of the story rather than impersonal description of a history. Such interpretation involves the kind of spiritual exegesis that Herbert's speaker rediscovers in "The H. Scriptures (II)" where the Christian appropriates and is appropriated by the Word. It is precisely this dimension of scripture that the speaker of "The bunch of grapes" loses sight of when he declares: "Gods works are wide, and let in future times; / His ancient justice overflows our crimes" (13–14). What is crucial here is the "our," the alienating sense of historical abstraction orienting his interpretive disposition. The speaker finds himself adopting a retrospective view in which the meaning of his present suffering has been locked in place through the story of Jewish exile which he apparently perceives from a God's-eye view. At the very moment he admits that he remains behind the Word temporally, he behaves as though he were ahead of it semiotically. As Luther warned, this is what happens when law absorbs gospel and letter freezes Spirit.

[36] Cited in Forde, *Law and Gospel*, 242. Italics are Forde's.

The grip of law begins to loosen in the penultimate stanza of "The bunch of grapes" when the focus shifts from God's commands to his gifts:

> Then have we too our guardian fires and clouds;
> Our Scripture-dew drops fast:
> We have our sands and serpents, tents and shrowds;
> Alas! our murmurings come not last.
> But where's the cluster? where's the taste
> Of mine inheritance? Lord, if I must borrow,
> Let me as well take up their joy, as sorrow. (15–21)

As Chana Bloch observes, "The question [where's the taste / Of mine inheritance?] carries within itself an implicit answer: 'O taste and see how gracious the Lord is'; 'The Lord himselfe is the portion of mine inheritance, and of my cup'" (Pss. 34:8, 16:6).[37] In this context, the word *taste* bears the sense of embodied foreknowledge much as the Latin term *sapere* ("to know") does. At this point, Herbert's speaker has no feeling, no embodied awareness, of God's saving presence, those "pledges of love" that Herbert addresses in *The Country Parson*,[38] hence the searchingly bewildered tone of "Alas! our murmurings come not last" and the falling rhythm of "Our Scripture-dew drops fast." Revealingly, Herbert's use of the term *taste* is very similar to the meaning that Sibbes gives it in his commentary on 2 Corinthians when he explains that Christians can rejoice in their afflictions precisely insofar as their assurance of God's graciousness rests on an underlying awareness of his spiritually nourishing presence. According to Sibbes,

> So good is God, that in the worst estate he gives his children matter of rejoicing in this world. He gives them a taste of heaven before they come there. He gives them a grape of Canaan, as Israel. They tasted of Canaan, what a good land it was, before they came thither. So God's children, they have their rejoicing. St Paul sweares and protests it, 1 Cor. xv. 31, 'By our rejoicing in Christ Jesus I die daily.' As verily as we joy in all our afflictions, so this is true that I say, that I die daily. (3.206)[39]

---

[37] Bloch, *Spelling the Word*, 144.
[38] See Chap. 2.
[39] Daniel Doerksen makes a related point with reference to Sibbes in *Conforming to the Word*, 131. For a parallel passage in Andrewes, see 3.161.

In the penultimate stanza, the speaker has not yet assimilated the full force of Paul's paradox as he still feels caught within the grip of a deadening law. Although his interpretive stance has broadened to include the tension between gospel and law, he has not yet fully avowed its saving or sanctifying effects.

These effects do not begin to register until the final stanza when the speaker achieves his first fully mature articulation of the tension between Moses and Christ, justice and mercy. At this point, the speaker arrives at a rather humble and hesitating epiphany:

> But can he want the grape, who hath the wine?
> I have their fruit and more.
> Blessed be God, who prosper'd *Noahs* vine,
> And made it bring forth grapes good store.
> But much more him I must adore.
> Who of the laws sowre juice sweet wine did make,
> Ev'n God himself, being pressed for my sake. (22–28)

For the first time in the poem, law discloses gospel; hence the speaker's first-person response to Christ's sacrifice "for my sake." This shift from the alienating "our" of the penultimate stanza to the "my" of the final line marks the point at which the speaker starts to become a living character within the Christian story, one who is no longer penned down by a deadening letter. In other words, the speaker now comes to see that the law is not "against the promises of God" (Gal. 3:21) but operates as the "law of Christ" (Gal. 6:2), the "spiritual law" (Rom. 7:14). By tasting the wine made from the law's sour-sweet juice, the speaker demonstrates a lived-understanding of the Pauline idea that the fulfillment of the law comes through those who "walk not according to the flesh but according to the Spirit" in faith (Rom. 8:3). Furthermore, Herbert's phrasing in the final stanza's opening question recalls Andrewes' teaching in his 1623 Easter Day sermon that in the winepress of Isaiah 63, Christ "was Himself trodden and pressed; He was the grapes and clusters Himself," thereby occasioning the "'year of redemption' [which] is already come, and is now" (3.70; 3.78). In other words, Andrewes preaches what Herbert's speaker slowly discovers.

For many critics, the ending of "The bunch of grapes" feels forced and unpersuasive. There is perhaps something too intellectual, too unemotional about it, as if the speaker were arguing himself into joy.[40] But Herbert, we

---

[40] See, for example, Vendler, 191, Cited in Wilcox, 448; and Strier, *Love Known*, 159.

should remember, was aware of the danger of being "argu'd into hopes" ("Affliction," 15). When this happens in "Affliction," it occurs because his "thoughts reserved / No place for grief or fear" (15–16) as he deluded himself into thinking that the state of grace excludes suffering. This is exactly where we were at the beginning of "The bunch of grapes" when the speaker assumed that joy can be defined in the negative through a lack of shame, sin, and law. In this respect, the speaker's spiritual crisis flowed from a blinkered view of what Herbert elsewhere calls "true Christian joy" ("Self-condemnation" 8). As Herbert reminds us in "The Invitation," true Christian joy is not to be confused with commonsense notions of pleasure or peace. Unlike conventional notions of happiness, Christian joy involves an eschatological dimension that transcends earthly happiness:

> Come ye hither all, whom joy
>   Doth destroy,
> While ye graze without your bounds:
> Here is joy that drowneth quite
>   Your delight,
> As a floud the lower grounds. (19–24)

In his commentary on 2 Corinthians, Sibbes similarly differentiates common sense views of joy from true Christian joy, teaching that Christians have "peace with God, and joy in tribulation'" (3.19). For Sibbes, Christian joy is as much a mystery as conversion; or as he puts it: "It is a mystery for a man to be tossed up and down, and yet to have a contended mind" (5.461). Viewed in these contexts, it becomes clear that what the speaker of "The bunch of grapes" learns is that Christian joy is not an affective coloring or feeling tone that comes and goes; instead, it is the attitude toward life that a mature faith makes possible.

This view of joy is largely rooted in Johannine teachings. In the Gospel of John, Christ presents a joy that is distinct from all worldly joys in its being a "kinetic reality" rather than a "static condition," a promise that orients one now but which shall be fulfilled later (15: 11; 17:13).[41] This is the view of joy that Sibbes endorses when he observes that "The word in the original is more than joy, for it is χαυχησις, a glorying ... let others rejoice in riches, in honours, in the favour of men; let them rejoice in what they please, my joy is another kind of joy" (3.206–7). In the course of

---

[41] Rudolf Bultmann, *Theology of the New Testament Volume Two* trans. Kendrick Gobel (London: SCM Press, 1955), 83.

"The bunch of grapes," the speaker does not move from affliction to joy but from an unrealistic and immature view of joy as a permanent state of happiness to a recognition that Christian joy is an eschatological phenomenon that can coincide with sorrow, grief, and tribulation. These paradoxes recall Herbert's parable poem "Peace," particularly the speaker's realization that although Christ "sweetly liv'd; yet sweetnesse did not save / His life from foes" (25–6). As these lines intimate, true Christian "peace" does not involve anything as naïve as exemption from suffering, hence Christ's teaching in John: "These things I have spoken unto you, that in me ye might have peace, in the world ye shall have tribulation" (16:33).

What is perhaps most striking about "The bunch of grapes" is the way it depicts a spiritual crisis as a crisis in reading. The resolution to its conflict, incomplete as all such resolutions necessarily are, comes when the speaker arrives at a more mature understanding of the relation between faith and joy through a specific kind of figural interpretation of the Old Testament. He rediscovers, for himself, the typological link between the cluster of grapes in Numbers to the messianic prophecy of the grape press in Isaiah and thus to Christ in the gospels.[42] Applying these typological patterns to himself at this specific moment of spiritual pain, he rediscovers the continuity in difference between the law of Moses and the law of Christ. By trying to "lock-up" joy, the speaker of "The bunch of grapes" inadvertently locked himself out of the promissory dimension of scripture, thus making the error Paul warns against in Galatians: "*Is* the law then against the promises of God? God forbid" (3:21). As Luther often warned, this is what happens when scripture is perceived entirely as a set of commandments summoning the faithful to action. But in Herbert's poem, this crisis is implicitly initiated by the opposite, more antinomian, error of suppressing law. In "The bunch of grapes," the speaker is driven into speech by an overconfident expectation of constant joy and the felt-experience of ever-present grace. Given the poem's initiating crisis, the hesitating tone of its ending is entirely appropriate. After all, Herbert's challenge in the poem is to provide a resolution that avoids the triumphalism that instigated the crisis in the first place. Instead of unmitigated hope, the speaker comes to learn with Sibbes that "Joy enlargeth the soul, but grief straitenth it" (7.341). Ultimately, the speaker rediscovers that Christological joy "is not

---

[42] For a fuller articulation of these biblical allusions in the poem, see Bloch, *Spelling the Word*, 141–146.

something that can be realized in the external conditions of life or in some state of mind"[43] but by and through hope, faith, and love.

From a spiritual and exegetical standpoint, "The bunch of grapes" is a more complicated variation on issues addressed earlier in the sequence in the dreamlike lyric "Love-joy." In this much shorter poem, an overly self-assured speaker who is "never loth to spend [his] judgment" is also led from third-person abstraction to first-person participatory reading:

> As on a window late I cast mine eye,
> I saw a vine drop grapes with *J* and *C*
> Anneal'd on every bunch. One standing by
> Ask'd what it meant. I (who am never loth
> To spend my iudgment) said, It seem'd to me
> To be the bodie and the letters both
> Of *Joy* and *Charitie*. Sir, you have not miss'd,
> The man reply'd; It figures *JESUS CHRIST.*

Tone is everything here. The self-satisfied speaker is subtly taught that subtending abstract virtues like charity is the living presence of Christ. The ending's implication is that biblical reading is inherently participatory; one must be personally rooted in Christ in order to participate in the virtues that he embodies and communicates. Otherwise, religious truth resides, Sibbes warns, "not in the heart, but only in the brain" (7.310).

Consistent with Jeremy Taylor's exegetical sensibility, "Love-joy" suggests that acts of spiritual reading are necessarily partial and incomplete. At some level, they almost always reflect where the interpreter stands at the particular moment of interpretation. If the speaker of "Love-joy" begins by assuming a strong distinction between the subject who interprets and the sacred text being interpreted, the poem's ending narrows this distinction by suggesting that reader and Word interpenetrate one another. In this sense, the speaker rediscovers that revelation is a *mysterion*, a term that in its essence identifies precisely this interpenetration of reader and Word. To understand Herbert's poetics of discovery and the biblical hermeneutics underpinning, it is to recognize how Herbert continually exposes the many dangers that arise when Christians lose sight of the interpenetration of reader and Word. Much of this is communicated in "Love-joy" through tone. Where the speaker stands aloof from himself and his acts of

---

[43] Bultmann, *Theology of New Testament Volume 2*, 83.

reading, suggesting a degree of false assurance on his part, the voice who corrects him speaks in a calmly authoritative manner with feet firmly on the ground. Such use of tonal variation is one of Herbert's major contributions to the religious lyric as a genre. In this instance, Herbert's shifting tone suggests that he clearly understood that the resonance of someone's voice often reveals whether they deeply believe and fully understand what they are saying or not, a principle all good country parsons and psychoanalysts presumably know.

We are now in a position to observe a slight but significant difference between Herbert's "The bunch of grapes" and Sibbes' theology of joy. For Sibbes, Christological joy

> *is permanent.* Other men's joy and rejoicing is but as a flash of thorns, as the wise man calls it, as it were, a flame in thorns; as the crackling of thorns, which is sooner gone ... A holy Christian hath that in himself, and that which is more excellent than himself, to glory in. (3.207)

Unlike the more puritan Sibbes, Herbert rarely, if ever, speaks of any particular state of the soul as "permanent," even one that is not, strictly speaking, affective in nature. In "Peace," for example, he locates repose in Christ who is mysteriously figured as the "grain" from which "bread" may be made (see 37–42). In this respect, Herbert follows Hooker's insight that oftentimes despair arises from a misapprehension of the nature of faith as a permanent emotional condition. Indeed, the following passage from Hooker's "The Certainty and Perpetuity of Faith in the Elect" perfectly captures the implied backstory of "The bunch of grapes." According to Hooker,

> an error groweth, when men in heaviness of spirit suppose they lack faith, because they find not the sugared joy and delight which indeed doth accompany faith, but so as a separable accident, as a thing that may be removed from it; yea there is a cause why it should be removed. The light would never be so acceptable, were it not for that usual intercourse of darkness. (3.474)

It is exactly the "sugared joy and delight" that the speaker of Herbert's poem finds lacking at the outset. Misconstruing this new emotional state as a sign of Christ's absence, the speaker finds himself in a state of spiritual and interpretive crisis.

Ultimately, the speaker of "The bunch of grapes" finds his way back into the promissory dimension of scriptural narrative by reopening the channels of *sacra doctrina*, thereby rediscovering that faith, in its Pauline essence, "is the condition for the receipt of 'righteousness'."[44] For Herbert such a condition enables Christians to rejoice in the midst of tribulation. It is precisely this ability to joy in tribulation (and not an abstract theological problem) which provides the exigency for "The Water-course":

> Thou who dost dwell and linger here below,
> Since the condition of this world is frail,
> Where of all plants afflictions soonest grow;
> If troubles overtake thee, do not wail:
> For who can look for lesse, that loveth $\begin{cases} \text{Life} \\ \text{Strife.} \end{cases}$ (1–5)

This is the dilemma that the ending of "The Banquet" answers when Herbert encourages his readers to "take up my lines and life" and to "Hearken under pain of death, / Hands and breath" so as to "Strive in this, and love the strife" (51–2, 54). From this perspective, Christological joy is the very opposite of stasis; it is the wisdom of knowing how to take moments of affliction as the occasion of mortification that Herbert describes as characteristic of the "Christian Soldier" in "The Parson Condenscending" (284). By situating worldly strife within the eschatological and hermeneutic context of faith, Christians can face up to the impenetrable mystery that concludes "The Water-course," the mystery that God

> gives to man, as he sees fit $\begin{cases} \text{Salvation} \\ \text{Damnation.} \end{cases}$ (10)

The Temple's emphasis on the dialectic of joy in sorrow is in keeping with Andrewes' wariness about the eclipse of mystery in the English church. Like Andrewes, Herbert exposes the way that spiritual overconfidence results in a foreshortening of scriptural narrative, a deadening of the living Word of God. Ultimately, Herbert shared the view that the pursuit of godliness could only be sustained in a way that is true to human

---

[44] Bultmann, *Theology of the New Testament*, 314.

suffering if scripture remains an ongoing story as well as a true history, a book of mysteries as well as a collection of promises. If *Briefe Notes on Valdesso* exposes the negative consequences of historicism and radical spiritualism, and if "The H. Scriptures (I) and (II)" correct the desire for a totalizing view of scripture, then "The bunch of grapes" discloses how presumption inadvertently makes scripture appear "weak and unprofitable" (Andrewes, 1.287). Taken together, these various pressures constitute some of the major pastoral exigencies motivating Herbert's work.

Exegesis and Fellowship: The Country Parson and Musae Responsoriae

As Herbert's response to the antinomian dimensions of Valdés' theology suggests, he was alert to the political and social consequences of a narrowed biblicism. For Herbert, any foreshortening of the scriptural narrative necessarily impinges on what *The Book of Common Prayer* calls, after Ephesians, the fellowship of the mystery. On his account, reductive reading practices can be as spiritually and politically dangerous as bad theology. This is why Herbert strongly stresses the extent to which Christian fellowship is rooted in an experience of nescience as well as on a general set of scripturally derived beliefs. In Herbert's view, the church is akin to the human soul insofar as it is a process more than a product. Like the soul, the church is an ongoing and inherently flawed pursuit of truth and holiness in the context of history, custom, and experience as well as revelation. Central to this ecclesiastical vision is a commitment to the interpenetration of reader and Word such that many exegetical acts are, at some level, provisional and thus subject to change. As Herbert makes clear in *The Country Parson* and *Musae Responsoriae*, his conception of the church as an evolving process mediated by context and custom differs from more purist conceptions of Christian fellowship in ways that are broadly consonant with his spiritual aesthetic.

As we have begun to see, ecclesiastical debate in Herbert's world occurred between conformists who saw the church as evolving slowly over time through shifting cultural contexts in which disagreement was inevitable and reformers who sought to return to the fixed ideal of the apostolic period.[45] Generally speaking, conformists took it for granted that

---

[45] Prior, *Defining the Jacobean Church*, 260 and Hunt, *Art of Hearing*, 39.

the church was an inherently imperfect institution mediated by the transformations of time and persons. Reformists, on the other hand, sought to recuperate the original perfection of the apostolic church regardless of changing circumstances. In developing the conformist side of this debate over ecclesiastical orthodoxy, Herbert stresses the centrality of nescience and mystery to religious life at all levels from personal reading practices and sermon-going to the life of common prayer. But he does so in a way that was designed to appeal to rather than alienate more rigorous reformists.

Herbert develops his particular take on the conformist vision of the church in *The Country Parson* in a number of ways. Of particular importance is the manner in which he construes the priest's role in cultivating social bonds. According to *A Priest to the Temple*, the social bonds holding the community together are grounded on a carefully articulated but deeply felt sense of human limitations more than they are on a pursuit of certainty or absolute perfection per se. In place of unqualified certainty, Herbert's treatise on *The Country Parson*, like his poetry, advocates learned ignorance (*docta ignorantia*), a cultivated sense of one's intellectual limitations.[46] Herbert articulates this point in the chapter on "The Parson's Knowledge" by first asserting the importance of the priest's learning only to radically qualify it later. According to Herbert,

> The Countrey Parson is full of all knowledg ... He condescends even to the knowledge of tillage, and pastorage, and makes great use of them in teaching, because people by what they understand, are best led to what they understand not. (228)

As with his poetry, the end of this chapter moves in a surprising direction as he roundly qualifies the idea of the parson's being full of "all knowledg."[47] By the end of the chapter, Herbert stresses the necessarily collective and interpersonal nature of the pursuit of truth within the context of an evolving Christian fellowship:

---

[46] Christopher Hodgkins situates Herbert in relation to a distinctly Calvinist view of learned ignorance in *Authority, Church, and Society* 12–16. While there are important continuities between this context and Herbert's work, there are also, as Prior has subsequently shown, significant spiritual and ecclesiastical differences.

[47] Ronald W. Cooley makes much the same point in '*Full of all knowledg': George Herbert's Country Parson and Early Modern Social Discourse* (Toronto: University of Toronto Press, 2004), 47.

...as one Countrey doth not bear all things, that there may be a Commerce; so neither hath God opened, or will open all to one, that there may be a traffick in knowledg between the servants of God, for the planting both of love, and humility. Wherefore [the Parson] hath one Comment at least upon every book of Scripture, and ploughing with this, and his own meditations, he enters into the secrets of God treasured in the holy Scripture. (229)

This passage implies a theory of fellowship in which it is impossible for church leaders to fully recover the lost perfection of the apostolic age. Instead of emphasizing the extent to which fellowship is grounded in the certitude of the Spirit, Herbert endorses a notion of Christian fellowship that is centered on mutually experienced wise ignorance. From this perspective, the interpersonal relations among Christians should be grounded in an acknowledgment that each person of good faith brings something edifying for others to learn, hence the view that the parson's responsibility is to make scripture his own; he must assimilate "doctrine and life, colours and light" into himself so as to bring a uniquely authoritative view of scripture into the *corpus mysticum*.

Herbert's concern with the socially dangerous consequences of presumption self-consciously replays some of the issues Augustine confronts in the preface to *On Christian Doctrine*. In the prologue to his treatise on scriptural exegesis, Augustine critiques those who claim that only direct inspiration from the Holy Spirit and not human teaching can communicate the truth of the gospel. Augustine's critique is both social and pedagogical in nature as he points out how overstated claims to inspiration undermine the cultivation of charity and fellowship in communion. We should thus beware, Augustine warns,

of most proud and most dangerous temptations of this kind and think rather that the Apostle Paul himself, although prostrated and taught by the divine and heavenly voice, was nevertheless sent to a man that he might receive the sacraments and be joined to the church.[48]

While conformists and reformists all share this Augustinian heritage, writers such as Herbert, Sanderson, and Taylor place an unusual degree of emphasis upon it. Indeed, Augustine's reminder that even Paul, who enjoyed direct contact with the Spirit, learned from human

---

[48] *On Christian Doctrine* trans. D.W. Robertson Jr. (Upper Saddle River, New Jersey: Prentice Hall, 1958), 5.

teaching concludes with an insight that clearly resonated for Herbert as he responded to the kind of radical spiritualism exemplified by Valdés. According to Augustine, "Charity itself, which holds men together in a knot of unity, would not have a means of infusing souls and almost mixing them together if men could teach nothing to men."[49] This is precisely the Augustinian vision that Taylor breathes new life into when he suggest that the complexity of scripture provides occasion and opportunity for "our mutual charity and toleration to each other and humility in ourselves," just as much as "the repositories of faith, and furniture of creeds, and articles of belief" do.[50] What passes between Augustine and Taylor, however, is a much more developed humanistic sense of historical and cultural difference. Highly attuned to the inevitability of historical and cultural change, Taylor takes Augustine's view of fellowship as resting on a process of ongoing pedagogy much further than is normally the case in protestant ecclesiology. Although Herbert did not go quite as far down the road of nescience as Taylor would, he nevertheless saw that the certainties provided by spiritual intuition can be dangerous insofar as they uproot the space within which mystery and fellowship flourish.

By placing the limits of knowledge at the center of Christian fellowship, Herbert goes at least as far as Hooker in insisting that imperfect faith and vaguely articulated confessional loyalties are acceptable within Christian communion. For them, as for Augustine, the church is a *corpus permixtum*, an imperfect assembly of the holy and the wretched with no clear demarcation between the two groups. This ethos is discernible in *Musae Responsoriae*, particularly Herbert's wry neo-Latin response to Andrew Melville's Presbyterian critique of the English church as imperfect. Rather than contradicting Melville's accusation that the English church is flawed, Herbert turns the tables by agreeing with him:

> You reproach us for
> Imperfections, stains.
> Why? Is it so strange?
> We are Travelers.
> What is Christ's blood for, save
> To wash stains off,
> Which the body's clay, too intimate,
> Sprinkles on the spirit?

---

[49] Ibid., 6.
[50] Taylor, *Works*, 5.410.

> You are therefore pure! (*Vos ergo puri!*) ...
> "On spots and stains" (*De labe maculisque*). (30–31)

There is a distant family resemblance, if not a direct line of continuity, between this wry response to Melville and Anthony Trollope's affectionate satire of the English church in the *Chronicles of Barsetshire* especially, I would say, the quasi-allegorical description of the flawed architecture of Plumstead Episcopi in *The Warden*. According to Trollope's narrator, although "the old priests who built [the church], built it wrong, one cannot bring oneself to wish that they should have made it other than it is."[51] While the general parallel here is not to be overstated, the similarity lies in a shared attitude toward religious controversies, one that is more easily enjoyed by conservatives than reformers.

CONCLUSION: THE FLOWER

As the Latin poem just prior to "On spots and stains" suggests, Herbert diagnosed his age as one of diminishing fellowship. Adopting the European-wide perspective he takes in "Church-rents and schisms," Herbert addresses his audience in the prophetic tone that he would later adopt in "The Church Militant":

> O gracious age! On every side
> The brothers stand around.
> Puritans and Papists have
> Each their own. So now there are
> Good brothers everywhere, though nothing
> Can be rarer than a brother's love. (*nil fraterno rarius esse queat*)
> (30–31)

Having studied Augustine in the context of seventeenth-century Europe, Herbert felt that a narrowed scripturalism leads to a narrowed theology and hence to a divisive fellowship. Stressing the idea of scripture as the living voice of God, he also felt that the extremes of "feeling faith" must be mitigated by a tempered protestant version of "historical faith," the shared faith, that is, of tradition as passed on by fallible instructors. Among other things, this view of Christianity helps explain why Herbert's

---

[51]Anthony Trollope, *The Warden* (London: J.M. Dent & Sons Limited, 1957), 175.

poetry is preoccupied with his own fallibility as an instructor of *doctrina*, an anxiety that registers in early lyrics such as "Perseverance" as well as late ones such as "The Flower."

Many of the themes addressed in this chapter find full expression in "The Flower," a poem in which the following epiphany brings the speaker into sudden, awe-struck, speech: "We say amisse, / This or that is: / Thy word is all, if we could spell" (19–21). For Herbert, losing sight of the "if" here means losing the foundation upon which common prayer is built. After all, creative dynamism is the very essence of the revealed Word; it cannot be frozen in place once and for all such that we can confidently assert that "This or that is." Viewed in this context, it becomes clear that "The Flower" reverses and resolves the spiritual conflicts of "The bunch of grapes." Instead of resisting the transformations of the Word, the speaker of "The Flower" has become newly vivified by the delighted confusion that it brings. Openly responsive to spiritual change and the provisionality of scriptural understanding, the speaker of "The Flower" restates the ending of "The bunch of grapes" with greater wisdom. The thought of a future stillness beyond time is now enough to allow him to enjoy a sense of wonder amidst tribulation. After all, this is the only real paradise available to the wayfaring Christian; or as he says in the poem's final stanza:

> These are thy wonders, Lord of love,
> To make us see we are but flowers that glide:
>   Which when we once can finde and prove,
> Thou hast a garden for us, where to bide.
>   Who would be more,
>   Swelling through store,
> Forfeit their Paradise by their pride. (43–49)

By this point in *The Temple*, we know that the paradise which the proud forfeit is the capacity to rejoice in affliction, what Vaughan calls, in a slightly different context, our "transplanted paradise" ("Sone-days," 11). What the ending of "The Flower" does not refer to is God's final judgment, of which the speaker knows he knows nothing. According to the diagnosis carried out in the poem, the danger of pride is that it constitutes a kind of psychological and interpretive clenching, an attempt to hold oneself still, strong, and secure even in the face of the Word's overwhelmingly transformative power. A common ailment of intellectuals like Herbert's speaker, this defensive posture is finally overcome in the loose, flowing assonance of "These are thy wonders, Lord of love, / To make us see we are but flowers that glide" (43–4).

As I have argued in this chapter, Herbert saw the prideful impulse to be "past changing" as a spiritually and aesthetically destructive temptation. In it, he saw the undoing of everything from Christian joy and fellowship to a true appreciation of the provisional dimensions of scriptural understanding. For Herbert, as for Hooker and Sanderson, the desire for security can undermine the unity of the human soul as well as that of the community. Unlike them, however, he saw in lyric poetry a uniquely powerful way of articulating these interrelated dynamics. Absent of these distinctly seventeenth-century exigencies, Herbert would not have developed a poetics of correction and revision in the specific way that he did; nor would he have put the love sonnet tradition to the specific uses that he did. While the threats posed by radical spiritualism and the eclipse of mystery extend back into the sixteenth century, they became increasingly pressing in early Stuart England. Viewed in this context, it becomes clear that Herbert's poetics of process is as much an aesthetic response to the spiritual and social tensions of seventeenth-century English Christendom as it is a personal record of his own religious struggles. Though ultimately, the two are probably inextricable from one another.

In order to further appreciate the peculiar way in which the experience of discovery enhances rather than diminishes the experience of mystery in Herbert's work, and in order to better understand the specific exigencies motivating his pursuit of neatness, we turn now to his response to Christian rationalism, especially as expressed by Lord Cherbury.

CHAPTER 6

Lord Cherbury in *The Temple*: Faith, Mystery, and Understanding

If Herbert's experience of dogmatism sensitized him to the disenchanting dimensions of post-reformation culture, then so too did the experience of having an older brother. One of the most intellectually independent men of his age, Lord Herbert of Cherbury (1583–1648) articulated a philosophical vision that threatened the very ground on which Augustinian Christianity rests, if not that of Christianity itself. In doing so, he showed the way toward a more full-throated deism later in the century.[1] Developing neo-Stoic ideas about natural religion that were well known in the period, particularly those expressed in Cicero's *The Nature of the Gods*, Cherbury sought to displace revelation as the center of religious life with universal reason.[2]

This influential vision necessarily involved attacking widely held notions of Christian mystery, something he did with a subtle irony and

---

[1] For Cherbury's subtle relation to deism, see R.D. Bedford, *The Defence of Truth: Herbert of Cherbury and the seventeenth century* (Manchester: Manchester UP, 1979).

[2] For discussions of the intellectual background to Cherbury's work, see Louis I. Bredvold, "Deism before Lord Herbert" *Papers of the Michigan Academy of Science, Arts, and Letters* 4 (1924), 431–442; Basil Willey, *The Seventeenth Century Background: Studies in the Thought of the Age in Relation to Poetry and Religion* (New York: Doubleday, 1934), 125–138; Harold R. Hutcheson ed. and trans., *Lord Herbert of Cherbury's De Religione Laici* (New Haven: Yale UP, 1944), 3–84; and C.J. Butts, *Early Deism in France*. For the stoic origins of Cherbury's ideas, see Book II Sections 43–45 of Cicero's *The Nature of the Gods*.

© The Author(s) 2017
G. Kuchar, *George Herbert and the Mystery of the Word*,
DOI 10.1007/978-3-319-44045-3_6

an oftentimes oblique mode of argumentation.[3] Central to his attack on
mystery is a sustained critique of priest-craft, which he saw as little more
than a cynical means of attaining worldly power. And although Cherbury
comes very close to denying the atonement outright in his posthumously
published *A Dialogue Between a Tutor and His Pupil* (1768), he cannot
be said to have rejected Christianity altogether.[4] Instead, he did something
much more threatening: he redefined the meaning of inherited belief by
downplaying the authority of historical faith in favor of universally shared
and thus highly general religious ideas. In other words, rather than rejecting Christian orthodoxy, he sought to redefine it within the growing prob-
lematic of global religion, the dawning realization that Christianity is one
faith among many and one of the most violently self-destructive at that.

While Cherbury's philosophical vision posed a substantial threat to
Augustinian Christianity, it is important not to overstate the subversive intent of his overall effort. Generally speaking, Cherbury's project
was ecumenical in orientation. His aim was to provide a foundation for
Christianity that would allow it to avoid internecine conflict by overcoming the twin tyrannies of Roman Catholic authoritarianism and protestant
dogmatism. In this restricted sense, his project belongs to the constructive,
pragmatic mode of rational Christianity that in England runs from John
Hales and The Great Tew circle to John Locke. In this respect, his work
arguably differs from the more truly subversive variety that largely begins
with John Toland's *Christianity not Mysterious* (1696). Nevertheless,
this distinction provides little solace for those working within orthodox
Augustinian Christianity such as Richard Baxter who ends his critique of
De Veritate with the telling prayer: "Lord save this Land and the darker
world from Infidelity and its fruits."[5] As Baxter recognized, the rationalist
defense of Christianity engenders more problems than it resolves. Once
the Augustinian privileging of faith over reason is compromised, then the
door is open to the subverting of revelation as an important category of
religious experience, a point not lost on Sir John Suckling who satirized

[3] For a sustained assessment of Cherbury's irony, see Eugene D. Hill, *Edward, Lord Herbert of Cherbury* (Boston: Twayne, 1987). See also Bredvold, "Deism Before Lord Herbert", 433.
[4] The authorship debate about this work seems to have been settled in favor of his having penned it. See Bedford, *A Defence*, 189.
[5] Richard Baxter, *Animadversions On ... De Veritate* (London: 1672), 168.

The Great Tew circle in *An Account of Religion by Reason*.[6] No less wary of rationalism than Baxter, George Herbert responded critically to his brother's highly intellectualized brand of rationalist Christianity, especially its reductive view of scripture.

DE VERITATE: REASON AND FAITH

Posterity has largely agreed with Cherbury's view that his most important work was his 1624 treatise *De Veritate*. By no later than 1714, "On Truth" was seen as the major forerunner of English deism, specifically the radically unorthodox idea that true religious knowledge was best gained through reason rather than scripture.[7] At bottom, *De Veritate* was an attempt to overcome the simultaneous and often mutually implicating rise of Calvinist fideism and Pyrrhonist skepticism. The book's primary aim is audible in its subtitle, which indicates that it shall differentiate "Revelation, Probability, Possibility, and Error" in order to establish a sure method for arriving at truth. Despite ostensible enervations to the contrary, Cherbury includes religious truth within the compass of his analysis. This philosophical project places Cherbury near the center of a European-wide effort to provide some kind of infallible method for arriving at certain knowledge above and beyond that given through historical faith or ongoing spiritual revelation. As with related philosophical efforts, Cherbury's project was designed to provide a way of avoiding religious schism which, as ambassador to France (1619–1624), he saw culminate in what would become the Thirty-Years War. This ecumenical effort is expressed in many of his works, including his 1649 history of Henry VIII, commissioned by Charles I, as well as his autobiography, first published by Horace Walpole in 1764. In his history of Henry Tudor, Cherbury interrupts his narrative to assert that a rationally grounded religion based on commonly shared ideas "dispose[s] us to a generall Concord and Peace," a point he reiterates while telling his own life story.[8] At the heart of Cherbury's thought lies the dream of such concord and with it a general contempt for religiously motivated conflict.

---

[6] Fredrick C. Beiser, *The Sovereignty of Reason: The Defense of Rationality In the Early English Enlightenment* (Princeton: Princeton UP, 1996), 132.

[7] See Thomas Halyburton, *Natural Religion Insufficient* (Edinburgh: 1714).

[8] Edward Herbert, *The Life and Raigne of King Henry the Eighth* (London: 1649), 296 and *The Life of Edward, First Lord Herbert of Cherbury* ed. J.M. Shuttleworth (London: Oxford UP, 1976), 24–25, 29–31.

George Herbert's response to his elder brother's philosophy remains a major question for literary scholars as well as for seventeenth-century intellectual history more generally.[9] To properly gauge this response, we must first consider how Cherbury subtly critiqued Augustine's prioritizing of faith over reason. After all, this reversal effectively forecloses Pauline-Augustinian interpretations of Christian mystery fundamentally differentiating Cherbury's religion from the kind of spirituality depicted in *The Temple*. When read in the context of Cherbury's work, it becomes apparent that *The Temple's* emphasis on mystery as a central category of religious faith is not simply a predictable reiteration of an Augustinian status quo. On the contrary, it constitutes a reaction to one of the most powerfully ecumenical, if subtly disenchanting, philosophies of the day.

The earliest extant manuscript of *De Veritate* is dedicated to George Herbert and to Cherbury's secretary at Paris, William Boswell, "on the understanding that they should expunge anything which they found in it contrary to good morals or the true Catholic faith."[10] As with Cherbury's work generally, it is difficult to know how to read this dedication. Evasive and provocative at once, it downplays the work's radical nature in the very act of admitting that it could be perceived as unorthodox. Something similar occurs in the final dedication which is pointedly addressed to "every sane and unprejudiced reader" (ET LECTORI CVIVIS, integri & illibati Iudicii dicavit) (1633 title page). Both dedications indicate how Cherbury sustains the illusion of orthodoxy in the very act of critiquing and thereby redefining it.

As the manuscript edition implies, Cherbury explicitly maintains that he is doing philosophy not theology and that nothing he says is intended to undermine orthodox faith. But the very fact that he felt the need to make the claim betrays the extent to which the last five chapters of the work, for which the treatise is now mostly known, violates this distinction. As critics routinely note, *De Veritate's* "central meaning and purpose

[9] For a discussion of Herbert and Cherbury in their tense familial context, see Jeffrey Powers-Beck, *Writing the Flesh: The Herbert Family Dialogue* (Pittsburgh: Duquesne UP, 1998), 119–164.
[10] Cited in Margaret Bottral, *George Herbert* (London: Murray, 1954), 18. See also *De Religione Laici*, ed. Hutcheson, 20. According to John Drury, who sees more similarities than differences in the spiritualities of the two Herberts, "most of [*De Veritate*] was written in England with his brother George to hand," *Music at Midnight*, 103.

is essentially religious, and not epistemological at all."[11] What appears as "overt epistemology or psychology is, in fact, covert religious polemic."[12] As Eugene Hill has shown, Cherbury's polemic against the orthodoxies of historical faith is expressed through the kind circumspection that we might expect of a diplomat. Without an ear for such "diplomatic irony," readers may easily miss the foundation-shattering nature of Cherbury's rationalist vision that so deeply inspired deists later in the century.

Nowhere is Cherbury's polemic against historical faith more discernible than in the way *De Veritate* reverses the long-held axiom, based on Isaiah 7:9, "Believe so as to understand" (*crede ut intelligas*). While Cherbury explicitly undermines this principle in *A Dialogue Between A Tutor and his Pupil*, he does so obliquely in chapter nine of *De Veritate* where he outlines his five common notions or the universally shared assumptions about religious truth visible in all normal human beings. The notions are as follows: (1) there is some kind of supreme deity, (2) this divinity is to be worshipped, (3) virtue and piety constitute the fundamentals of religion, (4) evil deeds must be repented, and (5) God rewards the virtuous and punishes the evil after death. A highly consequential move, Cherbury's founding of religious life upon a rational intuiting of common ideas rather than faith in scriptural revelation fundamentally transforms the nature of Christianity, particularly its grounding in the incarnation and Trinity. He effects this transformation by asking:

> If we do not advance towards truth upon a foundation of Common Notions, assigning every element its true value, how can we hope to reach any but futile conclusions? ... So we must establish the fundamental principles of religion by means of universal wisdom, so that whatever has been added to it by the genuine dictates of Faith may rest on that foundation as a roof is supported on a house. (290)

It is surely no coincidence that in the prefatory letter to Cherbury's posthumous 1665 collection of poems, Henry Herbert reminds his nephew, Cherbury's grandson and namesake, that in traditional Christianity men do "not believe because they know, but know because they believe.

---

[11] Charles Lyttle, "Lord Herbert Apostle of Ethical Theism" *Church History* 4.4 (1935), 247–267, 254.
[12] Hill, *Edward, Lord Herbert of Cherbury*, 28.

Faith must precede knowledge."[13] As this not-so-subtle reminder suggests, Cherbury reversed a basic axiom of Christian thought and in doing so envisioned a stripped-down religion in which faith clarifies and verifies rational intuitions about commonly held beliefs rather than vice versa. As Henry Herbert's prefatory letter intimates, the consequences of this move are far more radical than Cherbury admits. To start with, he is suggesting that universal providence is no different than the wisdom of nature, both of which are to be found in the "Church of Common Notions" (*De Veritate*, 303).

Cherbury's subordination of faith to reason is concomitant with his critical attitude toward Pauline-Augustinian notions of biblical mystery. Throughout his work, Lord Cherbury speaks derisively of mystery as a religious category, often describing it as a cynical ploy that priests have historically used for the sake of power and prestige. Accordingly, he subordinates mystery to the rational intuiting of virtue as in his autobiography when he claims to have "found [that] all Mistereys Sacraments and Revelations cheefely tended to the Establishment of these five Articles."[14] Typical of Cherbury, this idea that divine revelation supplements and clarifies the common notions implies the subversive possibility that revelation is not only secondary but ultimately superfluous. Thus, when he attacks mystery outright, Cherbury displays the kind of circumspection we should expect. In *A Dialogue*, for instance, the tutor begins by insisting that he will not discuss religious "mysteries" (22). Nevertheless, by the end of the treatise the audacious pupil arrives at the shocking conclusion that religious sacrifices are an example of the "mysterious cozenage that ever priests imposed upon mankind," implicitly calling into question the validity of the atonement (198). Cherbury's sharply critical attitude toward priest-craft and dogma may go some way in explaining John Aubrey's claim that Cherbury was insouciant about receiving communion on his deathbed.[15] In any case, Cherbury's critique of the standard Christian practice of privileging faith over reason is concomitant with his broader undermining of the Augustinian idea that Christianity is a mystery. After all, Augustine's understanding of *mysterion* is part and parcel with his insistence that belief provides the charitable basis on which true understanding

---

[13] Edward Herbert, *The Poems of Lord Herbert of Cherbury* ed. John Churton Collins (London: Chatto and Windus, 1881; rpt. 1970), xxxviii.

[14] Edward Herbert, *Life of Edward Herbert*, 31.

[15] See John Drury, *Music at Midnight*, 311.

and thus genuine fellowship arises. Without the priority of faith over reason, mystery, in Augustine's sense, disappears, and with it fellowship as he defined it.

We can set Cherbury's critique of mystery in its proper context by observing how he obscured a crucial dimension of Augustine's definition of the faith/reason dialectic. Augustine, we must recall, does not simply claim that faith precedes reason in the realm of revelation or religious belief; instead, he argues that a basic element of nonverifiable trust undergirds the whole of human life generally. In the realm of human relations, Augustine thought, reason is largely helpless without trust because so much of life cannot be known on a first-hand basis. At almost every step in human experience we implicitly rely on others, so much so that we are mostly unconscious of it. This basic condition of human life leads Augustine to the view that in the absence of unverifiable trust, relations among humans are not, in principle, humane.

The phrase Augustine uses to describe the implicit condition of faith in one another which human beings must assume is *sacramentum amoris*. For Augustine, the mystery of love denotes the condition in which a community qua community lives and moves, be it a family, a group of friends, or a church. He makes this point in *On Faith in Things Unseen* when he envisions what a community composed of members who only believe what they know through first-hand observation would actually look like. His point is that any genuine community presupposes faith in things unverifiable by observation as a condition of its own possibility. According to Augustine,

> If this faith in human affairs is removed, who will not mark how great will be their disorder and what dreadful confusion will follow? For, who will be cherished by anyone in mutual charity, since love itself is invisible, if what I do not see I ought not to believe? Friendship, then, will wholly perish, since it rests upon nothing more than mutual love. What of this will one be able to receive from another, if it shall be believed that nothing of it can be shown?[16]

On this account, reason alone is too weak a force to ground a genuinely humane community. This is not to say that reason has no place

[16] Augustine, *On Faith in Things Unseen* trans. Roy Joseph Deferrari and Mary Francis McDonald in *The Fathers of the Church* Vol 4. (New York: Fathers of the Church, 1947), 454.

in Augustine's account of ethical social relations. On the contrary, we would not believe in the first place, Augustine claims, were we not rational creatures. Accordingly, we should believe in a way that seeks a reasonable account of and for our belief.[17] From this nonfideist perspective, reason clarifies rather than simply contrasts belief. When working properly, rationality continuously discloses, without ever fully comprehending, the contexts in which it operates, including those of faith. This dialectical relation between faith and reason is concomitant with Augustine's concept of mystery. In his view, the term *mystery* identifies the conditions of life within the *sacramentum amoris*, a form of fellowship rooted not in first-hand knowledge or intuitive reason but in commonly extended trust.

Cherbury's *De Veritate* takes direct aim at Augustine's thesis about the primacy of belief over reason in a chapter called "On Probability." All belief, Cherbury writes,

> though corrupted in the course of centuries, must in the last resource rest on the knowledge or understanding of the author from whom the belief originated. So here, too, knowledge precedes and confirms belief. (315)

A decisive difference between Augustine's and Cherbury's modes of argumentation emerges here. While Augustine is speaking from a first-person point of view, revealing the extent to which life as lived depends on trust in authority, Cherbury adopts an objective point of view, arguing that from a strictly logical standpoint that someone's knowledge always has priority over a subsequent person's belief. While this may be true in principle, it misses Augustine's point. Augustine is talking about life as it actually lived; he is not talking about life as it may be abstractly reconstructed from a perspective outside of human agency. In this respect, Cherbury argues from the interpretive position that is implicitly assumed and then corrected in "The bunch of grapes." As we saw, the speaker of that poem begins by adopting the abstracted, transcendent view that Cherbury assumes. By the end of the poem, however, Herbert's speaker realizes his immanence within the narrative of divine revelation, a move that reorients his faith in light of a more mature conception of the dialectic of law and gospel.

---

[17] On this point, see Augustine, Letter 120, in *Saint Augustine's Letters Volume 2* trans. Sister Wilfrid Parsons (Washington D.C.: Catholic University of America Press, 1953), 300–316.

Although Cherbury's elision of Augustine's mode of argumentation goes unremarked, it is nevertheless decisive for his overall philosophy and its broader reception in subsequent rationalist thought. After all, it allows him to render scriptural revelation (or what he circumspectly calls "history") secondary to the common notions. In effecting this reversal, Cherbury does nothing less than redefine orthodox notions of fellowship. For him, religious community is rooted in the transparent ground of rational intuition and is supported by universal reason rather than a non-empirical bond of love and trust in and through which souls are perfected over time. In helping pave the way toward the Enlightenment view that we trust in reason, Cherbury silently elides Augustine's argument that, given our existential limitations, human beings inevitably reason in trust.[18]

The consequences of this elision would prove decisive for subsequent debates about mystery. By adopting a strictly logical point of view in his analysis of the faith/reason dialectic and by demystifying Pauline notions of *mysterion* as a political and economic ploy by greedy priests, Cherbury eschewed the issue of sanctification normally thought to be central to mystery as a context of spiritual life. Whether it was his intent or not, Cherbury systematically obscured the subjective or spiritual dimension of biblical mystery as a theological category. This is why his eighteenth-century critic Thomas Halyburton is essentially correct to suggest that Cherbury "reduces religion to mere morality."[19] For Cherbury, scripture offers a set of universally applicable rules rather than an ethically variegated and potentially unpredictable context for spiritual life as lived in the first person.

CHERBURY'S SCRIPTURE

Because Cherbury's privileging of common notions over revelation runs the risk of rendering scripture superfluous, he is forced in *De Veritate* to repeatedly say what would normally go without saying, such as: "Faith in the sacred records is not abolished or disparaged by these considerations. With the greater part of mankind I fully accept these accounts" (315). Similarly, at one moment he insists that "while knowledge is perpetually refreshed by the spring waters of the Common Notions, and faith is

---

[18] I heard the Cambridge-based philosopher Edmond Wright use the phrase "reason in trust" in a closely related context. For Wright's Nietzschean account of faith in productive fictions, see *Narrative, Perception, Language, and Faith* (New York: Palgrave, 2005), Ch. 6.

[19] Halyburton, *Natural Religion*, 24.

nourished by miracles, the whole inner man is stirred to life by this Book," the bible (316). Yet, moments later he demurs: "The miracles which have been invented to establish some new and often unworthy belief or dogma have always seemed to me to suggest imposture: in the same way I have always had respect for any law or religion which is supported not by miracles but by virtue" (316). As these passages suggest, his most orthodox statements have a peculiar way of betraying highly unorthodox implications. Almost every time he endorses scriptural revelation, he qualifies or even undermines the claim with a subsequent comment. Read closely, he clearly privileges intuitive reason and personal spiritual experience over biblical authority. Hence his assertion that "under the guidance of the inner consciousness I maintain that the principle of good actions spring from Common Notions or the divine wisdom within us" (311). The parallels between this and Juan de Valdés must have deeply struck George Herbert. Like the Spanish reformer, Cherbury reduces scripture from a book of mysteries to an ethical treatise, preferring the authority of his own private experience over supposed miracles disclosed to others in the ancient past. In doing so, he set the stage for the broader reduction of religion to morality that occurred in the eighteenth-century tradition of pragmatic rationalist Christianity.

By grounding his philosophical edifice on common notions rather than revelation, Cherbury marginalized scripture in an even more profound way than Valdés. One of his most revealing attempts to soft-pedal the unorthodox dimensions of his thought occurs in *De Religione Laici* where he responds to criticisms of his approach to scripture. Intriguingly, some of these criticisms appear to have originated with his younger brother George, who is perhaps vaguely alluded to here:

> But those of our country may say that I ought to speak more eloquently of the Holy Scriptures. To whom I reply that no one thinks more nobly of them, for I have asserted strongly that the best laws for living rightly and happily, or eternally, are delivered in the Scriptures. (129)

This is by no means a reversal of position. Cherbury's defense of his philosophy amounts to the view that scripture is primarily valuable for its moral lessons or "laws." Such a view is ultimately antithetical to Herbert's conception of faith as resting in the vitality of Christian narrative as a living story in which one participates in the pursuit of holiness.

The defensive posture in *De Religione Laici* arises from Cherbury's unusually liberal attitude toward scripture, particularly as evinced in the final chapters of *De Veritate*. At one point in Chap. 11, for example, he defends the use of the common notions as an "analogy of faith" or exegetical touchstone by which to weigh scriptural meaning. Here again, the unspoken implication is that revelation, strictly speaking, is, at best, secondary, at worst, superfluous:

> But if carelessness or the or the passage of time has allowed to creep into a sacred or profane book any passage which maligns God or calls in question those divine attributes which are universally recognized, why should we not agree either to amend the work—and this has been done before—or to charge its interpreters with error, in that they have departed from the writer's meaning and even from the analogy of faith, since they have stated views which conflict with Common Notions? (316)

In Augustinian Christianity, as we have seen, Christ is the "hypothesis" of scripture, its central point of reference or *scopus*. In Cherbury's thought, however, common notions perform this hermeneutic function. To this extent, Cherbury implicitly raises the question of why scripture and the incarnation are necessary in the first place. After all, the clear implication here is that scripture is not even remotely self-interpreting. Even worse, it implies that the bible should not be read through ecclesiastical tradition which is subject to priestly perversion. Instead, it can be clarified with reference to rational intuitions shared across time and space. In the end, such intuitions both ground and supplement faith in a way that wholly obscures any sense of the bible as the living Word of God.

HEAVEN AND ECHO IN A CHURCH

In light of Cherbury's remarkable reduction of scripture, it is surely no coincidence that Herbert expresses the idea that the bible is the living Word of God in a poetic genre directly associated with his brother Edward. Herbert's technically masterful "Heaven," the penultimate lyric in "The Church," is generally recognized to be a response to Cherbury's "Echo in a Church," which is likely the earliest devotional usage of the form in the vernacular.[20] Where Edward's penitent speaker seeks to discharge his guilt for sin, thereby keeping with common notion 4, George's speaker rediscovers

[20] Wilcox citing Mary Ellen Rickey, 179.

the salvific promise of scripture, its pointing the way toward "Heaven" for him personally. In this way, Herbert's poem focuses on a feature of Christian faith that remains irreducible to reason, including the vaguely generalized common notion 5 which states that the virtuous are rewarded and the guilty punished after death. Few of Herbert's poems more effectively convey the sense in which scripture is a mysteriously living presence than "Heaven." Simultaneously comforting and beguiling, "Heaven" neatly emphasizes precisely those aspects of scripture which Cherbury's philosophy elides, particularly the idea that it is the *Viva Vox Dei*:

> O who will show me those delights on high?
> *Echo.*   *I.*
> 3   Thou Echo, thou art morall, all men know.
> *Echo.*   *No.*
> Wert thou not born among the trees and leaves?
> *Echo.*   *Leaves.*
> And are there any leaves, that still abide?
> *Echo.*   *Bide.*
> What leaves are they? impart the matter wholly.
> 10   *Echo.*   *Holy.*

Silence, space, and breath reverberate in the tension between these two voices, especially through the circulation of aspirates and assonance. The effect is to convey presence as much as to bear meaning. Both palpable and ineffable, the voice of Echo somehow feels near and far at the same time. It intimates the living presence of the Holy Spirit speaking through the leaves of scripture as a voice that is neither fully exterior nor interior but something else entirely. Through the tight restrictions of the echo form and in a mode that is as elusive as it is simple, Herbert neatly expresses the view that the believing Christian is a living participant in a scriptural narrative that is dialogical and surprising. Particularly significant is the play between abide and bide, which suggests that Echo's story continually endures. All of this contrasts with Cherbury's "Echo," which appears in his lyric as an internal voice rather than a scripturally mediated spirit. As Jeffrey Powers-Beck observes, Cherbury's poem "suggests that the place for confession is not limited to any church 'built of clay or stone or living rock or even of marble,' but is in the internal space of the conscience ... or the 'human mind informed by the Common Notions.'"[21] Having established the ongoing vitality of Echo's leaves as the living presence of the eternal Word, "Heaven" concludes by associating scripture with illumination, peace, and the equanimity of faith. In doing so, Herbert further recalls the way his brother's philosophy reduces holiness to ethics thereby disclosing the extent to which a narrowed biblicism undermines Christian spirituality:

> 11 Are holy leaves the Echo then of blisse?
> *Echo. Yes.*
> Then tell me, what is that supreme delight?
> *Echo. Light.*
> Light to the minde: what shall the will enjoy?
> *Echo. Joy.*
> But are there cares and businesse with the pleasure?
> *Echo. Leisure.*
> Light, joy, and leisure; but still they persever?
> 20 *Echo. Ever.*

Much more than a bare set of laws or moral principles, scripture appears in the poem as a living presence whose persevering light shows the way toward heavenly bliss in all of its senses. Given that he is now writing in the context of last things, Herbert pushes the meaning of Christian joy to the furthest limits of language. Throughout the poem as a whole, but especially in its final lines, Herbert somehow manages a tone that is comforting and estranging at once.

The difference between Cherbury's blunter, more obvious ending and that of "Heaven" is instructive. Cherbury's "Echo in a Church" concludes:

> Since now with crying I am grown so weak,
> I shall want force even to crave thy name.
> O speak before I wholly weary am.
> *Echo*—I am. (22–25)

Cherbury's conclusion lacks the delicate, hard-to-grasp quality of Herbert's closing lines. Where "Heaven" makes God's presence ephemeral yet authoritative, Cherbury's poem rather oddly gives us Jehovah's "I am"

---

[21] Powers-Beck, *Writing the Flesh*, 145. The inset quote is from *De Veritate* 303–304.

in lieu of the still small voice that Elijah hears in 1 Kings which would seem more appropriate here. In any event, Herbert's poem does not construe scripture as a collection of predicate statements that one can follow like a map of physical space. Instead, it is an abiding presence receding into and then back out of silence. Read in the wider context of *The Temple*, "Heaven" shows Herbert intimating the spiritual limitations and hermeneutic reductiveness of Cherbury's religion.

THE AGONIE

As "Heaven" confirms, George Herbert's poetry routinely emphasizes the spiritual consequences involved in degrading mysteries into problems, of turning a relationship or living presence into a riddle one might solve once and for all. In at least two closely related poems in *The Temple*, Herbert addresses these issues thematically, speaking to them directly rather than implicitly as he does in "Heaven." The first is "The Agonie" and the second is "Divinitie." In both, the threat of Cherbury's rationalism can be felt.

"The Agonie" begins by claiming that natural philosophical problems can be fully measured while religious mysteries involve matters so personal that they may be infinitely sounded without ever being fully grasped. The poem begins by setting two types of "mysteries" against one another. On the one hand, there are the mysteries of nature and statecraft. And on the other, there are the scriptural mysteries of Sin and Love, both of which are capitalized so as to indicate that they are not reducible to objects or things in the world. Adopting the tone characteristic of Old Testament wisdom literature, Herbert teaches:

> Philosophers have measur'd mountains,
> Fathom'd the depths of seas, of states, and kings,
> Walk'd with a staffe to heav'n, and traced fountains:
>   But there are two vast, spacious things,
> The which to measure it doth more behove:
> Yet few there are that sound them; Sinne and Love. (1–6)

As the typography of line 6 implies, Sin and Love constitute two of the major mysteries expressed in the New Testament (2 Thess. 2:7; Eph. 6.32). The difference between these mysteries and the secular mysteries like statecraft is intimated in the shifting meaning of "measure" between lines one and five. In the first instance, measure means "to calculate," while in the second it implies "to put into metre" (OED, 16). The second meaning of "measure" is verified by the word *sounding*, which implies singing and searching rather than tracing and weighing. Herbert thus warns against overly literal readings of scriptural uses of the word *measure* in much the way Calvin does in his commentary on Isaiah 40:12, which Herbert is partly glossing. The passage from Isaiah reads: "Who hath measured the waters in the hollow of his hand, and meted out heaven with the span, and comprehended the dust of the earth in a measure, and weighed the mountains in scales, and the hills in a balance?" According to Calvin,

> When [God] names 'measures', which are used by men in very small Matters, he accommodates himself to our ignorance; for thus does the Lord often prattle with us ... for his greatness far exceeds all creatures, so that heaven, and earth, and sea, and all that they contain, however vast may be their extent, yet in comparison with him are nothing.[22]

Yet, there is more to Herbert's diction in this stanza. The shift between the epistemological problems of calculation and the ontological mysteries of Sin and Love are further evinced in the word *behove*. The term implies that the latter mysteries are proper to human beings, that they are morally appropriate to who or what human beings are in their essence. In this respect, Herbert's conception of love parallels the one expressed in Joseph Beaumont's lyric "*Loves Mysterie.*" Beaumont's poem begins with the speaker asking saints and lower angels "What kind of thing is Love"? only to be told "They could not tell ... They Liv'd in its Flames, but could not say." He then turns to the heavenly seraphim, who reply:

> Who ... more than Wee
> Should know, that *Love's* a *Mysterie*?
> Hid under his owne flaming Wing
> Lies *Love* a secret open thing.
> And there lie Wee, all hid in Light,
> Which gives Us, & denies Us Sight.[23]

[22] Calvin, *Commentary on Isaiah* trans. William Pringle (Grand Rapids: Baker Books, 2009), 8:218.
[23] *The Minor Poems of Joseph Beaumont* (1616–1699) ed. Eloise Robinson (Boston: Houghton Mifflin, 1914), 11.

For Beaumont, divine mystery is not a problem to be resolved but a condition in which one finds oneself. This is what "The Agonie" as a title implies. Sin and Love are the conditions in which we struggle and thrive; they are the site of our "agon" not accidental qualities we might or might not possess. As such, Sin and Love demand a different kind of response than mountains and rivers. Ultimately incalculable, they demand contemplation or meditative understanding not analytical circumscription. Sin and Love are not so much what we know as what we live through, hence Sibbes' exhortation that "every one of us should be skillful in this double mystery, the mystery of the corruption of nature … as well as of the gospel" (7.399). In this respect, "The Agonie" presents a religious vision similar to the one encapsulated in Jeremy Taylor's assertion that "Theology is rather a divine life than divine knowledge. In heaven indeed we shall first see, and then love; but here on earth we must first love … and we shall then see and perceive and understand."[24] This is precisely the approach to theology that Cherbury reverses. For him, knowledge and reason ground faith which is understood as a series of intellectual commitments more than a lived agony.

No less importantly, the distinction between human and divine mysteries set out in the first stanza of "The Agonie" intimates a theory of poetry that is expounded in detail in the course of *The Temple*. For Herbert, poetry differs from natural philosophy because its *raison d'être* lies in its concern with phenomena that we are too immanent within to fully comprehend once and for all. For Herbert, we write poems about things that we cannot, in principle, fully comprehend. Thus, rather than being antithetical to natural philosophy, poetry begins where science ends. If Love and Sin are known at all, "The Agonie" suggests, they are known at the level of first-hand experience, not the level of abstract knowledge. Thus, those who "would know Sinne" are told to meditate upon Christ's suffering at Mount Olivet and those who would know Love are told to taste Christ's blood, "that juice, which on the crosse a pike / Did set again abroach" (14–15). In this poem, little, if anything, contradicts the remark sometimes mistakenly attributed to Galileo that "The intention of the Holy Ghost is to teach us how one goes to heaven, not how heaven goes." In fact, Herbert reasserts a distinction that Francis Bacon himself routinely makes, namely that the mysteries of nature should not be confused with the mysteries of faith.

---

[24] Cited in A.S. Mcgrade "Reason" in *The Study of Anglicanism*, 127.

If Herbert is taking aim at anyone in "The Agonie," it is the rationalism of his brother and not the empiricism of his friend. Unlike Bacon, who defends revelation by defining its proper sphere of influence, Cherbury tends to collapse the distinctions Herbert makes in the opening of "The Agonie," especially the difference between a first-person experience of immanence within the mystery of scripture and a third-person grasping of its overall meaning as message. Rather than being an uncontroversial reiteration of Augustinian views, "The Agonie" is a self-conscious attempt to keep open the difference between problems and mysteries at an historical moment when such distinctions came under increasing pressure.

The final couplet of "The Agonie" sustains these spiritually vital distinctions by emphasizing how, as John Donne writes in the context of 1 Timothy 3:16, "mystery and manifestation make the text" (3.206). In other words, the poem ends by reiterating how scripture both reveals and conceals its meaning: "Love is that liquour sweet and most divine, / Which my God feels as bloud; but I, as wine" (17–18). Presented in the forms of blood and wine, love is both disclosed and hidden to human view. On the one hand, love appears in the historical materiality of God's suffering in a form where his divinity is concealed under his humanity. On other hand, it appears sacramentally through the collective recalling of Christ's sacrifice in the eucharist as wine materially conceals but spiritually reveals Christ's presence to participants. In both cases, love is simultaneously hidden and disclosed.

By concluding the poem with a celebration of divine love, Herbert confirms Sibbes' view that "there is a greater height and depth and breadth; there are greater dimensions in love and mercy in Christ than there is in our sins and miseries; and all this is gloriously discovered in the gospel" (4:241). The rationalist tradition fostered by Cherbury had little patience for the conviction that gospel mysteries are hidden and yet revealed in this manner. In his chapter "On Revelation" in *De Veritate*, for example, Cherbury strictly delimits the conditions under which true revelation can be said to occur. To start with, he insists that "revelation must be given directly to some person; for what is received from others as revelation must be accounted not revelation but tradition or history" (308). This startling claim explains why Cherbury tends to refer to biblical narrative as "history" rather than revelation. In his view, revelation is what happens to me, while history is what happens to you. Although the exegetically skeptical implications of this particular view are never fully stated by Cherbury, their corrosive force will be developed later in the century in writers such as Arthur Bury and John Toland. Also important is Cherbury's claim that "revelation must recommend some course of action which is good; in this way genuine revelations may be distinguished from false and wicked temptations" (308). The implication here is that revelation cannot suspend the ethical values embodied in the common notions; they can only reinforce them. Ignoring the implications of this claim for stories such as Abraham and Isaac, Cherbury applies it to the Decalogue. In his view, the ten commandments simply authorize the previously known common notions "since their injunctions are implicit in every kind of law and religion" (312). In the beginning, Cherbury claims, was not the Word as event but intuitive, universal reason.

As I have noted, this logical displacing of revelation behind common notions forecloses the interpretive space in which standard Augustinian notions of mystery operate. If everything crucial in scripture can be reduced to a set of reasonable and predictable propositions, then the kind of interpretive commitment demanded by participatory exegesis is either beside the point or simply a means of reinforcing what is already known. Cherbury's reduction of participatory exegesis, which is precisely the kind of development that Andrewes warned against, would become more fully explicit later in the century in works such as Arthur Bury's *The Naked Gospel* (1690). Rector of Exeter College, Oxford, Bury presented a disquisition on the meaning of *mysterion* that wholly rejected the type of mystery faith articulated by Browne, Donne, and Herbert. Rather than defining Christianity as an extended mystery, as Sibbes did, Bury asks incredulously:

> You say, Religion hath *Mysteries*; let us therefore consider what a *Mystery* is. In the Old Testament we find not the word; in the New, we find it consist in two parts; the one Open, the other Secret.[25]

The crucial point comes when Bury sharply qualifies this standard definition by adding:

> So the word plainly importeth two contrary Aspects upon two different Persons; hid to the one, and open to the other: But that it should at the same Time, and to the same Persons, be both hid and open, is more than a hidden Mystery; it is an open Contradiction, and it is no less so, that I must believe what is hidden from my understanding.[26]

---

[25] Arthur Bury, *The Naked Gospel* (London: 1690), 56.
[26] Ibid., 56–57.

For Bury, the Augustinian dialectic of manifestation and mystery amounts to nothing more than implicit faith, the dreaded scholastic doctrine that believers who do not understand the complexities of Catholic teaching can nevertheless trust the authority of the institution. He thus conflates the Catholic notion of implicit faith, which in scholastic thought is normally reserved for those who are intellectually incapable of grasping Christian teachings, with Augustine's broader conception of trust as a basic condition of a humane social existence. This allows him to narrow the gap between faith and reason, making belief a rational action no different in kind from ratiocination. Developing Cherbury's approach to revelation, Bury further obscures the idea that reading scripture is analogous to participating in the sacraments in the sense that it is intellectually and ethically edifying. For if faith is no different in kind than knowledge, then scripture offers information for consumption. What it does not offer is a narrative context for spiritual development over the course of one's life.

Bury's eliding of the difference between belief and reason is most vividly expressed in his bombastic critique of Sir Thomas Browne's Tertullian distinction between faith and knowledge. As far as Bury is concerned, Browne's view of faith "is a certain symptom of madness" no better "than the Ravings in *Bedlam*."[27] Only decades after Browne wrote, his kind of mystery faith began to appear utterly lunatic. While Cherbury is never quite as forthright about these matters as Bury, the general implications are clear enough. They approach John Toland's view that the totality of scripture can be comprehended with certainty. For Toland, the idea that scripture contains mysteries that cannot be fully grasped or comprehended is incoherent obscurantism. He can thus answer his question, "Is it possible for us to understand those [biblical] *Mysteries* at last, or not?" with absolute certitude: "If it be, then all I contend for is gain'd ... But if it be impossible after all to understand them, this is such a piece of Folly and Impertinence as no sober Man would be guilty of."[28] While this black-and-white approach to hermeneutics is worlds away from the Augustinianism of Sibbes and Herbert, it is not far from Cherbury's rationalism which Toland openly champions.

This shift in attitudes reflects the general degradation of Augustinian notions of mystery over the course of the seventeenth century. By the time Toland addressed the question of mystery in 1696, the concept itself had lost much of its hermeneutical meaning. No longer identify-

[27] Ibid., 56.
[28] Toland, *Christianity not Mysterious*, 86.

ing the reader's participatory immanence within a diachronically unfolding revelation, the term simply came to synchronically denote something
which cannot be, or has not yet been, comprehended. Even those who
sought to defend Augustinian Christianity from deists began to conceive
of *mysterion* as an epistemological problem rather than an ontological
condition, hence the exigency behind later-twentieth-century developments such as the *nouvelle theologie* which sought to recover the hermeneutical dimensions of premodern theologies of mystery. A full history
outlining this degradation of biblical concepts of mystery in seventeenth-
century England still remains to be told. But when it is, Cherbury and
Toland will play leading roles.[29]

As we have seen, Herbert's "Agonie" expresses the exegetical vitality
of the Augustinian conception of mystery as a dialectic between secrecy
and revelation. In doing so, Herbert was not simply repeating noncontroversial orthodoxies. Instead, he was exposing the spiritual implications
involved in failing to distinguish between two kinds of mysteries: those
that define the context in which we live and those which can be resolved
through effective technique. If there is one figure in early Stuart Britain
most responsible for collapsing this distinction, it is Lord Cherbury.
Like Sibbes, Herbert recognized the implications of Christian rationalism for a biblically centered spiritual life. To understand poems such as
"The Agonie" and "Heaven" is to understand how their exigency partly
lies in the hermeneutic reductions inherent in rationalist approaches to
Christianity such as found in Cherbury's philosophy.

DIVINITIE

If one poem in *The Temple* errs more on the side of certainty than mystery, it is "Divinitie," the lyric most closely associated with "The Agonie."
The two poems form a kind of diptych, with one emphasizing wonder
and the other confidence. John Drury recognizes this when he suggests
that "Divinitie" mocks "mystery-mongers and complexity-lovers."[30] Yet,
"Divinitie" itself is not a straightforward poem. Taken as a whole, it is an
exquisitely beguiling dramatic monologue in which claims to scriptural
simplicity are made in difficult to understand ways. The result is a poem

---

[29] For a discussion of the new theology, see Hans Boersma, *Nouvelle Théologie and
Sacramental Ontology: A Return to Mystery* (Oxford: Oxford UP, 2009).
[30] Drury, *Music at Midnight*, 108.

that makes an interpretively challenging claim about textual simplicity. More than an inadvertent irony on Herbert's part, this tension between form and meaning is consistent with the way the lyric qualifies each of its claims to certainty. Ultimately, the assurance in simplicity that the speaker enjoys occurs after he recognizes, *pace* Cherbury, that faith is a Tertullian leap that grounds and contextualizes human reason. The final result is a poem in which we rediscover Herbert's commitment to neatness, the idea that in scripture plainness and mystery coincide.

In the process of arriving at this insight about the relationship between faith and reason, the speaker of "Divinitie" engages in a subtle defense of holistic thinking. This spiritual and intellectual adventure begins in the first two stanzas where the speaker does more than critique the application of reason to revelation: he establishes the poem's defense of avowing the immanence of the human thinker within the discursive context in which he meditates. The speaker begins this apology of holistic thought by identifying an element of magical thinking lurking at the root of otherwise reasoned astronomical speculation:

> As men, for fear the starres should sleep and nod,
>   And trip at night, have spheres suppli'd;
> As if a starre were duller then a clod,
>   Which knows his way without a guide:
>
> Just so the other heav'n they also serve,
>   Divinities transcendent skie:
> Which with the edge of wit they cut and carve.
>   Reason triumphs, and faith lies by.

Herbert's speaker is here concerned with two sets of holistic patterns found in the universe: the heavenly bodies of stars and planets and scriptural revelation. In his view, the reduction of these holistic patterns into their constituent parts is symptomatic of an anxious desire for control and domination over both natural and supernatural worlds. He thus senses a psychological motive underlying empiricist reductionism. In making this critique, he endorses the Aristotelian-Platonic idea that heavenly bodies move according to an inherent intelligence or occult quality. The assumption here is that the heavenly bodies are alive and conscious not mechanical; hence the speaker's disgust at the practice of cutting and carving up something that is a living creation, be it the heavens or the divine Word. For him, such reductive thinking amounts to a form of idolatry in which the observer unnecessarily imposes his own limitations on the observed.

Crucial to stanza two is the biting sarcasm of the word *serve* at the end of line one: "Just so the other heav'n they also serve." The implication here is that theologians-cum-natural philosophers have violated the warning that John Chrysostum makes in his commentary on Paul's description of apostles as stewards of the mysteries. According to Chrysostum, a priest must not usurp "what belongs to his master by claiming it for himself as if he were master."[31] This is precisely what the rationalist theologians criticized in "Divinitie" do when they cut and carve *sacra doctrina* as though she were a cadaver upon a table rather than a mystery into which one is initiated. Herbert's anatomical image conjures up the relatively familiar idea that early modern anatomies were carried out in a mock-sacramental or quasi-liturgical manner. The implication of the image is that rather than playing the role of steward (*oikonomos*) or *mystagogue*, the rationalist theologian dissects the sacred environment that he should initiate other Christians into. At stake in these opening stanzas is the difference between objective comprehension and subjective initiation, the difference, that is, between understanding something and the process of becoming more understanding. This is poetry in defense of mystagogy.

Stanza three of "Divinitie" continues the trajectory of thought as the speaker calls attention to the distinction between *sapientiae* and *scientiae*: eternal wisdom and temporal knowledge. Just as "The Agonie" warned against collapsing the difference between two kinds of mysteries, so "Divinitie" warns against collapsing two distinct modes of knowledge. For this speaker, the eternal wisdom of revelation demands reverence and wonder not scholastic disputation:

> Could not that wisdome, which first broacht the wine,
>   Have thicken'd it with definitions?
> And jagg'd his seamless coat, had that been fine,
>   With curious questions and divisions? (9–12)

Figured here as Christ's "seamless coat," divine love is said to be a gift in which humans participate, especially during the eucharist. To reduce

---

[31] Judith L. Kovacs, *1 Corinthians: Interpreted by Early Medieval Christian Commentators* (Grand Rapids: Eerdmans, 2005), 71.

this spiritual context to "curious questions and divisions" is to misconstrue eternal wisdom for temporal knowledge, something with which we participate and something we might dominate. On this account, divinity denotes a set of actions one does more than a set of abstractions that one knows; or more precisely, it is something one comes to know by doing. For this speaker, divinity is more like learning how to improvise on an instrument than it is like memorizing a set of rules.

Having identified the limits of human knowledge vis-à-vis divinity, the poem then emphasizes the clarity of *sacra doctrina*. But the poem does not reduce this clarity to straightforward simplicity like that of a catechism. Instead, it offers its own variation of doctrine as a "secret open thing," describing doctrine as blindingly bright, as clear, apparently, as heaven:

> But all the doctrine, which he taught and gave,
>   Was cleare as heav'n, from whence it came.
> At least those beams of truth, which onely save,
>   Surpasse in brightnesse any flame. (13–16)

For a stanza that follows on a critique of overly fine theological distinctions, these lines offer a series of surprisingly careful qualifications and rather beguiling images. Indeed, the imagery here recalls the kinds of distinctions Sibbes makes when he asserts that there are "degrees of discovery of heavenly things":

> First in the *doctrine of them*; and so they are hid to them that are out of the church. And then, secondly, in the *spiritual meaning of them*; and so they are hid to carnall men in the church. And then, thirdly, in regard of *the full comprehension of them*, as they are indeed; and so they are reserved for heaven. We have but a little glimpse of them, a little light into them in this world. (4.165)

Even more directly, Herbert's paradox recalls Luther's claim that "the Holy Scriptures are a spiritual light far brighter than the sun itself, especially in things that are necessary to salvation."[32] As we have seen, this is a standard idiom used to express the play of revelation in concealment presupposed by Augustinian hermeneutics and hence by Herbert's understanding of poetic neatness.

---

[32] Luther, *Bondage of the Will*, 159.

Such idioms qualify and contextualize the claims to simplicity made in the following stanza:

> *Love God, and love your neighbour. Watch and pray.*
> *Do as ye would be done unto.*
> O dark instructions; ev'n as dark as day!
> Who can these Gordian knots undo? (17–20)

From a strictly intellectual standpoint, there is nothing particularly complicated about the biblical proclamation to love one's neighbor announced here. In practice, however, the commandment is impossibly difficult, as the speaker of "Unkindnesse" admits when he deplores how he lets "the poore" "starve at doore" (13–14). Stanza five thus implies a degree of dialectical irony. From the standpoint of external meaning, the image of the "Gordian knot" is comic hyperbole. Yet, from the standpoint of personal significance, the image is a highly revealing category error. Loving one's neighbor is nothing like a "Gordian knot" because it is not something one could finish with through a single, final bold gesture. This dramatic irony is expressed in the Bodleian manuscript through the typographical emphasis placed on "Gordian."[33] Rather than being a once-and-for-all responsibility, loving one's neighbor is a goal that one aims at without ever fully realizing. At this point in the poem, the speaker of "Divinitie" is stumbling toward the realization that biblical mystery is "not just ... the focus for *our* questioning and investigating, but mystery [is] that which *questions us,* which calls us to account."[34] As Augustine would have it, in "assimilating the mystery," the Christian "will be assimilated by it." Or as John Hales puts it, scripture "interprets the interpreter."[35] This implicit interpenetration of reader and text becomes clearer in the following stanza.

Veering away from scripture's ostensible clarity, the speaker is suddenly struck by its terrible strangeness in stanza six. It is almost as though the theological idioms he has been rehearsing are beginning to slowly seep in and affect his outlook as he now reaches something of a stumbling block:

[33] *George Herbert The Temple: A Diplomatic Edition of the Bodleian Manuscript (Tanner 307)* With Introduction and Notes by Mario A. Di Cesare (Binghamton: MRTS, 1995), 203.

[34] Andrew Louth, *Discerning the Mystery: An Essay on the Nature of Theology* (Oxford: Clarendon Press, 1983), 145.

[35] Augustine paraphrased by Henri de Lubac in *Theological Fragments* trans. Rebecca Howell Balinski (San Francisco: Ignatius Press, 1984), 67. John Hales, *Sermon ... Concerning The Abuses of obscure and difficult places of holy Scripture* (Oxford: 1617), 4.

But he doth bid us take his bloud for wine.
Bid what he please; yet I am sure,
To take and taste what he doth there designe,
Is all that saves, and not obscure. (13–16)

The first line returns us to the dialectic of manifestation in mystery that concluded "The Agonie" earlier in the sequence. Here again, the speaker confronts the question of how blood and wine, history and sacrament, law and gospel, constitute the ongoing forms in which revelation occurs. Indicating a startling shift in tone, this line suggests a degree of befuddlement on the speaker's part. It is as if as he were saying: "Wait a second, there is nothing simple or clear about being told to take his blood as wine? Doesn't this part of scripture violate my natural reason?" This shift in tone signals the realization that the commandments of scripture cannot always be fully comprehended intellectually, and that it is precisely at such moments that a true leap of faith is called for. Confronted with noncomprehension, the speaker declares a willingness to participate in scripture even when he does not really grasp it. But in doing so, he does not fully avow the mystery inherent in such a leap. Sophie Read is thus right to note that the speaker's tone betrays a "suspicious complacency that the mystery is 'not obscure.'"[36] Read this way, stanza five need not be bemoaned as unfortunately obscure. On the contrary, such obscurity is part and parcel with the way that the poem's dialectical irony betrays the interpenetration of reader and sacred text which the speaker only half-consciously realizes. At this point in the poem, the speaker rediscovers the necessary priority of faith over knowledge that Cherbury sought to reverse. The irony of the poem is that the speaker does not fully recognize the principle of neatness that he has rediscovered, the way plainness and mystery are thought to coincide in scripture. Rather than denying mystery, "Divinitie" shows a speaker in the early stages of discovering it through the dialectical irony of protestant hermeneutics, the way in which the text can be a mystery for us personally even when it is clear from a general intellectual standpoint.

"Divinitie" ends with a stanza that has the status of a charm. On the one hand, the final stanza breaks the enchantments of magical thinking identified in the first two stanzas. But on the other, it initiates readers into the mystery of the fellowship and the enchantments of faith associated with it. Rather than arguing on behalf of mystagogy, the final stanza becomes an instance of it:

[36] Sophie Read, *Eucharist and the Poetic Imagination in Early Modern England* (Cambridge: Cambridge UP, 2013), 121.

> Then burn thy Epicycles, foolish man;
> Break all thy spheres, and save thy head.
> Faith needs no staffe of flesh, but stoutly can
> To heav'n alone both go, and leade. (25–28)

Given the popularity of Ante-Nicene fathers in seventeenth-century England, it is probably no coincidence that the ending of "Divinitie" is simultaneously enchanting and disenchanting in much the same way as Clement's *Protrepticus* (*Exhortation to the Heathen*).[37] Like Clement's exhortation to the Greeks, Herbert's warning to rationalists echoes Paul's appeal to the Corinthians to place faith in the Christian mystery prior to the claims of philosophy or pagan tradition. In his second-century patristic work, Clement exhorts his sophisticated Greek readers to abandon pagan philosophy and Hellenistic mystery rites in order to enter into the *mysterion* of Christian faith. Somewhat paradoxically, he concludes his highly demystifying anthropology of pagan culture by turning to the language of charm and song:

> Come, O madman, not leaning on the thyrsus, not crowned with ivy; throw away the mitre, throw away the fawn-skin; come to thy senses. I will show thee the Word, and the mysteries of the Word, expounding them after thine own fashion ... Come thou also, O aged man ... I give thee the staff [of the cross] on which to lean ... O truly sacred mysteries! O stainless light! My way is lighted with torches, and I survey the heavens and God; I become holy whilst I am initiated.[38]

Though "Divinitie" has none of the gnosticism that colors Clement's Alexandrian brand of Christianity, it nevertheless ends by dissolving philosophical illusions so as to illuminate the mysteries of faith in much the way the *Protrepticus* does. What begins as a catechistical warning in "Divinitie" ends as an invitation to a sacred feast. The poem thus concludes by affirming Clement's distinction between the personally invested knowledge

---

[37] For the rise in popularity of Ante-Nicene fathers among seventeenth-century English clergymen, see Jean-Louis Quantin, *The Church of England and Christian Antiquity: The Construction of a Confessional Identity in the 17th Century* (Oxford: Oxford UP, 2009), 9, 79.

[38] Clement of Alexandria, "Exhortation to the Heathen" in *The Ante-Nicene Fathers Volume 2* trans. and ed. Alexander Roberts and James Donaldson with notes by A. Cleveland Coxe (Edinburgh: T & T Clark, 1994), 204.

gained through initiation into mystery and the impersonal knowledge gained through philosophical analysis.

The tension between clarity and mystery presented in Herbert's "Divinitie" revealingly parallels not only Andrewes' sermon on the mystery of Godliness discussed earlier but also Donne's sermon on the same text. One passage in particular serves as an effective gloss on the last four stanzas of "Divinitie." Like Herbert's poem, Donne's sermon carefully balances between different forms of simplicity and difficulty. What is more, Donne emphasizes the question of how the mystery of scripture arises from the difference between faithful and empirical perception. Like Hooker, Donne emphasizes the distinction between a mode of perception that is institutionally and contextually mediated versus one that is wholly private and unmediated. The result is a vision that carefully balances between two sets of virtues. On the one hand, Donne emphasizes the hermeneutical virtues of realizing that authoritative interpretation involves some form of institutional consensus, an idea that Cherbury rigorously downplays. But on the other, Donne avows the spiritual virtues inherent in the personal experience of scripture. Speaking of the doctrine of salvation, Donne preaches:

> But yet, as clear as it is, it [godliness] is a Mystery, a Secret; not that I cannot see it, but that I cannot see it with any eyes that I can bring: not with the eye of Nature: *Flesh and blood has not revealed this unto thee*, sayes Christ to *Peter:* not with the eye of Learning; *Thou hast hid these things from the wise*, sayes Christ to his Father ... nor with the eye of a private sence ... for ... no Scripture is of private interpretation. I see not this mystery by the eye of Nature, of Learning, of State, of mine private sense; but I see it by the eye of the Church, by the light of Faith, that's true ... this Church is that which proposes to me all that is necessary to my salvation, in the Word, and seals all to me in the Sacraments. (3.9.210)

Donne's emphasis on the ecclesiastical mediation of mystery maps perfectly onto Herbert's analogy between doctrine and sacrament in "Divinitie." After all, the sacramental imagery in the poem does more than emphasize the importance of personally experiencing the Word, though it does do that; it also emphasizes how the encounter with the Word happens in and through the church. Richard Strier admits the possibility of this reading in order to refute it when he notes that "Herbert is not contrasting 'the great wheele of the Church' with the vagaries of private judgment," as Thomas Browne does in *Religio Medici*; instead, he is confuting the "efforts of reason in the realm of 'divinitie'."[39] The truth, however, is that Herbert is doing both at the same time. Like *Religio Medici*, "Divinitie" avoids the ignorance of an implicit faith that is void of scriptural knowledge while nevertheless embracing an ecclesiastically mediated historical faith, much as Browne endorses:

> In Philosophy where truth seemes double-faced, there is no man more paradoxical then my self; but in Divinity I love to keep the road, and though not in an implicite, yet an humble faith, follow the great wheele of the Church, by which I move.[40]

Ultimately, "Divinitie" is in keeping with a poem such as "Lent," which strongly celebrates the authoritative role of "thy Mother" church in determining doctrine and practice, so much so that in it Herbert teaches how "The humble soul compos'd of love and fear / Begins at home, and layes the burden there, / When doctrines disagree" (7–9). Indeed, nowhere does Herbert more clearly resist the scripturally and ecclesiastically unmediated visions of Valdés and Cherbury in favor of orthodoxy than in "Lent." This is especially true of its penultimate stanza which may call attention to more than puritan dissent; it may also point out the striking absence of any Christological dimension to his brother's writing, be his poetry or prose: "Who goeth in the way which Christ hath gone, / Is much more sure to meet with him, then one / That travelleth by-wayes" (37–39).

CONCLUSION: FAITH, REASON, AND BIBLICAL FELLOWSHIP

Lurking behind the work of both Valdés and Cherbury is the specter of Socinian rationalism, the heretical threat that Robert Sanderson warned against in a sermon on 1 Timothy 3:16 delivered at Berwick on 16 July, 1639. Closely recalling the idioms that Herbert uses in "The Agonie" and "Divinity," Sanderson rails against Socinians who make "*Reason* the sole *standard*, whereby to measure both the *Principles* and *Conclusions* of Faith. *Mysteries* are not to be measured by *Reason*."[41] As Sanderson's

---

[39] Strier, *Love Known*, 47.

[40] Sir Thomas Browne, "Religio Medici" in *Sir Thomas Brrowne: The Major Works* ed. C.A. Patrides (New York: Penguin, 1977), 66.

[41] Robert Sanderson, *XXXVI Sermons* (London: 1689 8th edn.), 485.

sermon suggests, the exigency behind Herbert's attacks on reason likely lies as much in post-reformation forms of rationalism as it does in medieval scholasticism, especially those forms he encountered closest to home. One of the most intriguing heirs of Herbert's hermeneutic approach to scripture is Thomas Traherne whose self-consciously anti-dogmatic exegetical sensibility is encapsulated in his fragmentary poem "On the Bible." On the one hand, the exigency of Traherne's rejection of dogmatic approaches to scripture likely arises from works such as William Twisse's *The Doubting Conscience Resolved ... Or that a Christian may be infallibly certain of his Faith and Religion by the Holy Scriptures* (1652).[42] As its title suggests, Twisse's book offers the infallible religious certainty that Laud's somewhat troublesome Godson William Chillingworth rejected as impossible in his hugely influential 1638 treatise *The Religion of Protestants*. According to Chillingworth, the best humans can hope for in the realm of religious ideas is moral certainty, the kind of knowledge requisite for getting on in the world. What we cannot hope for is infallible religious knowledge. Writing in the wake of Chillingworth's very wide post-Restoration reception, Traherne gives strikingly unguarded expression to the open-ended view of scripture that Herbert articulates more circumspectly. Traherne's unfinished poem reads:

I.

When Thou dost take
   this sacred Book into thy hand;
Think not that Thou th' included sence dost understand.

2.

It is a signe
   though wantest sound Intelligence;
If that Thou think
   thy selfe to understand the Sence.

---

[42] Traherne responds respectfully but critically to Twisse in *A Sober View of Dr Twisses his Considerations* in *The Works of Thomas Traherne Volume 1* ed. Jan Ross (Cambridge: D.S. Brewer, 2005), 45–230.

3.

Bee not deceived
    Thou then on it in vain mayst gaze
The way is intricate
    that leads into a Maze.

4.

Heer's nought but whats Mysterious
    to an understanding Eye:
Where Reverence alone stands Ope,
    And Sence stands By.

These verses very neer, to
strangely seen in ...[43]

While rejecting Twisse's brand of certainty, Traherne's approach to scripture also precludes the kind of rationalist certainty that increased in popularity during his lifetime. In this and other ways, Traherne extended some of the ways that Herbert's *The Temple* balanced between dogmatism and rationalism opting instead for a more open-ended Augustinian approach to scripture. As Traherne understood, what is at stake in such Augustinianism is a conception of fellowship that is rooted in a spiritually and hermeneutically robust sense of the Christian *mysterion*. On this point, Herbert and Cherbury differed in subtle but significant ways. Although Herbert shared his older brother's ecumenical spirit, he differed as to how Christians should establish a widely held and peaceful fellowship. Like Augustine, Herbert thought cool reason too weak a force to serve as a foundation for human community. More powerful than reason, Herbert thought, is the experience of wise ignorance, the belief that human limitations constitute the condition in which charity flourishes within the context of God's love. Again and again, his poems show speakers discovering that "Thy word is all, if we could spell." But rather than serving as the occasion for interpretative frustration or the more full-throated liberalism of the Great Tew Circle, this insight ultimately provides the space in

---

[43] Thomas Traherne, *Centuries, Poems, And Thanksgivings* ed. H.M. Margoliouth (Oxford: Clarendon Press, 1958), 2.205.

which Herbert's speakers discover the spiritually productive inevitability of doubt, uncertainty, and mystery in the life and strife of faith. And while Herbert's poetics of mystery may be conventionally Augustinian in its general outlines, it is nevertheless a response to forms of rationalism that differ, in crucial respects, from the Hellenistic traditions with which Augustine vied. Most importantly, Herbert reacted against the claims of intuitive reason on which Cherbury based his philosophical and religious system. In this respect, Cherbury's *De Veritate* is an early example of a distinctly late seventeenth-century understanding of "Religion" as a universal phenomenon. After all, it is only in the Enlightenment that a concept of "Religion" emerges such that one could impartially and systematically study various kinds of "religion" as essentially one and the same type of thing.[44] It is precisely this tendency to strive for impartiality, this practice of adopting a third-person stance vis-à-vis the question of revelation, that most shockingly distinguishes Cherbury's thought from his predecessors and immediate contemporaries. It is also what most perturbed George Herbert who saw in it nothing less than the demise of Christian mystery as such. What ultimately worried Herbert is the way Cherbury's system collapses the difference between the ontological process of becoming understanding and the epistemological process of understanding something, a collapse that would eventually be fulfilled in the work of John Toland and those who followed in his wake. Rather than emphasizing the unity of all knowledge, as Peter Ramus did, Herbert carefully distinguished between different types of knowing. In doing so, he continually explored the crucial, if sometimes intellectually elusive, difference between edification and information-transfer. And as he demonstrates, few mediums do this better than lyric poetry.

The powerful appeal that Cherbury's argument had for many seventeenth-century intellectuals is clear from the responses it generated decades after *De Veritate* was published, be it the positive response of Toland or the critical reaction of Toland's other philosophical hero, John Locke. If Cherbury seems like an alien figure in the history of English thought, it is partly because Locke's empiricism in *An Essay Concerning Human Understanding* begins as a systematic critique of Cherbury's common notions. As a result, it is difficult now to read Cherbury without Locke mediating our view of him. But prior to Locke's empiricist critique

---

[44] This is the main thesis of Peter Harrison's, *Religion and the Religions in the English Enlightenment* (Cambridge: Cambridge UP, 1990).

of Cherbury's rationalism lay Herbert's Augustinian reaction to the eclipse of mystery implicit in *De Veritate*. For Herbert, his elder brother Cherbury presented a system that ultimately led to the same foreshortening of scriptural mystery that could be found in trivializing fideists such as Valdés. Viewed in these terms, it becomes apparent that Herbert's poetics, along with the exegetical and social visions it supports, constitutes a reaction to two different ways of approaching scripture as a closed-ended text that one may fully and totally comprehend rather than be comprehended by. Central to this spiritual aesthetic is not only the process of correction and revision long associated with Herbert's verse but also a deep awareness of the spiritually productive role of error, to which we now turn.

CHAPTER 7

Truth and Method: Error and Discovery in *The Temple*

The processes of correction and revision characteristic of Herbert's poetry have been productively read in a variety of contexts, including protestant notions of regeneration, Augustinian sign theory, and eucharistic theology.[1] What happens, though, when we turn from the frisson of discovery to the experience of being in error? How, exactly, does Herbert conceive of error as a necessary feature of Christian experience? Are there specific ideas about error that Herbert inherited? And if so, what relation pertains between the experience of being in error and the process of rediscovering the mysteries in Herbert's poetry?

An answer to these questions can be found in the way Herbert poeticizes what Augustine calls a "blessed failing," a theme that is related to, but should not be uncritically confused with, the *felix culpa* motif initiated by Ambrose's Easter proclamation. Where the fortunate fall motif is predominantly dogmatic in its claim that Adam's guilt happily occasioned Christ's incarnation and redemption, Augustine's blessed error motif is predominantly hermeneutic. For Augustine, the sweet mistake motif has less to do with dogma than with processes and modes of understanding, especially those involved in the mystery of godliness. Sibbes summarizes this aspect of Augustine's thought when he remarks that God makes man

---

[1] See respectively Strier, *Love Known*; Richard Todd, *The Opacity of Signs: Acts of Interpretation in George Herbert's The Temple* (Columbia: University of Missouri Press, 1987); and Read, *Eucharist and the Poetic Imagination*, 98–126.

© The Author(s) 2017
G. Kuchar, *George Herbert and the Mystery of the Word*,
DOI 10.1007/978-3-319-44045-3_7

"good by his slips, which is a strange course to make a man better by. Saith St. Austin, 'I dare say, and stand to it, that it is profitable for some men to fall; they grow more holy by their slips'" (3.137). So although Augustine's insights into the potentially productive dimensions of error emerge against the background of the *felix culpa* motif, they remain irreducible to it.

More important in this context than the *felix culpa* principle is Augustine's broader concern with learned ignorance. Throughout his poetry, Herbert's speakers continually rediscover that there is no predictable or even repeatable means by which one can fully understand the living Word. In *The Temple,* the process of spiritual discovery remains irreducible to methdologization; there is no systematic means of arriving at a spiritual epiphany. Although the habits of faith are crucial for religious life, they do not guarantee any sort of sanctifying insight.[2] In this sense, the learned ignorance that T.S. Eliot said is inherent to the act of writing poetry very much applies to Herbert's spiritual aesthetic. As far as poetry goes, Eliot says in "East Coker," "Every attempt Is a wholly new start ... each venture ...a new beginning" and all "a different kind of failure."[3]

Rather than being a doctrinal thematization of the *felix culpa* motif, Herbert's appropriation of Augustine's concept of "blessed error" is part of a larger hermeneutic vision in which the experience of understanding is concomitant with nonunderstanding, truth with error. In many respects, Herbert's fascination with Augustine's "blessed error" has more in common with William Empson's "fortunate confusion" than it does with Ambrose's "happy fault."[4] For Herbert, authentic understanding often happens in excess of human willing or expectation as the event of truth arises through various forms of misunderstanding and the experience of mortal limitations attendant therein. On this account, it is in the nature of spiritual and hermeneutic experience to reverse one's expectations, shift one's perspective, and thereby change one's heart. Even more, though, Herbert often assumes that the experience of holy mystery is concomitant with the experience of being in error, much as he assumes that the act of reading scripture is coincident with misreading it. The result is a spiritual aesthetic in which the "experience of 'being in error,' so inevitably

---

[2] See, for example, Sibbes 1.47.

[3] T.S. Eliot, "The Four Quartets," in *The Complete Poems and Plays* 1909–1950 (New York: Harcourt, Brace, & World, 1971), 128.

[4] See Empson's fifth type of ambiguity in *Seven Types of Ambiguity* (Chatto and Windus, 1930 rpt; New York: Penguin, 1995).

accompanies the perception of beauty that it begins to seem one of its abiding structural features," as Elaine Scarry has dared to say of beauty generally.[5]

Viewed from this perspective, it becomes clear that Herbert's representation of the experience of being in error needs to be seen against the background of renaissance pursuits of method. After all, the pursuit of reliable forms of repeatable knowledge occurred in the arts as well as the sciences, in rhetoric as well as in dialectic, in theology as well as in devotion itself. This drive toward methodologically reproducible knowledge was so central to early modern culture that it became the party slogan of renaissance intellectuals.[6] As a highly trained orator, Herbert was no doubt familiar with one of the main proponents of renaissance method: Peter Ramus. A crucial context for the rise of Baconian science, Ramist logic has also been said to have influenced Elizabethan and Jacobean poetry, specifically its fascination with dialectic and other processes of ratiocination.[7] Yet, as Walter Ong has pointed out, there is a fundamental tension between the objectifying orientation of Ramus' spatialization of knowledge within a scopic regime and the inherently dialogical character of Elizabethan and Jacobean poetry. Where Ramus' visual schematizations of all kinds of knowledge engender an objectivizing attitude in which the knower becomes a disembodied spectator, early modern poetry tends to place readers into the situation of living dialogue, making them auditors of persons rather than possessors of objects.[8] On this account, Herbert's poetry is less anti-rhetorical than it is anti-Ramist. Instead of following the monological route with Ramist thinkers like William Perkins, Herbert went in a decidedly dialogical direction, one in which Augustine's nonmethodological approach to hermeneutics and his accompanying investment in error as an inevitable feature of hermeneutic experience came to play important roles.

Although we know Herbert was a great reader of Augustine, what is perhaps less appreciated is the extent to which his response to the Bishop of Hippo was mediated by two major events in the history of hermeneutics:

---

[5] Elaine Scarry, *On Beauty and Being Just* (Princeton: Princeton UP, 1999), 28.

[6] Neal W. Gilbert, *Renaissance Concepts of Method* (New York: Columbia Press, 1960), 66.

[7] For a discussion of Ramus' influence on Bacon, see Lisa Jardine, *Francis Bacon: Discovery and the Art of Discourse* (Cambridge: Cambridge UP, 1974), 41–47, 52–53. For Ramus' possible influence on poetry, see Rosemund Tuve, *Elizabethan and Metaphysical Imagery: Renaissance Poetic and Twentieth-Century Critics* (Chicago: University of Chicago Press, 1947), Chap. 12.

[8] Walter Ong, *Method and the Decay of Dialogue* (Cambridge: Harvard UP, 1958), 287.

the protestant Reformation and the natural philosophy of Francis Bacon. Bacon's phenomenology of error, especially as expressed in *The New Organon* (1620), has been rightly celebrated as a major hermeneutical achievement, one that is of some consequence for the poetics of discovery in Herbert's *The Temple*.[9] In the process of translating Bacon's *The Advancement of Learning* from English into Latin at the author's request, Herbert came to recognize some of the important differences between Augustine's and Bacon's theories of knowledge, including their strikingly different attitudes toward the role of error in the experience of discovery.[10] Thus, in order to understand how Herbert depicts the experience of rediscovering the mysteries in *The Temple*, we need to consider how his response to Augustine is mediated by Bacon's pursuit of method, particularly his discussion of the idols of the mind. To do this, we first need to first consider how Herbert's The New Year Sonnets set the agenda for his poetics of discovery. From there, we will move back into *The Temple* in order to appreciate why truth and method are often so incommensurable with one another in Herbert's work. This will allow us to see that instead of participating in the post-reformation search for certitude, Herbert critically distanced himself from the early modern cult of method.

BEGINNINGS AND ENDINGS: THE NEW YEAR SONNETS

Herbert's fascination with questions of poetic method goes back to his earliest extant poetry. In the two New Year Sonnets that he sent to his mother at the age of 17, which Izaac Walton first printed, Herbert announces his vocation as a religious poet. In doing so, he defines poetry as a mode of spiritual discovery very similar in nature to Augustine's teaching that Christians should "always seek [God's] face; so that discovery may not bring an end to this quest, whereby love is meant, but, as love increases, let the quest for what has been discovered increase as well."[11] What is more, though, Herbert gives this Augustinian economy of inexhaustible spiritual discovery a distinctly alchemical inflection. The result is Herbert's first-known depiction of Augustine's conception of the inner spiritual life

---

[9] See Hans-Georg Gadamer, *Truth and Method* 2nd Edition. Trans. Joel Weinsheimer and Donald G. Marshall (New York: Continuum, 2002), 348–350, 356.

[10] For an informed discussion of Herbert's relation to Bacon, see Miller, *George Herbert's 'Holy Patterns'*, 77–118.

[11] *On The Trinity* 15.2 as cited in Lubac, *Medieval Exegesis*, 2.193.

as a process in which increasing, broadly progressive discovery enhances rather than exhausts the mystery of God's love. This subtly paradoxical view of spiritual life would later become an organizing principle of *The Temple* as a whole.

The alchemical dimensions of the New Year Sonnets are signaled at the opening of sonnet one when Herbert asks God's inspiring flame to kindle sanctifying desires in the hearts of English poets:

> My God, where is that ancient heat towards thee,
> Wherewith whole showls of *Martyrs* once did burn,
> Besides their other flames. Doth Poetry
> Wear *Venus* Livery? Only serve her turn? (1–4)

Helen Wilcox has identified a crux in the word *showls* from line two, noting that it "is difficult to reconcile with the surrounding metaphors of fire ('heat', 'burn,' 'flames')" (4). The missing context here is alchemy as the coexistence of fire and water in sonnet one is a hermetic expression of the spiritual refinement associated with martyrs who, by this definition, reach a state in which opposites are united. Herbert's imagery emphasizes the traditional idea that a martyr is first and foremost a fully realized spiritual soul bearing witness to the truth and only secondarily a sacrificial victim of the Christian faith. This distinction is crucial because it occurs in the context of Herbert's allusion to the alchemical poetics of the poet-martyr Robert Southwell. The only other English poet to have dedicated himself entirely to devotional verse, Southwell looms large in The New Year Sonnets as a significant precursor.[12] While the highly popular Southwell used alchemy as a mildly veiled code for recusant experience and post-Tridentine theology, Herbert now uses it to redefine poetry in light of Augustine's spiritual aesthetic.[13] In dedicating his poetic talents to the greater glory of God, as he says in the letter in which the sonnets were sent

---

[12] For discussions of Herbert's nonalchemical echoes of Southwell in these sonnets and the letter in which they first appeared, see F.E. Hutchinson, *the Works of George Herbert* (Oxford: Clarendon Press, 1959), 549–550 and Gary M. Bouchard "The Roman Steps to the Temple: An Examination of the Influence of Robert Southwell, SJ, upon George Herbert" *Logos* 10. 3 (2007), 131–150, 138–139.

[13] For a discussion of Southwell's alchemical poetics, see my "Alchemy, Repentance, and Recusant Allegory in Robert Southwell's *St Peters Complaint*" in *Remapping Early Modern English Catholicism* ed. Lowell Gallagher (Toronto: University of Toronto Press, 2010), Chap. 7.

(thereby appropriating the motto of the Jesuit order), Herbert invokes Southwell's alchemical poetics in order to forward a different theory of poetry as a medium of spiritual discovery. In the process, he also develops a different notion of the poet as martyr.

As the fire and water imagery of sonnet one suggests, alchemy is generally understood as a process of uniting opposites, be they chemical, elemental, or spiritual, hence its description as the *mysterium conjunctionis*. In the context of Herbert's two poems, the alchemical *conjunctio* that is alluded to in reference to the burning "showls of *Martyrs*" implies that the martyrs exemplify the most spiritually elevated form of existence possible. They burn not just with any fire but with a heat that emerges at the final stages of the alchemical opus, one that coincides with its opposite element. Rooted in the chemical practice of trying to refine base metals into silver and gold (*chrysopoeia*), spiritual alchemy is a symbolic code that medieval and renaissance Christians used to describe processes of regeneration. Expressed through a variety of metaphorical modes of representation, spiritual alchemy describes the transforming effects of divine love as an ongoing process of dissolution and coagulation, the breaking down of impurities and the building up of increasing perfection. As we have seen, this process of dying to rise again is a basic poetic impulse in Herbert's poetry. The basic idea of *solve et coagula* is that God's love is like a purifying fire that refines impure elements of the soul, thereby raising the heart to a more divine state. This is the underlying process alluded to in the opening of sonnet two when Herbert declares:

> Sure Lord, there is enough in thee to dry
> Oceans of *Ink*, for, as the Deluge did
> Cover the Earth, so doth thy Majesty:
> Each Cloud distills thy praise, and doth forbid
> *Poets* to turn it to another use. (1–5)

The image of the cloud distilling God's praise intimates a relatively technical use of the alchemical idea that the mercurial rain, or what is referred to as the 'dew of grace,' washes the material at the bottom of the alchemical vessel so as to make "it ready to receive the 'seed' of gold ... leading to the conception and birth of the philosopher's stone."[14]

---

[14] Lyndy Abraham, *A Dictionary of Alchemical Imagery* (Cambridge: Cambridge UP, 1998), 42.

But the general point here is essentially the one Richard Sibbes makes when he says that "the Grace of God is a blessed Alcumist, where it toucheth it makes good, and religious."[15] Consistent with the alchemical fire imagery of its opening, sonnet one ends with a prayer complaint that poets be purified with the love of divine fire: "Why doth that fire, which by thy power and might / Each breast does feel, no braver fuel choose / Than that, which one day, Worms, may chance refuse" (12–14).

Sonnet two concludes on a similar note, except now Herbert draws out the spiritual and aesthetic consequences of his key distinction between sacred and profane verse. In doing so, Herbert participates in a long tradition of employing alchemy as a way of expressing the transformative power of verse.[16] He does this by declaring that true beauty lies not in physical form but in the spiritual process of "sounding" God. Stating his case somewhat baldly, the teenaged Herbert concludes sonnet two by distinguishing the attractions of the female muse from the everlasting beauty inherent in the process of seeking God's love. In the process, he confirms the view expressed in an anonymous seventeenth-century alchemical treatise which declares that God is "the true Alchymist [who] excludes all vulgar operations to extract internal beauty"[17]:

> Why should I *Womens eyes* for Chrystal take?
> Such poor invention burns in their low mind
> > Whose fire is wild, and doth not upward go
> > To praise and on thee Lord, some *Ink* bestow.
> Open the bones, and you shall nothing find
> > In the best *face* but *filth*, when Lord, in thee
> > The *beauty* lies, in the discovery. (8–14)

---

[15] Cited Stanton J. Linden *Darke Hierogliphicks: Alchemy in English Literature from Chaucer to the Restoration* (Lexington: University Press of Kentucky, 1996) 93. See also Strier, *Love Known*, 208.

[16] For studies of how alchemy inflects early modern poetics, see Lynn Veach Sadler, "Relations Between Alchemy and Poetics in the Renaissance and Seventeenth Century, With Special Glances at Donne and Milton" *Ambix* 24.2 (1977), 69–76 and Peggy Munoz Simonds, "Love is a spirit all compact of fire': Alchemical *Coniunctio* in *Venus and Adonis*" in *Emblems and Alchemy* eds. Alison Adams and Stanton J. Linden (Glasgow: Glasgow Emblem Studies, 1998), 133–156.

[17] An anonymous seventeenth-century alchemical treatise cited in Linden, *Darke Hieroglyphickes*, 251.

The coincidence of opposites conveyed at the beginning of sonnet one has now come full circle as the sanctifying fire alluded to in the earlier lyric is revealed to be the expression of divine wisdom traditionally associated with martyrdom. From the patristic period onward, sanctifying fire is generally associated with the mode of purifying wisdom that defines martyrdom as a spiritual condition rather than as a literal act.[18] By tying the two sonnets together around the word *discovery*, Herbert clarifies that the sanctifying fire of sonnet one refers to a mode of inspired wisdom, one that purifies the soul to the point of perfection rather than literal death. In this respect, the poems end by coming full circle as the coincidence of beauty and knowledge at the end of sonnet two discloses at a conceptual level the coincidence of opposites that is expressed at an imagistic level in the opening of sonnet one through fire and watery imagery. Through this circular structure, Herbert displays the protestant tendency to emphasize the figure of the martyr as writer and reader rather than simply a bodily sufferer.[19] What is far more important to Herbert's poems than the physical suffering of the martyrs is a conception of the poet as bearing literate witness to the truth. Crucially, then, Herbert links poetry to martyrdom in ways that play to his favor over and against that of his invoked precursor: Robert Southwell. Evoking Southwell's alchemical poetics in order to displace it, Herbert redefines devotional poetry and the figure of the devotional poet in subtly but significantly different terms.

The underlying circular structure of these precocious poems follows the alchemical pattern of spiritual transformation symbolized by the ouroboros or self-consuming snake. These poems thus present Herbert's first extant depiction of the basic movement that would serve as the organizing principle of *The Temple*, what Daniel Doerksen describes as "that mysterious spiraling movement (neither simply linear nor purely cyclical) which [Herbert] sees as the Christian's inner life."[20] As Herbert clearly recognized, the alchemical pattern of spiritual transformation symbolized by the ouroboros parallels Augustine's call to "always seek [God's] face; so that discovery may not bring an end to this quest, whereby love is meant, but, as love increases, let the quest for what has been discovered increase

---

[18] See, for example, Clement of Alexandria's, *Stromata*, 532.

[19] Brian Cummings, *Mortal Thoughts: Religion, Secularity & Identity in Shakespeare and Early Modern Culture* (Oxford: Oxford UP, 2013), 99, 107, 130–132.

[20] Doerksen, *Picturing Religious Experience*, 189.

as well."[21] Heather Asals is thus entirely correct to see the concluding phrase of sonnet two as channeling Augustine's theory of discovery in *On The Trinity*. According to Augustine, "If we ... trace back the origin of the word 'discovery' [*inventio*], what else does it mean, than that to discover is to come [*venio*] into [*in*] that which is sought?"[22] The crucial implication here is that "knowing about" something, for Augustine, is a species of "participating in" it. Like the biblical idiom "to know," Augustinian discovery presumes intimacy, relationality, a blending of knower with known. In this model of knowledge, the truth event is less about ostensive reference per se than it is about achieving a proper form of participation between knower and known. Virtually all ancient and medieval epistemology presupposes some form of this basic theory of knowing, especially the alchemical tradition.[23] So too does Herbert when he makes religious beauty coextensive with discovery. Rather than being an external property of something, beauty is the consequence of an achieved relation between persons. This is beauty as process rather than as product. Only in the early modern period, with the rise of empirical science and the pursuit of method, does the desire for pure objectivity become a significant cultural force. For Herbert, as for Andrewes, the act of seeking God's sanctifying presence involves a totally different ontology and temporality than the pursuit of objective knowledge. As Andrewes teaches, echoing Augustine: "For sure as we seek God to save us, He saveth us to seek Him; if when we seek Him we are saved, when we are saved we should seek Him. The time of His saving is the time of our seeking; and one hour then is better than four and twenty" (1.315).

AUGUSTINE AND THE BLESSINGS OF ERROR

The New Year Sonnets give us our first glimpse of how Augustine's theory of discovery would prove crucial to Herbert's view that spiritual transformation and aesthetic beauty are inextricably related phenomena. Later in his career, Herbert would adapt Augustine's ideas of error into his broader

---

[21] Cited in Lubac, *Medieval Exegesis*, 2.193.

[22] Cited in Heather A.R. Asals, *Equivocal Predication: George Herbert's Way to God* (Toronto: University of Toronto Press, 1981), 62.

[23] See Louis Dupre, *Passage to Modernity: An Essay on the Hermeneutics of Nature and Culture* (New Haven: Yale UP, 1993), 32–34.

spiritual aesthetic recognizing, all the while, the close relation among error, discovery, beauty, and mystery in Augustine's thought.

From early philosophical texts such as *Answer to the Skeptics* and *De Ordine*, to mature works such as *On The Trinity* and *The City of God*, Augustine remained deeply preoccupied with the experience of being mistaken. Augustine's practice of parsing the various ways in which human beings err was partly occasioned by his desire to counter the radical skepticism espoused by members of the Second Academy. Seeking to refute the Pyrrhonist view that we do not have access to any certain truths, including even the truth of our own existence, Augustine arrived at the *Si fallor, sum* principle which he expressed in *The City of God* this way: "I have no fear of the arguments of the Academics. They say, 'Suppose you are mistaken [that you exist]?' I reply 'If I am mistaken, I exist'. A nonexistent being cannot be mistaken; therefore I must exist, if I am mistaken."[24] This proto-Cartesian refutation of radical skepticism suggests one way in which error can be an aspect of knowledge rather than simply a veering from it. Resting his rebuttal of skepticism on the idea of a philosophically productive mistake, Augustine confronted the inherently limited nature of human understanding without relinquishing claims to truth. While acknowledging that human apprehension is structured by our finite perspective, Augustine nevertheless shows how understanding can happen in and through the experience of error.

If *The City of God* identifies intellectually productive forms of erring, then his *Enchirdion* interrogates the ethics of error. In a chapter wholly dedicated to the problem, Augustine encourages his readers to avoid error whenever possible while nevertheless acknowledging that "there are points on which ignorance is better than knowledge."[25] Tellingly, Augustine communicates this point by turning from the third-person standpoint of philosophical abstraction to the first-person stance of biographical narration:

> It has happened to myself to take the wrong road where two ways met, so that I did not pass by the place where an armed band of Donatists lay in wait for me. Yet I arrived at the place whither I was bent, though by a roundabout route; and when I heard of the ambush, I congratulated myself on my mistake, and gave thanks to God for it. Now, who would not rather be the traveler who made a mistake like this, than the highwayman who made no mistake?[26]

[24] St. Augustine, *City of God* trans. John O'Meara (New York: Penguin, 1984), 11.26.460
[25] St. Augustine, *Enchiridion on Faith, Hope, and Love* ed. Thomas S. Hibbes (Washington D.C.: Regnery, 1996), 19.
[26] Ibid.

In this example, momentarily losing one's way nevertheless serves the purpose of truly finding it. As a result, Augustine's destination is reached in a manner that utterly transforms his perspective on where he has been and thus where he has truly arrived. Given the hermeneutic implications of this process, it is perhaps no surprise that Augustine returns to this anecdote in his major discussion of scriptural interpretation.

In Book One of his treatise on biblical exegesis *On Christian Doctrine*, Augustine argues that the first-person ethical application of the text is an inherent part of scriptural understanding rather than a specific type of reading. Instead of being an activity that follows upon interpretation, the application of scripture to one's life is thought to be concomitant with interpretation itself. This idea is captured in the figure of scripture as mirror commonly expressed in medieval literature which we saw in "H. Scriptures (I)." As St. Gregory the Great writes, "The Holy Scripture offers itself to our soul like a mirror. We can contemplate in it our inner face."[27] The same principle attaches to the claim made by another medieval commentator that "it is not man who explicates Scripture, but rather man uses Scripture to explain himself to himself, so as to surpass himself."[28] From this Augustinian perspective, all understanding of scripture is in a very broad sense a mode of self-understanding. For the text to be understood, there must be an interpenetration of reader and text. To test whether this interpenetration has occurred properly or not, readers need to consider if their interpretation has engendered charity or *caritas*. The contrast with Edward Herbert now comes into full relief. For Lord Cherbury, readers can test the validity of scriptural interpretation against the objectivity of the five common notions, a move that effectively nullifies the spiritual dimension of biblical reading that Augustine assumes is fundamental. For Augustine, interpretation of scripture is true if it brings divine love into the world. And as we have seen, such acts of reading are said to provide the kind of assurance central to the Johannine tradition, assurance through the manifestation of love among those in fellowship with one another.

Augustine's rule of charity makes the phenomenon of blessed failing an important dimension of Christian hermeneutics, hence his return to the story of the wayfaring traveler in Book Two of *De Doctrina* in the context of interpretive erring. According to Augustine,

---

[27] Saint Gregory the Great, *Morals on the Book of Job*, 1.II.67; cited in Chretién, *Under the Gaze*, 27.

[28] Chatillon cited in Lubac, *Medieval Exegesis*, 2.142.

> Anyone with an interpretation of the scriptures that differs from that of the writer is misled, but not because the scriptures are lying. If ... he is misled by an idea of the kind that builds up love, which is the end of the commandment, he is misled in the same way as a walker who leaves his path by mistake but reaches the destination to which the road leads by going through a field.[29]

This passage shows Augustine identifying a kind of middle ground between understanding and noncomprehension, an experience of truth within error. Revealingly, Augustine warns against the habitualization or systematization of this phenomenon for fear one should "go astray or even adrift."[30] This means that while the experience of "blessed error" can be spiritually and hermeneutically productive, it cannot be integrated into a workable, repeatable method of interpretation. Augustine asserts that there is no way of incorporating such errors into a *modus inveniendi*.[31] After all, such errors are simply too unpredictable to be manipulated or controlled in advance. Though they can be helpful retrospectively, there is no question of making them happen on purpose. This is not reading by trial and error.

According to Brian Stock, Augustine's positive evaluation of interpretive erring was unprecedented in classical culture. The thesis that there is a middle ground between understanding and nonunderstanding "introduces a new idea into ancient interpretive theory—the notion that reading's ethical value can take place in a situation of perceived estrangement from truth."[32] In *De Doctrina*, Augustine speaks as though blessed erring were a somewhat unfortunate but not especially fatal response to the task of scriptural interpretation. Elsewhere, however, he implies that such erring is an inevitable, if nevertheless still unpredictable, dimension of how Christians experience truth. Without this exegetical approach, it is difficult to imagine the hermeneutic dynamics of Herbert's *The Temple* taking shape as they did.

[29] Augustine, *On Christian Teaching*, trans. R.P.H. Green (Oxford: Oxford UP, 1997), 27.
[30] Ibid.
[31] For a related analysis of Augustine, see Gerald Bruns, *Hermeneutics Ancient and Modern*, 159.
[32] Brian Stock, *Augustine the Reader: Meditation, Self-Knowledge, and the Ethics of Interpretation* (Cambridge: Harvard UP, 1998), 169.

AUGUSTINE AND PSALM 119

If one biblical text played an especially crucial role in the development of Augustine's hermeneutics, it was Psalm 119. More than one scriptural text among others, Psalm 119, for Augustine, was paradigmatic of what Herbert would later call scripture's neatness.

The longest psalm in the psaltery and the longest chapter in the Hebrew bible, Psalm 119 is organized acrostically with each of the 22 letters of the Hebrew alphabet beginning eight lines of poetry.[33] Yet it was not the psalm's length so much as its depth that most perplexed Augustine. What most puzzled Augustine about Psalm 119 was not just that it is difficult, but that it is difficult in very peculiar ways. In terms of diction, syntax, idioms, and grammar, it is not especially obscure. Even more strangely, the psalm's basic meaning is not unusually difficult to grasp. What troubled Augustine is that even after all the parts of the work are put together, something troublingly elusive remains, something he cannot clearly identify, let alone explain, via commentary. In the experience of failing to understand Psalm 119, Augustine discovered something about the very nature of textual understanding as such. As he explains:

> I put off the CXIXth Psalm, as well on account of its well-known length, as on account of its depth being fathomable by few. And when my brethren deeply regretted that the exposition of this Psalm alone, so far as pertaineth strongly pressed me to pay this debt, I yielded not to them, though they long entreated and solicited me; because as often as I began to reflect upon it, it always exceeded the utmost stretch of my powers. For in proportion as it seemeth more open, so much the more deep doth it appear to me [*Quanto enim videtur apertior, tanto mihi profundor videri solet*]; so that I cannot show how deep it is. For in others, which are understood with difficulty, although the sense lie hid in obscurity, yet the obscurity itself appeareth; but in this, not even this is the case; since it is superficially such, that it seemeth not to need an expositor, but only a reader and listener. And now that at length I approach its interpretation, I am utterly ignorant what I can achieve in it: nevertheless, I hope that God will aid me with His Presence, that I may effect something. (560)

---

[33] Robert Alter, *The Book of Psalms: A Translation with Commentary* (New York: W.W. Norton, 2007), 419. References to Augustine's commentary on Psalm 119 are given in text by page number and are from *Expositions on the Book of Psalms Nicene and Post-Nicene Fathers: First Series Volume 8*. ed. A Cleveland Coxe (New York: Cosimo Classics, 2007).

Augustine casts himself here in the role Paul played before the Corinthians. Standing before his brethren in weakness, fear, and trembling, Augustine finds himself so fully absorbed by the holy book that he is unable to locate a vantage point that is sufficiently capacious enough to provide a point of view from which to understand the text. Brought to the limits of his own capacity as a reader, Augustine is forced to reflect back on his own situation as an interpreter of scripture. He thus admits the necessarily provisional nature of his commentary: "Now that … I approach its interpretation, I am utterly ignorant what I can achieve in it" (560). Part of the psalm's power for Augustine lies in the way that it thematizes participatory exegesis, raising general questions about the very nature of sacred reading. In particular, Augustine notes the psalmist's desire to incarnate the law so fully as to become a living instance of it. What is at issue for him is not only how to read Christian mystery but how to allow oneself to be read by it.

Augustine here hits on one of the most striking features of *The Country Parson*, namely Herbert's insistence, in Kristine A. Wolberg's words, that "holy living establishes the truth of … doctrine."[34] But rather than being alien to orthodox Christianity, this concern with "doing" rather than simply "knowing" truth is one of Augustine's major preoccupations and a central question in post-reformation Christendom. Throughout his career, Augustine engaged in a sustained meditation on different modes of understanding *sacra doctrina*. Indeed, what really strikes Augustine about Psalm 119 is the way it expounds the different modes of understanding proper to spiritual life. In particular, Augustine is fascinated by the way the psalm dilates on the differences between intellectually apprehending God's law and actually fulfilling it through one's actions and person. As he explains:

Many learn the righteousnesses of God, and learn them not, For they know them in a certain way; and again do not know them from a kind of ignorance, since they do them not. In this sense the Psalmist therefore is to be understood to have said, 'That I might learn Thy righteousnesses,' meaning that kind of knowledge whereby they are performed. (571)

Importantly, Augustine is led to the view that learning the righteousness of God necessarily involves an experience of error, weakness, and even

[34] Kristine A. Wolberg, *'All Possible Art': George Herbert's The Country Parson*. Madison: Fairleigh Dickinson, 2008.

failure. Likely working from a corrupted translation of the *Caph* section of this longest of the psalms, Augustine finds himself needing to explain an error that appears to arise from the strength of David's faith rather than from a weakness of character or intelligence. Zeroing in on the phrase "My soul hath failed for Thy salvation," [*Defecit in salutare tuum anima mea*],[35] Augustine discovers something about the nature of spiritual reading generally:

> 'My soul hath failed for Thy salvation: and I hoped because of Thy word' ...
> It is not every failing that should be supposed to be blameable or deserving
> punishment: there is also a failing that is laudable or desirable ... This losing
> ground is therefore good: for it doth indicate a longing after good, not as
> yet indeed gained, but most eagerly and earnestly desired. (573)

What Augustine essentially discovers in David is the realization that genuine understanding often arises at the very limit of comprehension, at the point where knowledge ceases and wonder and even confusion begin. In light of Psalm 119, Augustine came to see that spiritual understanding is not the result of interpretation per se, so much as the consequence of the failure of interpretation to yield reliable results.[36] Augustine comes to this realization about the value of error and misreading vis-à-vis David's frustration with God's Word. Disappointed in the hopes of finding consolation in God's promise, David is forced to rethink the relationship between faith and hope. Rather than searching out the meaning of this or that aspect of the Word, David, according to Augustine, is forced to rethink how he stands with respect to God's future promise. What he encounters in the process is the way in which the Christian *mysterion* unfolds in unpredictable and often very ironic ways. In this way, nothing less than the psalmist's entire relationship to the Word as a relationship of faith, hope, and understanding is at stake in the blessed erring of Psalm 119 as Augustine conceives it.

---

[35] *Patrologiae cursus completus ... series latina*, ed. J-P Migne et al. (Paris, 1844–1903), v. 37, p. 1555. The King James translation reads: "My soul fainteth for thy salvation: *but* I hope in thy word"

[36] For Gadamer's treatment of these themes, see Bruns, *Hermeneutics Ancient and Modern*, 205 and Joel C. Weinsheimer, *Gadamer's Hermeneutics: A Reading of Truth and Method* (New Haven: Yale UP, 1985), 8.

In his state of utter noncomprehension, Augustine reevaluates how he stands in the concrete situation that he finds himself in the act of interpretation much as he thinks David does in Psalm 119. According to Augustine, David does this by maintaining a belief in consolation without delimiting what exactly divine consolation may actually come to mean at a point in the future. Read this way, David is thought to embody a feature of *epektasis* that remains consistent across Jewish and Christian dispensations. That is, David exemplifies the experience reaching out in hope and trust toward a future promise whose full meaning remains obscure. From this perspective, a Christian must place hope and trust in God's Word without pretending to comprehend the specific form its eventual return might take or what exact effect it may have upon oneself. Even the experience of holding out hope for consolation means opening oneself to the possibility that consolation will arrive in a form that one does not currently recognize as consolatory. As Sibbes says, God "brings his promises to pass strangely above the reach of man ... God brings his children to heaven by strange ways, yea, by contrary ways" (6.84). As we have seen, this is precisely what happens in "The bunch of grapes" and "Peace." In these poems, "comfort" has less to do with pacification or relief and more to do with becoming present to God by achieving equanimity in the face of hardship. In these poems, Herbert's speakers encounter the Word as a *mysterion*, a divine revelation that constitutes the inexhaustible context in which believers must continually reestablish the terms of hope, faith, and love.

David's experience of blessed erring helps to account for Augustine's unparalleled fascination with Psalm 119. In reading this psalm, Augustine came to believe that David's experience exemplifies the hermeneutical situation as one that is fundamentally characterized by disappointment in the unpredictable movements of the Word. Such movement is characterized by the way "disappointment itself gives rise to hope, as hope leads to disappointment," for in this cycle is the nature of scriptural experience as such.[37] Moving back into *The Temple* we will now see that this is precisely the hermeneutic pattern orienting the passion sequence running from "The Sacrifice" to "The Reprisall," a sequence which is then expanded and reprised in the closely related poems "Easter" and "Jordan (II)."

---

[37] Weinsheimer, *Gadamer*, 201.

HERBERT'S PASSION: THE SACRIFICE TO THE REPRISALL

The productive error motif is first introduced in *The Temple* during the Good Friday reproaches of "The Sacrifice."[38] Hearing the audience at the crucifixion cry out for his blood, Herbert's Christ responds by introducing a form of irony that will recur throughout the sequence:

> Yet still they shout, and crie, and stop their eares,
> Putting my life among their sinnes and fears,
> And therefore wish *my bloud on them and theirs*:
>   Was ever grief like mine?

> See how spite cankers things. These words aright
> Used, and wished, are the whole worlds light:
> But hony is their gall, brightnesse their night:
>   Was ever grief like mine? (105–112)

Like Christ in the Gospel of Luke, Herbert's Jesus diagnoses his persecutors as being guilty of false consciousness. They do not understand how their sadistic cry to be covered in Christ's blood conceals a much truer meaning: used and wished aright, their cry for blood betrays a need to have their sins blotted out. More than simply scriptural, though, this irony turns on the distinction between the objective work that the passion accomplishes and the subjective working of those responsible for it. As the twelfth-century theologian Peter of Poitiers explains: "So God approved of the passion of Christ carried out by the Jews, insofar as it was the Jews' work done [*opus iudaeorum operatum*], but did not approve the Jews' doing of the work [*opera iudaeorum operantia*]."[39] For Herbert, this distinction applies to Christ as priest rather than the stewards of the eucharist as it does in the Roman Catholic tradition.

---

[38] For the poem's medieval liturgical contexts, see Rosemund Tuve, *A Reading of George Herbert* (Chicago: University of Chicago Press, 1952), 19–99. For a competing view of the poem, see Ilona Bell, "Setting Foot into Divinity: George Herbert and the English Reformation," in *Essential Articles for the study of George Herbert's Poetry* ed. John R. Roberts (Hamden: Archon Books, 1979), 63–86. For a subtle reconsideration of Herbert's passion poems, see also Robert Whalen, *The Poetry of Immanence: Sacrament in Donne and Herbert* (Toronto: University of Toronto Press, 2002), 149–154.

[39] Peter of Poitiers, *Sententiae* 1.16 as cited in Agamben, *Opus Dei*, 23.

This providential irony is both corrected and confirmed later in "Sunday." A celebration of the Christian Sabbath, "Sunday" occurs against the unspoken backdrop of attiring oneself for church. Although this context is not explicitly stated, there is a distinct sense in which the speaker addresses us while readying himself for church, especially in the penultimate stanza where Herbert compares and contrasts a secular idiom for dressing and a biblical idiom for regeneration and salvation. Blending the physical act of "making oneself gay" for a service with the spiritual act of becoming "fit for Paradise," this stanza gives the horror of "The Sacrifice" an understated, retrospective twist as spiritual regeneration is now subtly conflated with the homely act of prepping for a church service:

> Christs hands, though nail'd, wrought our salvation,
>   And did unhinge that day.
>
>   The brightnesse of that day
> We sullied by our foul offence:
> Wherefore that robe we cast away,
> Have a new at his expence,
> Whose drops of blood paid the full price,
> That was requir'd to make us gay,
>   And fit for Paradise. ("Sunday," 48–56)

Just as Christians cast away the "robe" of sin by wearing Christ's flesh, so they make themselves "gay" for church in thanks for having been made "fit for Paradise." Herbert thus estranges a common scriptural idiom by implicitly literalizing it vis-à-vis a secular idiom associated with physical clothing. Recalling "The Sacrifice," this stanza shows how an ordinary act subtly bears the terrible, if redemptive, weight of providential irony.

Ilona Bell has done much to help us appreciate the estranging dimension of Herbert's Christological poetics in the opening poems of *The Temple*. As Bell shows, Herbert's decision to begin *The Temple* with a poem based on the Good Friday reproaches of the medieval liturgy was designed to unsettle and alienate readers, rather than conform to their expectations of liturgical tradition.[40] What Bell perhaps does not emphasize enough, however, is the extent to which Christ's paschal reproaches have always been inherently unsettling and that it is these aspects which Herbert's poem

---

[40] Bell, "Setting foot into Divinity."

emphasizes. Just because a tradition is familiar does not mean it is without the power to estrange and upset. Yet Herbert does much more than stress the intrinsically unsettling features of the Good Friday reproaches; he also exposes certain dangers inherent within the imitation of Christ tradition. But in doing so, he accomplishes something far more consequential than confessional polemicizing; he further exposes the dangers of trying to fully grasp Christian narrative by exempting oneself from it. The result is a broadly applicable and fully empathic diagnosis of certain interpretive and spiritual errors that Christians sometimes fall into when trying to imitate Christ, especially, but not exclusively, those working from pre-reformation and post-Tridentine traditions.

Instead of demonizing medieval practices as the ungodly other in the sequence running from "The Sacrifice" to "The Reprisall," Herbert suggests that they can give rise to a "blessed error," an excess rather than an absence of faith, as it were. The role that holy error plays in these poems comes into view in "The Thanksgiving" when the speaker, in a state of profound confusion, asks:

> But how then shall I imitate thee, and
>   Copie thy fair, though bloudie hand?
> Surely I will reuenge me on thy love,
>   And trie who shall victorious prove. (15–18)

The petition here amounts to an inadvertently subversive variation of the psalmist's "What shall I render unto the Lord: *for* all his benefits towards mee?" (116:12). But rather than trying to imitate Christ, the well-meaning yet erring speaker wants to appropriate Christ's salvific power for himself. The thought of "revenge" is attractive to him because it would mean being freed from the torturous bond of guilt and debt he owes Christ, a feeling that gets repeated in the gut-wrenching ending of "Dialogue." Implicit in "The Thanksgiving," however, is an awareness that imitation and rivalry engender relationship-destroying violence. As René Girard explains, "If the appropriative gesture of an individual named A is rooted in the imitation of an individual named B, it means that A and B must reach together for one and the same object."[41] Herbert's speaker

---

[41] Rene Girard, "Mimesis and Violence," in *The Girard Reader* ed. James G. Williams (New York: Crossroad, 2001), 9–19, 9.

is on the verge of engendering exactly this kind of mimetic rivalry as he wants not only to imitate but quite literally double Christ by taking possession of God's salvific power.

Seeking to become Christ's doppelganger, the speaker of "The Thanksgiving" focuses obsessively on Christ's redeeming grace to the exclusion of all the other objects of desire that are suddenly listed including, wealth, honor, marriage, and friendship (19–30). So, in the very act of identifying with Christ, the speaker forecloses on human life altogether, envisioning a morbidly monastic future. Rather than giving life, this mode of *imitatio christi* effectively annuls it. Not only does such mimesis undermine his relationship to Christ through envious rivalry, but it also results in a pathological desire for martyrdom that he implicitly rejects in The New Year Sonnets, the kind of self-destructive desire that Donne warns against in *Pseudo-Martyr* when he recapitulates arguments about the dangers of romanticizing death that go back as far as the patristic period; hence the exasperated cry of confused disappointment that Herbert's speaker lets out when he is finally confronted with the logical consequences of his literalism: "Then for thy passion—I will do for that— / Alas, my God, I know not what" (49–50).

The different stanza forms structuring "The Sacrifice" and "The Thanksgiving" are intimately related to their respective diagnoses of mimetic rivalry. "The Sacrifice" consists of 63 four-lined stanzas with a repeated refrain ending each of them, giving the poem a neat liturgical structure. The ironically titled "The Thanksgiving," however, consists of one rather bulky, stanzaically nondifferentiated, 50-line poem. Such stanzaic nondifferentiation confirms Girard's claim that oftentimes "rituals begin with a mimetic free-for-all during which hierarchies disintegrate, prohibitions are transgressed, and all participants become each other's conflictual doubles or 'twins'."[42] Consistent with this ritual logic, the speaker's failure to respect Christ's unique authority is reflected in "The Thanksgiving's" relative absence of stanzaic structure, a strategy Herbert also employs in the metrical breakdowns of "The Collar." In this way, the speaker of "The Thanksgiving" fails to heed the warning expressed in "The Church-porch": "Envie not greatnesse: for thou mak'st thereby / Thy self the worse, and so the distance greater" (259–260). Succumbing to exactly this temptation, the speaker of "The Thanksgiving" finds himself in search of liturgy rather than one maturely participating in one, hence the

[42] Ibid., 10.

confusion of stanzaic form. Read anthropologically, we should expect this conflict to be resolved through a reinstantiation of both poetic/liturgical form and spiritual hierarchy. Though by no means fully complete, this is precisely what begins to happen in the following poem: "The Reprisall."

Like Augustine's David, Herbert's speaker in "The Reprisall" begins to find his way by first losing it. Abandoning the futile desire to overtake Christ, he acknowledges his own limitations in a way that is spiritually liberating:

> I have consider'd it, and finde
> There is no dealing with thy mighty passion:
> For though I die for thee, I am behinde;
> My sinnes deserve the condemnation. (1–4)

Everything in *The Temple* may be said to turn on the realization that with respect to Christ "I am behinde." At this moment, the insight begins to free him from the pathological desire for martyrdom which Herbert diagnoses as arising from the narrowly construed attachments of mimetic rivalry. The epiphany that he is necessarily "behinde" Christ further dawns on him in the following stanza of "The Reprisall" as he continues to feel himself being disburdened of his illusions of glory even as he lingers over them: "O make me innocent, that I / May give a disentangled state and free: / And yet thy wounds still my attempts defie, / For by thy death I die for thee" (5–8).

In the final stanza of "The Reprisall," the speaker finally realizes how Christ's sacrifice was done for the sake of reestablishing a relationship with humankind and not for his own glory as classically construed. Crucially, this realization breaks the spell of mimetic rivalry. What the speaker now sees is that God is the very condition of fellowship, the very body of the church rather than one part of it. As Herbert says in *The Country Parson*, Christ is "not only the feast, but the way to it" (257–258). Viewed this way, one can no more be in competition with God than one can compete with the air one breathes or the water in which one swims. Having corrected his category error, the speaker of "The Reprisall" reaches the point where understanding and initiation become the same thing:

> Yet by confession will I come
> Into the conquest. Though I can do nought
> Against thee, in thee I will overcome
> The man, who once against thee fought. (13–16)

Although the idioms of conquest and self-overcoming suggest that a degree of spiritual straining is still going on here, the poem ends by fully breaking the bonds of mimetic rivalry. In doing so, the speaker reopens the possibility of a mystical marriage between the soul and Christ realized at various intervals in "The Church," especially, as we have seen, in "Love (III)."

In the course of the passion sequence, the speaker disburdens himself of a series of wrong-headed assumptions about his relationship with Christ. Through this process, he undergoes the kind of experience that is paradigmatic of understanding in the strict hermeneutical sense of the term. As Gerald Bruns explains, true hermeneutical understanding

> cannot be contained within propositions or underwritten by the law of contradiction. It has the universality of proverbs rather than of principles. It is never rule-governed. Experience is inevitably painful, because it entails the defeat of will or desire, the breakdown of design or expectation, of power or projection, but this breakdown is also an opening, even a sort of emancipation or releasement. Gadamer thinks of it in terms of insight, where insight means less a metaphysical grasp of something, however, and less an illumination of transcendence than an 'escape from something that had deceived us and held us captive' ... a releasement, say, from some prior certainty or ground, some vocabulary or framework or settled self-understanding; or say that the hermeneutical experience always entails an 'epistemological crisis' that calls for the reinterpretation of our situation, or ourselves, a critical dismantling of what had been decided.[43]

The religious literalisms animating the passion poems constitute a defensive posture against such painful forms of understanding. After all, the desire to return Christ's gift amounts to an early attempt to "fix [God's] chair of grace," to control the dynamic play of Word and Spirit ("The Temper (II)," 9). Rather than comprehending the Word, Herbert's speakers have to allow themselves to undergo the process of being apprehended by it. Instead of entirely losing or erasing themselves, however, such letting go allows them to understand that the "mystery of Christ" is the context in which they live, move, and breathe. As Augustine teaches in sermon 117, deploying somewhat unusual idioms, if you want to buy the Word, you must "give yourself" but "when on paying it you do not lose yourself,

---

[43] Bruns, *Hermeneutics Ancient and Modern*, 183–184.

and you acquire the Word for which you pay over yourself, and you acquire yourself in the Word to whom you pay yourself."[44] Though often dismaying, such self-dispossession is figured at the opening of "The Church" as a spiritually liberating release into a wider, richer, horizon of experience than had previously shown itself.

EASTER OR THE JOY OF BEING WRONG[45]

As Herbert's passion sequence suggests, his speakers often betray a deep-seated confusion about what should presumably be a relatively straight-forward matter: how to participate in liturgical worship. Yet, if we recall that the eucharist neatly contains within it all of scripture's teachings and promises as "The Banquet" suggests, then it is, by definition, an over-whelmingly rich event. As such, it is no wonder that communicants might shrink from the Lord's Supper in the way the speaker of Herbert's "Easter" does. In this lyric, the ostensibly simple matter of participating in the Easter liturgy gives rise to a profound spiritual and hermeneutic crisis, one that further demonstrates the importance of the sweet error motif to Herbert's poetics of discovery.

Originating with Ambrose's Easter Proclamation, the *felix culpa* motif has long been associated with the Easter liturgy. Herbert even exploits this association in "Easter-Wings," which immediately follows "Easter," when his speaker asks to rise with Christ so that "the fall shall further the flight in me" (10). The *felix culpa* paradox alluded to here charged the medieval religious imagination, giving rise to iconographical traditions and literary variations. It even inspired a verbal idiom used for any kind of mistake that turns out to have a good or happy effect.[46] In "Easter," Herbert draws on Augustine's development of this motif in hermeneutic terms.

Revealingly, the spiritual crisis staged in the revised version of "Easter" parallels some of the challenges Herbert identifies in "The Parson in Sacraments." According to Herbert, ministers "at Communion times" are often "in a great confusion, as being not only to receive God, but to break,

---

[44] *Works of Augustine*, 13.210.
[45] I echo the title of James Alison's *The Joy of Being Wrong: Original Sin Through Easter Eyes* (New York: Crossroad, 1998).
[46] James T. Bretzke, *Consecrated Phrases: A Latin Theological Dictionary* (Collegeville Minnesota, 1998), 49.

and administer him" (257). Faced with this confusion, there is nothing the minister can do but kneel before the authority of the revealed mystery and hope that the activity itself will give rise to understanding:

> Neither findes he any issue in this, but to throw himself down at the throne of grace, saying, Lord, thou knowest what thou didst, when thou appoint-edst it to be done thus; therefore doe thou fulfill what thou dost appoint; for thou art not only the feast, but the way to it. (257–8)

A very particular variation of this crisis occurs in the ante-penultimate stanza of "Easter":

> I got me flowers to straw thy way;
> I got me boughs off many a tree:
> But thou wast up by break of day,
> And brought'st thy sweets along with thee. (19–22)

Much like the speaker of the previous poem "Sepulchre," this speaker feels himself to be in the position of Mary Magdalene at the empty tomb. Having already arisen, Christ appears to have taken his "sweets" with him, leaving no need for further offerings. In the wake of feeling himself to be behind an absent Christ, the speaker of "Easter" cannot figure what it means to rise with him as required by the liturgical cycle: "Rise heart; thy Lord is risen. Sing his praise." Just as Christ refuses Magdalene's desire to touch him in the Gospel of John, so the speaker feels unsure of how to consume God's flesh by participating in communion.

This anxiety about participating in communion diminishes in the following stanza in a way that closely recalls the lessons learned in the passion sequence:

> The Sunne arising in the East,
> Though he give light, & th' East perfume;
> If they should offer to contest
> With thy arising, they presume. (23–26)

Etymologically, to presume means "to consume beforehand, to take upon oneself beforehand, to anticipate" (OED, *praesumere*). As in "The Thanksgiving," this is the presumptuous desire that prevents the speaker from sacramental participation. Now, however, the speaker begins to realize that Christ is not one person within the Christian fellowship but the very condition of fellowship as such. As Sibbes says, "We are now come to the banquet, and Christ is the founder of it; nay, he is the feast itself. He is the author of it, and he it is that we feed upon" (2.451).

"Easter" thus further clarifies the distinction between contesting and communing with Christ initiated in the early passion sequence. In doing so, it provides the speaker with a widened appreciation of the mode of Christ's grounding presence in the eucharist. Through this process, Herbert's speaker reencounters, and to some extent reworks, the paradox of Christian liturgy that Augustine expresses while defining the nature of sacramental signification. Writing to Bishop Boniface sometime between 408 and 413, Augustine asks: "Has not Christ been sacrificed once in himself, and yet in the mystery [*sacramento*] he is sacrificed for the people, not only during all the solemnities of Easter, but every day"?[47] This idea that the single event of the passion repeats itself on all subsequent days suggests that Augustine sees the atonement as a new creation in a way that complements his account of the beginning of things in *On the Literal Meaning of Genesis*. For Augustine, the seven days of creation involve six repetitions of the one primordial act of creation, none of which refer to days in the normal, quotidian, sense of the term. As he explains: "In all the days of creation there is one day, and it is not to be taken in the sense of our day, which we reckon by the course of the sun; but it must have another meaning, applicable to the three days mentioned before the creation of the heavenly bodies."[48] In other words, the primordial act of creation establishes the conditions for quotidian time rather than being an instance of it. This is precisely the realization that the speaker of "Easter" makes in the blessed error of the poem's concluding stanza as the resurrection now appears as a new creation:

> Can there be any day but this,
> Though many sunnes to shine endeavour?
> We count three hundred, but we misse:
> There is but one, and that one ever. (27–30)

---

[47] "Letter 98:9," *Works of Saint Augustine*, 431.

[48] Augustine, *The Literal Meaning of Genesis* trans. John Hammond Taylor, S.J. (New York: Paulist Press, 1982), 134.

The speaker here discovers what Paul means in the second letter to the Corinthians: "Behold, now is the accepted time, behold, now is the day of salvation" (6:2). But in doing so, he offers a striking example of how the experience of holy mystery is often concomitant in *The Temple* with the experience of being in error. An essential feature of his spiritual vision, this aspect of Herbert's poetics is much more than a bare application of the *felix culpa* motif. It is a hermeneutical insight that guards against the reductive drive for religious certainty of whatever variety. By the end of "Easter," we are left with the sense that what Andrewes says of Magdalene at the empty tomb goes also for Herbert's speaker, namely that there was "error in her love, but there was love in her error too" (3.12). For him the resurrection happens every day not because the eucharist is a literal corporal sacrifice via transubstantiation (a view that can only be anachronistically attributed to Augustine), but because it is the ground or basis on which all future days come to spiritually rest.

Given this general parallel with Andrewes, it is perhaps not surprising that the ending of "Easter" crescendos in a similar manner as many of Andrewes' high-holiday sermons. For example, his 1604 Good Friday sermon concludes by praising how Easter Friday focuses the kind of spiritual attention believers should strive for on all days. Deploying similarly Augustinian idioms as Herbert, Andrewes teaches that

> this, as at all other times, for no day is amiss but at all times some time to be taken for this duty, so specially on this day; this day, which we hold holy to the memory of His Passion, this day to do it; to make this day, the day of God's wrath and Christ's suffering, a day to us of serious consideration and regard of them both. (2.156–7)

Andrewes focuses attention in much the same way in a 1596 Lenten Sermon, when he preaches, with reference to the crucifixion:

> That this *now* shall be still *now*, and never have an end; and this *cruciaris* be *cruciaris* for ever, and never declined into a preter tense, as *recepisti* was. This is an exaltation of the cross, above all else; none shall ever come down from it, none shall ever beg our body to lay it in our sepulchre. (2.85)

Like the final stanza of "Easter," Andrewes' liturgical sensibility closely follows long-standing conceptions of the paschal mystery in which "it is in this Christian soul, it is *each day*, it is *today*, that the mystery, by being interiorized, is accomplished. 'It existed historically then; today it exists spiritually.' *Moraliter, intrinsecus* and *quotidie* are three adverbs that go together."[49] The long-standing tradition of spiritual reading that Henri de Lubac here explains stands behind the visionary epiphany of Herbert's "Easter" and its related paschal poems.

When "Easter" is viewed in these contexts, it becomes clear that Ilona Bell overstates things when she suggests that in Herbert's liturgical poems the speaker is placed in a "protestant world of history and sequence rather than a medieval or Catholic world of ritual reenactment and timelessness."[50] By exaggerating differences between the Church of England's liturgy and the specific medieval traditions still animating it, Bell commits exactly the eclipse of mystery that Herbert and Andrewes sought to resist. Just as "The bunch of grapes" exposes the spiritual dangers of seeking gospel without law, so "Easter" exposes the liturgical and hermeneutic consequences of reducing everything to "history and sequence." To experience Christ in the paschal liturgy, for Augustine and Herbert, is not to experience him historically and temporally but spiritually and eternally: "Can there be any day but this, ... / There is but one, and that one ever." The capacity to make this hermeneutic movement from history to mystery is the very thing Herbert and Andrewes were worried was disappearing from English protestant culture.

JORDAN (II) AND THE IDOLS OF THE MIND

If the speakers of "The Thanksgiving" and "Easter" adopt a literalist mentality that momentarily forecloses participation in Christ, then the speaker of "Jordan (II)" goes to the opposite extreme. Originally titled "Invention" in the Williams manuscript, "Jordan (II)" stages a "then versus now story" in which the speaker confesses his old penchant for extreme, self-absorbed poetic figuration. The result is a poem about how he arrived at a more mature approach to poetic composition through the imitation of Christ. Here again, the question of poetic method is front and center.

In telling his story, the speaker adopts Baconian idioms derived from the idols of the mind in order to articulate a decidedly Augustinian poetics of prayer. Central to his spiritual aesthetic is a conception of "copying"

[49] Lubac, *Medieval Exegesis*, 2.138.
[50] Bell, "Setting Foot," 80.

that markedly differs from the literalistic one of "The Thanksgiving." In this respect, the ending of "Jordan (II)" corrects not only the first half of the lyric but also the literalistic mentalities expressed in the passion sequence at the opening of "The Church." Here is the poem in full:

> When first my lines of heav'nly joyes made mention,
> Such was their lustre, they did so excell,
> That I sought out quaint words, and trim invention;
> My thoughts began to burnish, sprout, and swell,
> Curling with metaphors a plain intention,
> Decking the sense, as if it were to sell.
>
> Thousands of notions in my brain did runne,
> Off'ring their service, if I were not sped:
> I often blotted what I had begunne;
> This was not quick enough, and that was dead.
> Nothing could seem too rich to clothe the sunne,
> Much lesse those joyes which trample on his head.
>
> As flames do work and winde, when they ascend,
> So did I weave my self into the sense.
> But while I bustled, I might heare a friend
> Whisper, *How wide is all this long pretence!*
> *There is in love a sweetnesse readie penn'd:*
> *Copie out onely that, and save expense.*

In the first Jordan poem, the speaker asks if all beauty must be in a "winding stair," recalling Bacon's warning in "Of Great Place" that "'All Rising to *Great Place*, is by a Winding Staire.'"[51] "Jordan (II)" returns to Bacon but now it is his idols of the mind that Herbert echoes, not the essays. In particular, Herbert recalls how Bacon thought that "human understanding is like an uneven mirror receiving rays from things and merging its own nature with the nature of things, which thus distorts and corrupts it,"[52] hence Bacon's use of the term *idola* to describe ungrounded speculations about nature. By *idola* Bacon does not mean idols but something much closer to the Greek term *eidwla*, which denotes the false impositions that

[51] Cited in D.M. Hill, "Allusion and Meaning in Herbert's Jordan I" *Neophilologus* 56.3 (1972), 344–352, 350.
[52] Bacon, *The New Organon*, 41.

the human mind projects onto the things of nature.[53] One of the main characteristics of the idols, according to Bacon, is that they are unproductive. They do not provide any light for further knowledge, leading only to airy speculations and fruitless verbiage. And because the idols constitute human projections onto natural phenomena, they turn nature into a mirror in which we gaze at ourselves rather than showing the truth of things. The result is a kind of demonic variation on the idea of scripture as a mirror that reveals the inner truth of things. This notion of idolatrous thought as unproductive is central to "Jordan (II)," only now the issue is poetic fruitfulness rather than scientific productivity.

"Jordan (II)" unfolds by developing two key images, both of which convey pointless activity: poet as bawd and poet as vainly phallic. The first image develops the motif of poetry as meretricious in "Jordan (I)," which is then picked up again in the thematically related lyric "The Forerunners." Now in "Jordan (II)," the poet is said to give birth to dead or dying figures which have the effect of "prostituting" the divine meaning that is intended, hence their lewd offer of "service" in stanza two: "Thousands of notions ... did runne ... Off'ring their service, If I were not sped." This image suggests that the poet's activity is as prurient as that of the "fleet Astronomer" in "Vanitie," who surveys the stars as though he were a "potential customer outside a brothel" (Wilcox, 308). Despite the speaker's "plain intention" in "Jordan (II)," he finds himself clothing God in his own image rather than discovering God's image in himself (line 11). The proper roles thus get reversed here as it is Christ who spiritually clothes the old man with new flesh as we saw in "Sunday" (Rom. 13:14, 1 Cor. 15:53, Gal. 3:27). Getting his role backward, the speaker admits that he has been guilty of idolatry, worshiping idols of his own making rather than disclosing God through prayerful verse. The result is a series of still and demonic births that are blotted out, as though in demonic parody of Christ's regenerative blotting out of sin in Colossians 2:14.

In the case of the second, phallic image the poet's thoughts "swell" "sprout" and "burnish" without ever taking seed, a point that is exposed in the friend's cutting suggestion to "save expense." Bearing the same connotation as Shakespeare's "an expense of spirit in a waste of shame," the friend's phrase rebukes the poet's unfertile male ego: "*There is in love a*

[53] Iain M. Mackenzie, *God's Order and Natural Law: The Work of Laudian Divines* (Aldershot: Ashgate, 2002), 47.

sweetnesse readie penn'd: / Copie out onely that, and save expense" (17–18).
Both images of sterility disclose the extent to which true spiritual and
poetic productivity rests in the fecundity of the divine Word. The poet's
major error, then, is to have circumvented the Word by projecting himself
into the sense, a point he explicitly confesses in the opening of stanza
three: "As flames do work and winde, when they ascend, / So did I weave
my self into the sense" (13–14).

Initially, this idolatrous process looks like it is going to result in a birth as
his thoughts "burnish" in the sense of "grow plump" (OED, 3). Yet, this
meaning turns out to be more apparent than real, as the verb really means
"to gloss" or "to polish" (OED, 2). The same double meaning applies to
the verb "sprout," which first appears to mean "to grow" or "to issue"
(OED, 3) but eventually signifies "to gush" or "to squirt" (OED, 4).
So although the poet's thoughts multiply, they have no real substance
or life-giving power. These are the kinds of thoughts that Bacon refers
as the *idols of the marketplace*, those thoughts that are based on empty
verbiage rather than sound and productive knowledge. Bacon warns that
such "words beget words" doing "violence to the understanding" which
is, itself, "ceaselessly active, and cannot stop or rest ... seek[ing] to go
further; but in vain."[54] These prodigiously mental births are all very dangerous, Bacon asserts, because the "human understanding is most affected
by things which have the ability to strike and enter the mind all at once
and suddenly, and to fill and expand the imagination."[55] Echoing Bacon,
Herbert conceives of the imagination as a womb that is susceptible to infil-
tration by unproductive notions that arise from within the mind itself. The
result is a picture of the mind swelling rather than expanding.

Like Bacon's scientifically unproductive ideas, the speaker's inventions
are ceaselessly in motion but without any purpose or aim, hence the poet's
admission that he "bustles," meaning, "To move or work vigorously but
aimlessly" (OED, 1); "To be fussily or noisily active; to move about in an
energetic and busy manner; to make a show of activity" (OED, 2a). For
Bacon, true philosophical induction begins when the purging of the idols
ends. Similarly for Herbert's speaker, true poetic writing begins when
the poet ceases to weave himself into the sense in a spiritually aimless or
purposeless manner. The parallel lies in the principle that the process of
discovery is impeded by the misapprehensions of the prejudiced human

[54] Bacon, *New Organon*, 48, 43, 42.
[55] Ibid., 43.

mind. Once those prejudices are removed, the mind gains greater, less mediated, access to the object it seeks to know.

Yet, this parallel between poetic composition and Baconian induction collapses in the poem's devastatingly ironic and richly beguiling conclusion.

Given the speaker's depiction of his mind as a vulnerable womb which impregnates itself with dead thoughts, the friend's suggestion to "save expense" is as doubly gendered as the three key verbs in line four are. The spiritual motion brings the poet out of his fantasy of autonomous productivity long enough to see that true poetic activity does not consist in creating what Shakespeare calls, in a very similar context, "new found methods," but in the living Word which is "ev'ry day a new Creatour." The implication is that the unproductive poet-bawd should open himself to the Word so as to become impregnated by it. In this respect, "Jordan (II)" assumes the patristic notion of the Word as *Logos Spermatikos*, the inseminating power of spiritual creation which Andrewes assumes when he says that good works "beget and bring forth" the mystery of the Word through a kind of "birth or generation" (1.42). According to "Jordan (II)," true poetry involves precisely this rebirthing of the Word through the poet's participation in it. Crucially, then, participation means imitation as reproduction or birthing not imitation as copying or engraving. We are thus reminded here of Andrewes' commentary (discussed in Chap. 3) on the epistle of James' insistence that Christians must be "doers of the word" as the Greek phrase *poitèai logou* bears the sense of "poets of the Logos."[56] Importantly, the term *poitèai* is "opposed to the simple *akroatès*, the poet in the Greek sense of him who makes or does."[57] For Herbert, the religious poet must be more like a midwife or mother than a self-contained masculine ego. After all, the Christian poet must further the living Word rather than give rise to a dead letter.

Read in terms of its guiding imagery, "Jordan (II)'s" revised title becomes easier to understand. Jordan is the site of spiritual rebirth, the place where regeneration begins. Viewed this way, "Jordan (II)" defines poetry as the renewing of the divine Word as the source of spiritual life within the poet's soul. In this respect, Herbert's poem implicitly identifies a fundamental difference between Baconian and Augustinian discovery. Where the natural philosopher empties himself of prejudice, purifying his

[56] Chretién, *Under the Gaze*, 24.
[57] Ibid.

mind of the idols so as to see nature clearly, the poet empties himself of vainly human creations so as to be filled with the Word, thereby allowing him to participate in spiritual reality. And while Herbert's speaker follows Bacon in rejecting human language as a site of discovery, he turns to the divine Word in its place. What the poem thus stages is the speaker's birth as a religious poet. By the end of the lyric, the speaker recognizes himself as the midwife of the Word. Viewed this way, it becomes clear that "Jordan (II)" brings the themes of poetic discovery and beauty explored in the New Year Sonnets to their fullest, most mature expression.

Responding to the various misunderstandings that have occurred in the poem thus far, the final stanza of "Jordan (II)" challenges us to rethink what it might mean "to copy" the Word. Given the mysteriousness of "love" and the lexical richness of sweetness—not to mention the lessons learned in "The Thanksgiving"—copy cannot mean transcribe.[58] It can only take its figurative sense of "To make or form an imitation of (anything); to imitate, reproduce, follow" (OED, 3a.). In keeping with the poem's imagery, "reproduce" is the best choice here. Ultimately, the friend reminds the poet that Christ is to be *reproduced* not contested, *followed* not literally transcribed. Here we see Herbert stressing both the vitality and the vulnerability of the living Word. To make the divine Word live, the poet must do more than engrave it; he must make it his own by reproducing it anew. While the overall vision here is deeply rooted in Augustinian hermeneutics, it is expressed through a careful reworking of Baconian idioms. Herbert deploys Baconian idioms in order to contrast two completely distinct modes of knowing and erring. In one form of knowing, the subject stands above and outside the known, gaining access to it through trial and error. But in the other form, the knower participates in and with the known, clarifying the nature of such participation through patterns of correction and revision. The end result is a poetics that is adequate to a spiritual vision in which truth and beauty are processes one experiences as an immanent participant within Christian narrative as it unfolds in specific contexts. Herbert's conception of poetry as divine impregnation is consistent with his broader exegetical vision of scripture as the living Word.

---

[58] For a discussion of the aesthetic connotations of sweetness in medieval and early modern thought, see Mary Carruthers, "Sweetness," *Speculum* 81.4 (October 2006), 999–1013.

THE QUIDDITIE

"Jordan (II)" is not the only poem in *The Temple* that deploys Baconian idioms as a way of addressing the question of poetry in Augustinian terms. A similar dynamic also unfolds in the ironically named lyric "The Quidditie."

Although its neo-Aristotelian title leads us to expect a definition of poetry's essence along scholastic lines, "The Quidditie" ultimately defines verse in terms of its spiritual utility or devotional use rather than its "whatness." It begins and ends this way:

> My God, a verse is not a crown, 1
> No point of honour, or gay suit,
> No hawk, or banquet, or renown,
> Nor a good sword, nor yet a lute ... 4
>
> But that which while I use 11
> I am with thee, and *Most take all.* 12

The un-signaled turn at the end involves an unusually sophisticated irony. Herbert here alludes to the way that Aristotelian science was failing in mid-seventeenth-century Europe because of its misguided pursuit of essences. As Peter Harrison notes, "Aristotelian science had foundered because it sought the essences and qualities of things. God, said Pluche, 'has given us Abilities and Powers to discern clearly the Use and Fitness of things' but 'he has cast a veil over their essences'."[59] Exploiting the failure of Aristotelian scholasticism to advance our understanding of the world through its focus on essence, Herbert defines poetry not as a static thing or *quidditie* but as a dynamic and fruitful process, namely an unpredictable two-way conversation with God. In doing so, Herbert articulates a long-standing view of divine reading as a spiritually transformative activity in an idiom that is consistent with the reformed emphasis on utility and productivity. Moreover, Herbert's attitude toward reading is consistent with the broader view that in the Renaissance it was common for the literate to read for use rather than entertainment, though here the usefulness is spiritual and edifying rather than professional or utilitarian.[60]

---

[59] Peter Harrison, *The Bible, Protestantism, And The Rise of Natural Science* (Cambridge: Cambridge UP, 1998), 170.
[60] Kevin Sharpe, *Reading Revolutions*, 189.

Intriguingly, Herbert's application of negative theology in "The Quidditie" is closely tied to its deployment of Baconian insights. Bacon's approach to scientific understanding involved a process of progressive elimination that was partly inspired by the tradition of addressing God's radical transcendence through negation.[61] In Bacon's view, understanding nature without distortion necessarily involves a process of progressively eliminating that which it is not, just as understanding God's transcendence requires processes of negation. Herbert's subtly articulated critique of the scholastic pursuit of essences rests on the anti-Aristotelian consequences of Baconian eliminative induction. In other words, the process of discovery that unfolds in "The Quidditie" is not simply an adaptation of the *via negativa* to the question of poetry; rather, it is a poetic adaptation of Bacon's translation of the *via negativa* to natural philosophical uses but with one crucial twist. The method of negation pursued in "The Quidditie" results in a definition of poetry as something that is entirely nonmethodological. In this way, "The Quidditie" is broadly consistent with "Jordan (II)" and the two New Year Sonnets, each of which assumes that Christian poetry must be responsive to the experience of mystery in a way that any methodologically derived mode of understanding cannot be. To this extent, Herbert's approach to negative theology in "The Quidditie" sustains Augustine's sense of the unpredictable and nonmethodological dimension of both Christian prayer and Christian hermeneutics.

Despite its highly intellectual qualities, "The Quidditie" is written in anti-courtly language that is self-consciously homely. This is especially true of the lyric's final phrase which closely recalls Hugh Latimer's enormously popular 1529 Christmas sermons, first published in Fox's *Acts and Monuments*: "On the Cards." In the first of these sermons, Latimer distinguishes card games in which there is only one winner from "Christ's rule" in which everyone has the opportunity to win. With a warmth and wit similar to Herbert, Latimer told his Cambridge audience:

---

[61] See Steven Matthews, "Francis Bacon and the Divine Hierarchy of Nature," in *The Invention of Discovery*, ed. James D. Fleming *The Invention of Discovery, 1500–1700* (Burlington: Ashgate, 2011), 29–44 and Michael McCanles, "The New Science and the Via Negativa: A Mystical Source for Baconian Empiricism" in Julie Robin Solomon and Catherine Gimelli Martin (eds.), *Francis Bacon and the Refiguring of Early-Modern Thought* (Burlington: Ashgate 2005), 45–68.

The game that we will play at shall be called the triumph, which if it be well played at, he that dealeth shall win; the players shall likewise win; and the standers and lookers upon shall do the same; insomuch that there is no man that is willing to play at this triumph with these cards, but they shall be all winners, and no losers.[62]

Recalling Latimer's homely comparison of Christianity to a card game, Herbert concludes his method of negation in "The Quidditie" with a positive assertion about the universality of Christ's mercy, hence its availability via a poetics based on the presence of the living Word.

CONCLUSION: HERBERT'S MODERNITY

The basic difference between Augustine's and Bacon's analyses of error turns on the question of methodologization. While Augustine warns against any attempt to hermeneutically systematize error, Bacon develops a mode of inquiry characterized by the systematic use of trial and error. The views on error which Augustine expresses in *On Christian Teaching* also occur in his treatise *On Order.* In this text, Augustine finds himself struck by a change in the sound of running water in the plumbing system of his house. Noticing that the movement of water sounds much slower one day than it previously was, Augustine wonders what the cause of this erring may be. Taking this error as paradigmatic of the phenomenon, Augustine presupposes that ultimately mistakes suggest apparent rather than real disorder. As a result, his task, as G.R. Evans explains, "is to arrive at an understanding of the nature of order which will hold all this together and make accidents or mistakes fall in with God's plans and become in a humble way, something like *felices culpae,* bad things made good."[63] In this deductive system of analysis, individual errors arise out of the background assumption of providential order and are retrospectively resolved with reference to it. Within such a regime, there could be no question of causing error to arise through experimental manipulation so as to better understand the larger question of order. God uses error as a heuristic means of bringing humans into a fuller understanding of their place within an inexhaustible and thus constitutively mysterious order.

[62] Hugh Latimer, *Works,* 1.8.
[63] G.R. Evans, *Getting it wrong,* 20.

To try to generate error for the sake of comprehending the cosmos would be equivalent to playing God. On this point, Bacon disagreed.

Central to Bacon's project is an attempt to overturn Aristotle's view that individual errors in nature do not have a metaphysical cause and are thus philosophically inconsequential. In rejecting this Aristotelian view, Bacon simultaneously overturned Augustine's position that errors cannot be methodologically engendered. For Bacon, errors are more than a by-product of experimental procedures; they are an essential, structural feature of the inductive method. Bacon believed that "knowledge of nature can appear only when nature is 'vexed' or errs from its usual course"[64]—a point Herbert echoes in "The Pearl" when he says he knows what "willing nature speaks, what forc'd by fire" (6). One form of such erring involves what Bacon calls "Deviant Instances" (*Instantiae Deviantes*). Sensitively distinguishing between kinds of errors and the forms of knowledge made available by each, Bacon describes deviant instances as

> errors of nature, freaks and monsters, where nature deflects and declines from its usual course. Errors of nature differ from *unique instances* in the fact that unique instances are wonders of species, whereas errors of nature are wonders of individuals. But their use [in natural philosophy] is pretty much the same, because they fortify the intellect in the face of the commonplace, and reveal common forms... for errors in one direction show and point the way to errors in and deviations in all directions.[65]

Bacon's originality lies in breaking from Aristotle's belief that accidents in nature result from no clear pattern of causation and as a result do not answer to philosophical analysis. As Michael Witmore explains:

> Whereas with Aristotle, any deviation from the regular course of nature had to be without a metaphysical cause and so could never become the object of purposeful human deliberation (all regularity being underwritten by meta-physically principled *per se* causes), Bacon's disaggregation of Aristotelian species forms into simple ones allows for the accidental deviation to be reproduced deliberately.[66]

[64] Michael Witmore, *Culture of Accidents: Unexpected Knowledges in Early Modern England* (Stanford: Stanford UP, 2001), 114.

[65] Bacon, *New Organon*, 148.

[66] Witmore, *Culture of Accidents*, 120.

In other words, the Baconian scientist proceeds by making nature veer or err from its regular course. From this perspective, error can be assimilated into a methodical regime or system of knowledge. Once this occurs, errors give rise to knowledge rather than understanding, to conceptual control rather than participatory revelation.

These types of distinctions between different forms of error and the modes of discovery proper to them provide the exigency of Herbert's "Vanitie." Similar to "The Agonie," Herbert's "Vanitie" calls attention to the difference between problems and mysteries, or what, in this instance, he refers to more polemically, and with another echo of Bacon, as "death" and "life." The first three stanzas define scientific knowledge as the pursuit of domination and control as the "fleet Astronomer," "nimble Diver," and "subtil Chymick" seek to penetrate, survey, exploit, strip, and rape the natural world. All of these actions presuppose a fundamental gap between knower and known, subject and object. Herbert's point is that such knowledge is good for controlling the world but not for understanding oneself or one's place in the cosmos. To understand oneself, the last stanza contends, is to listen and respond to the law as written upon the human heart. Thus, while scientific knowledge is grasped and gained, religious understanding is heard and given:

> What hath not man sought out and found,
> But his deare God? who yet his glorious law
> Embosems in us, mellowing the ground
> With showres and frosts, with love & aw,
> So that we need not say, Where's this command?
> Poore man, thou searchest round
> To finde out *death,* but missest *life* at hand. (22–28)

This is arguably Herbert's most explicit warning against turning mysteries into problems. In seeking everything but God, he warns, natural philosophers nevertheless reaffirm that God is the condition of all discovery. In other words, by seeking to control nature, Herbert's scientists overlook their position within a divinely sanctioned *life*—that is, their existence within the compass of an all-encompassing God. As with several poems we have seen, the final stanza reverses perspective by placing the scientists within the circle of God's spiritual creation, his revealed law and Word. In doing so, Herbert reasserts the distinction between apprehending one's place in a divinely revealed mystery and comprehending some aspect of the world.

As Charles Whitney explains in his essay "Bacon and Herbert as
Moderns," the conclusion of "Vanitie (I)" echoes *The Great Instauration*.
In particular, "Vanitie" uses

> the same biblical incident to help define man's true calling that Bacon uses
> to define the philosopher's scientific calling: the angels before the empty
> tomb of Christ asking the searchers within, 'Why seek ye the living among
> the dead?' (Luke 24:5). In 'Vanitie' 1 from *The Temple* Herbert remarks,
> 'Poore man, thou searchest round / To find out *death*, but missest *life*
> at hand' ... To try to find scientific truth by reading scripture, Bacon had
> said in the *Instauratio*, is '*inter viva quaerentes mortuus*' ('seeking the dead
> among the living'): to try to find theological truths in natural philosophy,
> he had said in the Latin version of the *Advancement* that Herbert helped to
> translate, represents the opposite mistake.[67]

Whitney then goes on to criticize Herbert for not acknowledging the parallels between his project and that of Bacon's. In Whitney's view, Herbert
participates in the modern search for epistemological grounds. Placing
Herbert in the same tradition as Bacon and Descartes, Whitney reads
Herbert as pursuing certainty. My burden throughout this book is to suggest that this is exactly what Herbert does not do.

On the contrary, Herbert continually distinguishes different modes
of discovery and the varying forms of understanding proper to them.
And in doing so, he deploys Baconian idioms and ideas for poetic and
spiritual ends which are essentially Augustinian. Unlike Bacon, Herbert
does not seek the stability of first principles or philosophical methods.
Instead, he seeks to keep open the experience of mystery, carefully distinguishing knowledge-as-certainty from understanding-as-initiation-
into-the-mystery. In this way, Herbert's poetry cannot be said to share
in the Ramist desire to unify all learning that so excited early modern
intellectuals. At no point does Herbert seek to synthesize modes of discovery and invention by transcending distinctions among logic, poetry,
and dialectic so characteristic of seventeenth-century thought. If not
anti-Baconian in any strict sense, Herbert nevertheless sought to sustain
distinctions between information-transfer and spiritual awareness, the

---

[67] Charles Whitney, "Bacon and Herbert: Bacon and Herbert as Moderns" in *Like Season'd
Timber: New Essays on George Herbert* eds. Edmund Miller and Robert DiYanni (New York:
Peter Lang, 1987), 231–240, 232.

very distinctions that disappear when we conflate Herbert's Augustinian approach to *invenio* with Bacon's concept of discovery.

Whitney's conclusions about Herbert are consistent with his deconstructive approach. By viewing Herbert within a definition of modernity derived from Nietzschean genealogy, he collapses the distinctions that are the very lifeblood of Herbert's poetics of mystery and then criticizes Herbert for not doing the same. If Herbert is a modern as Whitney claims (and indeed I think he is), then he belongs to the modernity of Kierkegaard, Heidegger, and Gadamer not that of Derrida, Foucault, and de Man.[68] Seen this way, Herbert's interpretive vision appears more amenable to the tradition of phenomenological hermeneutics than deconstruction. The fundamental difference here turns on what Gerald Bruns describes as a hermeneutics of teaching versus a hermeneutics of meaning. In the patristic tradition of Origen and Augustine, "To understand Scripture is not to understand what it *means* but what it *teaches* ... where the notion of teaching is to be understood as the initiation of one 'who is capable of being taught'."[69] In this model, scriptural reading is more like learning how to be in a relationship than it is like learning how to describe a chemical reaction.

Gadamer's philosophy constitutes a modernist revival of this pre-enlightenment hermeneutics of teaching, where there is no possibility of unprejudiced or de-contextualized analysis and in which language is an event that occurs within the horizon of a living tradition experienced by individuals in dialogue rather than a reflection that necessarily distorts an objective world. As Herbert tells us in "The Quiddition," poetry is a form of social and spiritual practice that occurs within the context of a Christian fellowship; it is not a means of mirroring third-person, impartial realities. In this kind of spiritual aesthetic, erring is central rather than antithetical to the pursuit of truth and beauty. Concomitantly, an exaggerated sense of security is downplayed in favor of ever-renewing initiation and the modes of provisional understanding attendant upon it.

If Herbert is modern, it is because he diagnosed the turn to epistemology taking place in seventeenth-century intellectual culture and reacted against it through the medium of the religious lyric. Recognizing a powerful instance of this turn in the rationalism of his older brother and a

---

[68] For an account of the coexisting modernities of the post-Enlightenment world, see Charles Taylor, *A Secular Age* (Cambridge: Harvard UP, 2007).

[69] Bruns, *Hermeneutics Ancient and Modern*, 154.

far-less threatening one in Bacon's empiricism, Herbert kept alive an Augustinian poetics of error that remains irreducible to systematization precisely insofar as it is modeled on dialogue rather than method. Viewed this way, Herbert's echo of Bacon in the conclusion of "Vanitie" reveals a greater understanding of the difference between scientific and hermeneutical discovery than some have suggested. While scientific discovery occurs through rigorous methodological control and impersonal observation, hermeneutical discovery happens through a necessarily personal initiation into an evolving disclosure of truth. This is the difference between scientific method and an evolving Christian *paideia*. Rather than seeking to ground his knowledge claims so as to gain epistemological certainty, Herbert seeks to rediscover and renew the believer's position within an unfolding mystery. Herbert's project, I would submit, is not to ground first principles for the sake of religious security. Instead, his project is to find a spiritually vital way into religious faith at an historical moment when it was becoming possible to imagine a "Christianity not mysterious."

Little wonder, then, that Herbert appears to have taken Augustine's experience of Psalm 119 as paradigmatic of scriptural revelation as such. In the wake of the Reformation's insistence on the bible's monological character, the idea that there is a mode of simplicity which possesses inexhaustible richness became newly significant. In a certain sense, everything came to depend upon it. Responding to post-reformation exigencies, Herbert sought a poetics that would make readers feel something very much like the dread and the joy that Augustine describes in relation to Psalm 119: How can something so apparently simple be so hard and so strangely mysterious? How can something so ostensibly open remain, nevertheless, opaque, and in need of constant re-reading? And when is true knowledge no longer a matter of gaining more information? By making us ask such questions, Herbert was doing more than crafting exquisitely neat poems. He was negotiating the competing impulses of mystery and certainty so characteristic of English reformation culture. In doing so, he helped generate the conditions for a fully mature biblical literature at the very moment when the concept of scripture as the living Word of God came under unprecedented pressure, hence the relative decline of biblical, if not necessarily religious, literature in subsequent centuries.

Viewed this way, Herbert's poetry appears as a response to the epochal changes in modes of reading and belief happening within post-reformation England. Responding to these changes, Herbert asked how the religious lyric could serve as a mode of prayer in which one discovers the mysteries anew. In particular, Herbert's poetics of discovery is an attempt to mitigate pressures arising from reformation exegesis, including the view that scripture is somehow darkest at the very moment it shines most bright. What is ultimately at stake in *The Temple*, then, is not simply a plain-style poetry that invites repeated soundings, but the very existence of an interpretive community that has ears to hear.

CHAPTER 8

The Mystery of Hearkening: Listening for *The Odour*

If *The Temple* was partly designed to cultivate an audience with the ears to hear, there remains the question of what this may have meant exactly within an early modern context. What does it mean to *listen* to mystery of the Word in Herbert's culture? And how do ideas about early modern listening animate Herbert's practice of mystagogy? In asking such questions we inevitably broaden our understanding of the protestant Reformation as a revolution in reading. While we know that the Reformation witnessed an increase in biblical literacy as scripture was read in various European vernaculars by an increasing number of believers, it is important to remember that most people in early modern England heard the bible more often than they read it. In fact, hearing the bible in church was so important that the producers of the Authorized Version made sure to read their translations aloud to one another to ensure its effectiveness as an oral text.[1] For them, the idea that faith comes by hearing was not a theological abstraction but a perfectly quotidian reality orienting the work of scriptural translation.

    Arnold Hunt has even gone so far as to suggest that the general privileging of speech over writing in post-reformation England "led to an emphasis on preaching over and above the written word of scripture; a distrust of printed books; and a belief that 'bare reading', even the reading

---

[1] Gordon Campbell, *Bible: The Story of The King James Version 1611–2011* (Oxford: Oxford UP, 2010), 80.

© The Author(s) 2017
G. Kuchar, *George Herbert and the Mystery of the Word*,
DOI 10.1007/978-3-319-44045-3_8

of the Bible, could not suffice for salvation."[2] However strongly phrased this thesis may be, the early modern English bible very much remained an oral text, one that was routinely heard in sermons, in the liturgy, in acts of common prayer, and in domestic settings.

Although Herbert scholars have attended closely to the musical dimensions of *The Temple*, no one, to my knowledge, has stepped back to ask the more general question of how sound and hearing function in it.[3] What happens when we read *The Temple* by listening to its representation of sound and hearing not only as transhistorical phenomena shared through a common biology but also as they were understood in the early modern period? How does *The Temple* resonate differently when we attend to early modern ideas about the physics, physiology, and theology of sound, ideas that bring with them "protocols of listening, remarkably different from ours"?[4]

By tuning into early modern frequencies, we will discover that hearing and sound sometimes mean different things in the seventeenth century than they do for us and that such differences have crucial consequences for Herbert's poetics of mystery. At the same time, however, there are certain phenomenological givens that continue to animate the power of fascination that Herbert's poems possess. In this chapter, I shall examine Herbert's understanding of what it means to *hearken* by attending to the historical differences between him and us, while, at the same time, not denying the basic givens of human biology that continue to make his poetry vital. By doing so, we shall see that the dialogical dimensions of his prayerful art consist of much more than the spiritual motions explored in previous chapters. They also consist of a specific understanding of what it means to hear the Word as an embodied being. For Herbert, early modern ideas about sound and hearing mediate practices of prayer and reading in ways that are so fundamental they usually go without saying. And yet, to ignore them is to overlook some of the most constitutive features of *The Temple's* spiritual aesthetic, especially its depiction of poetry as a species of prayer in which one rediscovers that "Faith cometh by hearing, and

---

[2] Hunt, *Art of Hearing*, 21.

[3] For major statements on Herbert and music, see John Hollander, *The Untuning of the Sky: Ideas of Music in English Poetry, 1500–1700* (Princeton: University of Princeton Press, 1961), 245–331 and Diane Kelsey McColley, *Poetry and Music in Seventeenth-Century England* (Cambridge: Cambridge UP, 1997), 134–174.

[4] Bruce R. Smith, *The Acoustic World of Early Modern England. Attending to the O-Factor* (Chicago: University of Chicago Press, 1999), 8. This chapter builds on Smith's practice of historical phenomenology.

hearing by the Word of God" (Rom. 10:17). Such an approach will help us see that Herbert shared his culture's general feeling that the act of hearkening involves a renewed appreciation of one's immanence within the revealed Word, an immanence that is somatic as it is soulful, and as quotidian as it is mysterious.

HEARKEN UNTO A VERSER: THE CHURCH-PORCH

Lancelot Andrewes spoke for much of English protestant culture when he taught, in his 1620 Easter Day sermon, that

> Christ is the word; hearing then, that sense, is Christ's sense … In matters of faith the ear goes first ever, and is of more use, and to be trusted before the eye. For in many cases faith holdeth, where sight faileth. (3.21)

Such sentiments recall Luther's slightly less refined declaration that "the church is not a pen-house but a mouth-house," the "Gospel should not be written but screamed" (*LW,* 56.63–64). It is with these assumptions in mind that Herbert begins *The Temple* by calling readers to attention as though they were about to hear a sermon:

> Thou, whose sweet youth and early hopes inhance
> Thy rate and price, and mark thee for a treasure;
> Hearken unto a Verser, who may chance
> Ryme thee to good, and make a bait of pleasure.
>   A verse may *finde* him, who a sermon flies,
>   And turn delight into a sacrifice. (1–6)

Right at the beginning of "The Church-porch," Herbert tells us to listen with the kind of ear an auditor should possess before the pulpit. This emphasis on hearing spoke so deeply to Herbert's protestant readership that another poet writing later in the period cited this passage from "The Church-porch" on the frontispiece of his own collection of poems.[5] The force of such an emphasis on aurality was no doubt strong in a culture where being "read to was the normal experience of reading for the aristocracy and gentry, as well as for the illiterate common folk."[6] If Herbert's *The Temple* was collectively heard in the seventeenth century at least as

---

[5] Thomas Washbourne, *Divine Poems* (London: 1654).
[6] Sharpe, *Reading Revolutions,* 173.

often as it was privately read, then the phrase "Hearken unto a Verser" would have resonated for original audiences much more literally than for subsequent generations of Herbert lovers.

Perhaps this is why only moments after figuring his poetry as a supplement to sermons, Herbert again emphasizes the centrality of listening. Only now he reminds his readers that virtue has a tendency to enter through the ear, while sin often comes through the eye:

> In time of service seal up both thine eies,
> And send them to thine heart; that spying sinne,
> They may weep out the stains by them did rise:
> Those doores being shut, all by the eare comes in.
>
> ("The Church-porch" 415–418)

Just as one often goes to *hear* rather than *see* a play in early modern England, so one enters *The Temple* by hearkening unto a verser so as to discover oneself through the power of the poet's voice insofar as it is an expression of the living Word.

Although Herbert is celebrated for his use of visual typography, he was very much of his culture in maintaining the spiritual priority of hearing over sight. This general emphasis on hearing as the source of faith makes great sense in a culture as highly oral in character as early modern England.[7] As Martin Elsky has noted, Herbert's poems were composed "during a time of transition when oral and written approaches to textuality continued to intersect in the written and typographic word."[8] The orality to which Elsky refers is evinced in the *Perirrhanterium* by the typicality of the imagined listener: a sweet youth whose early hopes make him both valuable and vulnerable. Such typicality of character is a distinguishing feature of writing that remains close to oral culture.[9] Like proverbs, it stamps the work with a public dimension, making the text function as

---

[7] For Walter Ong's thesis that the early modern period undergoes a clear transition from orality to literacy, see *Orality and Literacy: The Technologizing of the Word* (London: Routledge, 2002). For balanced reassessments of this claim, see Adam Fox, *Oral and Literature Culture in England 1500–1700* (Oxford: Oxford UP, 2002) and Arnold Hunt, *Art of Hearing*, 59.

[8] Martin Elsky, *Authorizing Words: Speech, Writing, and Print in the English Renaissance* (Ithaca: Cornell UP, 1989), 149.

[9] See Ong, *The Presence of the Word: Some Prolegomena for Cultural and Religious History* (New Haven: Yale UP, 1967).

a means of uniting readers into a community rather than distinguishing them as discrete individuals. Oral modes of communication tend toward the collective and the didactic. Recognizing this, Herbert begins his most explicitly didactic poem in *The Temple* by drawing on his experience as university orator and perhaps his skills as a preacher. Exploiting the oral-aural qualities of catechism, Herbert fashions his ideal reader, at least initially, in the form of a catechumen, instructing him in how to hearken to the Word. As this prefatory material suggests, orality forms an essential part of Herbert's mystagogy.

Herbert's molding of the reader as a kind of auditor occurs against the backdrop of the varying soundscapes associated with temple life, many of which echo throughout *The Church* such as catechisms, psalm singing, sermons, public prayer, confession, bell ringing, hymns, and other religious vibrations. Seventeenth-century English church life was awash in sound, and these audio presences form part of the verbal and aural texture of Herbert's verse. Such sounds are further audible in the residually oral modes of writing that Herbert deploys in his poetry, most notably commonplace book conventions and proverbs, both of which are rooted in oral culture.[10]

Needless to say, "The Church-porch" is not literally a catechism any more than it is literally a sermon, drama, or dialogue. Nevertheless, it shares with each of these forms an implicit awareness that sound more than vision orients us in relation to other persons and the spaces they inhabit. As Francis Bacon writes in his 1627 work *Sylva Sylvarum*, sight "worketh in right lines, and maketh several cones; and so there can be no coincidence in the eye or visual point: but sounds, that move in oblique and arcuate lines, must needs encounter and disturb the one the other."[11] In other words, sound interpenetrates with itself and its environment blurring distinctions between bodies in space rather than illuminating them.[12]

---

[10] For discussion of Herbert's use of common place books, see Anne Ferry "Titles in George Herbert's 'little book'" *ELR* 23 (1993), 314–344 and Matthias Bauer, "Herbert's Titles, Common Place Books, and the Poetics of Use: A Response to Anne Ferry." *Connotations* 4.3 (1994–1995), 266–279.

[11] Francis Bacon, *The Works of Francis Bacon*. Ed. James Spedding, Robert Leslie Ellis, and Douglas Denon Heath. Vol 2. (London: Longman, 1859), 241.

[12] For a related discussion of Bacon, see Bruce Smith, *The Key of Green: Passion and Perception in Renaissance Culture* (Chicago: University of Chicago Press, 2009), 168–207. For a modern confirmation of Bacon's basic views on sound, see Don Ihde, *Listening and Voice: A Phenomenology of Sound* (Athens: Ohio UP, 1976).

On this account, sight and sound differ insofar as the visual sense remains exterior to objects, while the aural sense penetrates into and becomes part of them. This means that while "the visible doth not mingle in the medium … the audible doth." As a result, "voices or consorts of music do make an harmony by mixture, which colours do not."[13] Like scent, but unlike sight, Bacon contends, sound interfuses with its environment, becoming part of the medium in which it moves. As he explains,

> The sweetest and best harmony is, when every part or instrument is not heard by itself, but a conflation of them all; which requireth to stand some distance off. Even as it is in the mixture of perfumes; or the taking of the smells of several flowers in the air.[14]

If sight aspires toward clarity and distinctness, Bacon claims, sound and scent find their perfection in concinnity. Sound and scent thus offer modes of discovery that enhance the participation of knower with known rather than distinguishing them, as Bacon would seek to do within the realm of natural philosophy. Given Herbert's investment in pre-Enlightenment forms of discovery in which knowing involves a deepened initiation into and participation with the known, these qualities of sound and smell take on significant spiritual and poetic significance. As he declares in the second of his New Year Sonnets, "Lord, in thee / The *beauty* lies, in the discovery" (13–14).

Herbert's Baconian awareness that sound pulls one into the world of others helps provide the speaker of "Prayer (II)" with a degree of assurance that God is always accessible to the human voice. Rediscovering Christ's promise, "Ask, and it will be given you" (Matt. 7:7; Luke 11:9), the speaker of "Prayer (II)" expresses surprise at God's readiness to hear the call of supplication:

> Of what an easie quick accesse,
> My blessed Lord, art thou! how suddenly
> May our requests thine ear invade!
> … Thou canst no more not heare, then thou canst die. (1–3, 6)

Although Herbert quickly corrects the point about God not being able to die, the point about hearing remains. This is because for Herbert, God's

---

[13] Bacon, *Works*, 420–421.
[14] Ibid.

willingness to hear is not just a consequence of his omniscience, but much more immediately it is a sign of his immanence. More precisely, it is an effect of prayer as the gift of *parrhesia* the uninhibited speech of the bold soul before the Almighty. What better proof that God is in the world, "Prayer (II)" seems to say, than that God hears and in hearing is pulled into a relation with the speaker as though through the visceral force of sound itself. Bearing these various accounts of hearing and sound in mind, I would hazard to say that there are phenomenological reasons for phrases like *prêter l'oreille* just as there are phenomenological reasons for the Pauline principle that faith comes through hearing (Rom. 10:17), a principle that animates some of the most important features of Herbert's *The Temple*.

LISTENING FOR THE ODOUR, 2. COR. 2

One of the more surprising results of Herbert's commitment to the principle that faith comes through hearing is the assumption that God is often a full-body experience. This idea is rooted in St. Paul's placing of the body within the realm of spiritual life (Rom. 12:1). As Richard Sibbes says of this Pauline principle, "The soul is in the whole man. It is diffused over all the members. It is in the foot, in the eye, in the heart, and in the brain" (7.87). This is why the divine Word is often presented as infusing Herbert's speakers in both body and soul, especially when it is presented in the form of sound. In "The Odour, 2. *Cor.* 2," for example, Herbert envisions an act of ideal listening in which the soul undergoes a richly synesthetic encounter with God through the divinely charged phrase *My Master*:

> How sweetly doth *My Master* sound! *My Master*!
>   As Amber-greese leaves a rich sent
>   Unto the taster:
>   So do these words a sweet content,
> An orientall fragrancie, *My Master*.
>
> With these all day I do perfume my minde,
>   My minde ev'n thrust into them both;
>   That I might finde
>   What cordials make this curious broth,
> This broth of smells, that feeds and fats my minde.

My Master, shall I speak? O that to thee
        My *servant* were a little so,
                As flesh may be;
        That these two words might creep & grow
To some degree of spiciness to thee!

Then should the Pomander, which was before
        A speaking sweet, mend by reflection,
                And tell me more:
        For pardon of my imperfection
Would warm and work it sweeter then before.

For when *My Master,* which alone is sweet,
        And ev'n in my unworthinesse pleasing,
                Shall call and meet,
        My servant, as thee not displeasing,
That call is but the breathing of the sweet.

This breathing would with gains by sweetning me
        (As sweet things traffick when they meet)
                Return to thee.
        And so this new commerce and sweet
Should all my life employ, and busie me.

To understand the multisense experience expressed in "The Odour, 2. *Cor. 2*" and the act of spiritual listening that gives rise to it, we need to situate the poem in the context of a distinctly early modern sensorium or ratio of senses. After all, Herbert's sensorium differs from ours for a host of reasons. As I have noted, his culture's ethical privileging of sound over sight on pastoral grounds occurred at an historical moment when early modern England remained residually, if not predominantly, oral. No less importantly, Herbert's conception of mind is grounded in Augustine's sacralization of ancient theories of perception. Thus, to read a poem such as "The Odour," we need to reconstruct its theology and physiology of sense perception; only then will we really appreciate what Herbert is saying at the beginning of "The Church" when he invites us to "Hearken unto a Verser" ("The Church-porch," 3).

The embodied experience of divinity that Herbert expresses in "The Odour" and related poems has nothing to do with rare flights of mysticism and everything to do with quotidian but nevertheless mysterious experiences of praise and regeneration. In this respect, Herbert's theology of sound is consistent with the one envisaged in Richard Braithwaite's 1620 work, *Essaies Upon the Five Senses*. The revised second edition of Braithwaite's text (1635) concludes with a divine sonnet in which he encourages readers to employ all five of their senses in praise. By doing so, Braithwaite teaches, believers will participate in "that *sacred-secret mysterie* of *his* five wounds, *curing and crowning our* five Sences":

> Let *eye, eare, touch, taste, smell,* let every *Sence,*
> Employ it selfe to praise *his* providence,
> Who gave an *eye* to see; but why was't given?
> To guide our feet on earth, our soules to heaven.
> An *Eare* to heare; but what? no jest o'th' time,
> Vaine or prophane, but melody divine.
> A *touch* to feele …
> A *taste* to relish …
> A *smell* to breath; and what? flowers that afford
> All choyce content, the *odours* of *his* Word.
> 'If our *five Sences* thus employed bee,
> Wee may our Saviour *smell, taste, touch, heare, see.*[15]

Braithwaite's phrase "odours of his Word" reflects early modern usage of the term *odour,* which usually suggests a pleasant smell and which bears the etymological sense of an impression that a person makes upon another (*OED*). This play of meanings underwrites Braithwaite's conflating of hearing and smelling the Word; in particular, the idea that the conflation of hearing and smelling suggests that both senses involve receptiveness, especially a pleasingly self-transforming receptiveness.

Absent from the 1620 edition of the *Essaies,* Braithwaite's poetic conflating of smelling and hearing the *odours* of the Word may very well derive from Herbert's synesthetic vision in "The Odour, *2. Cor. 2,*" which begins thus: "How sweetly doth *My Master* sound! *My Master!*" (1). In this context, the word *sweetly* takes its standard sixteenth-century meaning of "perfectly tuned" or "pleasing unto the ear."[16] The phrase *My Master* resonates for Herbert in perfect pitch, generating what in the

---

[15] Richard Braithwaite, *Essaies Upon The Five Senses* 2nd ed. (London: 1635), 209. Subsequent references are given in text by page number.

[16] John Hollander, *Untuning the Sky,* 152 and OED 4a.

previous poem "Aaron" is referred to as "Another musick, making live not dead" (13). So, despite its olfactory title, "The Odour" begins as a *sounding*, both a listening to and a searching for. Such sounding rests on the assumption Braithwaite expresses when he says that "our *Eare* can best judge of sounds, so hath it a distinct power to sound into to the centre of the heart" (7). If, for Herbert, the echo of the heart forms "Another musick" a specifically spiritual form of sound, then, for Braithwaite, it generates "another note" as indicated in his summary of hearing's spiritual responsibilities:

> my *eare* must bee tuned to another note, that my edifying Sence may discharge her peculiar office; not to affect novelities, or chuse varieties, but to dedicate her inward operation to the mindes comfort (to wit) the *Melodie of Heaven*. (33)

Like Herbert's "The Odour," Braithwaite's analysis presupposes sound's capacity to do two things. First, it emphasizes sound's ability to incorporate listener into it, to draw listener and sound together, as it were, into one "body"; and second, his analysis alludes to sound's capacity to penetrate into the interiority of objects in space, thereby discovering their hidden depths. Braithwaite thus agrees with George Hakewill's claim in *The Vanitie of the Eie* (1608) that the ear is superior to the eye insofar as it can perceive "the soundesse of timber, the emptinesse of vessels," whereas the eye observes only their "crust and surface."[17] In these respects, Herbert's poetics, like Braithwaite's ethics, rests on sound's capacity to, in a word, *sound*. This sensitivity to sound's power of revelation helps explain why Herbert elsewhere defines both poetry and prayer as privileged modes of listening and hence as mediums of spiritual discovery. In "Prayer (I)," prayer is said to be "The Christian plummet sounding heav'n and earth" (4), while in the first of the two New Year Sonnets he asks why poets do not "sound out" God's praise "As well as any she?" playing on the rhetorical meaning of *invention* as "discovery" (7). For Herbert, poetry and prayer are, in their very essence, means of hearkening to the invisible.

Although Braithwaite's privileging of hearing is typical of protestant culture, he is unusually invested in empirical observation and the

---

[17] George Hakewill, *The Vanitie of the Eie* (Oxford: 1608), E4r as cited in Hunt, *Art of Hearing*, 23.

experimental knowledge arising from it. Such an investment makes his treatise a highly rewarding context for Herbert's own spiritual and poetic investments in particularities, especially as they manifest through specific sensory experience. Braithwaite displays his natural philosophical credentials early in the treatise, advertising his quasi-empirical method, which, he explains, consists of

> Theses, Or Generall rules drawne by Art, from the line of Nature tried by the touch-stone of infallible experience, and applied as observances to these present times; having reference to the *five Senses*, (proper subjects) to which they are restrained. (1)

Although protestant theologians often followed late-medieval Nominalists in emphasizing the authority of experience, Braithwaite's view of empirical phenomena as infallible is somewhat extreme for a work religious ethics from the mid-seventeenth century. Bacon, for example, would not offer so optimistic a formulation. Anticipating the focus on observation and empirical phenomenon that is characteristic of later writers, such as Thomas Traherne, Braithwaite's explanation of religious phenomena is remarkably concrete. It offers ethical and theological insights that are often poetic in their striking particularity.

Braithwaite's treatise begins with a study of vision, where we are reminded that the physical posture of the eye was thought to substantiate man's conscious awareness of his indebtedness to God. As Lactantius remarks, the Greeks called man *anthropon* ("one looking upward") because of his physical posture.[18] Yet, despite the ethical promise afforded by the eye, Braithwaite warns that it is particularly susceptible to temptations and dangers. The moral threat posed by sight is apparently so great that even if we close our eyes as a way of tempering ocular desire, the eye can produce imaginary sights to feed upon. "If the *eye* chance to be restrained," Braithwaite warns, "and want an *object* outwardly, it makes it self a mirror represented inwardly, and sometimes *Narcissus*-like doates for want of a *substance*, on an imaginarie *shadow*: it is jealous, and that is the cause, it is ever prying into others secrets" (4–5). Braithwaite thus recalls the medieval tendency to define *curiositas* as "desire of the eyes."[19]

---

[18] Lactantius. *The Divine Institutes Books I- VII*. Trans. Sister Mary Francis McDonald, O.P. (Washington, D.C.: Catholic U of America P, 1964), 97.
[19] See G.R. Evans, *Getting it Wrong*, 114.

We later learn that the ear can help save us from the envy and narcissism generated by the eye's capacity to trap the soul in the shadows of the imaginary. Hearing, in Braithwaite's ratio of senses, orients and orders other modes of perception. For him, the ear serves as what John Donne calls "the bones of the soul," organizing, commanding, and reorienting the other senses (*Sermons*, 6.4.101). "A discreet *eare*," Braithwaite writes, "seasons the understanding, marshals the rest of the senses wandring, renewes the minde, preparing her to all difficulties" (11, 1635). Whereas Braitwaite perceives the well-tuned ear as "seasoning" the other senses, Herbert presents the words *My Master* as "perfuming" and "sweetening" the psyche. Through this perfuming, Herbert hopes to "finde / What cordials make this curious broth, / This broth of smells, that feeds and fats my minde" (8–10). In both Herbert and Braithwaite, the ethical person does not transcend or annihilate his senses, but rather concentrates and tunes them. Following the basic Pauline credo *fides ex auditu*, this process of concentration begins with hearing. As Herbert tells us in "The Church-porch" and as he shows us in "The Odour 2 *Cor. 2*," poetry can play a role in tuning the senses in precisely this way. In this very concrete sense, Herbert conceives of poetry as a spiritual and sensual discipline.

Indeed, Braithwaite's championing of sound as a means of discovering the heart further explains Herbert's description of poetry and prayer as forms of spiritual sounding. Both Herbert and Braithwaite presuppose the feature of sound that Walter Ong explains when he notes:

> *Sound is a special sensory key to interiority.* Sound has to do with interiors as such, which means with interiors as manifesting themselves, not as withdrawn into themselves, for true interiority is communicative.[20]

Herbert's culture had a specific word for the kind of listening that exposes interiors without any kind of violence, one that greatly preoccupied John Donne.

THE BONES OF THE SOUL: HEARKENING IN DONNE

The kind of listening that can expose and transform the psyche in the way that "The Odour 2 *Cor. 2*" and Braithwaite's treatise describe is generally referred to as hearkening. John Donne explains this specific form of

---

[20] Ong, *Presence of the Word*, 117.

listening in a 1624 sermon on Psalm 34.11 "Come Ye Children, Hearken Unto me, I will Teach you the Fear of the Lord." According to this sermon, hearing and hearkening denote more than two modes of listening; they signify two distinct ways of being in the world. Listening, Donne says, becomes hearkening when sound is translated into action, when what is heard actually transforms one's relation to the world, one's mode of attunement. The ethics of hearing that Donne expresses in this sermon conforms to the general patristic view summarized by Gregory the Great in the context of bible reading. According to Gregory's *Moralia on Job*, "We should transform what we read within ourselves, so that the mind, roused by the ears, brings together and puts into practice what we have heard by means of our way of life."[21] Writing at a time of increased interest in experience and experimental knowledge, Donne places even greater emphasis on what it feels like to be "roused by the ears" during an act of hearkening than does Gregory whom Jean Leclercq has praised as one of the great phenomenologists of Christian experience.[22] Bearing this in mind, if we can recover the full meaning of the verb "hearken" as Donne and Herbert present it, we will go a long way in understanding their respective depictions of religious and literary experience as, in a rather fundamental way, experiences of sound.

For Donne, hearing becomes hearkening when the soul reorients itself in relation to God via sound much as the body reorients itself in space through sound: when I hear a person cry for help in the street or a wolf howl in the woods, I suddenly become aware of where I am in relation to other beings. Similarly, when I hear a preacher addressing my own spiritual failings, I suddenly become aware of my relation to God in a new and potentially renewing way. At such moments I have begun to hearken.

Donne arrives at his key distinction through a sacred anatomy, an analysis of the body's relation to the soul and hence to God. Reflecting upon the body–soul relation, he explains how both seeing and hearing play integral roles in the acquisition and implementation of religious knowledge:

> *The soul hath bones as well as the body*. And in this Anatomy, and dissection of the soul, as the bones of the soul, are the constant and strong resolutions thereof, and as the *seeing* of the soul is *understanding* ... so the *Hearing* of

---

[21] Cited in Brian Stock, *After Augustine: The Meditative Reader and the Text* (Philadelphia: University of Pennsylvania Press, 2001), 14–15.

[22] Jean Leclercq, *The Love of Learning and The Desire for God: A Study of Monastic Culture*. Trans. Catharine Misrahi (New York: Fordham UP, 1961), 31–44.

the *soul* is *hearkening;* in these religious exercises, we doe not *hear*, except we *hearken;* for *hearkening* is the *hearing* of the soul. (6.4.1010)

True hearing is to the soul what bones are to the body: it orients the soul's movement, its direction, and thus its strength. Religion is in its essence listening precisely insofar as hearing the Word yokes or ligatures the soul to God.

Having decided between hearing and hearkening, Donne then tests his audience to discover who is listening to him right *now* at the very moment he is speaking about the art of listening. Adopting a theatrically engaging form of reflexivity, Donne warns his audience not to undergo a "perverse ecstasy" in which body and soul separate due to ennui rather than rapture:

> It were a strange and a perverse extasie, that the body being here, at a reli-gious exercise, and in a religious posture, the soul should be gone out to the contemplation, and pursuit of the pleasures or profits of this world. You come hither but to your own funeralls, if you bring nothing hither but your bodies; you come but to be *enterred*, to be *laid in the earth*, if the ends of your comming be *earthly respects*, prayse, and opinion, and observation of men; you come to be *Canonized*, to grow *Saints*, if your souls be here ... Thou art good, O Lord, to that soul that seeks thee; It is *St. Augustines* note, that it is put in the singular, *Animae*, to *that soul.* (6.4.101–2)

As with the meaning of prayer, the full significance of a sermon only comes retrospectively. It is only after the preacher speaks that we will know if you have been hearkening:

> We cannot see *now*, whether thy soul be here *now*, or no; but, to *morrow*, *hereafter*, in the course of thy life, they which are near thee ... [and] know whether thy soul use to be at Sermons, as well as thy body uses to go to Sermons. *Faith comes by hearing*, saith the Apostle; but it is by that hearing of the soul, *Hearkening, Considering.* (6.4.102)

Donne's sensitivity to sound's animating of the relation between faith and works becomes most remarkable in the sequence that follows. Donne now sets up a series of analogies between sound, faith, and works, each of which explains how these various phenomenon orient us in both physical and spiri-tual space. He does this by implicitly connecting the omnidirectionality of sound to the fully diffused nature of the soul within the body, which, in turn, grounds the diffusion of faith in works. In other words, just as hearing is diffused in all directions throughout our body's relation to the world, so the soul is diffused throughout the body and so is faith diffused in our works. In this play of analogy, Donne sees the ethical poignancy of the Word working to orient Christians in relation to God and to one another:

> As the soul is infused by God, but diffused over the whole body, and so there is a *Man*, so *Faith* is infused from God, but diffused into our *works*, and so there is a *Saint*. Practise is the *Incarnation* of *Faith*, Faith is incorporated and manifested in a body, by works; and the way to both, is that *Hearing*, which amounts to this *Hearkening*, to a diligent, to a considerate, to a profitable *Hearing*. (6.4.102)

Hearing is the way to the fulfillment of the faithful soul because its diffusion in time and space orients us in relation to the world, to one another, and most of all to God. This is a theology of, in, and by the body as a receptor of sound.

Herbert closely echoes Donne's emphases in "The Prayer before Sermon" in *The Country Parson* when he teaches parsons to pray in the following manner:

> O make thy word a swift word, passing from the ear to the heart, from the heart to the life and conversation: that as the rain returns not empty, so neither may thy word, but accomplish that for which it is given. O Lord hear, O Lord forgive! O Lord, hearken. (289)

Lancelot Andrewes locates the key distinction at stake in each of these discussions in the epistle of St. James. Warning against the dangers of sermon mongering, he stresses the importance of doing the word as well as simply hearing it. This means that Christians must not be "ακουσται 'bare hearers', but . . . ακροαται 'attentive hearers'; that in so doing you do well" (5.191).

TOUCHING THE ODOUR: THE PHYSICS OF EARLY MODERN SOUND

Alongside the theology of hearing explored by Herbert, Braithwaite, and Donne is a shared physics of sound that is very different from our own.[23] Once understood, this physics further deepens Arnold Hunt's startling

---

[23] The following account of early modern theories of sound derives from Gretchen Ludke Finney, *Musical Backgrounds for English Literature: 1580–1650* (New Brunswick: Rutgers

insight that "when Protestant writers declared that hearing was preferable to sight, they meant it quite literally."[24]

In our scientific world, the objective phenomenon of sound and the subjective act of hearing are two substantially different things. We now recognize the mental event of hearing to be a translation of sound waves such that the physics and physiology of sound have become two different phenomena. This was not the case in Herbert's culture. In Herbert's world, the ear was generally thought to literally receive sound in the form of rarified air particles. Following Aristotle, Herbert's culture associated the senses with the four elements in a system of correspondences, connecting the eye with water, smell with fire, touch with earth, and the ear with air. Believing sound to be rarified air particles moving between mind and world, Herbert's readers came to *The Temple* as they went to a sermon, with a kind of preconscious belief in an isomorphism of sound. In hearing the world, Herbert's readers believed that they were, in effect, touching it.

This belief that hearing is a form of spiritualized touching gives a word like *hearken* an immediacy, an intimacy, in short, a force, that it does not have for those of us who hear in the word *sound* a disjunction between physics and physiology, to say nothing of physics and theology. Indeed, the entire language of sense experience means something different in the early modern period than it does for us. By bearing this difference in mind, it is perhaps not too much to say that early modern culture was more amenable to the Pauline belief that hearing the Word makes one intimate with God than we are today. After all, in hearing the Word early modern auditors thought that they were directly encountering it physically, much as the Virgin Mary does in visual depictions of the annunciation in which she receives the Word into her ear via a banderole. All of which helps explain the early modern belief that to hearken to the divine Word is to undergo a virtual annunciation. As Richard Sibbes teaches,

> We must have Christ as it were born in us, 'formed in us' ... We must labour that Christ may be 'manifest' in our understandings, in our affections, that he may be manifest to us, and conceived, as it were, in us ... Even as the virgin Mary, she conceived Christ when she yielded her assent. (5.486)

UP, n.d), 139–160 and Louis Vinge, *The Five Senses: Studies in a Literary Tradition* (Lund: Royal Society of Letters, 1975), 15–46, 71–103.
[24] Hunt, *Art of Hearing*, 24.

This is precisely what Herbert suggests when he describes the words *My Master* as perfuming his mind. According to the *OED*, to perfume means "to impregnate with a (usually pleasant) odour" (2) "To fill or impregnate with the smoke or vapour of a burning substance" (1a.). Thus just as Mary is traditionally inseminated by the Holy Spirit through the ear, signifying her role as ideal servant, so Herbert longs to feel himself a servant of God by means of a kind of aural impregnation. It is on the basis of these assumptions that early modern poets often took the Virgin Mary as a model for the poet-priest as servant of God, as Herbert implicitly does in "The Odour." Moreover, it is on the basis of these assumptions that both "Jordan (II)" and "The Odour" depict poetic and spiritual vocations as forms of impregnation and reception.[25]

Part of "The Odour's" power lies in how it creates the effect that the speaker's process of spiritual rebirth is happening as he prays. In the course of the poem, the words *My Master* and *My Servant* give the effect of *creeping* and *growing* together even as the speaker petitions for this to be so. A kind of word magic unfolds in the poem as *My Master* and *My Servant* become increasingly aligned. Herbert signals this process visually in the penultimate stanza through the spatial and typographical alignment of the two terms:

> For when *My Master*, which alone is sweet,
>> And ev'n in my unworthinesse pleasing,
>>> Shall call and meet,
>> *My Servant*, as thee not displeasing,
> That call is but the breathing of the sweet.

"My Master" calls and meets "My Servant" both typographically and verbally here. In this way, aural and visual registers begin to work together much as sound and smell have up to this point. Through this process, God becomes ("As flesh may be") incarnate in the speaker's vocation as ministering servant. By hearing the words *My Master*, Herbert is not only touched but is spiritually impregnated by them so as to be reborn as God's servant. The word magic developed in the poem creates the effect that God is answering the prayer even as Herbert is offering it. Herbert thus enacts the birth of Christ in the heart that Henry Vaughan pleads for

---

[25] See Theresa M. DiPasquale, *Literature & Sacrament: The Sacred and the Secular in John Donne* (Pittsburgh: Duquesne UP, 1999), 76 and my *Poetry of Religious Sorrow*, Chapter 4.

when he cries, in "Christ's Nativity," "let once more by mystic birth / The
Lord of life be born on earth" (29–30), and which is further developed in
"The Banquet" when Herbert praises "God, who gives perfumes, / Flesh
assumes, / And with it perfumes my heart" (22–24).

Taken together, the distinctly pre-Cartesian combination of physics and theology animating "The Odour 2 Cor. 2" helps explain why
prayer was so often thought to have the physically enjoyable effects
dramatized in Herbert's poem. Such enjoyable effects are also a function of how Herbert's theory of mind remains grounded in Augustine's
sacralization of Aristotle's *sensus communis*. In the early modern world,
after sound enters the ear it goes to the *sensus communis* where it combines with other senses in order to become a fully realized thought. The
sensually unifying function performed by the *sensus communis* tends
to delimit hard and fast distinctions among the senses. This is why
Aristotelian-inflected accounts of sense experience are often synesthetic
in nature. In the case of "The Odour," Herbert's depiction of how the
Word transforms one in both body and soul recalls Augustine's claim in
Homilies on the Gospel of John that in the Word "seeing and hearing are
not diverse things … but hearing is sight, and sight is hearing."[26] In the
course of his commentary, Augustine sacralizes his culture's pagan conception of the psyche by imagining what it looks like after having been
regenerated as an image of the Word. According to Augustine, when
sense experience becomes unified in the regenerated heart, the soul
perceives the world in a way that conforms more closely to that of the
synesthetic totality that is the Word. "In thy flesh," Augustine writes,
"thou hearest in one place, seest in another; in thy heart, where thou
seest, there thou hearest."[27] For Augustine, spiritual insight is characterized by its unification of sensory phenomena. He expresses this point
in a sermon that describes how a soul in a state of blessedness delights
in justice through a spiritualization of the senses:

if you have got interior senses, all these interior senses, are delighted by the
delights of justice. If you have got interior eyes, observe the light of justice
… If you have interior ears, try to hear justice. Such were the ears he was
looking for, the one who said: Whoever has ears to hear, let him hear (Lk.

[26] St. Augustine, *Gospel of John, First Epistle of John, and Soliloquies*. Nicene and Post-
Nicene Fathers. Ed. Philip Schaff (New York: Cosimo Classics, 2007), 121.
[27] Ibid.

8:8). If you have an interior sense of smell, listen to the apostle: For we are the good odor of Christ for God everywhere (2 Cor 2:15). If you have an interior sense of taste, listen to this: Taste and see that the Lord is sweet (Ps. 34:9).[28]

Following this general Augustinian tradition, what Herbert gives us in "The Odour" is a picture of the human psyche beginning to undergo the process of regeneration through a hearkening of the Word. As in Augustine's *De Trinitate*, Herbert's "The Odour" presents the production of spiritual knowledge as the begetting of a true word, a word that transcends the diversification of senses even as it first comes into us through sound.[29] Through this spiritually refining process of rebirth, Herbert's mind takes on the synesthetic characteristics attributed to the Word itself.

The prayerful dimensions of "The Odour *2 Cor. 2*" are similar to an instruction that Erasmus gives in the *Enchiridion*. In his handbook for Christians, Erasmus teaches readers to approach the word *Christ* by listening for all of the meanings embedded in it, as though it were a richly layered symbol or emblem rather than a word. "Do not think of 'Christ'," Erasmus declares, "as an empty word, but that it stands for charity, simplicity, patience, purity, in brief, all that he has taught."[30] If the word *Christ* bears within it all the teachings of the gospel, then the words *My Master* embody the promise of divine service, which is not one thing but all the things that make up a meaningful life. As we have seen, a number of words in *The Temple* are figured as possessing this Christological power to unite human and divine, including *Son*, *Jesu*, and now *My Master*.

There may also be a sense, however vague, in which Herbert's "The Odour" assumes Luther's belief that scripture has something like the power of a medieval sacrament. As we have seen, Luther maintained the view that "the words of Christ are sacraments by which he works our salvation" because "the Gospel words and stories are a kind of sacrament, that is, *a sacred sign, by which God effects what they signify* in those who believe."[31] On this account, the words of scripture received in faith have sacramental efficacy of the sort Herbert describes in "The Odour." At the

---

[28] Sermons 159.4.4 as cited in T.J. Van Bavel, *The Longing of the Heart: Augustine's Doctrine on Prayer* (Leuven-Walpole: Peeters, 2009), 59.

[29] See *On the Trinity Books 8–15*. Ed. Gareth B. Matthews. Trans. Stephen McKenna (Cambridge: Cambridge UP, 2002), 15.12.193.

[30] Erasmus, *Collected Works: Spiritualia* v. 66, p. 61.

[31] See footnote 45 Chap. 2.

very least, it is difficult to imagine the word magic that transpires in "The Odour" between "My Master" and "My Servant" having been written without something like this elevated conception of biblical revelation lurking in the background of his poetics.

By depicting the experience of regeneration as a unifying of sense experience, "The Odour" constitutes a poetic and deeply participatory exegesis of 2 Corinthians 2:15: "For wee are unto God, a sweet savour of Christ." As the words *My Master* enter into his ear, the speaker fuses with the Word as the servant of the Father, thereby becoming an echo of divinity. Should God accept his service by breathing the words *My servant* in response to Herbert's call to "My Master," then "this breathing would with gains by sweetning me (As sweet things traffick when they meet) / Return to thee." While this intercourse of human and divine voices rests on a theology of the Word as both sound and vision, it also arises from a conception of hearing as the literal receiving of sound into oneself. The conception of the psyche informing this poem provides a readymade means of establishing a sense of intimacy with Christ as sound. This is why the poem involves a kind of annunciation: the speaker is being impregnated with the Word through the ear so as to give birth to good works in employment. Herbert's use of the phrase "My Master" exemplifies the belief that "there is a savour in the very terms of Scripture, a sweet taste in the very language of the Holy Ghost," which in turn is mediated by early modern conceptions of sensory experience (Sibbes, 3.276).

The traffic between human and divine voices envisioned in "The Odour" rests, in part, on the idea that divine service (like true prayer) is an echo of the voice of the Word, an idea very similar to the one expressed in "Heaven":

> Are holy leaves the Echo then of blisse?
> *Echo.*   *Yes.* (11–12)

The idea that scripture is the voice of God and that true prayer is echo of that voice lies behind the way the pattern of call and response gets played out in the final three stanzas of "The Odour *2 Cor. 2*," especially the penultimate one:

> For when *My Master*, which alone is sweet,
> And ev'n in my unworthinesse pleasing,
> Shall call and meet,
> *My servant*, as thee not displeasing,
> That call is but the breathing of the sweet.

God's hoped-for response to Herbert's call of "My Master" will result in the mending of the soul "by reflection" mentioned in stanza four. Yet, this divine response signals a more primordial beginning than the word *response* implies. This is because God's hoped-for response ultimately takes the circular form of "Gods breath in man returning to his birth." This circular view of God's Word is expressed in the final stanza when God's "breathing" the words *My Servant* is said to ultimately "Return to thee" (27–29). The final stanza thus implies that the call "My Master" is from the very outset an echo of the Word alluded to in the poem's subtitle. In this way, the dialogical pattern of call and response in the poem turns out to have been subtended by a circular pattern of God's voice echoing itself in and through Herbert's prayer. This makes perfect sense, given that the words *My Master* only properly apply to Herbert if God accepts him as his servant. Here again, God's answer to prayer will determine what the prayer meant in the first place. As Herbert says in "Praise (III)": "When I did call, / Thou heardst my call, and more" (23–24). This "more" signifies the temporal as well as the semantic generosity of God's hearkening of humans.

Herbert's rediscovery that the Word in prayer is "God's breath in man returning to his birth" accords with Donne's sense that

the Scriptures are Gods Voyce: The Church is his Eccho; a redoubling, a repeating of some particular syllables, and accents of the same voice. And as we harken with some earnestnesse, and some admiration at an Eccho, when perchance we doe not understand the voice that occasioned that Eccho; so doe the obedient children of God apply themselves to the Eccho of his Church, when perchance otherwise, they would lesse understand the voice of God, in his Scriptures, if that voice were not so redoubled unto them. (6.11.223)

Herbert's hope in "The Odour" is to redouble the Word through acts of obedience, which will occupy him all his life in true employment before and in commerce with God: "And so this new commerce and sweet / Should all my life employ, and busie me" (30–31).

Like Donne, Herbert envisions such service through a diffusion of God throughout the body's senses. Indeed, just as Donne presents good works as the result of the Word's diffusing itself into the psyche through a proper hearkening of a sermon, so Herbert perfumes his mind with the word's *My Master*, thereby fattening the soul. Through this infusing of the Word, Herbert hopes that God will then become diffused in his acts of service to him:

> With these all day I do perfume my minde,
>   My minde ev'n thrust into them both;
>   That I might finde
>   What cordials make this curious broth,
> This broth of smells, that feeds and fats my minde.

While the image of thrusting himself into the words *My Master* may conjure up the act of eagerly smelling flowers, it is also an entirely appropriate description of attentive listening; for the sound made by the words enter into the ear in the form of oscillating air that literally fills up the "wickets of the soul" with spiritual sense as "all by the ear comes in" ("The Church-porch," 418). More technically, the words enter the *sensus communis* in the form of sound where they blend with other senses in the production of thought. Such blending results in a "curious broth" "that feeds and fats" his mind. This fusing with the Word does not result in a transcendence of the body or of the world. On the contrary, it initiates a reorientation of the self in physical and spiritual space, hence the hope for lifelong employment expressed in the final stanza.

"The Odour" powerfully exemplifies Ong's observation that "words consist not of corpuscular units but of evanescent sound" whose meanings "are never fully determined in their abstract signification but have meaning only with relation to man's body and to its interaction with its surroundings."[32] Language's necessary investments in the body and in human action help explain why the poem concludes with the hope of remaining in a state of spiritual employment, in ongoing and sensually oriented expressions of faithful works. By the end of "The Odour" the soul hopes for the same kind of synesthetic tuning expressed at the end of "Christmas" where Herbert blends Petrarchan eye imagery with renaissance ideas of harmony as he prays that Christ's "beams shall cheer my breast, and both so twine, / Till ev'n his beams sing, and my musick shine" (33–34).

Conclusion: Orality and Literacy in The Temple

Ultimately, "The Odour" exemplifies Ong's insight that ideal listening aspires not to "clarity and distinction" as ideal sight does but to "harmony" and incorporation.[33] Witness the poem's conclusion, in which Herbert

[32] Ong, *Interfaces of the Word: Studies in the Evolution of Consciousness and Culture.* (Ithaca: Cornell UP, 1977), 56.
[33] Ong, *Orality and Literacy*, 71.

hopes that his newly tuned senses will occasion a renewed relation to God and that the experience "Should all my life employ, and busie me" (30). The final stanza shows "The Odour" doing very much what one 1613 writer says should be accomplished by acts of spiritual reading. In such acts, we should "seek not only information concerning spiritual matters but preferably in addition their flavor and emotional content."[34] Behind such statements is the broader concern that post-reformation Christianity was being reduced to whatever could be taught and learnt, to mere information transfer. It is precisely this concern that gives Herbert's depiction of hearing and sound much of its spiritual and historical exigency. If the act of divine hearkening only really happens when it evokes the *gustum* and *affectum* of thought as a sensual experience, then what better way to teach spiritual reading than through poetry?

These parallels between the sensuality of spiritual reading and the physiology of sacred listening may offer us a glimpse of the mutually reinforcing relations between orality and literacy at work in *The Temple*. After all, the lived experience of orality underlies the sequence's psalmic and liturgical dimensions, its echo poems and antiphonic verses, and its catechistical and dialogical elements. Moreover, its proverbial and allegorical features arise from formulaic patterns typical of oral traditions. Indeed, even the titles of Herbert's poems have been linked to the orally based tradition of commonplace books.[35] So, by becoming more self-conscious about how richly invested Herbert's poetry is in oral modes of communication and their accompanying forms of historically and phenomenologically mediated sense experience, *The Temple* will reveal itself to us in ways that are at once familiar and yet new.

The aim of this chapter has been to show how Herbert's insistence that the Christian narrative is a mystery in which believers immanently participate is reinforced by the physics, physiology, and theology of early modern concepts of sound. If Herbert shares Jeremy Taylor's view that the complex richness of the Word should serve as the basis for Christian fellowship, then he also recognized the inherently communal and dialogical dimensions of the Word that Ong sees as crucial to the best of renaissance poetics. This is why the liturgical features of *The Temple* are so integral to its spiritual aesthetic, especially its focus on faith and poetry as kines-

---

[34] J. Alvarez de Paz *De Exterminatione Maeli et Promotione Boni libiri*, 3.5.2.2 Cited in Stock, *After Augustine*, 107.

[35] See Ferry, "Titles" 314–344 and Bauer, "Herbert's Titles," 266–279.

thetic processes that move in time, space, and bodies.[36] Importantly, such kinesthetic features further show that Herbert's poetry was nourished by an increasing emphasis on scripturally mediated experiences of mystery and wonder with the sense of provisionality and perspectival awareness attendant therein. To hear the Word, Herbert insists, following Augustine, is to hear it from somewhere in time and space.

[36] For studies that emphasize the centrality of liturgy to Herbert, see John Wall, *Transformations of the Word: Spenser, Herbert, Vaughan* (Athens: University of Georgia Press, 1988) and Ramie Targoff, *Common Prayer: The Language of Public Devotion in Early Modern England* (Chicago: University of Chicago Press, 2001). For a competing view, see Doerksen, *Conforming to the Word*.

CHAPTER 9

Conclusion

If the growing emphasis on mystery in early seventeenth-century English protestant culture was neither universal enough nor fully realized enough to prevent subsequent sectarian conflict, it nevertheless helped engender some of the nation's best religious literature. As works such as Donne's *Holy Sonnets* and Milton's *Paradise Lost* indicate, there seems to be an intimate relation between theological ambiguity and literary greatness in the period, one that may deserve greater generalized reflection. In the case of *The Temple*, Herbert's emphasis on mystery is often visible in the way his poems operate as acts of exegesis, mini-dramas of spiritual reading in which speakers undergo a form of discovery that has the structure of an initiation. In many cases, such acts of exegesis are figured as prayers in the broad sense that they are pleas for "help," expressions of "thanks," and exclamations of "wow."[1] Like the exegetical dimensions of Herbert's poetry, his prayerful dimensions constitute a post-reformation reinvention of Augustinian assumptions and practices. In particular, Herbert learned from Augustine that it is very difficult to be dogmatic if one remains in a state of awe at the gap between one's self and the image of perfection reflected in the mirror of scripture.

Revealingly, such nondogmatic attitudes inform Augustine's approach to prayer as well as to hermeneutics. For instance, when Augustine summarizes the essence of prayer in the opening of the *Soliloquies* as the desire

---

[1] I allude here to Anne Lammott's disarmingly simple typology of prayer in *Help, Thanks, Wow: Three Essential Prayers* (New York: Penguin, 2012).

© The Author(s) 2017
G. Kuchar, *George Herbert and the Mystery of the Word*,
DOI 10.1007/978-3-319-44045-3_9

to "know God and the soul" (*Deum et animam scire cupio*), he brings a major feature of Herbert's nondogmatic poetics into focus.[2] According to the *Soliloquies*, prayers for understanding constitute the ur-genre of prayer, the very archetype of prayer itself. Rather than being merely one kind of prayer among a host of possible types, like thanksgiving, praise, complaint, or repentance, prayers for understanding—such as in Solomon's dream vision in 1 Kings 3 or David's in Psalm 119—constitute the very essence of prayer. For Augustine, prayer is always at some basic level a method of discovery, a *modus inveniendi*. This means that prayer is less a means of petitioning God than it is first and foremost a way of receiving him. As Joseph Hall asserts, "Prayer is our speech to God, so is each good meditation ... God's speech to the heart: the heart must speak to God, that God may speak to it."[3] From this perspective, there is no radical distinction between prayer and spiritual reading; the two are inherently bound up with one another. As Origen says, "What is most necessary for understanding [scripture] is prayer."[4] This is especially true in the more advanced states of sanctification that Saint Anthony assumes when he asserts, "He who knows that he is praying has not yet begun to pray."[5] Such is the state to which Herbert aspires when he asks to see God in all things, thereby making even "drudgerie divine" ("The Elixir," 18). In a fully realized state of holiness, all acts are a form of prayer, including acts of spiritual reading. If Herbert's *The Temple* can be said to aspire to one fundamental thing, it is this state of complete immersion within the divine mystery. Perhaps this is why at least 20 of the 164 poems in "The Church" are explicitly structured as prayers of understanding including such key poems as "The Elixir," which begins, "Teach me, my God and King, / In all things thee to see" (1–2), and "Faith," which opens: "Lord, how couldst thou so much appease / Thy wrath for sinne, as when mans sight was dimme, / And could see little, to regard his ease, / And bring by Faith all things to him?" (1–4).

More than a theme per se, this broad understanding of prayer as a form of spiritual discovery orients the structure, movement, and experience of Herbert's poems. That is, it animates his very conception of poetry as a

---

[2] Saint Augustine, *Soliloquies*, trans. Gerard Watson (Warminster: Aris and Phillips, 1990), 30–31.

[3] Cited in John Booty, *Three Anglican Divines On Prayer: Jewel, Andrewes, Hooker* (Society of St. John the Evangelist: Cambridge, MA, 1977), 35.

[4] Cited in Lubac, *History and Spirit: The Understanding of Scripture According to Origen* trans. Anne Englund Nash (San Francisco: Ignatius Press, 2007), 89.

[5] Cited in Bouyer, *Christian Mystery*, 279.

species of prayer in which we are offered an opportunity for sanctification. For Herbert, the challenge of the devotional poet is to make the aesthetic experience coincide with the pursuit of religious perfection. In his view, a religious lyric should return us to the point where prayer and poetry were the same thing, hence his insistence that process is all. This means, in effect, that Herbert's practice of correction and revision encourages the same mode of hearkening that prayer and spiritual reading do. With this in mind, it becomes apparent that some of the most decisive formal strategies in Herbert's lyrics encourage, rather than simply express, the kind of nondogmatic spirituality depicted in *The Temple*. After all, there is something of a dialectical relation between the lyric as a medium and Herbert's overall spiritual vision. If he cultivated a spiritual poetics, he also, in turn, engendered a poetic spirituality.

To put this another way, the process of composing and refining the figural dimensions of his poetry likely made Herbert more sensitive to what Thomas Cooper calls *The Wonderful Mystery of Spiritual Growth* (1622). Indeed, the following passage from Cooper's treatise amounts to an implicit explanation of why poetry is the best medium for expressing the experience of sanctification:

> I call it *a Mysterie of growing in grace:* because it pleaseth the Spirit to resemble it unto us by *Mysteries*. And the way to discern the *truth* and *manner* thereof, and so to attaine the *measure* of the same, is still *in* and *by a Mysterie*: By the Mysterie of the Word preached.[6]

When Herbert tells us that poetry is "that which while I use / I am with thee," he intimates a dialectical relation between the lyric as a medium and the mystery of spiritual growth. He suggests that the lyric as a form mediates his understanding of Christian spirituality as revealed through images, conceits, metaphors, figures, parables, and so on. Rather than simply depicting prayer, Herbert conceived of poetry as a species of prayer for understanding vis-à-vis poetic figuration and composition. To this extent, Herbert shared Augustine's view that prayer involves listening for what one knows without knowing that one knows it. As Augustine explains in his Letter to Proba, prayer often arises out of an underlying experience of precognition because the Holy Spirit

---

[6] Thomas Cooper, *The Wonderful Mystery of Spiritual Growth* (London: 1622), B1.

makes the saints ask with unspeakable groanings, breathing into them the desire of this great thing, as yet unknown, which we await in patience. For, how could it be put into words when what is desired is unknown? On the one hand, if it were entirely unknown, it would not be desired; and on the other, if it were seen, it would not be desired or sought with groanings.[7]

On this account, the very desire for God bears within it a "pre-instinctual" or unconscious knowledge of God and the holiness he makes possible, hence Herbert's use of dramatic irony. If we hear more than his speakers intend, it is often because the Holy Spirit is figured as speaking through his poems.

Rather than being Wordsworthian recollections, Herbert's poems are carefully crafted spiritual exercises in which we overhear the speaker in dialogue with God even as we remain immanent participants with the scriptural drama unfolding in *The Temple*. Here I am in general agreement with Kristine Wolberg who proposes that

> Rather than imagining Herbert as either transcribing a past spiritual experience into poetry or as imagining him as merely using religious materials for a higher aesthetic end, perhaps we ought to conceive of Herbert as first shaping poetic and religious forms, which then create corresponding experiences. That is, instead of thinking of Herbert's poems as records of past thoughts or events, we might think of the poems as actual precursors or catalysts to spiritual events, insights, or dramas.[8]

Wolberg arrived at this consequential thesis by focusing on Herbert's emphasis on the habits of faith, especially as expressed in *A Priest to the Temple*. In doing so, she independently confirmed Paul Cefalu's ground-breaking thesis that early modern protestant theologians seeking to develop coherent notions of sanctification had recourse to medieval concepts of habit in ways that often compromised reformed concepts of justification.[9]

[7] See Saint Augustine, *Letters Volume 2*, trans. Sister Wilfrid Parsons (Washington D.C. Catholic University of America Press, 1966), 399 and Clarke, *Theory and Theology*.

[8] Kristine A. Wolberg, '*All Possible Art*', 133. For a related view of the medieval religious lyric see Judson Boyce Allen, "Grammar, Poetic Form, and the Lyric Ego: A Medieval *A Priori*" in *Vernacular Poetics in the Middle Ages*. ed. Lois Ebin (Western Michigan University Press: Kalamazoo, 1984), 227–248.

[9] Paul Cefalu, *Moral Identity in Early Modern English Literature* (Cambridge: Cambridge UP, 2004), chapter 5.

On these accounts, Herbert is committed to the post-Aristotelian theory that outward actions can have an effect on inward spiritual realities, an ethical philosophy that sits very uneasily alongside any strongly reformed emphasis on faith alone or *solifidianism*. While this crucial aspect of Herbert's work remains to be fully integrated into our understanding of his poetics, it is nevertheless important to bear in mind his equal emphasis on the unpredictability of spiritual motions and the irreducible mystery of a scripturally mediated faith.

In *The Country Parson* Herbert teaches that prayer should be a daily practice or spiritual habit in which one tries to cultivate and edify the soul in some of the ways that medieval monks and saints did ("The Parson's State of Life"). At the same time, however, he remained sensitive to the principle the Spirit can no more be controlled or predicted in advance than can the living Word. For him, the value of devotional habits does not preclude the mysterious unpredictability of the Spirit's motions or inexhaustible significance of scripture. Thus, if Herbert saw the religious lyric within the context of the habits of faith, then he nevertheless remained mindful of the unpredictable nature of any truly spiritual phenomena. For him, poetry, prayer, and biblical interpretation cannot be reduced to a method with predictable results, hence the importance of "blessed failing" and spiritual hearkening to his poetics.

In other words, it is not enough to say that Herbert's poetry is meditative, or that the test of a good early modern poem is whether or not readers can "'join' and make it their own."[10] What we require is a critical framework that is truly adequate to the different kinds of spiritual events depicted in and engendered by Herbert's poetry. Developing such a vocabulary will involve further research into Herbert's commitment to the habits of faith, particularly as espoused by thinkers such as Hooker and Andrewes. In doing so, we may arrive at a more nuanced appreciation of how he approaches the vital question of the origins of faith, the problem of *initium fidei* with which *The Temple* is so broadly preoccupied.

One possible way to begin such a project is to recognize that if Herbert situated poetry within the context of the habits of faith, he nevertheless avoided the two Augustinian extremes represented by Calvin and Pascal. Where Calvin strongly insists that inward states of faith are

[10] C.S. Lewis, *English Literature in the Sixteenth Century* (Oxford: Clarendon Press, 1965), 491.

logically and temporally prior to outward acts of devotion, Pascal allows
for the reverse. For Pascal, habit and custom can generate faith from the
outside in, whereas for Calvin they cannot.[11] These extremes constitute
two post-reformation attempts to disambiguate Augustine's tendency to
oscillate between these two positions, sometimes leaning one way and
sometimes the other depending on context and audience. What is clear
though is that Augustine viewed the very act of prayer as bearing within
it a zero-degree of spiritual knowledge. For him, the very medium of
prayer offers leverage on the peculiar relation human beings have with
divine transcendence. In his view, the dialogical nature of prayer opens a
space between understanding and ignorance, inside and outside, self and
Other. For Augustine, any act of true prayer involves an inherent dispos-
session of the self-reliant ego and that in that act of self-dispossession
one experiences at least the bare intuition of transcendence. Through
this intuition, the differences between presence and absence, knowledge
and ignorance, self and Other, become difficult, even impossible, to fully
parse. They become, if you like, the blurred coordinates by which one
discovers oneself in relation to a God who is both immanent and transcendent, both radically other than me and yet "more inward to me
than my most inward part." Hence the speculative prayer that opens
the *Confessions*: "Grant me Lord to know (*scire*) and understand (*intel-
legere*) which comes first—to call upon you or to praise you, and whether
knowing you precedes calling upon you."[12] Although this passage echoes
Psalm 119, it asks the opposite question that the psalmist does. Instead
of trying to move from knowing to doing the law, Augustine wants to go
from the act of prayer to forms of knowledge presupposed by it. In this
way, Augustine asks for intellectual comprehension of what one intuitively knows in the act of self-dispossessing prayer. In short, he wants to
unfold the logical priority that obtains among acts of calling, praising,
loving, and knowing God. Crucially, however, his question is not firmly
answered in *The Confessions*. Instead of definitively resolving the issue,
Augustine's prayer outlines the condition of uncertainty from which
desire for God arises in the first place.

Many of Herbert's poems occur within this Augustinian space between
understanding and ignorance, precognition and knowledge. Indeed, it is

---

[11] See Calvin *Institutes* 3.20.1.146 and Blaise Pascal, *Pensées*, trans. A.J. Krailsheimer (New
York: Penguin, 1995), 125.

[12] Saint Augustine, *Confessions* trans. Henry Chadwick (Oxford: Oxford UP, 1998), 3.

out of such indefinite transpersonal states that Herbert constructs spiritual dramas in which processes of correction and revision result in the difficult to describe modes of spiritual progress delicately traced in *On The Trinity*. Commenting on Isaiah, Augustine asks:

> Why, then, does he so seek if he comprehends that what he seeks is incomprehensible, unless because he knows that he must not cease as long as he is making progress in the search itself of incomprehensible things, and is becoming better and better by seeking so great a good, which is sought in order to be found, and is found in order to be sought? For it is sought in order that it may be found sweeter, and is found in order that it may be sought more eagerly.[13]

In Augustine's spiritual economy, prayer is a process of constant reinitiation; it consists of a movement back into the place from where one began but with a broadly increasing sense that both prayer and wisdom arise out of love. This is why Augustine repeatedly insists that *amor notitia est*: piety is wisdom precisely insofar as its expression through prayer is the medium in which love is intuitively expressed so as to become consciously known and thereby integrated at a higher level of awareness. Therein also lies the back-and-forth progressive structure of *The Temple*.

Viewed in these Augustinian contexts, Herbert's "generous ambiguity" appears to be something more than a historically contingent compromise formation on questions of doctrine. It begins to appear as a broader disposition toward faith as grounded on a notion of divine mystery as an unfolding action in time rather than fidelity to an impenetrable synchronic statement. As Sophie Read remarks with respect to the Lord's Supper, Herbert developed "a poetics that can posit a number of mutually exclusive doctrinal positions without having to decide between them. The poet retreats in humility from the need to formulate a consistent viewpoint, preferring rather to have faith in, than a precise understanding of, the mysteries of the sacrament."[14] Yet, it is important to remember that other churchmen of Herbert's day shared this Augustinian open-endedness.

For example, Herbert's depiction of his poetic art in "The Altar" rests on the same dynamic notion of the eucharistic mystery as the one

[13] Augustine, *On the Trinity*, 15.2.168.
[14] Read, *Poetry and the Eucharist*, 126.

expounded in John Buckeridge's funeral sermon for Lancelot Andrewes delivered in 1626. Rather than a purely inward offering of the heart divorced from communion, Herbert's "The Altar" constitutes a poetic variation on the kind of offering that Buckeridge explains when he asserts that "the Church, which is Christ's mystical body, offers not Christ's natural body ... but the Church offers *corpus mysticum*, 'Christ's mystical body,' that is, itself, to God in her daily sacrifice" (*Ninety-Six Sermons*, 5.263). Buckeridge thus stresses Cranmer's prayer of oblation in the communion service, the congregation's desire "to be a reasonable, holy, and lively sacrifice unto thee" so as to become "very membres incorporate in thy mistical body."[15] Drawing heavily on Augustine, Buckeridge productively blurs the distinction between eucharistic sacrifice "and all other sacrifices of the Church, external or spiritual," each of which "must be offered up and accepted *per Ipsum*, in, by, and through Christ" (5.262). Included here is the "*sacrificium cordis contriti*, 'the sacrifice of the contrite and broken heart'*" that Herbert's "The Altar" offers up (5.281). Buckeridge's pivotal point comes straight out of Augustine's *Contra Faustum*, a passage that has parallels not only to "The Altar" but also "To all Angels and Saints":

> praying and praising, we direct our signifying words to Him to Whom we offer the things signified in our hearts; so sacrificing, we know the visible sacrifice is to be offered to no other but to Him Whose invisible sacrifice in our hearts we ourselves ought to be ... Let us not sacrifice to them [angels, the elect, and glorious saints], but let us be a sacrifice to God together with them. (5. 264)

Buckeridge's sermon blurs the line between eucharistic worship and the daily sacrifice of the church in all its forms no less than Herbert's "The Altar" blurs the line between personal prayer and public rite. In this spiritual vision, all forms of prayer occur along a kind of eucharistic spectrum with the ritualized action of the Lord's Prayer standing as the foundation of religious life much as "The Altar" stands at the opening of "The Church." Ultimately, the same basic notion of eucharistic sacrifice as an utterly mysterious exchange of human prayer and divine grace expressed in Buckeridge's sermon structures Herbert's poem. Following the same logic as Buckeridge, Herbert offers up "A broken ALTAR ... / Made of a heart, and cemented with teares" only to conclude his shaped poem in

---

[15] Cummings, *Book of Common Prayer*, 138.

the hopes that Christ's "blessed SACRIFICE be mine" (1–2, 14). This productive ambiguity over the line between personal prayer and public rite arises from a shared conviction of the *corpus mysticum* as an ongoing action unfolding in time, one in which all of the church's devotional acts participate in a broadly conceived and purposefully ill-defined eucharistic vision. Yet, it also arises from the belief that the eucharist is "called a sacrifice inasmuch as it doth represent the passion of Christ" and likewise because "it is called *hostia*, 'an host,' inasmuch as it containeth Christ Himself, Who is *Hostia salutaris*" (5.261). In other words, the eucharist participates in the sacrifice of Calvary though it does not literally repeat it much as Herbert hopes his poems will participate in Christ's "blessed sacrifice" for the benefit of its readers. This qualified sense of participation in Christ's sacrifice was deepened when Herbert replaced the term *onely sacrifice* with *blessed* in the Williams manuscript version of "The Altar." Like Buckeridge, Herbert insists in a perfectly Augustinian manner on the singular nature of the crucifixion on Calvary while nevertheless allowing for a sense of participation with it. So, while I agree with Robert Whalen that for Herbert "Eucharistic topoi ... were not only necessary and effectual means of grace but also the conceptual and psychological framework within which to imagine its application to the human heart,"[16] I would nevertheless add one caveat: in adopting this kind of eucharistic vision Herbert was more consistent with the open-ended dimensions of the so-called avant-garde wing of the Jacobean church than is often thought. After all, the idea that internal religious experience was "a *distinctive feature* of both moderate and more radical puritan divinity" mistakes a puritan talking point for a firm truth.[17] As Buckeridge's sermon makes clear, the question at stake for ceremonialists is not whether to cultivate an inward, private religious life or not. (That counterreformers of all stripes almost universally did so should go without saying.) Instead, their concern is with what relationship pertains between internal religious experience and the public action of the church. To put Herbert's "The Altar" in context is to recognize how it situates private prayer within a broader eucharistic context in much the same way that Buckeridge does.

As with Luther's translation of *mysterion*, what is fundamentally at stake in Buckeridge's account of communion is the question of Christian

---

[16] Whalen, *Poetry of Immanence*, 112.
[17] See Ibid. My emphasis.

community. Deeply sensitive to the relationship between the eucharist
and the church, Buckeridge tries to avoid the pitfalls of post-reformation
debates "that obsess over the question of the presence of the body ... at
the cost of neglecting the question of the community that coalesces in
and through the ritual: the community that is itself the body of Christ,
and, according to the older ideals of the *corpus mysticum*, the most real
presence at stake in the celebration."[18] In presenting a eucharistic vision
in which the doctrinal emphasis lies on the mutually reinforcing relations between church and sacrament, more than the question of real
presence, Buckeridge is able to minimize differences among reformed,
patristic, and even some late medieval theologies (favorably quoting
Thomas Aquinas at one point in his sermon). In this respect, he follows
Andrewes in presenting a eucharistic discourse that is in keeping with
the more ambiguous and conservative 1549 *Prayer Book* which retains
the term *altar* than the more reformed 1559 version which uses the
term *table* instead.[19] As its title suggests, Herbert's "The Altar" expresses
the same kind of broadly conceived and productively obscure eucharistic
vision as the one Buckeridge presents. Rather than encouraging either
a thoroughly noneucharistic reading or a narrowly ritualized one, "The
Altar" ultimately seeks to accommodate both interpretations through its
sense of the *corpus mysticum* as the sacramental site in which the divine
mystery unfolds in time, hence its placement at the beginning of "The
Church." The result is a poetic vision built on the assumption that "participation in the Church, participation in the sacrament, and participation in Christ are inextricably bound together in acts at once single
and collective, outer and inner."[20] Viewed this way, it makes little sense
to say that Herbert's poetry is rooted in the eucharist rather than in
Augustinian prayer. Like Buckeridge, Herbert sees such acts of devotion
along a sacramental continuum in which public acts of worship involve an
edifying transformation of the heart, just as private acts of prayer involve
forms of communion most fully expressed in the eucharist, hence their
mutual importance to the poetics of *The Temple*. From this perspective,

[18] Rust, *Body in Mystery*, 37.
[19] For Andrewes' preferring of the 1549 BCP, see Davies, *Caroline Captivity* 61, and
Cummings, *Book of Common* Prayer, 769.
[20] David Aers and Sarah Beckwith, "The Eucharist," in *Cultural Reformations: Medieval
and Renaissance in Literary History* eds. Brian Cummings and James Simpson (Oxford:
Oxford UP, 2010), 153–165, 154.

the *mystical body* of Christ in which Herbert hopes *The Temple* will participate is understood as an evolving and growing community of believers and not a reflection of a static ideal.

A similarly nondogmatic sense of scripture and tradition as the one expressed in Buckeridge's funeral sermon for Andrewes finds expression in Herbert's "To all Angels and Saints." Directed at church papists and Catholic recusants, the poem is unusually controversial in substance. At the same time, however, it shows remarkable compassion for its presumptive audience. Like Buckeridge's sermon, it expresses a kind of double-movement toward Catholicism. On the one hand, Herbert expresses criticism of saint veneration; but on the other, he acknowledges continuity with and sympathy for those who practice it:

> Oh glorious spirits ...
>
> Not out of envie or maliciousness
> Do I forbear to crave your speciall aid:
>   I would addresse
> My vows to thee most gladly, blessed Maid,
> And Mother of my God, in my distresse ...
>
> But now (alas!) I dare not; for our King,
> Whom we do all joyntly adore and praise,
>   Bids no such thing:
> And where his pleasure no injunction layes,
> ('Tis your own case) ye never move a wing. (1, 6–10, 16–20)

Unusual for religious controversy in reformation Europe, Herbert actually seems interested in persuading those with whom he disagrees (the implicit condescension notwithstanding). But what is more, he concludes the poem by leaving open the possibility that angelic mediation may, at some future point, be sanctioned by a renewed understanding of "our Masters hand":

> Although then others court you, if ye know
> What's done on earth, we shall not fare the worse,
>   Who do not so;
> Since we are ever ready to disburse,
> If any one our Masters hand can show. (26–30)

Of all the remarkable things in this poem, none is more significant than the phrase "ever ready" in the lyric's penultimate line. In context, this concluding phrase expresses moderate confidence in the nature of true devotion; but much more, it gestures toward future dialogue, as though the speaker were saying: "over to you Roman Catholics." Like Hooker and Augustine, Herbert's "To all Angels and Saints" intimates the potential contingency of scriptural interpretation, including on matters of dogma. In doing so, the poem displays the same tendency as James I to play down the Church of England's differences with Roman Catholicism while nevertheless maintaining a strong sense of the state church's Protestantism.[21] Unlike men such as George Abbot, who referred to Catholics as "vassals of the Antichrist ... and ... adorers of the beast," James tended to equate puritan and Catholic threats as arising more from doctrinally indifferent questions of worship and policy than fundamentals of dogma.[22] The result was a subtle and even somewhat detached attitude toward Rome, one that generally avoided polemical extremes. It was most likely out of this distinctly Jacobean attitude toward Rome that Herbert's "To all Angels and Saints" was written.[23]

Herbert's relatively open-minded religious positioning reflects an intellectual culture that was becoming increasingly sensitive to Hooker's insight that no theological method or institution can be infallibly assured of its own correctness even when grounded on scripture alone.[24] Or as Hooker puts it: "It is not the worde of God which doth or possibilie can assure us, that wee doe well to thinke it his worde."[25] Consistent with this insight about the limits of the *sola scriptura* principle, "To all Angels and Saints" implies that what is scripturally sanctioned is not self-evident but subject to change through collective dialogue. While the poem presumes the primary authority of scripture for determining true worship, and while it articulates a relatively confident sense of what true worship is, its ending nevertheless allows for the possibility that on the question of saint veneration the interpretive tradition of the church may evolve through

[21] Fincham and Lake, "Ecclesiastical Policy of King James I," 182–183.
[22] Ibid., 182–183.
[23] The more hostile attitude toward Rome expressed in "The Church Militant" may reflect a subsequent breakdown in the conditions for such an attitude later in James' reign among many conformists. Though even there, Herbert sustains a view of the church as evolving over time in unexpected ways.
[24] See Egil Grislis, "The Hermeneutical Problem in Richard Hooker" in *Studies in Richard Hooker* ed. W. Speed Hill, 159–206, 179.
[25] Hooker, *Laws* 1:153-13-25 cited in N. Voak, "Richard Hooker and the Principle of Sola Scriptura" *Journal of Theological Studies* 59 (2008), 96–139, 131.

subsequent dialogue about scripture. So, like Calvin and the puritans, Herbert's lyric acknowledges that getting scripture wrong means violating God's authority. After all, "All worship is prerogative, and a flower / Of his rich crown" (21–22). Yet, like Hooker, the poem presumes that disagreement is inevitable because scriptural interpretations are necessarily subject to error, both collective and individual. As Herbert makes clear in *The Country Parson*, scripture often differs from itself in ways that patristic and other authorities help clarify: "For the Law required one thing, and the Gospel another: yet as diverse, not as repugnant: therefore the spirit of both is to be considered, and weighed" (229).

It is surely no coincidence that one of the period's closest parallels to Herbert's poem on angels and saints comes from an intellectual who loved to stress that the "whole Creation is a mystery, and particularly that of man." In *Religio Medici*, Sir Thomas Browne confessed:

> I should violate my owne arme rather then a Church, nor willingly deface the memory of Saint or Martyr. At the sight of a Crosse or Crucifix I can dispence with my hat, but scarce with the thought or memory of my Saviour; I cannot laugh at but rather pity the fruitlesse journeys of Pilgrims, or contemne the miserable condition of Friers; for though misplaced in circumstance, there is something in it of devotion.[26]

If Herbert and Browne present a more strongly fideist view of Christianity than Hooker does, they nevertheless emphasize nescience in a way that is broadly consistent with Hooker's approach to questions of authority and tradition. Like Hooker's *Laws*, Herbert's "To all Angels and Saints" was written out of an awareness that the problems of conscience in post-reformation England would have to be resolved through empathic understanding rather than by force or vitriol.

Crucially, then, if Herbert's use of the lyric as a medium moved him in a nondogmatic direction, so too did some of his contemporaries. It was partly this ecclesiastical context that helped him develop a poetics that was keenly attuned to the dynamics of mystery in the patristic sense of an unfolding action in time. Seeking to sustain this notion of mystery at the cusp of its fullest eclipse, Herbert helped cultivate the literary and religious conditions in which sacred poetry would come to full bloom in England.

---

[26] Browne, *The Major Works*, 105 and 63.

One example of this literary summer is the biblical poetics of Henry Vaughan. In his contribution to the scriptural love sonnet tradition initiated by *The Temple*, Vaughan effectively summarizes key features of Herbert's Augustinian vision. Figuring the bible as an alchemical process of sanctification, Vaughan's "H. Scriptures" praises the bible not just as a book of promises or sacred history, but as a living mystery in which one lives and moves. Its opening apostrophe reads:

> Welcome dear book, souls Joy, and food!   The feast
> Of Spirits, Heav'n extracted lyes in thee;
> Thou art lifes Charter, The Doves spotless neast
> Where souls are hatch'd unto Eternitie.
>
> In thee the hidden stone, the *Manna* lies,
> Thou art the great *Elixir*, rare, and Choice;
> The Key that opens to all Mysteries,
> The *Word* in Characters, God in the *Voice*. (1–8)

Although each of Vaughan's key metaphors for scripture remains irreducible to simple exposition, they all nevertheless refer to a specific idea in Augustinian interpretive theory. According to "H. Scriptures," the bible is a map or spiritual context for those in search of salvation and holiness ("Charter"). In it lies Christ, who is the *skopus* or goal toward which all ultimately culminates (*"Manna / Stone"*) and from which all originates (*"Elixir"*). Moreover, the material words on the page are the written text or *verbum engraphon* (as opposed to the unwritten word or *verbum agraphon* of oral tradition), which reveals the historical nature of God's revelation in time and place (*"Word* in characters"). Most importantly, each of these terms helps convey the voice of the living God ("God in the *Voice*") which gives birth to regenerate hearts ("souls … hatch'd unto Eternitie"). Taken as a whole, this scriptural economy makes spiritual reading possible, hence the speaker's description of scripture as the "Doves spotless neast," the place or site in which communion with the divine occurs (3). In context, the word "neast" figures scripture as the alchemical vessel in which spiritual transformation occurs, an idea that becomes clearer in the final quatrain's plea: "O that I had deep Cut in my hard heart / Each line in thee! Then would I plead in groans / Of my Lords penning" (9–11). Recalling Herbert's "The bunch of grapes," Vaughan puns on God's "penning" as both writing and embracing, revealing and framing. The pun suggests that the limitations God places on believers in scripture are spiritually vivifying in much the same way that highly disciplined poetic forms like the Elizabethan sonnet are aesthetically edifying. Just as poetry relies on the tension between familiarity and surprise, form and variation, so sanctification rests on the tension between the habits of faith and the freedom of the Spirit, predictable discipline and unpredictable transformation. In this way, "H. Scriptures" intimates the underlying continuity between spiritual and aesthetic life that is a central feature of *Silex Scintillans*.

The parallel between poetry and spirituality animating *Silex Scintillans* is part and parcel of the way Vaughan hopes his "sweetest Art" will do for others what he prays scripture will do for him (11), hence his daringly nondogmatic conflation of *Silex Scintillans* with scripture in the direct address to readers in the sonnet's closing couplet: "Read here, my faults are thine. This Book, and I / Will tell thee so; *Sweet Saviour thou didst dye!*" (13–14). Not only does Vaughan conflate his book with scripture here, he suggests that it serves the same mirroring function as Holy Writ. By incorporating his readers into the poem in this manner, Vaughan hopes that his lyrics will invite the kind of participatory reading practices normally associated with scripture as mirror.

The general outlines of Herbert's overall spiritual aesthetic find further expression in the literary theory that Vaughan summarizes in "Affliction," one of his admiringly insightful responses to *The Temple*. Balancing loose flowing assonance with quickly clipped consonants, Vaughan insists that both beauty and truth lie in the experience of spiritual transformation, even when such experience is as excruciating as torture. Following both scripture and Herbert, Vaughan construes beauty as something that happens more than as something that is.[27] For Vaughan,

> Beauty consists in colours; that's best
> Which is not fixt, but flies and flows;
> The settled *Red* is dull, and *whites* that rest
> Something of sickness would disclose.
> Vicissitude plaies all the game,
> Nothing that stirs,
> Or hath a name,
> But waits upon this wheel,

---

[27] For a discussion of scriptural conceptions of beauty as process, see Gerard von Rad *Old Testament Theology* vol. 1. *The Theology of Israel's Historical Traditions*, trans. D.M.G. Stalker (Harper and Row: New York, 1962), 367–369.

Kingdomes too have their Physick, and for steel,
   Exchange their peace, and furrs.
Thus doth God *Key* disorder'd man
      (which none else can,)
Tuning his brest to rise, or fall;
And by a sacred, needful art
Like strings, stretch ev'ry part
Making the whole most Musicall. (25–40)

In this response to the question, "Is there beauty in truth," the answer is
a formally mimetic yes: beauty and truth are inextricably related processes
not fixed, static products. Behind Vaughan's answer lies Augustine's biblical conception of mimetic inversion, the principle that the church grows
in beauty because she is rooted in the ugly, humiliated, flogged, and tortured Christ.[28] Only, rather than celebrating the beauty made possible by
Christ's suffering, Vaughan praises the sanctifying power of affliction upon
the soul. The underlying paradox is the same however: through the imitation of Christ ugliness can become beauty and discord harmony because
truth and beauty are dynamic, kinetic processes. This is beauty as *kenosis*,
the process of divine self-emptying that Christian exegetes see revealed
throughout the whole of scripture and which Herbert and Vaughan see at
work in both the church and the human soul.

As Vaughan clearly understood, Herbert's patterning of correction and
revision is inextricable from a religious vision in which beauty and truth
are both coextensive with the growing pains inherent to sanctification,
the process of learning how to "love the strife." From such a perspective,
truth and beauty are rooted in the experience of holiness as it unfolds in
time. As a result, they cannot be grasped or held onto from an abstract,
once-and-for-all third-person standpoint. For Herbert and Vaughan, truth
and beauty are scripturally revealed processes in which human beings
immanently participate. They are not fixed objects which we transcendently observe or just so much information which we internalize. To
understand Herbert's achievement as a religious writer is to understand
how he resisted the forces which undermined these fundamental features
of Augustinian Christianity.

---

[28] See *Works of Saint* Augustine, 44.244–245. For a discussion of Augustine's theory of
mimetic inversion, see Karl F. Morrison, *The Mimetic Tradition of Reform in The West*
(Princeton: Princeton UP, 1982), 95.

SELECT BIBLIOGRAPHY OF SECONDARY SOURCES

Aers, David, and Sarah Beckwith. 2010. The Eucharist. In *Cultural Reformations: Medieval and Renaissance in Literary History*, ed. Brian Cummings and James Simpson, 153–165. Oxford: Oxford University Press.

Agamben, Giorgio. 2013. *Opus Dei: An Archaeology of Duty*. Trans. Adam Kotsko. Stanford, CA: Stanford University Press.

Althaus, Paul. 1966. *The Theology of Martin Luther*. Trans. Robert Schultz. Philadelphia, PA: Fortress Press.

Asals, Heather. 1981. A.R. *Equivocal Predication: George Herbert's Way to God*. Toronto, ON: University of Toronto Press.

Bakhuizen, J.N. van den Brink. 1969. *Juan de Valdés: réformateur en Espagne et en Italie 1529–1541*. Genève: Librairie Droz.

Bauer, Matthias. 1994/1995. Herbert's Titles, Common Place Books, and the Poetics of Use: A Response to Anne Ferry. *Connotations* 4(3): 266–279.

Beale, G.K., and Benjamin L. Gladd. 2014. *Hidden But Now Revealed: A Biblical Theology of Mystery*. Downers Grove, IL: IVP Academic.

Bedford, R.D. 1979. *The Defence of Truth: Herbert of Cherbury and the Seventeenth Century*. Manchester: Manchester University Press.

Bell, Illona. 1979. Setting Foot into Divinity: George Herbert and the English Reformation. In *Essential Articles for the Study of George Herbert's Poetry*, ed. John R. Roberts, 63–86. Hamden, CT: Archon Books.

———. 1987. Herbert's Valdésian Vision. *ELR* 17: 303–328.

Bloch, Chana. 1985. *Spelling the Word: George Herbert and the Bible*. Berkeley, CA: University of California Press.

Bossy, John. 1987. *Christianity in the West 1400–1700*. Oxford: Oxford University Press.

© The Author(s) 2017   273
G. Kuchar, *George Herbert and the Mystery of the Word*,
DOI 10.1007/978-3-319-44045-3

Bouyer, Louis. 1990. *The Christian Mystery: From Pagan Myth to Christian Mysticism*. Trans. Illtyd Trethowan. Edinburgh: T&T Clark.
Bozeman, Theodore Dwight. 2004. *The Precisianist Strain: Disciplinary Religion & Antinomian Backlash in Puritanism to 1638*. Chapel Hill, NC: University of North Carolina Press.
Brown, Raymond E.S.S. 1968. *The Semitic Background of the Term 'Mystery' in the New Testament*. Philadelphia, PA: Fortress Press.
Bruns, Gerald. 1992. *Hermeneutics: Ancient and Modern*. New Haven, CT: Yale University Press.
Bultmann, Rudolph. 1955. *Theology of the New Testament Volume Two*. Trans. Kendrick Gobel. London: SCM Press.
Campbell, Gordon. 2010. *Bible: The Story of The King James Version 1611–2011*. Oxford: Oxford University Press.
Caragounis, Chrys C. 1971. *The Ephesian Mysterion: Meaning and Content*. Lund: CWK Gleerup.
Cary, Phillip. 2008a. *Inner Grace: Augustine in the Traditions of Plato and Paul*. Oxford: Oxford University Press.
———. 2008b. *Outward Signs: The Powerlessness of External Things in Augustine's Thought*. Oxford: Oxford University Press.
Cavell, Stanley. 2003. *Disowning Knowledge in Seven Plays of Shakespeare*. Cambridge: Cambridge University Press.
Cefalu, Paul. 2004. *Moral Identity in Early Modern English Literature*. Cambridge: Cambridge University Press.
———. Forthcoming. *The Johannine Renaissance in Early Modern English Literature and Religion*. Oxford: Oxford University Press.
Certeau, Michel de. 1992. *The Mystic Fable: The Sixteenth and Seventeenth Centuries*. Trans. Michael B. Smith. Chicago, IL: University of Chicago Press.
Chretien, Jean-Louis. 2014. *Under the Gaze of the Bible*. Trans. John Marson Dunaway. New York: Fordham University Press.
Clarke, Elizabeth. 1997. *Theory and Theology in George Herbert's Poetry: 'Divinitie, and Poesie, Met'*. Oxford: Oxford University Press.
Cohen, Charles Lloyd. 1986. *God's Caress: The Psychology of Puritan Religious Experience*. Oxford: Oxford University Press.
Collinson, Patrick. 1967. *The Elizabethan Puritan Movement*. Oxford: Clarendon Press, Reprint 2004.
———. 1982. *The Religion of Protestants: The Church in English Society 1559–1625*. Oxford: Clarendon Press.
———. 1988. *The Birthpangs of Protestant England: Religious and Cultural Change in the Sixteenth and Seventeenth Centuries*. Basingstoke: Macmillan.
Cooley, Ronald W. 2004. *'Full of All Knowledge': George Herbert's Country Parson and Early Modern Social Discourse*. Toronto, ON: University of Toronto Press.
Coolidge, John S. 1970. *The Pauline Renaissance in England: Puritanism and the Bible*. Oxford: Oxford University Press.

Couturier, C. 1953. 'Sacramentum Et Mysterium' Dans L'Oeuvre de Saint Augustine. In *Études Augustiennes*, 161–332. Paris: Aubier.

Crews, Daniel A. 2008. *Twilight of the Renaissance: The Life of Juan de Valdés.* Toronto, ON: University of Toronto Press.

Cummings, Brian. 2002. *The Literary Culture of the Reformation: Grammar and Grace.* Oxford: Oxford University Press.

———. 2013. *Mortal Thoughts: Religion, Secularity & Identity in Shakespeare and Early Modern Culture.* Oxford: Oxford University Press.

Cunnar, Eugene R. 1987. Herbert and the Visual Arts: *Ut Pictura Poesis:* An Opening in 'The Windows'. In *Like Season'd Timber: New Essays on George Herbert*, ed. Edmund Miller and Robert DiYanni, 101–138. New York: Peter Lang.

Davies, Julian. 1992. *The Caroline Captivity of the Church: Charles I and the Remoulding of Anglicanism 1625–1641.* Oxford: Clarendon Press.

Dever, Mark E. 2000. *Richard Sibbes: Puritanism and Calvinism in Late Elizabethan and Early Stuart England.* Macon, GA: Mercer University Press.

DiPasquale, Theresa M. 1999. *Literature & Sacrament: The Sacred and the Secular in John Donne.* Pittsburgh, PA: Duquesne University Press.

Doerksen, Daniel W. 1997. *Conforming to the Word: Herbert, Donne, and the English Church Before Laud.* Lewisburg, PA: Bucknell University Press.

———. 2011. *Picturing Religious Experience: George Herbert, Calvin, and the Scriptures.* Newark, NJ: University of Delaware Press.

Drury, John. 2013. *Music at Midnight: The Life and Poetry of George Herbert.* London: Allen Lane.

Elsky, Martin. 1989. *Authorizing Words: Speech, Writing, and Print in the English Renaissance.* Ithaca, NY: Cornell University Press.

Ferrell, Lori Ann. 1998. *Government By Polemic: James I, The King's Preachers, and the Rhetorics of Conformity 1603–1625.* Stanford, CA: Stanford University Press.

Ferry, Anne. 1993. Titles in George Herbert's 'Little Book'. *ELR* 23: 314–344.

Fincham, Kenneth, and Peter Lake. 1985. The Ecclesiastical Policy of King James I. *Journal of British Studies* 24(2): 169–207.

Firpo, Massimo. 2014. *Juan de Valdés and the Italian Reformation.* Trans. Richard Bates. Farnham: Ashgate.

Forde, Gerhard O. 1983. Law and Gospel in Luther's Hermeneutic. *Interpretation* 37(3): 240–252.

Fox, Adam. 2002. *Oral and Literate Culture in England 1500–1700.* Oxford: Oxford University Press.

Frei, Hans W. 1974. *The Eclipse of Biblical Narrative: A Study in Eighteenth and Nineteenth Century Hermeneutics.* New Haven, CT: Yale University Press.

Gardner, Helen. 1971. *Religion and Literature.* Oxford: Oxford University Press.

Geest, Paul van. 2011. *The Incomprehensibility of God: Augustine as a Negative Theologian.* Paris: Peeters.

Girard, Rene. 2001. Mimesis and Violence. In *The Girard Reader*, ed. James G. Williams, 9–19. New York: Crossroad.

Gordis, Lisa M. 1996. The Experience of Covenant Theology in George Herbert's 'The Temple'. *The Journal of Religion* 76(3): 383–401.

Haigh, Christopher. 1987. Anticlericalism and the English Reformation. In *The English Reformation Revised*, ed. Christopher Haigh. Cambridge: Cambridge University Press.

———. 2000. The Taming of Reformation: Preachers, Pastors, and Parishioners in Elizabethan and Early Stuart England. *History* 85(280): 572–588.

———. 2001. Success and Failure in the English Reformation. *Past and Present* 11(173): 28–49.

———. 2007. *The Plain Man's Pathways to Heaven: Kinds of Christianity in Post-Reformation England, 1570–1640*. Oxford: Oxford University Press.

Haller, William. 1938. *The Rise of Puritanism*. New York: Columbia University Press, Reprint Harper and Row, 1957.

Harrison, Peter. 1998. *The Bible, Protestantism, and the Rise of Natural Science*. Cambridge: Cambridge University Press.

Hill, Eugene D. 1987. *Edward, Lord Herbert of Cherbury*. Boston, MA: Twayne.

Hodgkins, Christopher. 1993. *Authority, Church, and Society in George Herbert: Return to the Middle Way*. Columbia, MO: University of Missouri Press.

Hunt, Arnold. 2010. *The Art of Hearing: English Preachers and their Audiences, 1590–1640*. Cambridge: Cambridge University Press.

Johnson, Bruce A. 1992. Theological Inconsistency and its Uses in George Herbert's Poetry. *George Herbert Journal* 15(2): 2–18.

Kendall, R.T. 1979. *Calvin and English Calvinism to 1649*. Oxford: Oxford University Press.

Knight, Janice. 1994. *Orthodoxies in Massachusetts: Rereading American Puritanism*. Cambridge, MA: Harvard University Press.

Kuchar, Gary. 2008. *The Poetry of Religious Sorrow in Early Modern England*. Cambridge: Cambridge University Press.

———. 2010. Alchemy, Repentance, and Recusant Allegory in Robert Southwell's St Peters Complaint. In *Remapping Early Modern English Catholicism*, ed. Lowell Gallagher, Chap. 7. Toronto, ON: University of Toronto Press.

Lake, Peter. 1982. *Moderate Puritans and the Elizabethan Church*. Cambridge: Cambridge University Press.

———. 1988a. *Anglicans and Puritans: Presbyterianism and English Conformist Thought from Whitgift to Hooker*. London: Unwin Hyman.

———. 1988b. Serving God and the Times: The Calvinist Conformity of Robert Sanderson. *Journal of British Studies* 27(2): 81–116.

———. 1991. Lancelot Andrewes, John Buckeridge, and Avant-Garde Conformity at the Court of James I. In *The Mental World of the Jacobean Court*, ed. Linda Levy Peck, 113–133. Cambridge: Cambridge University Press.

————. 1995. Predestinarian Propositions. *Journal of Ecclesiastical History* 46(1): 110–123.

————. 1996. 'A Charitable Christian Hatred': The Godly and their Enemies in the 1630's. In *The Culture of English Puritanism 1560–1700*, ed. C. Durston and J. Eales, 145–183. Basingstoke: Macmillan.

————. 2003. The Anglican Moment? Richard Hooker and the Ideological Watershed of the 1590's. In *Anglicanism and the Western Christian Tradition*, ed. Stephen Platten, 90–121. Norwich: Canterbury Press.

Lossky, Nicholas. 1991. *Lancelot Andrewes, the Preacher* (1555–1626): *The Origins of the Mystical Theology of the Church of England*. Trans. Andrew Louth. Oxford: Clarendon Press.

Louth, Andrew. 1983. *Discerning the Mystery: An Essay on the Nature of Theology*. Oxford: Clarendon Press.

Lubac, Henri de. 1998. *Medieval Exegesis: The Four Senses of Scripture Volume 2*. Trans. E.M. Macierowski. Edinburgh: Eerdmans.

————. 2006. *Corpus Mysticum: The Eucharist and the Church in the Middle Ages*. Trans. Gemma Simmonds. Notre Dame: University of Notre Dame Press.

————. 2007. *History and Spirit: The Understanding of Scripture According to Origen*. Trans. Anne Englund Nash. San Francisco: Ignatius Press.

MacCulloch, Diarmaid. 2006. The Latitude of the Church of England. In *Religious Politics in Post-Reformation England: Essays in Honour of Nicholas Tyacke*, ed. Kenneth Fincham and Peter Lake, 41–59. Woodbridge: Boydell Press.

MacDonald, Michael. 1992. The Fearefull Estate of Francis Spira: Narrative, Identity, and Emotion in Early Modern England. *Journal of British Studies* 31(1): 32–61.

Martz, Louis. 1989. The Generous Ambiguity of Herbert's *The Temple*. In *A Fine Tuning: Studies of the Religious Poetry of Herbert and Milton*, ed. Mary A. Maleski, 31–56. Binghamton, NY: MRTS.

McCullough, Peter, eds. 2005. *Lancelot Andrewes: Selected Sermons and Lectures*. Oxford: Oxford University Press.

McGee, J. Sears. 1976. *The Godly Man in Stuart England: Anglicans, Puritans, and the Two Tables, 1620–1670*. New Haven, CT: Yale University Press.

McMahon, Robert. 1992. Herbert's 'Coloss. 3.3' as Microcosm. *George Herbert Journal* 15(2): 55–69.

Miller, Greg. 2007. *George Herbert's 'Holy Patterns': Reforming Individuals in Community*. New York: Continuum.

Milton, Anthony. 1995. *Catholic and Reformed: The Roman and Protestant Churches in English Protestant Thought 1600–1640*. Cambridge: Cambridge University Press.

————. 2006. 'Anglicanism' by Stealth: The Career and Influence of John Overall. In *Religious Politics in Post-Reformation England: Essays in Honour of Nicholas*

Tyacke, ed. Kenneth Fincham and Peter Lake, 159–176. Woodbridge: Boydell Press.

Moore, Jonathan D. 2007. *English Hypothetical Universalism: John Preston and the Softening of Reformed Theology*. Grand Rapids, MI: Eerdmans.

Morgan, Irvonwy. 1957. *Prince Charles's Puritan Chaplain*. London: George Allen & Unwin Ltd.

Morrison, Karl F. 1982. *The Mimetic Tradition of Reform in The West*. Princeton, NJ: Princeton University Press.

Morrissey, Mary. 2002. Scripture, Style and Persuasion in Seventeenth-Century English Theories of Preaching. *The Journal of Ecclesiastical History* 53(4): 686–706.

Muller, Richard A. 1993. *Post-Reformation Dogmatics Volume 2. Holy Scripture: The Cognitive Foundation of Theology*. Grand Rapids, MI: Baker Books.

———. 2000. *The Unaccommodated Calvin: Studies in the Foundation of a Theological Tradition*. Oxford: Oxford University Press.

———. 2003. *After Calvin: Studies in the Development of a Theological Tradition*. Oxford: Oxford University Press.

Nicolson, Adam. 2004. *God's Secretaries: The Making of the King James Bible*. New York: Perennial.

Nieto, José C. 1970. *Juan de Valdés and the Origins of the Spanish and Italian Reformation*. Genève: Libraire Droz 11 Rue Massot.

Norton, David. 2000. *A History of the English Bible as Literature*. Cambridge: Cambridge University Press.

Ong, Walter. 1958. *Method and the Decay of Dialogue*. Cambridge, MA: Harvard University Press.

———. 1967. *The Presence of the Word: Some Prolegomena for Cultural and Religious History*. New Haven, CT: Yale University Press.

———. 1977. *Interfaces of the Word: Studies in the Evolution of Consciousness and Culture*. Ithaca, NY: Cornell University Press.

———. 2002. *Orality and Literacy: The Technologizing of the Word*. London: Routledge.

Pettit, Norman. 1966. *The Heart Prepared: Grace and Conversion in Puritan Spiritual Life*. New Haven, CT: Yale University Press.

Pitkin, Barbara. 1999. *What Pure Eyes Could See: Calvin's Doctrine of Faith in its Exegetical Context*. Oxford: Oxford University Press.

Porter, H.C. 1958. *Reformation and Reaction in Tudor Cambridge*. Cambridge: Cambridge University Press.

Powers-Beck, Jeffrey. 1998. *Writing the Flesh: The Herbert Family Dialogue*. Pittsburgh, PA: Duquesne University Press.

Prior, Charles W.A. 2005. *Defining the Jacobean Church: The Politics of Religious Controversy, 1603–1625*. Cambridge: Cambridge University Press.

Rahner, Hugo. 1971. *Greek Myths and Christian Mystery*. New York: Biblo and Tannen.

Read, Sophie. 2013. *Eucharist and the Poetic Imagination in Early Modern England*. Cambridge: Cambridge University Press.

Richey, Esther Gilman. 2011. The Property of God: Luther, Calvin, and Herbert's Sacrifice Sequence. *ELH* 78(2): 287–314.

Rust, Jennifer R. 2014. *The Body in Mystery: The Political Theology of the Corpus Mysticum in the Literature of Reformation England*. Evanston, IL: Northwestern University Press.

Scarry, Elaine. 1999. *On Beauty and Being Just*. Princeton, NJ: Princeton University Press.

Schreiner, Louise. 2011. *Are You Alone Wise: The Search for Certainty in the Early Modern Era*. Oxford: Oxford University Press.

Slyke, Daniel G. van. 2007. The Changing Meanings of *Sacramentum*: Historical Sketches. *Antiphon*. 11(3): 245–279.

Smith, Bruce R. 1999. *The Acoustic World of Early Modern England. Attending to the O-Factor*. Chicago, IL: University of Chicago Press.

———. 2009. *The Key of Green: Passion and Perception in Renaissance Culture*. Chicago, IL: University of Chicago Press.

Song, Eric B. 2007. Anamorphosis and the Religious Subject of George Herbert's 'Coloss. 3.3. *SEL 1500-1900* 47(1): 107–121.

Stock, Brian. 1998. *Augustine the Reader: Meditation, Self-Knowledge, and the Ethics of Interpretation*. Cambridge: Harvard University Press.

———. 2001. *After Augustine: The Meditative Reader and the Text*. Philadelphia, PA: University of Pennsylvania Press.

Strier, Richard. 1983. *Love Known: Theology and Experience in George Herbert's Poetry*. Chicago, IL: University of Chicago Press.

Summers, Joseph H. 1954. *George Herbert: His Religion and Art*. London: Chatto and Windus.

Todd, Richard. 1987. *The Opacity of Signs: Acts of Interpretation in George Herbert's the Temple*. Columbia, MO: University of Missouri Press.

Tuve, Rosemund. 1952. *A Reading of George Herbert*. Chicago, IL: University of Chicago Press.

Voak, Nigel. 2003. *Richard Hooker and Reformed Theology: A Study of Reason, Will, and Grace*. Oxford: Oxford University Press.

———. 2008. Richard Hooker and the Principle of Sola Scriptura. *Journal of Theological Studies* 59: 96–139.

Weinsheimer, Joel C. 1985. *Gadamer's Hermeneutics: A Reading of Truth and Method*. New Haven, CT: Yale University Press.

Whalen, Robert. 2002. *The Poetry of Immanence: Sacrament in Donne and Herbert*. Toronto, ON: University of Toronto Press.

White, James Boyd. 1995. *'This Book of Starres': Learning to Read George Herbert.* Ann Arbor, MI: University of Michigan Press.

White, Peter. 2002. *Predestination and Polemic: Conflict and Consensus in the English Church from the Reformation to the Civil War.* Cambridge: Cambridge University Press.

Whitney, Charles. 1987. Bacon and Herbert: Bacon and Herbert as Moderns. In *Like Season'd Timber: New Essays on George Herbert,* ed. Edmund Miller and Robert DiYanni, 231–240. New York: Peter Lang.

Witmore, Michael. 2001. *Culture of Accidents: Unexpected Knowledges in Early Modern England.* Stanford, CA: Stanford University Press.

Wolberg, Kristine A. 2008. *'All Possible Art': George Herbert's The Country Parson.* Madison, NJ: Fairleigh Dickinson.

Wood, Chauncey. 1979. A Reading of Herbert's 'Coloss. 3.3'. *George Herbert Journal* 2(2): 15–24.

INDEX[1]

[1] Note: Page numbers with "n" denote notes.

© The Author(s) 2017
G. Kuchar, *George Herbert and the Mystery of the Word*,
DOI 10.1007//978-3 319-44045-3

Printed by Printforce, the Netherlands